GENERAL EQUILIBRIUM MODELS OF MONETARY ECONOMIES

Studies in the Static Foundations of Monetary Theory

This is a volume in
ECONOMIC THEORY, ECONOMETRICS,
AND MATHEMATICAL ECONOMICS

Consulting Editor: Karl Shell, *Cornell University*

A list of recent titles in this series appears at the end of this volume.

GENERAL EQUILIBRIUM MODELS OF MONETARY ECONOMIES

Studies in the Static Foundations of Monetary Theory

Edited by

Ross M. Starr

Department of Economics
University of California, San Diego
La Jolla, California

Academic Press, Inc.

Harcourt Brace Jovanovich, Publishers

Boston San Diego New York
Berkeley London Sydney
Tokyo Toronto

ACADEMIC PRESS, INC.
1250 Sixth Avenue, San Diego, CA 92101

United Kingdom Edition published by
ACADEMIC PRESS INC. (LONDON) LTD.
24–28 Oval Road, London NW1 7DX

Library of Congress Cataloging-in-Publication Data
General equilibrium models of monetary economies
edited by Ross M. Starr.
(Economic theory, econometrics, and mathematical economics)
Bibliography: p.
Includes index.
1. Equilibrium (Economics) 2. Money. 3. Value.
I. Starr, Ross M. II. Series.
HB145.G44 1988 332.4 88–6182
ISBN 0-12-663970-1

m.r.

89 90 91 92 9 8 7 6 5 4 3 2 1
Printed in the United States of America

To
C. S. and D. E. S.

CONTENTS

Part I

Monetary Theory and Microeconomic Theory

1

MONEY IN FORMAL GENERAL EQUILIBRIUM ANALYSIS

This volume presents work developed primarily over the last two decades using mathematical general equilibrium theory to treat a classic problem of economic theory, the integration of the theory of money and the theory of value. Questions addressed include the functions money performs in the economy, how it promotes efficient allocation, and how the value of an intrinsically worthless fiat money is sustained in a market equilibrium. The analytic approach is the Arrow-Debreu model of Walrasian general equilibrium theory. Use of this detailed general equilibrium model is intended to provide a framework to represent money as a device for facilitating trade among economic agents. To provide a function for money, there must be sufficient variety in agents and goods to make trade desirable, and to generate impediments to trade so that money can ease the difficulty. Hence an inquiry into the foundations of the role of money necessarily requires modelling the interaction of multiple traders and goods. A smaller model—of partial equilibrium, of Robinson Crusoe, or of the Edgeworth box—is insufficient. A less detailed approach may adequately characterize interactions in a monetary economy when the properties of money and finance are assumed, but it cannot provide a foundation for a theory of money.

The Arrow-Debreu general equilibrium model is a formal analytic counterpart of a common classroom exercise, considering an economy without money. The model presents a smoothly functioning economy with no money or financial institutions. The conventional functioning of money is otiose in the Arrow-Debreu model because the functions of money and finance are

ISBN 0-12-663970-1

performed by the markets themselves. Futures markets execute the intertemporal allocation functions which would otherwise be performed using a store of value. Trade is not bilateral, but omni-lateral; all trade takes place in a single marketing instant and place where traders meet all other traders at once. Each household and firm executes only a single lifetime transaction. Hence no role for a medium of exchange can arise as a token of value carried between trades. The Arrow-Debreu theory positively denies a role for money as a store of value or as a medium of exchange. A class of models that so fully repudiates money seems a curious jumping-off place for a monetary theory. It was Hicks' suggestion (selection 2) that starting from this point, we should consider money as a device for overcoming "frictions" in the smooth functioning that the model assumed. In order to do this we must make the frictions explicit. Hicks urged the profession to "look the frictions in the face," suggesting that their analysis will not actually prove intractable. That is the research plan undertaken by this body of work. The Arrow-Debreu model assumes away all impediments to trade. Introduction of explicit difficulties of trade is a lever for deducing the peculiar functions of money. The frictionless non-monetary Arrow-Debreu world is a precise and exacting jumping-off point for looking directly at the frictions in trade that generate the role of money and finance.

A common alternative formulation to represent the demand for money is to put money as an argument in the household utility function. The studies of this volume reject that formulation as unhelpful at best. The object of these papers is to explain the function of money in an economy. Entering money as an argument of the utility function would transparently and uselessly assume the conclusion of the inquiry.

> "Imbedding money in preferences or technologies does nothing to explain its role as a store of value. Moreover, such reduced forms are at best poor proxies for their structural counterparts. Worst of all, to the extent that this maneuver is successful, it is also likely to be misleading." Cass and Shell (1980)

Principal classic functions of money are as a medium of exchange and as a store of value. We first consider how the Arrow-Debreu Walrasian model deals with these functions without the use of money. Compared to the bilateral trading process in actual economies the mechanism of trade in an Arrow-Debreu model is simplified in a way that implies that there is no role for a medium of exchange, money, in the trading process. The mechanism of trade is simply absent. There is no role for shops, retailers, wholesalers, credit or means of payment. All trade takes place between the individual and an abstract market. There is an abstract price formation mechanism, sometimes personified as the Walrasian auctioneer. Once general equilibrium prices have been announced, agents deliver their excess supplies to the market and withdraw their excess demands, consistent with budget constraint. Inasmuch as prices are market clearing, there is no unsatisfied excess demand. The agent's trade is a single transaction, the delivery of goods and withdrawal of demands. Some record keeping is required to ensure that budget constraints are fulfilled, but there is no explicit account in the model of the process by which such records are kept. Since each agent and firm's transaction takes place in a single exchange, there is no role for a token or carrier of value to be held between transactions, hence no role for a medium of exchange. The perfection and simplicity of trade in the model preclude a role for money as a facilitator of transactions. You can't improve on perfection.

The task of formalizing a demand for a medium of exchange consists of modelling the process of trade in a fashion that adds some difficulty, structure, and complexity. This analysis is presented in Part II of the collection. Trade is formalized as a succession of bilateral trades. Hence a role for a medium of exchange as a carrier of value between trades arises endogenously.

A distinctive element of the Arrow-Debreu model is the availability of a full set of futures markets for intertemporal allocation. A commodity is defined by its description *and* by its delivery date. A typical household endowment then consists of goods—including labor—dated for availability in the present (spot) and in the future. The intertemporal allocation process works in the following way. There is a single date of active trade. Trade takes place in dated commodities: current goods spot and futures contracts (goods contracted for delivery in the future). A typical household endowment consists of both current and future goods. Thus, a household whose principal endowment is labor would sell current labor and contracts to deliver labor in the future. In exchange for these sales the household would receive abstract purchasing power to be credited toward its purchases on the market. It would then purchase spot goods for current consumption and contracts for delivery of future consumption. The household goes to the market with a portfolio of securities representing its endowment and when all trades have been completed it leaves the market with a portfolio of securities representing its lifetime consumption plan. Prices are present discounted values of dated goods. The household budget constraint is that the value of all of its purchases must equal the value of its sales. The household budget constraint is hence a lifetime budget constraint expressed in terms of present discounted values of sales and purchases.

Two quite distinct functions are performed by the futures markets in this model. One is price determination. As an outcome of the equilibrium, all agents know the trade-off between present and future consumption and between goods at a variety of dates. The other function performed is a capital market function. The futures markets allow the timing of household consumption to be allocated independent of the timing of sales by the household or of firms it owns. This is the function that capital markets and debt instruments play in a monetary economy. When the equilibrium allocation is achieved, every household has arranged its desired consumption plan for the present through the future, subject to its lifetime budget constraint. Firms maximize the present discounted values of their profit streams. The allocation is Pareto efficient in terms of household lifetime utility functions. All trade takes place at a single initial date. The rest of economic activity consists of fulfillment of the contracted plans of households and firms.

There is no reopening of markets at subsequent dates. If the markets were reopened, they would be inactive—there would be no desired net trades. All intertemporal allocation takes place at a single date through the use of futures markets. An intertemporal store of value can perform no function here, since markets do not reopen over time. We conclude that a theory of money as a store of value requires a sufficient reason for the reopening of markets or, equivalently, a sufficient impediment to the use of futures markets. This impediment is formalized as a transaction cost structure that favors the use of spot markets. In a non-monetary economy, a breakdown in the efficiency of the equilibrium allocation follows. The resulting theory of intertemporal financial structure and money as a store of value is presented in Part III of the collection.

There is one essential step in moving from the Arrow-Debreu model to the models of bilateral trade (Part II) and intertemporal allocation (Part III) that allows distinct functions of money to emerge. The single lifetime budget constraint must be replaced by a succession of budget balance requirements. In each trade (Part II) and at each date (Part III) the value of sales is required to equal the value of purchases. This requirement so distorts the pattern of trade interpersonally and intertemporally as to result in possible misallocation. A solution to the difficulty is the provision of a financial asset (money), so that trade in the financial asset can sustain budget balance in each transaction without a corresponding change in resource allocation. The financial asset is identified as money, and restoration of efficient resource allocation in equilibrium is shown to result.

Virtually all of the studies presented in the collection portray pure exchange rather than production economies. This necessarily implies an attenuated treatment of capital markets. Nevertheless the essential issues of the inquiry, the role of money in facilitating reallocation over time and between agents, can be amply portrayed. The plan of the field is to retain the clarity, generality, and rigor of mathematical general equilibrium theory, while introducing sufficient difficulty of trade to create a demand for money and financial institutions. The studies of Parts II, III, and IV of this volume are chosen as representative of the success we have had in fulfilling this research agenda.

2

A SUGGESTION FOR SIMPLIFYING THE THEORY OF MONEY

by John R. Hicks

In this essay Professor Hicks argues for the use of the microeconomic theory of optimizing behavior as the basis of monetary theory. He calls for the same sort of marginalist revolution that formed the modern theory of value.

Hicks notes that monetary and financial behavior and institutions represent accomodation to imperfections, "frictions," in other markets, particularly asset markets. His research program then is "to look the frictions in the face, and see if they are really so refractory after all." This is certainly the essential methodological view of the technical papers in this volume. The subsequent papers add the recognition that money is a tool for economic interaction among agents and goods to Hicks' requirement that difficulties of trade be made explicit. Hence it necessarily requires a multiple agent-multiple good (*general* equilibrium) model. This is very much the framework in which Hicks viewed goods markets in *Value and Capital*.

The following is printed with permission from *Economica*, New Series, vol. 11, 1935.

ISBN 0-12-663970-1

A Suggestion for Simplifying the Theory of Money[1]

By J. R. Hicks

After the thunderstorms of recent years, it is with peculiar diffidence and even apprehension that one ventures to open one's mouth on the subject of money. In my own case these feelings are particularly intense, because I feel myself to be very much of a novice at the subject. My education has been mostly in the non-monetary parts of economics, and I have only come to be interested in money because I found that I could not keep it out of my non-monetary problems. Yet I am encouraged on reflection to hope that this may not prove a bad approach to the subject: that some things at least which are not very evident on direct inspection may become clearer from a cross-light of this sort.

It is of course very largely by such cross-fertilisation that economics progresses, and at least one department of non-monetary economics has hardly emerged from a very intimate affair with monetary theory. I do not, however, propose to resume this particular liaison. One understands that most economists have now read Böhm-Bawerk; yet whatever that union has bred, it has not been concord. I should prefer to seek illumination from another point of view—from a branch of economics which is more elementary, but, I think in consequence better developed—the theory of value.

To anyone who comes over from the theory of value to the theory of money, there are a number of things which are rather startling. Chief of these is the preoccupation of monetary theorists with a certain equation, which states that the price of goods multiplied by the quantity of goods equals the amount of money which is spent on them. This equation crops up again and again, and it has all sorts of ingenious little arithmetical tricks performed on it. Sometimes it comes out as $MV = PT$; and once, in its most stupendous transfiguration, it blossomed into $P = \frac{E}{O} + \frac{I' - S}{R}$. Now we, of the theory of value, are not unfamiliar with this equation, and there was a time when we

[1] A paper read at the Economic Club, November 1934. The reader is asked to bear in mind the fact that the paper was written to be read aloud, and to excuse certain pieces of mischief.

used to attach as much importance to it as monetary theorists seem to do still. This was in the middle of the last century, when we used to talk about value being "a ratio between demand and supply." Even now, we accept the equation, and work it, more or less implicitly, into our systems. But we are rather inclined to take it for granted, since it is rather tautologous, and since we have found that another equation, not alternative to the quantity equation, but complementary with it, is much more significant. This is the equation which states that the relative value of two commodities depends upon their relative marginal utility.

Now, to an *ingénu*, who comes over to monetary theory, it is extremely trying to be deprived of this sheet-anchor. It was marginal utility that really made sense of the theory of value; and to come to a branch of economics which does without marginal utility altogether! No wonder there are such difficulties and such differences! What is wanted is a "marginal revolution"!

That is my suggestion. But I know that it will meet with apparently crushing objections. I shall be told that the suggestion has been tried out before. It was tried by Wicksell, and though it led to interesting results, it did not lead to a marginal utility theory of money. It was tried by Mises, and led to the conclusion that money is a ghost of gold—because, so it appeared, money as such has no marginal utility.[1] The suggestion has a history, and its history is not encouraging.

This would be enough to frighten one off, were it not for two things. Both in the theory of value and in the theory of money there have been developments in the twenty or thirty years since Wicksell and Mises wrote. And these developments have considerably reduced the barriers that blocked their way.

In the theory of value, the work of Pareto, Wicksteed, and their successors, has broadened and deepened our whole conception of marginal utility. We now realise that the marginal utility analysis is nothing else than a general theory of choice, which is applicable whenever the choice is between alternatives that are capable of quantitative expression. Now money is obviously capable of quantitative expression, and therefore the objection that money

[1] A more subtle form of the same difficulty appears in the work of Marshall and his followers. They were aware that money ought to be subjected to marginal utility analysis; but they were so dominated by the classical conception of money as a "veil" (which is valid enough at a certain level of approximation) that they persisted in regarding the demand for money as a demand for the things which money can buy—"real balances." As a result of this, their invocation of marginal utility remained little more than a pious hope. For they were unable to distinguish, on marginal utility lines, between the desire to save and the desire to hoard; and they necessarily overlooked that indeterminateness in the "real balance" (so important in some applications of monetary theory), which occurs when the prices of consumption goods are expected to change. On the other hand, I must admit that some versions of the Marshallian theory come very close to what I am driving at. Cf. Lavington, *English Capital Market*, ch. vi.

has no marginal utility must be wrong. People do choose to have money rather than other things, and therefore, in the relevant sense, money must have a marginal utility.

But merely to call that marginal utility X, and then proceed to draw curves, would not be very helpful. Fortunately the developments in monetary theory to which I alluded come to our rescue.

Mr. Keynes' "Treatise," so far as I have been able to discover, contains at least three theories of money. One of them is the Savings and Investment theory, which, as I hinted, seems to me only a quantity theory much glorified. One of them is a Wicksellian natural rate theory. But the third is altogether much more interesting. It emerges when Mr. Keynes begins to talk about the price-level of investment goods; when he shows that this price-level depends upon the relative preference of the investor—to hold bank-deposits or to hold securities. Here at last we have something which to a value theorist looks sensible and interesting! Here at last we have a choice at the margin! And Mr. Keynes goes on to put substance into our X, by his doctrine that the relative preference depends upon the "bearishness" or "bullishness" of the public, upon their relative desire for liquidity or profit.

My suggestion may, therefore, be re-formulated. It seems to me that this third theory of Mr. Keynes really contains the most important part of his theoretical contribution; that here, at last, we have something which, on the analogy (the appropriate analogy) of value theory, does begin to offer a chance of making the whole thing easily intelligible; that it is from this point, not from velocity of circulation, natural rate of interest, or Saving and Investment, that we ought to start in constructing the theory of money. But in saying this, I am being more Keynesian than Keynes; I must endeavour to defend my position in detail.

II

The essence of the method I am proposing is that we should take the position of an individual at a particular point of time, and enquire what determines the precise quantity of money which he will desire to hold. But even to this simple formulation of the problem it is necessary to append two footnotes.

1. "Point of Time." We are dealing with an individual decision to hold money *or* something else, and such a decision is always made at a point of time. It is only by concentrating on decisions made at particular points of time that we can apply the theory of value to the problem at all. A very large amount of current controversy about money seems to me to be due to the attempt, superficially natural, but, in fact, highly inconvenient, to establish a close relation between the demand for money and *income*. Now the simple

consideration that the decision to hold money is always made at a point of time shows that the connection between income and the demand for money must always be indirect. And in fact the whole conception of income is so intricate and beset by so many perplexing difficulties, that the establishment of any connection with income ought only to be hoped for at a late stage of investigation.[1]

2. "Money." What sort of money are we considering? For the present, any sort of money. The following analysis will apply equally whether we think of money as notes, or bank deposits, or even metallic coins. It is true that with a metallic currency there is an ordinary commodity demand for the money substance to be considered, but it is relatively unimportant for most of our purposes. Perhaps it will be best if we take as our standard case that of a pure paper currency in a community where there are no banks. What follows has much wider application in reality. Only I would just ask you to keep this standard case in mind, since by using it as a basis for discussion, we may be able to save time a little.

An individual's decision to hold so much money means that he prefers to hold that amount of money, rather than either less or more. Now what are the precise contents of these displaced alternatives? He could reduce his holding of money in three ways:

1. by spending, i.e. buying something, it does not matter what;
2. by lending money to someone else;
3. by paying off debts which he owes to someone else.

He can increase his holding of money in three corresponding ways:

1. by selling something else which he owns;
2. by borrowing from someone else;
3. by demanding repayment of money which is owed by someone else.

This classification is, I think, complete. All ways of changing one's holding of money can be reduced to one of these classes or a combination of two of them—purchase or sale, the creation of new debts or the extinction of old.

If a person decides to hold money, it is implied that he prefers to do this than to adopt any of these three alternatives. But how is such a preference possible?

A preference for holding money instead of spending it on consumption goods presents no serious difficulty, for it is obviously the ordinary case of a preference for future satisfactions over present. At any moment, an individual will not usually devote the whole of his available resources to satisfying present wants—a part will be set aside to meet the needs of the future.

[1] Cf. Lindahl, *The Concept of Income* (Essays in honour of Gustav Cassel).

The critical question arises when we look for an explanation of the preference for holding money rather than capital goods. For capital goods will ordinarily yield a positive rate of return, which money does not. What has to be explained is the decision to hold assets in the form of barren money, rather than of interest- or profit-yielding securities. And obviously just the same question arises over our second and third types of utilisation. So long as rates of interest are positive, the decision to hold money rather than lend it, or use it to pay off old debts, is apparently an unprofitable one.

This, as I see it, is really the central issue in the pure theory of money. Either we have to give an explanation of the fact that people do hold money when rates of interest are positive, or we have to evade the difficulty somehow. It is the great traditional evasions which have led to Velocities of Circulation, Natural Rates of Interest, *et id genus omne*.[1]

Of course, the great evaders would not have denied that there must be some explanation of the fact. But they would have put it down to "frictions," and since there was no adequate place for frictions in the rest of their economic theory, a theory of money based on frictions did not seem to them a promising field for economic analysis.

This is where I disagree. I think we have to look the frictions in the face, and see if they are really so refractory after all. This will, of course, mean that we cannot allow them to go to sleep under so vague a title.

III

The most obvious sort of friction, and undoubtedly one of the most important, is the cost of transferring assets from one form to another. This is of exactly the same character as the cost of transfer which acts as a certain impediment to change in all parts of the economic system; it doubtless comprises subjective elements as well as elements directly priced. Thus a person is deterred from investing money for short periods, partly because of brokerage charges and stamp duties, partly because it is not worth the bother.

The net advantage to be derived from investing a given quantity of money consists of the interest or profit earned less the cost of investment. It is only if this net advantage is expected to be positive (i.e. if the expected rate of interest ± capital appreciation or depreciation, is greater than the cost of investment that it will pay to undertake the investment.

Now, since the expected interest increases both with the quantity of money to be invested and with the length of time for which it is expected that the

[1] I do not wish to deny that these concepts have a use in their appropriate place—that is to say, in particular applications of monetary theory. But it seems to me that they are a nuisance in monetary theory itself, that they offer no help in elucidating the general principles of the working of money.

investment will remain untouched, while the costs of investment are independent of the length of time, and (as a whole) will almost certainly increase at a diminishing rate as the quantity of money to be invested increases, it becomes clear that with any given level of costs of investment, it will not pay to invest money for less than a certain period, and in less than certain quantities. It will be profitable to hold assets for short periods, and in relatively small quantities, in monetary form.

Thus, so far as we can see at present, the amount of money a person will desire to hold depends upon three factors: the dates at which he expects to make payments in the future, the cost of investment, and the expected rate of return on investment. The further ahead the future payments, the lower the cost of investment, and the higher the expected rate of return on invested capital—the lower will be the demand for money.

However, this statement is not quite accurate. For although all these factors may react on the demand for money, they may be insufficient to determine it closely. Since the quantity of available money must generally rise to some minimum before it is profitable to invest it at all, and further investment will then proceed by rather discontinuous jumps for a while, we shall expect to find the demand for money on the part of private individuals, excepting the very well-to-do, fairly insensitive to changes of this sort. But this does not mean that they are unimportant. For among those who are likely to be sensitive, we have to reckon, not only the well-to-do, but also all business men who are administering capital which is not solely their own private property. And this will give us, in total, a good deal of sensitivity.

IV

Our first list of factors influencing the demand for money—the expected rate of interest, the cost of investment, and the expected period of investment—does, therefore, isolate some factors which are really operative; but even so, it is not a complete list. For we have also to take into account the fact, which is in reality of such enormous importance, that people's expectations are never precise expectations of the kind we have been assuming. They do not say to themselves "this £100 I shall not want until June Ist" or "this investment will yield 3.7 per cent"; or, if they do, it is only a kind of shorthand. Their expectations are always, in fact, surrounded by a certain penumbra of doubt; and the density of that penumbra is of immense importance for the problem we are considering.

The risk-factor comes into our problem in two ways: first, as affecting the expected period of investment; and second, as affecting the expected net yield of investment. There are certain differences between its ways of operation on these two lines; but, as we shall se, the resultant effects are broadly similar.

Where risk is present, the *particular* expectation of a riskless situation is replaced by a band of possibilities, each of which is considered more or less probable. It is convenient to represent these probabilities to oneself, in statistical fashion, by a mean value, and some appropriate measure of dispersion. (No single measure will be wholly satisfactory, but here this difficulty may be overlooked.) Roughly speaking, we may assume that a change in mean value with constant dispersion has much the same sort of effect as a change in the particular expectations we have been discussing before. The peculiar problem of risk therefore reduces to an examination of the consequences of a change in dispersion. Increased dispersion means increased uncertainty.

If, therefore, our individual, instead of knowing (or thinking he knows) that he will not want his £100 till June Ist, becomes afflicted by increased uncertainty; that is to say, while still thinking that June Ist is the most likely date, he now thinks that it will be very possible that he will want it before, although it is also very possible that he will not want it till after; what will be the effect on his conduct? Let us suppose that when the date was certain, the investment was marginal—in the sense that the expected yield only just outweighed the cost of investment. With uncertainty introduced in the way we have described, the investment now offers a chance of larger gain, but it is offset by an equal chance of equivalent loss. In this situation, I think we are justified in assuming that he will become less willing to undertake the investment.

If this is so, uncertainty of the period for which money is free will ordinarily act as a deterrent to investment. It should be observed that uncertainty may be increased, either by a change in objective facts on which estimates are based, or in the psychology of the individual, if his temperament changes in such a way as to make him less inclined to bear risks.

To turn now to the other uncertainty—uncertainty of the yield of investment. Here again we have a penumbra; and here again we seem to be justified in assuming that spreading of the penumbra, increased dispersion of the possibilities of yield, will ordinarily be a deterrent to investment. Indeed, without assuming this to be the normal case, it would be impossible to explain some of the most obvious of the observed facts of the capital market. This sort of risk, therefore, will ordinarily be another factor tending to increase the demand for money.

V

So far the effect of risk seems fairly simple; an increase in the risk of investment will act like a fall in the expected rate of net yield; an increase in the uncertainty of future outpayments will act like a shortening of the time which is expected to elapse before those out-payments; and all will ordinarily tend to increase the demand for money. But although this is what it comes down to in the end, the detailed working of the risk-factor is not so simple; and since these further complications have an important bearing upon monetary problems, we cannot avoid discussing them here.

It is one of the peculiarities of risk that the total risk incurred when more than one risky investment is undertaken, does not bear any simple relation to the risk involved in each of the particular investments taken separately. In most cases, the "law of large numbers" comes into play (quite how, cannot be discussed here), so that the risk incurred by undertaking a number of separate risky investments will be less than that which would have been incurred if the same total capital had been invested altogether in one direction. When the number of separate investments is very large, the total risk may sometimes be reduced very low indeed.

Now in a world where cost of investment was negligible, everyone would be able to take considerable advantage of this sort of risk-reduction. By dividing up his capital into small portions, and spreading his risks, he would be able to insure himself against any large total risk on the whole amount. But in actuality, the cost of investment, making it definitely unprofitable to invest less than a certain minimum amount in any particular direction, closes the possibility of risk-reduction along these lines to all those who do possess the command over considerable quantities of capital. This has two consequences.

On the one hand, since most people do not possess sufficient resources to enable them to take much advantage of the law of large numbers, and since even the large capitalist cannot annihilate his risks altogether in this manner, there will be a tendency to spread capital over a number of investments, not for this purpose, but for another. By investing only a proportion of total assets in risky enterprises, and investing the remainder in ways which are considered more safe, it will be possible for the individual to adjust his whole risk-situation to that which he most prefers, more closely than he could do by investing in any single enterprise. It will be possible, for example, for him to feel fairly certain that in particular unfavourable eventualities he will not lose more than a certain amount. And, since, both with an eye on future commitments with respect to debt, and future needs for consumption, large losses will lay upon him a proportionately heavier burden than small losses, this sort of adjustment to the sort of chance of loss he is prepared to stand will be very well worth while.

We shall, therefore, expect to find our representative individual distributing his assets among relatively safe and relatively risky investments; and the distribution will be governed, once again, by the objective facts upon which he bases his estimates of risk, and his subjective preference for much or little risk-bearing.

On the other hand, those persons who have command of large quantities of capital, and are able to spread their risks, are not only able to reduce the risk on their own capital fairly low—they are also able to offer very good security for the investment of an extra unit along with the rest. If, therefore, they choose to become borrowers, they are likely to be very safe borrowers.They can, therefore, provide the safe investments which their fellow-citizens need.

In the absence of such safe investments, the ordinary individual would be obliged to keep a very considerable proportion of his assets in monetary form, since money would be the only safe way of holding assets. The appearance of such safe investments will act as a substitute for money in one of its uses, and therefore diminish the demand for money.

This particular function is performed, in a modern community, not only by banks, but also by insurance companies, investment trusts, and, to a certain (perhaps small) extent, even by large concerns of other kinds, through their prior charges. And, of course, to a very large extent indeed, it is performed by government stock of various kinds.

Banks are simply the extreme case of this phenomenon; they are enabled to go further than other concerns in the creation of money substitutes, because the security of their promises to pay is accepted generally enough for it to be possible to make payments in those promises. Bank deposits are, therefore, enabled to substitute money still further, because the cost of investment is reduced by a general belief in the absence of risk.

This is indeed a difference so great-as to be properly regarded as a difference in kind; but it is useful to observe that the creation of bank credit is not really different in its economic effects from the fundamentally similar activities of other businesses and other persons. The significant thing is that the person who deposits money with a bank does not notice any change in his liquidity position; he considers the bank deposit to be as liquid as cash. The bank, on the other hand, finds itself more liquid, if it retains the whole amount of the cash deposited; if it does not wish to be more liquid, but seeks (for example) to restore a conventional reserve ratio, it will have to increase its investments. But substantially the same sort of thing happens when anyone, whose credit is much above the average, borrows. Here the borrowing is nearly always a voluntary act on the part of the borrower, which would not be undertaken unless he was willing to become less liquid than before; the fact that he has to pay interest on the loan means that he will be made worse off if he does not spend the proceeds. On the other hand, if the borrower's credit is good, the liquidity of the lender will not be very greatly impaired by his making the loan, so that his demand for money is likely to be at least rather less than it was before the loan was made. Thus the net effect of the loan is likely to be "inflationary," in the sense that the purchase of capital goods or securities by the borrower is likely to be a more important affair than any sale of capital goods or securities by the lender, made necessary in order for the lender to restore his liquidity position.

Does it follow that all borrowing and lending is inflationary in this sense? I do not think so; for let us take the case when the borrower's credit is very bad, and the lender is only tempted to lend by the offer of a very high rate of interest. Then the impairment of the lender's liquidity position will be very considerable; and he may feel it necessary to sell rather less risky securities to an even greater capital sum in order to restore his liquidity position. Here the net effect would be "deflationary."

The practical conclusion of this seems to be that while *voluntary* borrowing and lending is at least a symptom of monetary expansion, and is thus likely to be accompanied by rising prices, "distress borrowing" is an exception to this rule; and it follows, further, that the sort of stimulation to lending, by persuading people to make loans which they would not have made without persuasion (which was rather a feature of certain phases of the world depression), is a dubious policy—for the lenders, perhaps without realising what they are doing, are very likely to try and restore their liquidity position, and so to offset, and perhaps more than offset, the expansive effects of the loan.

VI

It is now time for us to begin putting together the conclusions we have so far reached. Our method of analysis, it will have appeared, is simply an extension of the ordinary method of value theory. In value theory, we take a private individual's income and expenditure account; we ask which of the items in that account are under the individual's own control, and then how he will adjust these items in order to reach a most preferred position. On the production side, we make a similar analysis of the profit and loss account of the firm. My suggestion is that monetary theory needs to be based again upon a similar analysis, but this time, not of an income account, but of a capital account, a balance sheet. We have to concentrate on the forces which make assets and liabilities what they are.

So as far as banking theory is concerned, this is really the method which is currently adopted; though the essence of the problem is there somewhat obscured by the fact that banks, in their efforts to reach their "most preferred position" are hampered or assisted by the existence of conventional or legally obligatory reserve ratios. For theoretical purposes, this fact ought only to be introduced at a rather late stage; if that is done, then my suggestion can be expressed by saying that we ought to regard every individual in the community as being, on a small scale, a bank. Monetary theory becomes a sort of generalisation of banking theory.

We shall have to draw up a sort of generalised balance sheet, suitable for all individuals and institutions. It will have to be so generalised that many of the individual items will, in a great many cases, not appear. But that does not matter for our purposes. Such a generalised balance sheet will presumably run much as follows.

Assets.	*Liabilities.*
Consumption goods —perishable	
Consumption goods —durable	
Money	
Bank deposits	
Short term debts	Short term debts
Long term debts	Long term debts
Stocks and shares	
Productive equipment (including goods in process)	

We have been concerned up to the present with an analysis (very sketchy, I am afraid) of the equilibrium of this balance sheet. This analysis has at least shown that the relative size of the different items on this balance sheet is governed mainly by anticipation of the yield of investments and of risks.[1] It is these anticipations which play a part here corresponding to the part played by prices in value theory.[2]

Now the fact that our "equilibrium" is here determined by subjective factors like anticipations, instead of objective factors like prices, means that this purely theoretical study of money can never hope to reach results so tangible and precise as those which value theory in its more limited field can hope to attain. If I am right, the whole problem of applying monetary theory is largely one of deducing changes in anticipations from the changes in objective data which call them forth. Obviously, this is not an easy task, and, above all, it is not one which can be performed in a mechanical fashion. It

[1] As we have seen, these risks are as much a matter of the period of investment as of the yield. For certain purposes this is very important. Thus, in the case of that kind of investment which consists in the starting of actual processes of production, the yield which is expected if the process can be carried through may be considerable; but the yield if the process has to be interrupted will be large and negative. Uncertainty of the period for which resources are free will therefore have a very powerful effect in interrupting production. Short-run optimism will usually be enough to start a Stock Exchange boom; but to start an industrial boom relatively long-run optimism is necessary.

[2] I am aware that too little is said in this paper about the liabilities of the above balance sheet. A cursory examination suggests that the same forces which work through the assets side work through the liabilities side in much the same way. But this certainly requires further exploration.

needs judgment and knowledge of business psychology much more than sustained logical reasoning. The arm-chair economist will be bad at it, but he can at least begin to realise the necessity for it, and learn to co-operate with those who can do it better than he can.

However, I am not fouling my own nest; I do not at all mean to suggest that economic theory comes here to the end of its resources. When once the connection between objective facts and anticipations has been made, theory comes again into its rights; and it will not be able to complain of a lack of opportunities.

Nevertheless, it does seem to me most important that, when considering these further questions, we should be well aware of the gap which lies behind us, and that we should bring out very clearly the assumptions which we are making about the genesis of anticipations. For this does seem to be the only way in which we can overcome the extraordinary theoretical differences of recent years, which are, I think very largely traceable to this source.

VII

Largely, but not entirely; or rather a good proportion of them seem to spring from a closely related source, which is yet not quite identical with the first. When we seek to apply to a changing world any particular sort of individual equilibrium, we need to know how the individual will respond, not only to changes in the price-stimuli, or anticipation-stimuli, but also to a change in his total wealth.[1] How will he distribute an increment (or decrement) of wealth—supposing, as we may suppose, that this wealth is measured in monetary terms?

It may be observed that this second problem has an exact counterpart in value theory. Recent work in that field has shown the importance of considering carefully, not only how the individual reacts to price-changes, but also how he reacts to changes in his available expenditure. Total wealth, in our present problem, plays just the same part as total expenditure in the theory of value.

In the theory of money, what we particularly want to know is how the individual's demand for money will respond to a change in his total wealth—that is to say, in the value of his net assets. Not seeing any *a priori* reason why he should react in one way rather than another, monetary theorists have often been content to make use of the simplest possible assumption—that the

[1] The amount of money demanded depends upon three groups of factors: (1) the individual's subjective preferences for holding money or other things; (2) his wealth; (3) his anticipations of future prices and risks. Changes in the demand for money affect present prices, but present prices affect the demand for money mainly through their effect on wealth and on price-anticipations.

demand for money will be increased in the same proportion as total net assets have increased.[1] But this is a very arbitrary assumption; and it may be called in question, partly for analytical reasons, and partly because it seems to make the economic system work much too smoothly to account for observed fact. As one example of this excessive smoothness, I may instance the classical theory of international payments; as another, Mr. Harrod's views on the "Expansion of Bank Credit" which have recently been interesting the readers of *Economica* and of the *Economist*.[2] It would hardly be too much to say that one observed fact alone is sufficient to prove that this assumption cannot be universally true (let us hope and pray that it is sometimes true, nevertheless)—the fact of the trade cycle. For if it were true, the monetary system would always exhibit a quite straightforward kind of stability; a diminished demand for money on the part of some people would raise the prices of capital goods and securities, and this would raise the demand for money on the part of the owners of those securities. Similarly an increased demand for money would lower prices, and this would lower the demand for money elsewhere. The whole thing would work out like an ordinary demand and supply diagram. But it is fairly safe to say that we do not find this straightforward stability in practice.

The analytical reason why this sort of analysis is unsatisfactory is the following: The assumption of increased wealth leading to a proportionately increased demand for money is only plausible so long as the value of assets has increased, but other things have remained equal. Now, as we have seen, the other things which are relevant to this case are not prices (as in the theory of value) but anticipations, of the yield of investment and so on. And since these anticipations must be based upon objective facts, and an unexpected increase in wealth implies a change in objective facts, of a sort very likely to be relevant to the anticipations, it is fairly safe to assume that very many of the changes in wealth with which we are concerned will be accompanied by a change in anticipations. If this is so, the assumption of proportionate change in the demand for money loses most of its plausibility.

For if we assume (this is jumping over my gap, so I must emphasise that it is only an assumption) that an increase in wealth will very often be accompanied by an upward revision of expectations of yield, then the change will set in motion at least one tendency which is certain to diminish the demand for money. Taking this into account *as well as* the direct effect of the increase in

[1] Of course, they say "income." But in this case "income" can only be strictly interpreted as "expected income." And in most of the applications which are made, this works out in the same way as the assumption given above.

[2] The above was written before reading Mr. Harrod's rejoinder to Mr. Robertson. As I understand him, Mr. Harrod is now only maintaining that the expansion of bank credit may work smoothly. With that I am in no disagreement.

wealth, the situation begins to look much less clear. For it must be remembered that our provisional assumption about the direct effect was only guesswork; there is no necessary reason why the direct effect should increase the demand for money proportionately or even increase it at all. So, putting the two together, it looks perfectly possible that the demand for money may either increase or diminish.

We are treading on thin ice; but the unpleasant possibilities which now begin to emerge are sufficiently plausible for their examination to be well worth while. What happens, to take a typical case, if the demand for money is independent of changes in wealth, so that neither an increase in wealth nor a diminution will affect the demand for money?

One can conceive of a sort of equilibrium in such a world, but it would be a hopelessly unstable equilibrium. For if any single person tried to increase his money holdings, and the supply of money was not increased, prices would all fall to zero. If any person tried to diminish his money holdings, prices would all become infinite. In fact, of course, if demand were so rigid, the system could only be kept going by a continuous and meticulous and adaptation of the supply of money to the demand.

Further, in such a world, very curious results would follow from saving. A sudden increase in saving would leave some people (the owners of securities) with larger money balances than they had expected; other people (the producers of consumption goods) with smaller money balances. If, in their efforts to restore their money holdings, the owners of securities buy more securities, and the producers of consumption goods buy less consumption goods, a swing of prices, consumption good prices falling, security prices rising, would set in, and might go on indefinitely. It could only be stopped, either by the owners of securities buying the services of producers, or by the producers selling securities. But there is no knowing when this would happen, or where prices would finally settle; for the assumption of a rigid demand for money snaps the connecting link between money and prices.

After this, we shall be fairly inured to shocks. It will not surprise us to be told that wage-changes will avail nothing to stop either an inflation or a deflation, and we shall be able to extend the proposition for ourselves to interference with conventional or monopolistic prices of any kind, in any direction. But we shall be in a hurry to get back to business.

VIII

These exercises in the economics of an utterly unstable world give us something too mad to fit even our modern *Spätkapitalismus*; but the time which economists have spent on them will not have been wasted if they have served as a corrective to the too facile optimism engendered by the first assumption we tried. Obviously, what we want is something between the two—but not, I think, a mere splitting of the difference. This would give the assumption that an increase in wealth always raises the demand for money, but less than proportionately; if we had time, it might be profitable to work out this case in detail. It would allow for the possibility of considerable fluctuations, but they would not be such absurd and hopeless fluctuations as in the case of rigid demand.

However, I think we can do better than that. The assumption which seems to me most plausible, most consistent with the whole trend of our analysis, and at the same time to lead to results which at any rate look realistic, is one which stresses the probable differences in the reactions of different members of the community. We have already seen that a considerable proportion of a community's monetary stock is always likely to be in the hands of people who are obliged by their relative poverty to be fairly insensitive to changes in anticipations. For these people, therefore, most of the incentive to reduce their demand for money when events turn out more favourably will be missing; there seems no reason why we should not suppose that they will generally react "positively" to changes in their wealth—that an increase in wealth will raise their demand for money more or less proportionately, a fall in their wealth will diminish it. But we must also allow for the probability that other people are much more *sensitive*—that an increase in wealth is not particularly likely to increase their demand for money, and may very well diminish it.

If this is so, it would follow that where the sensitive trade together, price-fluctuations may start on very slight provocation; and once they are under way, the rather less sensitive would be enticed in. Stock exchange booms will pass over into industrial booms, if industrial entrepreneurs are also fairly sensitive; and, in exactly the same way, stock exchange depressions will pass into industrial depressions. But the insensitive are always there to act as a flywheel, defeating by their insensitivity both the exaggerated optimism and the exaggerated pessimism of the sensitive class. How this comes about I cannot attempt to explain in detail, though it would be an interesting job, for one might be able to reconcile a good many apparently divergent theories. But it would lead us too deeply into Cycle theory—I will only say that I think the period of fluctuation turns out to depend, in rather complex fashion, upon the distribution of sensitivity and the distribution of production periods between industrial units.

Instead, I may conclude with two general reflections.

If it is the insensitive people who preserve the stability of capitalism, people who are insensitive (you will remember) largely because for them the costs of transferring assets are large relatively to the amount of assets they control, then the development of capitalism, by diminishing these costs, is likely to be a direct cause of increasing fluctuations. It reduces costs in two ways: by technical devices (of which banks are only one example), and by instilling a more "capitalistic" spirit, which looks more closely to profit, and thus reduces subjective costs. In doing these things, capitalism is its own enemy, for it imperils that stability without which it breaks down.

Lastly, it seems to follow that when we are looking for policies which make for economic stability, we must not be led aside by a feeling that monetary troubles are due to "bad" economic policy, in the old sense, that all would go well if we reverted to free trade and *laisser-faire*. In so doing, we are no better than the Thebans who ascribed the plague to blood-guiltiness, or the supporters of Mr. Roosevelt who expect to reach recovery through reform. There is no reason why policies which tend to economic welfare, statically considered, should also tend to monetary stability. Indeed, the presumption is rather the other way round. A tariff, for example, may be a very good instrument of recovery on occasion, for precisely the reason which free-traders deplore; that it harms a great many people a little for the conspicuous benefit of a few. That may be just the sort of measure we want.

These will be unpalatable conclusions; but I think we must face the possibility that they are true. They offer the economist a pretty hard life, for he, at any rate, will not be able to have a clear conscience either way, over many of the alternatives he is called upon to consider. His ideals will conflict and he will not be able to seek an easy way out by sacrificing either.

3

MONEY, CAPITAL, AND OTHER STORES OF VALUE

by James Tobin

Professor Tobin repeats Hicks' manifesto calling for a microeconomically based monetary theory. An essential element, he argues, is to formulate the demand for money as a stock variable among other forms of wealth holding. This leads to the requirement for a general equilibrium model of asset markets, a prescription that Professor Tobin and his colleagues subsequently fulfilled. In formal mathematical general equilibrium models however, this portion of Professor Tobin's design represents unfinished business of the field. Formal models, such as those in this collection, have not generally treated the general equilibrium of asset markets—including markets for shares, direct ownership of capital, and debt of various maturities—simultaneously with that of flow markets.

The following was reprinted with permission from *The American Economic Review*, vol. LI, No. 2, 1961. © 1961, American Economic Association.

ISBN 0-12-663970-1

MONEY, CAPITAL, AND OTHER STORES OF VALUE

By James Tobin
Yale University

I. *Monetary Economics and Rational Behavior*

The intellectual gulf between economists' theory of the values of goods and services and their theories of the value of money is well known and periodically deplored. Twenty-five years after Hicks's eloquent call for a marginal revolution in monetary theory [4] our students still detect that their mastery of the presumed fundamental, theoretical apparatus of economics is put to very little test in their studies of monetary economics and aggregative models. As Hicks complained, anything seems to go in a subject where propositions do not have to be grounded in someone's optimizing behavior and where shrewd but casual empiricisms and analogies to mechanics or thermodynamics take the place of inferences from utility and profit maximization.

From the other side of the chasm, the student of monetary phenomena can complain that pure economic theory has never delivered the tools to build a structure of Hicks's brilliant design. The utility maximizing individual and the profit maximizing firm know everything relevant about the present and future and about the consequences of their decisions. They buy and sell, borrow and lend, save and consume, work and play, live and let live, in a frictionless world; information, transactions, and decisions are costless. Money holdings have no place in that world, unless possession of green pieces of paper and yellow pieces of metal satisfies some ultimate miserly or numismatic taste. Wealth, of course, has the reflected utility of the future consumption it commands. But this utility cannot be imputed to money unless there are no higher yielding assets available. As Samuelson has pointed out [4, pages 122-24], in a world of omniscient households and firms, dealing in strictly perfect markets, all vehicles of saving in use must bear the same rate of return. If "money" bears that yield, wealth-holders will be indifferent between money and other stores of value—the demand for money will be indeterminate. If money fails to yield the going rate, no one will hold it. Even though money is required as a medium of exchange, transactors will suffer no cost or inconvenience by holding more lucrative assets at all times except the negligible microseconds before and after transactions.

The general sources of the "utility" of money have, of course, long been clear to monetary theorists. Lavington [9] and Pigou [13], for example, imputed to money a rate of return varying inversely with the size of money holdings relative to the transactions needs and total wealth of the holder. This return stands for the convenience and economy of having wealth readily available as means of payment, as well as the safety of money compared with other stores of value. The only alternative asset that these elders of the Cambridge School explicitly envisaged was capital investment. "This proportion [k] depends upon the convenience obtained and the risk avoided through the possession of [money], by the loss of real income involved through the diversion to this use of resources that might have been devoted to the production of future commodities. . . . k will be larger the less attractive is the production use and the more attractive is the rival money use of resources. The chief factor upon which the attractiveness of the production use depends is the expected fruitfulness of industrial activity" [13, pages 166, 168]. In short, an individual adjusts his money holding so that its marginal imputed return is equal to the rate available to him in capital investment. Paradoxically the Cambridge tradition did not build on these ideas of liquidity preference. Instead of being systematically related to the profitability of investment and to other variables affecting the rational calculations of wealth owners, the demand for money became a constant proportion of income. Marshall [11, page 47] had explicitly mentioned wealth as well as income, but somehow wealth was dropped from the tradition. (k is not the only instance in English economics where a variable coefficient left unprotected by functional notation has quickly evolved into a constant in everyday use.) Hicks's prescription for monetary theory in 1935 was in much the same spirit as the approach of Lavington and Pigou. His strictures were nonetheless timely; the spirit of the original Cambridge theory had become obscured by the mechanical constant-velocity tradition.

Recent developments in economic theory have greatly improved the prospects of carrying out Hicks's "simplifying" suggestions and deriving rigorously the imputed return or marginal utility of money holdings in relation to their size. In the past decade theory has begun a systematic penetration of the murky jungle of frictions, market imperfections, and uncertainties. The theory of optimal inventory holdings, for example, shows how transactions and delivery costs must be balanced against interest and carrying costs. Applied to inventories of cash, the theory gives precision to the relation of cash holdings to the volume of nonfinancial transactions, the costs of asset exchanges, and the yields available on alternative assets [1] and [17]. A parallel development has been the theory of choices involving risk. Applied to the general strategy of portfolio selection, the theory of risk aversion explains how money may find a place in a rationally diversified portfolio [10] and [18].

The new tools are constructing a bridge between general economic theory and monetary economics. More than that, they give promise at last of a general equilibrium theory of the capital account. Such a theory would explain both the balance-sheet choices of economic units as constrained by their net worths and the determination of yields in markets where asset supplies and demands are balanced. What characteristics of assets and of investors determine the substitutabilities or complementarities among a set of assets? Among the relevant properties with which the theory must deal are: costs of asset exchanges; predictability of real and money asset values at various future dates; correlations—positive, negative, or zero—among asset prospects; liquidity—the time it takes to realize full value of an asset; reversibility—possibility and cost of simultaneously buying and selling an asset; the timing and predictability of investors' expected needs for wealth.

In a world of financial assets and well-developed capital markets, Keynes [7, pages 166 and 168, pages 140-41] was right in perceiving the tactical advantage to the theorist of treating separately decisions determining total wealth and its rate of growth and decisions regarding the composition of wealth. A theory of the income account concerns what goods and services are produced and consumed, and how fast nonhuman wealth is accumulated. The decision variables are flows. A theory of the capital account concerns the proportions in which various assets and debts appear in portfolios and balance sheets. The decision variables are stocks. Income and capital accounts are linked by accounting identities—e.g., increase in net worth equals saving plus capital appreciation—and by technological and financial stock-flow relations. Utilities and preference orderings attach to flows of goods and services; the values of stocks are entirely derivative from their ability to contribute to these flows. Some stock-flow relationships are so tight that this distinction is pedantic: the only way an art collector can obtain the flow of satisfactions of owning a particular *chef d'oeuvre* is to own it. But there is a vast menu of assets whose yields are generalized purchasing power, nothing less or more—investors do not have intrinsic preferences among engravings of security certificates.

II. *The Capital Account in Aggregative Models*

Strictures on the Need for Explicit Assumptions. Aggregative models of the income account reduce the dimensions of general equilibrium theory, purchasing definiteness in results at the risk of errors of aggregation. Commodities, prices, and factors of production are limited to one or two. For similar reasons, it is fruitful to limit the number of assets in aggregative theory of the capital account.

The first requisite of a theory of wealth composition is that decisions about assets and debts must, in the aggregate as for the individual, add up to the net worth of the moment, neither more nor less. Monetary theory needs to specify explicitly what forms the nonmonetary parts of wealth can take. Many confusions and disagreements can be traced to ambiguities and differences in assumptions about the nature of wealth. A theory should state the menu of assets assumed available, specifying which are components of net private wealth (capital stock plus government debt) and which are intermediate assets (private debts). Moreover, the independent interest rates in an aggregative system should be enumerated. An independent rate is one that is not tied to another yield by an invariant relationship determined outside the system; e.g., by a constant risk differential.

The means of payment of a country—at least in part governmental in origin—are generally demand "debts" of the central government. But there are also means of payment of private manufacture; indeed it is possible to imagine a pure credit economy without government debts of any variety, where all means of payment are private debts backed by private debts. Likewise it is possible to imagine a wholly nonmonetary public debt.

Monetary discussions suffer from confounding the effects of changing the supply of means of payment with the effects of changing the net value of private claims on the central government. The second kind of change takes time and requires private saving, absorbed in fiscal deficit, or dissaving equal to fiscal surplus. The first type of change can be accomplished instantaneously by exchanges of assets. When an author proposes to discuss the effects of changing the supply of money, is he imagining aggregate net worth to change simultaneously by the same amount? Effects that are due to increases of private wealth in the form of government debt should not be attributed to money per se. Sometimes we are asked to imagine that everyone wakes up to find his cash stock has doubled overnight and to trace subsequent adjustments. This mental experiment is harmless and instructive, provided its results are not considered indicative of changes in money supply engineered by normal central bank procedures. The overnight miracle increases equally money stocks and net worth; the gremlins who bring the money are not reported to take away bonds or IOU's. The repercussions are a mixture of effects: partly those of an unanticipated increase in net worth in the form of assets fixed in money value (as if the gremlins had brought bonds instead); partly those of an increase in the supply of means of payment relative to transactions needs and to other assets. The theory of real balance effect [12] is at the same time much more and much less than the theory of money.

Established procedure in aggregative model building is to specify the quantity of money, M, as an exogenous variable determined by the "monetary authorities." The practice is questionable when part of the money supply is manufactured by private enterprise. Banks are not arms of government. The true exogenous variables are the instruments of monetary control: the quantity of demand debt available to serve as primary bank reserves, the supplies of other kinds of government debt, required reserve ratios, the discount rate. Once these instrument variables are set, the interaction of bank and public preferences determines the quantity of money. No doubt a skillful central bank can generally manipulate its controls to keep M on target, but part of the job of monetary theory is to explain how. A theory which takes as data the instruments of control rather than M, will not break down if and when there are changes in the targets or the marksmanship of the authorities.

Two Models, One Keynesian and One Not. The assets of a formal model of Keynes's *General Theory* [7] appear to be four or possibly five in number: (1) government demand debt, serving either as means of payment or as bank reserves, (2) bank deposits, (3) long-term government bonds, (4) physical capital, i.e., stocks of *the* good produced on the income-account side of the model, and possibly (5) private debts, serving along with bonds (3) and demand debt (1) as assets held by the banking system against its monetary liabilities (2). Net private wealth is the sum of (1), (3), and (4).

Though there are four or five assets in this model, there are only two yields: the rate of return on money, whether demand debt or bank deposits, institutionally set at zero, and *the* rate of interest, common to the other two or three assets. For the nonmonetary assets of his system, Keynes simply followed the classical theory of portfolio selection in perfect markets mentioned above; that is, he assumed that capital, bonds, and private debts are perfect substitutes in investors' portfolios. The marginal efficiency of capital must equal *the* rate of interest.

Keynes did not, of course, envisage literal equality of yields on consols, private debts, and equity capital. Indeed, he provides many perceptive observations on the sources and cyclical variations of the expectations and risk premiums that differentiate market yields. But in given circumstances these differentials are constants independent of the relative supplies of the assets and therefore inessential. Once one of the rates is set, the others must differ from it by appropriate allowances for risk and for expectations of price changes.

Thus Keynes had only one yield differential to explain within his theoretical model: the difference between the zero yield of money and *the* interest rate. This differential he explained in his theory of liquidity preference, which made the premium of bond yields above money depend on the stock of money relative to the volume of transactions and, presumably, aggregate wealth. Keynes departed from the classical model of portfolio choice and asset yields to explain money holdings, applying and developing an innovation borrowed from his own *Treatise* [8, pages 140-44, 248-57], a rate differential that depends systematically on relative asset supplies.

Post-Keynesian aggregative theorists, whether disciples or opponents or just neutral fanciers of models, have stuck pretty close to the Keynesian picture of the capital account. For example, Patinkin [12] explicitly includes all the assets listed above, and no more, in his most comprehensive model. Like Keynes, he has only one interest rate to determine. His difference from Keynes is his real balance effect.

As Hicks [5], Kaldor [6], and others have pointed out, there are apparently no short-term obligations of fixed money value in the Keynesian scheme. Recognition of these near-moneys would add one asset category and a second interest rate to the Keynesian model of the capital account. Transactions costs become the major determinant of the money-short rate differential, and considerations of speculation and risk for investors of different types affect the size and sign of the short-long differential.

An entirely different monetary tradition begins with a two-asset world of money and capital and ignores to begin with all closer money substitutes of whatever maturity. Significantly, the authors of the Cambridge tradition, as mentioned above, regarded direct capital investment as *the* alternative to money holdings. Why did they fail to carry into their monetary theory the clear inference that the demand for money depends not only on the volume of transactions but also on the yield of capital? Perhaps the best guess is that for these economists the yield of capital was in the short run a constant, explained by productivity and thrift. Money balances were adjusting to a rate already determined, not to a rate their adjustment might help to determine.

On its own logic, therefore, the constant-velocity approximation is of little applicability in models where the rate of return on capital is variable. It is not applicable to cyclical fluctuations, where variations of employment affect the productivity of the given capital stock. It is not applicable to secular growth, if capital deepening or technological change alters the yield of capital.

Neither is the constant-velocity assumption applicable where money substitutes other than capital are available and have endogenously variable yields, for then the demand for money would depend on those yields. Paradoxically, the model of greatest popularity in everyday analysis of monetary policy really has no room for monetary policy per se. In the two-asset, money-capital economy there are no assets which the central bank and the banking system can buy or sell to change the quantity of money.

What is the mechanism by which a change in the quantity of money brings about the proportional change in money income that constant-velocity theory predicts? Sometimes the mechanism as described seems to assume a direct relationship between money holdings and spending on income account: When people have more money than they need, they spend it. It is as simple as that. Patinkin [12, Chapter 8] rightly objects that spending on income account should be related to excess wealth, not excess money. If the mechanism is a real balance effect, then it works only when new money is also new private wealth, accumulated by the public as a result of government spending financed at the printing press or the mint.

A mechanism more in the spirit of the arguments of Lavington, Pigou, and Hicks is that owners of wealth with excess money holdings seek to restore the balance of their capital accounts. Trying to shift from money to capital, they bid up the prices of the existing capital stock; and since new capital goods and old must bear comparable prices, prices also rise in commodity markets. The process ends when, and only when, money incomes have risen enough to absorb the new money into transactions balances. The real rate of return on the capital stock remains unchanged.

This mechanism can apply to increases in M due to expansion of bank lending—with private debts added to the menu of assets—as well as to increases associated with net saving. One aspect of the mechanism is then the process of which Wicksell [19] gave the classical description. Banks expand the money supply by offering to lend at a rate—the market rate—lower than the yield of capital—the natural rate. Excess demand for capital by new borrowers bids up capital values, with the repercussions already described. Whether this process has an end or not depends on whether the banks' incentive to expand is extinguished by proportionate increases of money supply, money income, and prices. For a pure credit economy, where all means of payment are based on monetization of private debts, this model produces no equilibrium. The end to the Wicksellian process depends on banks' needs for reserves, whether enforced by legislation or by their own transactions and precautionary motives.

I have presented a modern version of a two-asset, money-capital economy in [16]. Money and government debt are one and the same, and there are no private debts. The proportions in which owners of wealth desire to split their holdings between money and capital depend upon the volume of transactions and on the rate of return on capital. The yield of capital is not a constant, as it seems to be in the Cambridge model, but depends on the capital intensity of current production. The differential between the yield of capital and that of money depends on the relative supplies of the two basic assets; the liquidity preference mechanism is applied to a money-capital margin rather than a money-securities margin. The price level adjusts the relative supplies to the portfolios investors desire, given the ruling marginal productivity of capital. This portfolio adjustment is like the mechanism of response to increase in the quantity of money described above for the constant-velocity model; but here it does not necessarily maintain the same velocity or the same yield of capital. A real balance effect on consumption can be added if desired.

A trivial extension of the money-capital model is to include other kinds of government securities, on the assumption that given certain constant rate differentials they are perfect portfolio substitutes for money proper. Then "money" in the model stands for the entire government debt, whether it takes the form of media of exchange or money substitutes. The differential between the return on capital and the yield of any government debt instrument is determined by the relative supplies of total government debt and capital.

By a similar extension private debts could be added to the menu of assets, again with the proviso that they are perfect substitutes for government debt instruments but not for capital equity. This addition does not change the requirement of portfolio balance, that the net private position in assets of fixed money value stands in the appropriate relationship to the value of the capital stock.

Thus extended, the money-capital model winds up with the same asset menu as the Keynes-Patinkin model. Each has only one interest differential to be explained within the model. But there is a vast difference. The Keynes-Patinkin model assumes that all debt instruments are perfect substitutes for capital. The interest rate to be explained is the rate common, with the appropriate constant corrections, to all assets other than money itself. What explains this rate is the supply of money relative to transactions requirements and to total wealth. Monetary policy, altering the demand debt component of government debt, can affect the terms on which the community will hold the capital stock. Expansion of the real value of unmonetized debt cannot do so, although in Patinkin's version it can influence the level of activity via the real balance effect on current consumption. The money-capital model, in contrast, casts debt instruments on the side of money and focuses attention on the relationship between the total real value of government debt, monetized or unmonetized, and the rate of return the community requires of the capital stock. It contains no role for monetary policy; only the aggregate net position of the public as borrowers and lenders is relevant, not its composition.

The two models give different answers to important questions. Does retirement of government long-term debt through taxation have expansionary or deflationary consequences? The question refers not to the temporary multiplier-like effects of the surplus that reduces the debt—these are of course deflationary—but to the enduring effects, through the capital account, of having a smaller debt. The instinctive answer of economists schooled in the Keynesian tradition is "expansionary." The supply of bonds is smaller relative to the supply of money; *the* rate of interest goes down, and investment is stimulated until the marginal efficiency comes down correspondingly. The answer of the money-capital model is, as indicated above, "deflationary." The assumed substitutability of bonds and money will keep the bond rate up. The decline in the government debt component of net private wealth means that investors will require a higher rate of return, or marginal efficiency, in order to hold the existing capital stock.

Granted that both models are oversimplified, which is the better guide to instinct? Are long-term government debt instruments a better substitute for capital than they are for short-term debt and money? Reflection on the characteristic properties of these assets—in particular how they stand vis-à-vis risks of price-level changes—surely suggests that if government securities must be assimilated to capital or money, one or the other, the better bet is money.

Towards a Synthesis. A synthesis of the two approaches must, of course, avoid the arbitrary choices of both, abandoning the convenience of assuming that all assets but one are perfect substitutes. The price of this advance in realism and relevance is the necessity to explain not just one market-determined rate of return but a whole structure. The structure of rates may be pictured as strung between two poles, anchored at one end by the zero own-rate conventionally borne by currency (and by the central bank discount rate) and at the other end by the marginal productivity of the capital stock. Among assets that are not perfect substitutes, the structure of rates will depend upon relative supplies. In general, an increase in the supply of an asset—e.g., long-term government bonds—will cause its rate to rise relative to other rates, but less in relation to assets for which it is directly or indirectly a close substitute—in the example, short-term securities and money—than in relation to other assets—in the example, capital.

In such a synthesis, monetary policy falls in proper perspective. The quantity of money can affect the terms on which the community will hold capital, but it is not the only asset supply that can do so. The net monetary position of the public is important, but so is its composition.

One lesson of the simple money-capital model should be retained. The strategic variable—the ultimate gauge of expansion or deflation, of monetary tightness or ease—is the rate of return that the community of wealth-owners require in order to absorb the existing capital stock (valued at current prices), no more, no less, into their portfolios and balance sheets. This rate may be termed the supply price of capital. If it is lower than the marginal productivity of capital, there will be excess demand for capital, stimulating increases in prices of capital goods and additions to the stock. If the supply price of capital is higher than its marginal productivity, demand for capital will be insufficient to absorb the existing stock; its valuation will tend to fall, discouraging production of new capital goods. The effects of deviation of supply price of capital from the marginal productivity of the existing stock are similar to those of discrepancies between Wicksell's market and natural rates.

In assessing policy actions and other autonomous changes, there is really no short-cut substitute for the supply price of capital. As the example of long-term debt retirement illustrates, *the* Keynesian interest rate, the long-term bond rate, can be a misleading indicator. Events that cause it to fall may cause the supply price of capital actually to rise. Another example of error due to concentration on the long-term bond rate is the following Keynesian argument: Expectation of a rise in *the* interest rate leads to liquidity preference and keeps the current interest rate high; a high interest rate discourages investment. However, what the marginal efficiency of capital must compete with is not the market quotation of the long-term rate, but that quotation less the expected capital losses. If the fact that the rate so corrected is close to zero causes substitution of money for bonds, should it not also cause substitution of capital for bonds?

If the long-term bond rate is an inadequate substitute for the supply price of capital, the same is true of another popular indicator: the quantity of money. The modern quantity-of-money theorist [2] (to be distinguished from the ancient quantity-theorist-of-money, who actually was a believer in the constancy of velocity), holds that virtually everything of strategic importance in the capital account can be studied by focusing on the supply and demand for money. This view, though seemingly endorsed by Shaw [15], has been persuasively opposed by Gurley and Shaw [3]. As they point out, it is not hard to describe events and policies that raise the supply price of capital while leaving the quantity of money unchanged or even increasing it. Why concentrate on variables other than those of direct central interest?

How far to go in disaggregation is, as always, a matter of taste and purpose; it depends also on the possibilities of empirical application and testing. A minimal program for a theory of the capital account relevant to American institutions would involve: (1) four constituents of net private wealth: government demand debt, government short debt, government long debt, and capital stock; (2) two intermediate assets: bank deposits and private debts; (3) two institutionally or administratively fixed interest rates: zero on bank deposits and demand debt, and the central bank discount rate; (4) four market-determined yields: the short-term interest rate, the long-term interest rate, the rate on private debts, and the supply price of equity capital.

In this model, the quantity of demand debt is divided between currency held outside banks and the net (unborrowed) reserves of banks. Required reserves depend on the volume of deposits. If required reserves exceed net reserves, banks must borrow from the central bank at the discount rate. The disposable funds of banks are their deposits less their required reserves. These are divided among net free reserves (net reserves less required reserves), short governments, long governments, and private debts in proportions that depend on the discount rate, the short rate, the long rate, and the private loan rate. The nonbank public apportions net private wealth among currency, bank deposits, the two kinds of interest-bearing government debt, private debt to banks (a negative item), and capital equity. All the yields except the discount rate are relevant to the public's portfolio choices. When the wealth constraints are allowed for, there are four independent equations in this system; e.g., a balance equation for each constituent of net private wealth. These equations can be used to find the four endogenous yields. The solution for the yield of capital is its supply price. There is equilibrium of the whole system, which would include also equations for the income account, only if the solution for the supply price of capital coincides with the marginal productivity of the existing stock.

References

1. W. J. Baumol, "The Transactions Demand for Cash: An Inventory Theoretic Approach," *Q.J.E.*, 1952, pp. 545-56.
2. Milton Friedman, *Studies in the Quantity Theory of Money* (Univ. of Chicago Press, 1956), Chap. 1.
3. J. Gurley and E. S. Shaw, *Money in a Theory of Finance* (Brookings Inst., 1960).
4. J. R. Hicks, "A Suggestion for Simplifying the Theory of Money," Chap. 2 of *Readings in Monetary Theory* (Irwin, 1951), reprinted from *Economica* NS II (1935), pp. 1-19.
5. *Ibid., Value and Capital* (Oxford, 1939), Chap. 13.
6. N. Kaldor, "Speculation and Economic Stability," *Rev. of Econ. Studies,* 1939-40, pp. 1-27.

7. J. M. Keynes, *The General Theory of Employment, Interest and Money* (Harcourt Brace, 1936).
8. *Ibid., A Treatise on Money*, I (Harcourt Brace, 1930).
9. Lavington, *The English Capital Market*, 3rd ed. (London: Methuen and Co., Ltd., 1941), Chap. 6.
10. H. Markowitz, *Portfolio Selection* (Wiley, 1959).
11. Alfred Marshall, *Money, Credit, and Commerce* (London: Macmillan, 1923), Chap. 4.
12. Don Patinkin, *Money, Interest, and Prices* (Row Peterson, 1956).
13. A. C. Pigou, "The Value of Money," Chap. 10 of *Readings in Monetary Theory* (Irwin, 1951), reprinted from *Q.J.E.*, 1917-18, pp. 38-65.
14. P. A. Samuelson, *Foundations of Economic Analysis* (Harvard Univ. Press, 1947).
15. E. S. Shaw, "Money Supply and Stable Economic Growth," Chap. 2 of *United States Monetary Policy* (American Assembly, 1958).
16. J. Tobin, "A Dynamic Aggregative Model," *J.P.E.*, 1955, pp. 103-15.
17. *Ibid.*, "The Interest-Elasticity of Transactions Demand for Cash," *Rev. of Econ. and Statis.*, 1956, pp. 241-47.
18. *Ibid.*, "Liquidity Preference as Behavior Towards Risk," *Rev. of Econ. Studies*, 1958, pp. 65-86.
19. K. Wicksell, *Lectures on Political Economy*, II (New York: Macmillan, 1935), pp. 190-208.

Part II

Bilateral Trade

SECTION 1
Classical Writers

4
BILATERAL TRADE: MONEY AS A MEDIUM OF EXCHANGE

The most elementary property of money is that it is used as a medium of exchange. One buys things with it and sells others for it, rather than exchanging goods directly for one another. The use of money facilitates the trading process—though it is not trivially obvious why the introduction of an additional and otherwise useless good should simplify and speed the mechanics of trade. This is the issue that the studies of this Chapter address.

Adam Smith's concern with the division of labor gave him a particular interest in the process of trade. When agents' output is specialized, they necessarily provide for their diverse consumption needs by trade. If exchange is difficult, that difficulty discourages division of labor. "Division of labor is limited by the extent of the market," and impediments to trade narrow the "extent" of the market. Smith's stated concern was the possible noncoincident timing across traders of desired purchases, nonsynchronization. A suitably durable and divisible good, money, was required to even out transactions between agents whose desired trades with one another were not of precisely equal value or coincident scheduling.

> "When the division of labour has been once thoroughly established, it is but a very small part of a man's wants, which the produce of his own labour can supply. He supplies the far greater part of them by exchanging that surplus part of the produce of his own labour, which is over and above his own consumption, for such parts of the produce of other men's labour as he has occasion for. Every man thus lives by exchanging. But when the division of labour first began to take place, this power of exchanging must frequently have been very much clogged and embarrassed in its operations. The butcher has more meat in his shop than he himself can consume, and the brewer and the baker would each of them be willing to purchase a part of it. But

General Equilibrium
Models of
Monetary Economies

ISBN 0-12-663970-1

they have nothing to offer in exchange, except the different productions of their respective trades, and the butcher is already provided with all the bread and beer which he has immediate occasion for. No exchange can, in this case, be made between them. He cannot be their merchant, nor they his customers; and they are all of them thus mutually less serviceable to one another. In order to avoid the inconveniency of such situations, every prudent man in every period of society, after the first establishment of the division of labour, must naturally have endeavored to manage his affairs in such a manner, as to have at all times by him, besides the peculiar produce of his own industry, a certain quantity of some one commodity or other, such as he imagined few people would be likely to refuse in exchange for the produce of their industry."

A more formal treatment of Smith's views would involve a model of production with indivisibility or other non-convexity, a resulting scale economy (Edwards and Starr, 1987), and transaction cost. A fully general treatment of the Smithian view of the interaction between money and specialization is still absent from the literature.

Jevons focused on the problems of coordinating trade among agents as the essential rationale for the use of a medium of exchange. He argued that without a medium of exchange, trade was necessarily limited to exchange of reciprocally desired goods —e.g., the trade between the hungry tailor and the ill-clad baker. Jevons called the situation where the supplier of good *A* is a demander of good *B* and *vice versa* a "double coincidence" of wants. *A priori* it appears that such double coincidences are rare even when we have established market-clearing prices ensuring that for every buyer there is a seller.

"The earliest form of exchange must have consisted in giving what was not wanted directly for that which was wanted. This simple traffic we call barter . . . and distinguish it from sale and purchase in which one of the articles exchanged is intended to be held only for a short time, until it is parted with in a second act of exchange. The object which thus temporarily intervenes in sale and purchase is money. At first sight it might seem that the use of money only doubles the trouble, by making two exchanges necessary where one was sufficient; but a slight analysis of the difficulties inherent in simple barter shows that the balance of trouble lies quite in the opposite direction . . . the first difficulty in barter is to find two persons whose disposable possessions mutually suit each other's wants. There may be many people wanting, and many possessing those things wanted; but to allow of an act of barter there must be a double coincidence, which will rarely happen."

A failure of double coincidence of wants is the more likely event: between two traders; one of whom is the supplier of a good (good *A*) that the other demands, the latter's excess supplies—though of sufficient value at market prices to purchase the desired good *A*—are of a good (*B*) that the former does not require. It can be shown (Ostroy-Starr, selection 12), assuming market clearing prices, that there is a sequence of trades fulfilling budget balance at each trade, starting with the supplier of *A* that will allow each trader eventually to deliver an excess supply and to receive his excess demand, but the sequence is long and complex. Hence, the restriction to trades fulfilling double coincidence is an implicit restriction to easily coordinated (decentralized) trading patterns. Jevons argues that it is to overcome the absence of double coincidence of wants that monetary trade is introduced. The supplier of A, though apparently reluctant to accept B in trade, will accept money. The supplier has no more use for money than he had for B but, by common consent, money can be traded directly for what the supplier of A demands. Menger notes,

> "It is obvious ... that a commodity should be given up by its owner in exchange for another more useful to him. But that every economic unit ... should be willing to exchange his goods for little metal disks apparently useless as such, or for documents representing the latter, is a procedure so opposed to the ordinary course of things, that ... [it is] downright 'mysterious.'"

The less formal literature did not make significantly more explicit than Jevons and Menger the function of a medium of exchange. Authors were generally content to allude to the "difficulties of barter."

Monetary trade, the use of a common medium of exchange, is explained by a need to overcome the inconvenience of barter. What inconvenience? The difficulty of barter derives from the bilateral structure of trade and two consequences of bilateral structure: needs for coordination, and multiple budget constraints. The bilateral trading process imposes the *quid pro quo* requirement. In each trading pair, traders should pay for what they receive. This amounts to a multiplicity of budget constraints, one on each trading pair. This succession of constraints is a much severer restriction on trade than the single lifetime budget constraint of the Arrow-Debreu model. Ostroy (selection 10) notes that the multiple budget constraints are not merely a matter of assumption or observation. They can be derived from more elementary considerations: the *quid pro quo* condition is necessary in order to keep traders honest in the bilateral setting. Absent the *quid pro quo* requirement there would be no effective check to assure that the budget constraint be fulfilled. In a bilateral trade model there are then two reasons to trade goods: (*i*) to arrange for them eventually to go to the agent demanding them, and (*ii*) as means of payment to fulfill the *quid pro quo* requirement. The difficulty of barter is that the combination of (*i*) and (*ii*) may overdetermine the demand for goods so that for relatively simple (informationally decentralized) trading processes, it may not be possible to fulfill both.

The function of money as a medium of exchange is to circumvent the overdeterminacy. Introduction of a monetary commodity (of sufficient value, held sufficiently widely) provides an extra degree of freedom so that the system is no longer overdetermined.[1] Provision of money can allow revision

[1] Martin Shubik refers to money in this context as a "strategic decoupler," a device to separate the necessarily interdependent decisions of unrelated agents.

of the trading process to permit implementation of the equilibrium allocation by decentralized pairwise trade in relatively short trading time.

Sorting out these issues in a more formal setting is the task of Ostroy (selection 10), Starr (selection 11), Ostroy-Starr (selection 12), and Starr (selection 13). The questions addressed include: the origins of the *quid pro quo* restriction (Ostroy, selection 10); to what extent the problems of a medium of exchange and the coordination of trade reflect the requirement that goods be paid for at purchase (*quid pro quo*) (Starr, selection 11); simplification in the coordination of trade provided by the use of a medium of exchange (Ostroy-Starr, selection 12); faster execution of trade from use of a medium of exchange (Starr, selection 13). These studies start where Arrow-Debreu general equilibrium theory leaves off. Prices have been established at which supplies of each good equal the demand for the good. The remaining task is to arrange for the goods to go from the holders of excess supplies to agents with excess demand. Trade takes place pairwise.

Starr (selection 11) formalizes Jevons' problem with the conditions, in addition to pairwiseness, of *quid pro quo* and monotonicity. The monotonicity requirement formalizes Jevons' concept of double coincidence of wants. It requires that in any trade, agents deliver only goods for which they have an excess supply and accept only goods for which they have an excess demand. It is not generally possible to move from an arbitrary initial excess demand and supply position to the equilibrium allocation while fulfilling these conditions. A simple example of three agents and three goods is sufficient to establish the impossibility result. In achieving an equilibrium allocation it is not possible in general to fulfill both *quid pro quo* and monotonicity; either can be fulfilled at the expense of the other. In order to fulfill both and achieve the equilibrium allocation, money is introduced as an $N + 1^{st}$ good, for which the monotonicity requirement is waived; money can be accepted though undesired, delivered though not in excess supply.

Ostroy (selection 10) and Ostroy and Starr (selection 12) develop the concept and implications of decentralization of the bilateral trading process. Jevons' double-coincidence condition is a special case of a class of informationally decentralized trading procedures. Trade is said to be decentralized if two traders, in deciding what trade to undertake, need consult only their own excess supplies and demands. Further information and coordination—implying centralization—would be required if traders had to take into account others' demands and supplies. It is shown that in a relatively short fixed trading time a centralized trading mechanism—requiring more information and coordination than a decentralized procedure—can achieve the equilibrium allocation. In a non-monetary economy, decentralized trade to the equilibrium allocation may be impossible in restricted time, though it can be approached as a limit in more extended time (Starr, selection 13). In general, the twin difficulties of delay or of centralized trade are unavoidable. It is not generally possible successfully to use a decentralized bilateral trading process to achieve the equilibrium allocation in a brief fixed trading time. Money is introduced as a good universally held in sufficient quantity to finance desired purchases. Then in a monetary economy there is a decentralized trading procedure that implements the equilibrium allocation in a brief fixed time. Hence the use of monetary trade allows economizing on time and organization. Implicit in the treatment is the view that the real resource costs of the complex organization associated with centralized trade are prohibitive and that monetary trade is preferable.

Feldman (selection 8) and Goldmann-Starr (selection 9) seek to implement an even more rudimentary view of the trading process. Feldman begins with initial holdings and tastes of trading agents but without prices or a price mechanism. Agents then meet together in pairs to trade. At each trade a pair reallocates current holdings to the contract curve for the pair. The two traders then separate, form new trading pairs, eventually meet again and so forth. The process converges to a pairwise optimum, an allocation so that there is no pair of traders who could be made better off by reallocating their current holdings within the pair. Simple three trader-three good examples however are sufficient to show that a pairwise optimal allocation need not be Pareto optimal. In the fragmented trading structure with corner solutions, a pairwise optimum need not imply common supporting Marginal Rates of Substitution (MRS), a necessary condition for Pareto optimality. However, if there is a good held by all traders—corresponding to money—this universal holding provides sufficient linkage among traders to ensure Pareto optimality of a pairwise optimal allocation. Any Pareto non-optimality of the allocation would eventually show up as a difference among traders of the MRS of a misallocated commodity for the monetary good. Such an inequality would then be arbitraged away in pairwise trade.

Goldman-Starr extend the analysis to economies where trade takes place not only in pairs but in small groups, of size *t*. Again the presence of a monetary (i.e., universally held) commodity is a sufficient condition for *t*-wise optimality to imply Pareto optimality. A weaker class of sufficient conditions and a corresponding class of necessary conditions are also developed. The sufficient conditions for *t*-wise optimality to imply Pareto optimality are systematically less demanding as *t* becomes large. This points up a trade-off between trading group size and allocative efficiency that can be overcome by the use of money (in these models, not so much a medium of exchange as a universally held good providing a standard of value). In particular, the implicit costliness of large group trade leads to small group trade and a corresponding need for a common monetary medium.

What do we conclude from the studies of this Chapter? Essentially, that implementing a general equilibrium allocation by bilateral trade is a tricky proposition, one made significantly easier by the introduction of a single medium of exchange, entering asymmetrically in the trading process. Pairwiseness implies three restrictions on the structure of trade:

1. *Quid pro quo*; a multiplicity of pairwise budget constraints.
2. Nonnegativity; traders in bilateral transactions can deliver only goods they have.
3. Informational decentralization; the information or coordination needed to implement trades must be available pairwise.

These conditions are familiar; they are fulfilled by the individual's single trade with the market in the Arrow-Debreu model. But here they are applied to each pairwise trade. The multiplicity of bilateral trades—and their interdependence—implies however that extending these conditions to the bilateral trading model is not innocuous. It so overdetermines the system that—in contrast to the Arrow-Debreu general equilibrium model—expeditious trade to equilibrium is not generally possible. This represents the inconveniences of barter. The introduction of money as a medium of exchange, in sufficient quantity to avoid the nonnegativity constraint binding, restores sufficient flexibility to allow all three conditions to be fulfilled and to allow trade to proceed to equilibrium. Hence the superiority of monetary trade.

5
OF THE ORIGIN AND USE OF MONEY
by Adam Smith

The use of money as a medium of exchange was an essential element for Smith in the division of labor. Specialized labor with diverse consumption demands provides for those requirements by trade, and money is needed to facilitate trade. Smith did not focus explicitly (as did Jevons and Menger a century later) on the problem of coincidence of wants. His immediate concern was with overcoming indivisibility of traded goods and accomodating differing timing (nonsynchronization) of traders' consumption requirements.

The following is reprinted from *An Inquiry into the Nature and Causes of the Wealth of Nations* by Adam Smith, Book I, Chapter IV.

General Equilibrium
Models of
Monetary Economies

ISBN 0-12-663970-1

An Inquiry into the Nature and Causes of the Wealth of Nations
by Adam Smith
Book I: Chapter IV

Of the Origin and Use of Money

When the division of labour has been once thoroughly established, it is but a very small part of a man's wants which the produce of his own labour can supply. He supplies the far greater part of them by exchanging that surplus part of the produce of his own labour, which is over and above his own consumption, for such parts of the produce of other men's labour as he has occasion for. Every man thus lives by exchanging, or becomes in some measure a merchant, and the society itself grows to be what is properly a commercial society.

But when the division of labour first began to take place, this power of exchanging must frequently have been very much clogged and embarrassed in its operations. One man, we shall suppose, has more of a certain commodity than he himself has occasion for, while another has less. The former consequently would be glad to dispose of, and the latter to purchase, a part of this superfluity. But if this latter should chance to have nothing that the former stands in need of, no exchange can be made between them. The butcher has more meat in his shop than he himself can consume, and the brewer and the baker would each of them be willing to purchase a part of it. But they have nothing to offer in exchange, except the different productions of their respective trades, and the butcher is already provided with all the bread and beer which he has immediate occassion for. No exchange can, in this case, be made between them. He cannot be their merchant, nor they his customers; and they are all of them thus mutually less serviceable to one another. In order to avoid the inconveniency of such situations, every prudent man in every period of society, after the first establishment of the division of labour, must naturally have endeavoured to manage his affairs in such a manner, as to have at all times by him, besides the peculiar produce of his own industry, a certain quantity of some one commodity or other, such as he imagined few people would be likely to refuse in exchange for the produce of their industry.

Many different commodities, it is probable, were successively both thought of and employed for this purpose. In the rude ages of society, cattle are said to have been the common instrument of commerce; and, though they must have been a most inconvenient one, yet in old times we find things were frequently valued according to the number of cattle which had been given in exchange for them. The armour of Diomede, says Homer, cost only nine oxen; but that of Glaucus cost an hundred oxen. Salt is said to be the common instrument of commerce and exchanges in Abyssinia; a species of shells in some parts of the coast of India; dried cod at Newfoundland; tobacco in Virginia; sugar in some of our West India colonies; hides or dressed leather in some other countries; and there is at this day a village in Scotland where it is not uncommon, I am told, for a workman to carry nails instead of money to the baker's shop or the ale-house.

In all countries, however, men seem at last to have been determined by irresistible reasons to give the preference, for this employment, to metals above every other commodity. Metals can not only be kept with as little loss as any other commodity, scarce any thing being less perishable than they are, but they can likewise, without any loss, be divided into any number of parts, as by fusion those parts can easily be reunited again; a quality which no other equally durable commodities possess, and which more than any other quality renders them fit to be the instruments of commerce and circulation. The man who wanted to buy salt, for example, and had nothing but cattle to give in exchange for it, must have been obliged to buy salt to the value of a whole ox, or a whole sheep, at a time. He could seldom buy less than this, because what he was to give for it could seldom be divided without loss; and if he had a mind to buy more, he must, for the same reasons, have been obliged to buy double or triple the quantity, the value, to wit, of two or three oxen, or of two or three sheep. If, on the contrary, instead of sheep or oxen, he had metals to give in exchange for it, he could easily proportion the quantity of the metal to the precise quantity of the commodity which he had immediate occasion for.

Different metals have been made use of by different nations for this purpose. Iron was the common instrument of commerce among the antient Spartans; copper among the antient Romans; and gold and silver among all rich and commercial nations.

Those metals seem originally to have been made use of for this purpose in rude bars, without any stamp or coinage. Thus we are told by Pliny,[1] upon the authority of Timæus, an antient historian, that, till the time of Servius Tullius, the Romans had no coined money, but made use of unstamped bars of copper, to purchase whatever they had occasion for. These rude bars, therefore, performed at this time the function of money.

The use of metals in this rude state was attended with two very considerable inconveniences; first with the trouble of weighing; and, secondly, with that of assaying them. In the precious metals, where a small difference in the quantity makes a great difference in the value, even the business of weighing, with

[1] Plin. Hist. Nat. lib. 33. cap. 3.

proper exactness, requires at least very accurate weights and scales. The weighing of gold in particular is an operation of some nicety. In the coarser metals, indeed, where a small error would be of little consequence, less accuracy would, no doubt, be necessary. Yet we should find it excessively troublesome, if every time a poor man had occasion either to buy or sell a farthing's worth of goods, he was obliged to weigh the farthing. The operation of assaying is still more difficult, still more tedious, and, unless a part of the metal is fairly melted in the crucible, with proper dissolvents, any conclusion that can be drawn from it, is extremely uncertain. Before the institution of coined money, however, unless they went through this tedious and difficult operation, people must always have been liable to the grossest frauds and impositions, and instead of a pound weight of pure silver, or pure copper, might receive in exchange for their goods, an adulterated composition of the coarsest and cheapest materials, which had, however, in their outward appearance, been made to resemble those metals. To prevent such abuses, to facilitate exchanges, and thereby to encourage all sorts of industry and commerce, it had been found necessary, in all countries that have made any considerable advances towards improvement, to affix a public stamp upon certain quantities of such particular metals, as were in those countries commonly made use of to purchase goods. Hence the origin of coined money, and of those public offices called mints; institutions exactly of the same nature with those of the aulnagers and stampmasters of woollen and linen cloth. All of them are equally meant to ascertain, by means of a public stamp, the quantity and uniform goodness of those different commodities when brought to market.

The first public stamps of this kind that were affixed to the current metals, seem in many cases to have been intended to ascertain, what it was both most difficult and most important to ascertain, the goodness or fineness of the metal, and to have resembled the sterling mark which is at present affixed to plate and bars of silver, or the Spanish mark which is sometimes affixed to ingots of gold, and which being struck only upon one side of the piece, and not covering the whole surface, ascertains the fineness, but not the weight of the metal. Abraham weighs to Ephron the four hundred shekels of silver which he had agreed to pay for the field of Machpelah. They are said however to be the current money of the merchant, and yet are received by weight and not by tale, in the same manner as ingots of gold and bars of silver are at present. The revenues of the antient Saxon kings of England are said to have been paid, not in money but in kind, that is, in victuals and provisions of all sorts. William the Conqueror introduced the custom of paying them in money. This money, however, was, for a long time, received at the exchequer, by weight and not by tale.

The inconveniency and difficulty of weighing those metals with exactness gave occasion to the institution of coins, of which the stamp, covering entirely both sides of the piece and sometimes the edges too, was supposed to ascertain not only the fineness, but the weight of the metal. Such coins therefore, were received by tale as at present, without the trouble of weighing.

The denominations of those coins seem originally to have expressed the weight or quantity of metal contained in them. In the time of Servius Tullius, who first coined money at Rome, the Roman As or Pondo contained a Roman pound of good copper. It was divided in the same manner as our Troyes pound, into twelve ounces, each of which contained a real ounce of good copper. The English pound sterling in the time of Edward I., contained a pound, Tower weight, of silver of a known fineness. The Tower pound seems to have been something more than the Roman pound, and something less than the Troyes pound. This last was not introduced into the mint of England till the 18th of Henry VIII. The French livre contained in the time of Charlemagne a pound, Troyes weight, of silver of a known fineness. The fair of Troyes in Champaign was at that time frequented by all the nations of Europe, and the weights and measures of so famous a market were generally known and esteemed. The Scots money pound contained, from the time of Alexander the First to that of Robert Bruce, a pound of silver of the same weight and fineness with the English pound sterling. English, French, and Scots pennies too, contained all of them originally a real pennyweight of silver, the twentieth part of an ounce, and the two-hundred-and-fortieth part of a pound. The shilling too seems originally to have been the denomination of a weight. *When wheat is at twelve shillings the quarter*, says an antient statute of Henry III. *Then wastel bread of a farthing shall weigh eleven shillings and four pence*. The proportion, however, between the shilling and either the penny on the one hand, or the pound on the other, seems not to have been so constant and uniform as that between the penny and the pound. During the first race of the kings of France, the French sou or shilling appears upon different occasions to have contained five, twelve, twenty, and forty pennies. Among the antient Saxons a shilling appears at one time to have contained only five pennies, and it is not improbable that it may have been as variable among them as among their neighbours, the antient Franks. From the time of Charlemagne among the French, and from that of William the Conqueror among the English, the proportion between the pound, the shilling, and the penny, seems to have been uniformly the same as at present, though the value of each has been very different. For in every country of the world, I believe, the avarice and injustice of princes and sovereign states, abusing the confidence of their subjects, have by degrees diminished the real quantity of metal, which had been originally contained in their coins. The

Romans As, in the latter ages of the Republic, was reduced to the twenty-fourth part of its original value, and, instead of weighing a pound, came to weigh only half an ounce. The English pound and penny contain at present about a third only; the Scots pound and penny about a thirty-sixth; and the French pound and penny about a sixty-sixth part of their original value. By means of those operations the princes and sovereign states which performed them were enabled, in appearance, to pay their debts and to fulfil their engagements with a smaller quantity of silver than would otherwise have been requisite. It was indeed in appearance only; for their creditors were really defrauded of a part of what was due to them. All other debtors in the state were allowed the same privilege, and might pay with the same nominal sum of the new and debased coin whatever they had borrowed in the old. Such operations, therefore, have always proved favourable to the debtor, and ruinous to the creditor, and have sometimes produced a greater and more universal revolution in the fortunes of private persons, than could have been occasioned by a very great public calamity.

It is in this manner that money has become in all civilized nations the universal instrument of commerce, by the intervention of which goods of all kinds are brought and sold, or exchanged for one another.

What are the rules which men naturally observe in exchanging them either for money or for one another, I shall now proceed to examine. These rules determine what may be called the relative or exchangeable value of goods.

The word VALUE, it is to be observed, has two different meanings, and sometimes expresses the utility of some particular object, and sometimes the power of purchasing other goods which the possession of that object conveys. The one may be called "value in use;" the other "value in exchange." The things which have the greatest value in use have frequently little or no value in exchange; and on the contrary, those which have the greatest value in exchange have frequently little or no value in use. Nothing is more useful than water: but it will purchase scarce any thing; scarce any thing can be had in exchange for it. A diamond, on the contrary, has scarce any value in use; but a very great quantity of other goods may frequently be had in exchange for it.

In order to investigate the principles which regulate the exchangeable value of commodities, I shall endeavour to shew,

First, what is the real measure of this exchangeable value; or, wherein consists the real price of all commodities.

Secondly, what are the different parts of which this real price is composed or made up.

And, lastly, what are the different circumstances which sometimes raise some or all of these different parts of price above, and sometimes sink them below their natural or ordinary rate; or, what are the causes which sometimes hinder the market price, that is, the actual price of commodites, from coinciding exactly with what may be called their natural price.

I shall endeavour to explain, as fully and distinctly as I can, those three subjects in the three following chapters, for which I must very earnestly entreat both the patience and attention of the reader: his patience in order to examine a detail which may perhaps in some places appear unnecessarily tedious; and his attention in order to understand what may, perhaps, after the fullest explication which I am capable of giving of it, appear still in some degree obscure. I am always willing to run some hazard of being tedious in order to be sure that I am perspicuous; and after taking the utmost pains that I can to be perspicuous, some obscurity may still appear to remain upon a subject in its own nature extremely abstracted.

6

MONEY AND THE MECHANISM OF EXCHANGE.

by W. Stanley Jevons

Jevons presents the original formal statement of the problem of double coincidence of wants.

> "The earliest form of exchange must have consisted in giving what was not wanted directly for that which was wanted. This simple traffic we call barter . . . and distinguish it from sale and purchase in which one of the articles exchanged is intended to be held only for a short time, until it is parted with in a second act of exchange. The object which thus temporarily intervenes in sale and purchase is money. At first sight it might seem that the use of money only doubles the trouble, by making two exchanges necessary where one was sufficient; but a slight analysis of the difficulties inherent in simple barter shows that the balance of trouble lies quite in the opposite direction . . . The first difficulty in barter is to find two persons whose disposable possessions mutually suit each other's wants. There may be many people wanting, and many possessing those things wanted; but to allow of an act of barter there must be a double coincidence, which will rarely happen."

Unlike Menger, writing later, Jevons did not make explicit the implied multilateral reallocation desired. He argued simply that money's function is to be accepted in trade—though not immediately desired—when other equally valuable but less universally acceptable goods would not be. Though the greater convenience of bilateral trade with this generally acceptable good appears clear, Jevons has not fully explained its function. In particular, consistency of the expectation that money can be successfully passed on, "parted with in a second act of exchange," and the corollary expectation that this would not be true of other goods require elaboration. Nevertheless, the underlying insights that form the basis of Ostroy and Starr's paper (selection 12) are developed here.

ISBN 0-12-663970-1

MONEY

AND THE MECHANISM OF EXCHANGE.

CHAPTER I

BARTER

Some years since, Mademoiselle Zélie, a singer of the Theatre Lyrique at Paris, made a professional tour round the world, and gave a concert in the Society Islands. In exchange for an air from *Norma* and a few other songs, she was to receive a third part of the receipts. When counted, her share was found to consist of three pigs, twenty-three turkeys, forty-four chickens, five thousand cocoa-nuts, besides considerable quantities of bananas, lemons, and oranges. At the Halle in Paris, as the prima donna remarks in her lively letter, printed by M. Wolowski, this amount of live stock and vegetables might have brought four thousand francs, which would have been good remuneration for five songs. In the Society Islands, however, pieces of money were very scarce; and as Mademoiselle could not consume any considerable portion of the receipts herself, it became necessary in the mean time to feed the pigs and poultry with the fruit.

When Mr. Wallace was travelling in the Malay Archipelago, he seems to have suffered rather from the scarcity than the superabundance of provisions. In his most interesting account of his travels, he tells us that in some of the islands, where there was no proper currency, he could not procure supplies for dinner without a special bargain and much chaffering upon each occasion. If the vendor of fish or other coveted eatables did not meet with the sort of exchange desired, he would pass on, and Mr. Wallace and his party had to go without their dinner. It therefore became very desirable to keep on hand a supply of articles, such as knives, pieces of cloth, arrack, or sago cakes, to multiply the chance that one or other article would suit the itinerant merchant.

In modern civilized society the inconveniences of the primitive method of exchange are wholly unknown, and might almost seem to be imaginary.

Accustomed from our earliest years to the use of money, we are unconscious of the inestimable benefits which it confers upon us; and only when we recur to altogether different states of society can we realize the difficulties which arise in its absence. It is even surprising to be reminded that barter is actually the sole method of commerce among many uncivilized races. There is something absurdly incongruous in the fact that a joint-stock company, called "The African Barter Company, Limited," exists in London, which carries on its transactions upon the West Coast of Africa entirely by bartering European manufactures for palm oil, gold dust, ivory, cotton, coffee, gum, and other raw produce.

The earliest form of exchange must have consisted in giving what was not wanted directly for that which was wanted. This simple traffic we call *barter* or *truck*, the French *troc*, and distinguish it from sale and purchase in which one of the articles exchanged is intended to be held only for a short time, until it is parted with in a second act of exchange. The object which thus temporarily intervenes in sale and purchase is money. At first sight it might seem that the use of money only doubles the trouble, by making two exchanges necessary where one was sufficient; but a slight analysis of the difficulties inherent in simple barter shows that the balance of trouble lies quite in the opposite direction. Only by such an analysis can we become aware that money performs not merely one service to us, but several different services, each indispensable. Modern society could not exist in its present complex form without the means which money constitutes of valuing, distributing, and contracting for commodities of various kinds.

Want of Coincidence in Barter

The first difficulty in barter is to find two persons whose disposable possessions mutually suit each other's wants. There may be many people wanting, and many possessing those things wanted; but to allow of an act of barter, there must be a double coincidence, which will rarely happen. A hunter having returned from a successful chase has plenty of game, and may want arms and ammunition to renew the chase. But those who have arms may happen to be well supplied with game, so that no direct exchange is possible. In civilized society the owner of a house may find it unsuitable, and may have his eye upon another house exactly fitted to his needs. But even if the owner of this second house wishes to part with it at all, it is exceedingly unlikely that he will exactly reciprocate the feelings of the first owner, and wish to barter houses. Sellers and purchasers can only be made to fit by the use of some commodity, some *marchandise banale*, as the French call it, which all are willing to receive for a time, so that what is obtained by sale in one case, may be used in purchase in another. This common commodity is called a *medium of exchange*, because it forms a third or intermediate term in all acts of commerce.

Within the last few years a curious attempt has been made to revive the practice of barter by the circulation of advertisements. *The Exchange and Mart* is a newspaper which devotes itself to making known all the odd property which its advertisers are willing to give for some coveted article. One person has some old coins and a bicycle, and wants to barter them for a good concertina. A young lady desires to possess "Middlemarch," and offers a variety of old songs, of which she has become tired. Judging from the size and circulation of the paper, and the way in which its scheme has been imitated by some other weekly papers, we must assume that the offers are sometimes accepted, and that the printing press can bring about, in some degree, the double coincidence necessary to an act of barter.

Want of a Measure of Value

A second difficulty arises in barter. At what rate is any exchange to be made? If a certain quantity of beef be given for a certain quantity of corn, and in like manner corn be exchanged for cheese, and cheese for eggs, and eggs for flax, and so on, still the question will arise—How much beef for how much flax, or how much of any one commodity for a given quantity of another? In a state of barter the price-current list would be a most complicated document, for each commodity would have to be quoted in terms of every other commodity, or else complicated rule-of-three sums would become necessary. Between one hundred articles there must exist no less than 4950 possible ratios of exchange, and all these ratios must be carefully adjusted so as to be consistent with each other, else the acute trader will be able to profit by buying from some and selling to others.

All such trouble is avoided if any one commodity be chosen, and its ratio of exchange with each other commodity be quoted. Knowing how much corn is to be bought for a pound of silver, and also how much flax for the same quantity of silver, we learn without further trouble how much corn exchanges for so much flax. The chosen commodity becomes *a common denominator* or *common measure of value*, in terms of which we estimate the values of all other goods, so that their values become capable of the most easy comparison.

Want of Means of Subdivision

A third but it may be a minor inconvenience of barter arises from the impossibility of dividing many kinds of goods. A store of corn, a bag of gold dust, a carcase of meat, may be portioned out, and more or less may be given in exchange for what is wanted. But the tailor, as we are reminded in several treatises on political economy, may have a coat ready to exchange, but it much exceeds in value the bread which he wishes to get from the baker, or the meat from the butcher. He cannot cut the coat up without destroying the value of his handiwork. It is obvious that he needs some medium of exchange, into which he can temporarily convert the coat, so that he may give a part of its value for bread, and other parts for meat, fuel, and daily necessaries, retaining perhaps a portion for future use. Further illustration is needless; for it is obvious that we need a means of dividing and distributing value according to our varying requirements.

In the present day barter still goes on in some cases, even in the most advanced commercial countries, but only when its inconveniences are not experienced. Domestic servants receive part of their wages in board and lodging: the farm labourer may partially receive payment in cider, or barley, or the use of a piece of land. It has always been usual for the miller to be paid by a portion of the corn which he grinds. The *truck* or barter system, by which workmen took their wages in kind, has hardly yet been extinguished in some part of England. Pieces of land are occasionally exchanged by adjoining landowners; but all these are comparatively trifling cases. In almost all acts of exchange money now intervenes in one way or other, and even when it does not pass from hand to hand, it serves as the measure by which the amounts given and received are estimated. Commerce begins with barter, and in a certain sense it returns to barter; but the last form of barter, as we shall see, is very different from the first form. By far the greater part of commercial payments are made at the present day in England apparently without the aid of metallic money; but they are readily adjusted, because money acts as the common denominator, and what is bought in one direction is balanced off against what is sold in another direction.

CHAPTER II

EXCHANGE

MONEY is the measure and standard of value and the medium of exchange, yet it is not necessary that I should enter upon more than a very brief discussion concerning the nature of value, and the advantage of exchange. Every one must allow that the exchange of commodities depends upon the obvious principle that each of our wants taken separately requires a limited quantity of some article to produce satisfaction. Hence as each want becomes fully satiated, our desire, as Senior so well remarked, is for variety, that is, for the satisfaction of some other want. The man who is supplied daily with three pounds of bread, will not desire more bread; but he will have a strong inclination for beef, and tea, and alcohol. If he happen to meet with a person who has plenty of beef but no bread, each will give that which is less desired for that which is more desired. Exchange has been called *the barter of the superfluous for the necessary*, and this definition will be correct if we state it as *the barter of the comparatively superfluous for the comparatively necessary*.

It is impossible, indeed, to decide exactly how much bread, or beef, or tea, or how many coats and hats a person needs. There is no precise limit to our desires, and we can only say, that as we have a larger supply of a substance, the urgency of our need for more is in some proportion weakened. A cup of water in the desert, or upon the field of battle, may save life, and become infinitely useful. Two or three pints per day for each person are needful for drinking and cooking purposes. A gallon or two per day are highly requisite for cleanliness; but we soon reach a point at which further supplies of water are of very minor importance. A modern town population is found to be satisfied with about twenty-five gallons per head per day for all purposes, and a further supply would possess little utility. Water, indeed, may be reverse of useful, as in the case of a flood, or a damp house, or a wet mine.

Utility and Value Are Not Intrinsic

It is only, then, when supplied in moderate quantities, and at the right time, that a thing can be said to be useful. Utility is not a quantity *intrinsic* in a substance, for, if it were, additional quantities of the same substance would always be desired, however much we previously possessed. We must not confuse the usefulness of a thing with the physical qualities upon which the usefulness depends. Utility and value are only accidents of a thing arising from the fact that some one wants it, and the degree of the utility and the amount of resulting value will depend upon the extent to which the desire for it has been previously gratified.

Regarding utility, then, as constantly varying in degree, and as variable even for each different portion of commodity, it is not difficult to see that we exchange those parts of our stock which have a low degree of utility to us, for articles which, being of low utility to others, are much desired by us. This exchange is continued up to the point at which the next portion given would be equally useful to us with that received, so that there is no gain of utility: there would be a loss in carrying the exchange further. Upon these considerations it is easy to construct a theory of the nature of exchange and value, which has been explained in my book* called "The Theory of Political Economy." It is there shown that the well-known laws of supply and demand follow from this view of utility, and thus yield a verification of the theory. Since the publication of the work named, M. Léon Walras, the ingenious professor of political economy at Lausanne, has independently arrived at the same theory of exchange, † a remarkable confirmation of its truth.

Value Expresses Ratio of Exchange

We must now fix our attention upon the fact that, in every act of exchange, a definite quantity of one substance is exchanged for a definite quantity of another. The things bartered may be most various in character, and may be variously measured. We may give a weight of silver for a length of rope, or a superficial extent of carpet, or a number of gallons of wine, or a certain horse-power of force, or conveyance over a certain distance. The quantities to be measured may be expressed in terms of space, time, mass, force, energy, heat, or any other physical units. Yet each exchange will consist in giving so many units of one thing for so many units of another, each measured in its appropriate way.

Every act of exchange thus presents itself to us in the form of *a ratio between two numbers*. The word *value* is commonly used, and if, at current rates, one ton of copper exchanges for ten tons of bar iron, it is usual to say that the value of copper is ten times that of the iron, weight for weight. For our purpose, at least, this use of the word value is only an indirect mode of expressing a ratio. When we say that gold is more valuable than silver, we mean that, as commonly exchanged, the weight of silver exceeds that of the

* "The theory of Political Economy." 8vo. 1871 (Macmillan).

† Walras, Éléments d'Économie politique pure. Lausanne, Paris (Guillaumin), 1874.

gold given for it. If the value of gold rises compared with that of silver, then still more silver is given for the same quantity of gold. But value like utility is no intrinsic quality of a thing; it is an extrinsic accident or relation. We should never speak of the value of a thing at all without having in our minds the other thing in regard to which it is valued. The very same substance may rise and fall in value at the same time. If, in exchange for a given weight of gold, I can get more silver, but less copper, than I used to do, the value of gold has risen with respect to silver, but fallen with respect to copper. It is evident that an intrinsic property of a thing cannot both increase and decrease at the same time; therefore value must be a mere relation or accident of a thing as regards other things and the persons needing them.

CHAPTER III

THE FUNCTIONS OF MONEY

WE have seen that three inconveniences attach to the practice of simple barter, namely, the improbability of coincidence between persons wanting and persons possessing; the complexity of exchanges, which are not made in terms of one single substance; and the need of some means of dividing and distributing valuable articles. Money remedies these inconveniences, and thereby performs two distinct functions of high importance, acting as—

(1) A medium of exchange.

(2) A common measure of value.

In its first form money is simply any commodity esteemed by all persons, any articles of food, clothing, or ornament which any person will readily receive, and which, therefore, every person desires to have by him in greater or less quantity, in order that he may have the means of procuring necessaries of life at any time. Although many commodities may be capable of performing this function of a medium more or less perfectly, some one article will usually be selected, as money *par excellence*, by custom or the force of circumstances. This article will then begin to be used as a measure of value. Being accustomed to exchange things frequently for sums of money, people learn the value of other articles in terms of money, so that all exchanges will most readily be calculated and adjusted by comparison of the money values of the things exchanged.

A Standard of Value

A third function of money soon develops itself. Commerce cannot advance far before people begin to borrow and lend, and debts of various origin are contracted. It is in some cases usual, indeed, to restore the very same article which was borrowed, and in almost every case it would be possible to pay back in the same kind of commodity. If corn be borrowed, corn might be paid back, with interest in corn; but the lender will often not wish to have things returned to him at an uncertain time, when he does not much need them, or when their value is unusually low. A borrower, too, may need several different kinds of articles, which he is not likely to obtain from one person; hence arises the convenience of borrowing and lending in one generally recognized commodity, of which the value varies little. Every person making a contract by which he will receive something at a future day, will prefer to secure the receipt of a commodity likely to be as valuable then as now. This commodity will usually be the current money, and it will thus come to perform the function of a *standard of value*. We must not suppose that the substance serving as a standard of value is really invariable in value, but merely that it is chosen as that measure by which the value of future payments is to be regulated. Bearing in mind that value is only the ratio of quantities exchanged, it is certain that no substance permanently bears exactly the same value relatively to another commodity; but it will, of course, be desirable to select as the standard of value that which appears likely to continue to exchange for many other commodities in nearly unchanged ratios.

A Store of Value

It is worthy of inquiry whether money does not also serve a fourth distinct purpose—that of embodying value in a convenient form for conveyance to distant places. Money, when acting as a medium of exchange, circulates backwards and forwards near the same spot, and may sometimes return to the same hands again and again. It subdivides and distributes property, and *lubricates* the action of exchange. But at times a person needs to condense his property into the smallest compass, so that he may hoard it away for a time, or carry it with him on a long journey, or transmit it to a friend in a distant country. Something which is very valuable, although of little bulk and weight, and which will be recognised as very valuable in every part of the world, is necessary for this purpose. The current money of a country is perhaps more likely to fulfil these conditions than anything else, although diamonds and other precious stones, and articles of exceptional beauty and rarity, might occasionally be employed.

The use of esteemed articles as a store or medium for conveying value may in some cases precede their employment as currency. Mr. Gladstone states that in the Homeric poems gold is mentioned as being hoarded and treasured up, and as being occasionally used in the payment of services, before it became the common measure of value, oxen being then used for the latter purpose. Historically speaking, such a generally esteemed substance as gold seems to have served, firstly, as a commodity valuable for ornamental purposes; secondly, as stored wealth; thirdly, as a medium of exchange; and, lastly, as a measure of value.

Separation of Functions

It is in the highest degree important that the reader should discriminate carefully and constantly between the four functions which money fulfils, at least in modern societies. We are so accustomed to use the one same substance in all the four different ways, that they tend to become confused together in thought. We come to regard as almost necessary that union of functions which is, at the most, a matter of convenience, and may not always be desirable. We might certainly employ one substance as a medium of exchange, a second as a measure of value, a third as a standard of value, and a fourth as a store of value. In buying and selling we might transfer portions of gold; in expressing and calculating prices we might speak in terms of silver; when we wanted to make long leases we might define the rent in terms of wheat, and when we wished to carry our riches away we might condense it into the form of precious stones. This use of different commodities for each of the functions of money has in fact been partially carried out. In Queen Elizabeth's reign silver was the common measure of the value; gold was employed in large payments in quantities depending upon its current value in silver, while corn was required by the Act 18th Elizabeth, c. VI. (1576), to be the standard of value in drawing the leases of certain college lands.

There is evident convenience in selecting, if possible, one single substance which can serve all the functions of money. It will save trouble if we can pay in the same money in which the prices of things are calculated. As few people have the time or patience to investigate closely the history of prices, they will probably assume that the money in which they make all minor and temporary bargains, is also the best standard in which to register debts and contracts extending over many years. A great mass of payments too are invariably fixed by law, such as tolls, fees, and tariffs of charges: many other payments are fixed by custom. Accordingly, even if the medium of exchange varied considerably in value, people would go on making their payments in terms of it, as if there had been no variation, some gaining at the expense of others.

One of our chief tasks in this book will be to consider the various materials which have been employed as money, or have been, or may be, suggested for the purpose. It must be our endeavour, if possible, to discover some substance which will in the highest degree combine the characters requisite for all the different functions of money, but we must bear in mind that a partition of these functions amongst different substances is practicable. We will first proceed to a brief review of the very various ways in which the need of currency has been supplied from the earliest ages, and we will afterwards analyse the physical qualities and circumstances which render the substances employed more or less suited to the purpose to which they were applied. We may thus arrive at some decision as to the exact nature of the commodity which is best adapted to meet our needs in the present day.

7

ON THE ORIGIN OF MONEY

by Karl Menger

The riddle of money as a medium of exchange is "that every economic unit . . . should be ready to exchange his goods for little metal disks apparently useless as such, or for documents representing the latter . . . ." This appears to be irrational and calls for systematic explanation. Menger's analysis appears to represent the first formal explicit recognition that, in bilateral trade, at least three agents and three goods are needed to set up the problem that is solved by a medium of exchange. This allows mutually advantageous reallocations for the economy as a whole to be characterized as a sequence of bilateral trades, not all of which—considered separately—are mutually desirable. "Even in the relatively simple . . . case, where an economic unit. A, requires a commodity possessed by B, and B requires one possessed by C, while C wants one that is owned by A—even here, under a rule of mere barter, the exchange of the goods in question would as a rule be of necessity left undone."

Money is used as a token in trade to reassure traders in such a sequence that they are not making an egregiously bad deal. This leads to an alternate line of investigation, recognition that a theory of a medium of exchange is *inter alia* a theory of the liquidity or saleability (*Absatzfahigkeit*) of commodities.

The following is reprinted from *On the Origin of Money*, Economic Journal, Vol 2, 1892.

ISBN 0-12-663970-1

ON THE ORIGIN OF MONEY

I.—Introduction

There is a phenomenon which has from of old and in a peculiar degree attracted the attention of social philosophers and practical economists, the fact of certain commodities (these being in advanced civilizations coined pieces of gold and silver, together subsequently with documents representing those coins) becoming universally acceptable media of exchange. It is obvious even to the most ordinary intelligence, that a commodity should be given up by its owner in exchange for another more useful to him. But that every economic unit in a nation should be ready to exchange his goods for little metal disks apparently useless as such, or for documents representing the latter, is a procedure so opposed to the ordinary course of things, that we cannot well wonder if even a distinguished thinker like Savigny finds it downright 'mysterious.'

It must not be supposed that the *form* of coin, or document, employed as current-money, constitutes the enigma in this phenomenon. We may look away from these forms and go back to earlier stages of economic development, or indeed to what still obtains in countries here and there, where we find the previous metals in an uncoined state serving as the medium of exchange, and even certain other commodities, cattle, skins, cubes of tea, slabs of salt, cowrie-shells, etc.; still we are confronted by this phenomenon, still we have to explain why it is that the economic man is ready to accept a certain kind of commodity, *even if he does not need it, or if his need of it is already supplied*, in exchange for all the goods he has brought to market, while it is none the less what he needs that he consults in the first instance, with respect to the goods he intends to acquire in the course of his transactions.

And hence there runs, from the first essays of reflective contemplation in social phenomena down to our own times, an uninterrupted chain of disquisitions upon the nature and specific qualities of money in its relation to all that constitutes traffic. Philosophers, jurists, and historians, as well as economists, and even naturalists and mathematicians, have dealt with his notable problem, and there is no civilized people that has not furnished its quota to the abundant literature thereon. What is the nature of those little disks or documents, which in themselves seem to serve no useful purpose, and which nevertheless, in contradiction to the rest of experience, pass from one hand to another in exchange for the most useful commodities, nay, for which every one is so eagerly bent on surrendering his wares? Is money an organic member in the world of commodities, or is it an economic anomaly? Are we to refer its commercial currency and its value in trade to the same causes conditioning those of other goods, or are they the distinct product of convention and authority?

II. Attempts at Solution Hitherto

Thus far it can hardly be claimed for the results of investigation into the problem above stated, that they are commensurate either with the great development in historic research generally, or with the outlay of time and intellect expended in efforts at solution. The enigmatic phenomenon of money is even at this day without an explanation that satisfies; nor is there yet agreement on the most fundamental questions of its nature and functions. Even at this day we have no satisfactory theory of money.

The idea which lay first to hand for an explanation of the specific function of money as a universal current medium of exchange, was to refer it to a general convention, or a legal dispensation. The problem, which science has here to solve, consists in giving an explanation of a general, homogeneous course of action pursued by human beings when engaged in traffic, which, taken concretely, makes unquestionably for the common interest, and yet which seems to conflict with the nearest and immediate interests of contracting individuals. Under such circumstances what could lie more contiguous than the notion of referring the foregoing procedure to causes lying outside the sphere of individual considerations? To assume that certain commodities, the precious metals in particular, had been exalted into the medium of exchange by general convention or law, in the interest of the commonweal, solved the difficulty, and solved it apparently the more easily and naturally inasmuch as the shape of the coins seemed to be a token of state regulation. Such in fact is the opinion of Plato, Aristotle, and the Roman jurists, closely followed by the mediæval writers. Even the more modern developments in the theory of money have not in substance got beyond this standpoint.[1]

Tested more closely, the assumption underlying this theory gave room to grave doubts. An event of such high and universal significance and of notoriety so inevitable, as the establishment by law or convention of a universal

[1] *Cf.* Roscher, *System der Volkswirthschaft*, I. § 116; my *Grundsätze der Volkswirtschaftslehre*, 1871, p. 255, *et seq.*; M. Block, *Les Progre's de la Science economique depuis A. Smith*, 1890, II., p. 59, *et seq.*

medium of exchange, would certainly have been retained in the memory of man, the more certainly inasmuch as it would have had to be performed in a great number of places. Yet no historical monument gives us trustworthy tidings of any transactions either conferring distinct recognition on media of exchange already in use, or referring to their adoption by peoples of comparatively recent culture, much less testifying to an initiation of the earliest ages of economic civilization in the use of money.

And in fact the majority of theorists on this subject do not stop at the explanation of money as stated above. The peculiar adaptability of the precious metals for purposes of currency and coining was noticed by Aristotle, Xenophon, and Pliny, and to a far greater extent by John Law, Adam Smith and his disciples, who all seek a further explanation of the choice made of them as media of exchange, in their special qualifications. Nevertheless it is clear that the choice of the precious metals by law and convention, even if made in consequence of their peculiar adaptability for monetary purposes, presupposes the pragmatic origin of money, and selection of those metals, and that presupposition is unhistorical. Nor do even the theorists above mentioned honestly face the problem that is to be solved, to wit, the explaining how it has come to pass that certain commodities (the precious metals at certain stages of culture) should be promoted amongst the mass of all other commodities, and accepted as the generally acknowledged media of exchange. It is a question concerning not only the origin but also the nature of money and its position in relation to all other commodities.

III. The Problem of the Genesis of a Medium of Exchange

In primitive traffic the economic man is awaking but very gradually to an understanding of the economic advantages to be gained by exploitation of existing opportunities of exchange. His aims are directed first and foremost, in accordance with the simplicity of all primitive culture, only at what lies first to hand. And only in that proportion does the value in use of the commodities he seeks to acquire, come into account in his bargaining. Under such conditions each man is intent to get by way of exchange just such goods as he directly needs, and to reject those of which he has no need at all, or with which he is already sufficiently provided. It is clear then, that in these circumstances the number of bargains actually concluded must lie within very narrow limits. Consider how seldom it is the case, that a commodity owned by somebody is of less value in use than another commodity owned by somebody else! And for the latter just the opposite relation is the case. But how much more seldom does it happen that these two bodies meet! Think, indeed, of the peculiar difficulties obstructing the immediate barter of goods in those cases, where supply and demand do not quantitatively coincide; where, *e.g.*, an indivisible commodity is to be exchanged for a variety of goods in the possession of different persons, or indeed for such commodities as are only in demand at different times and can be supplied only by different persons! Even in the relatively simple and so often recurring case, where an economic unit, A, requires a commodity possessed by B, and B requires one possessed by C, while C wants one that is owned by A—even here, under a rule of mere barter, the exchange of the goods in question would as a rule be of necessity left undone.

These difficulties would have proved absolutely insurmountable obstacles to the progress of traffic, and at the same time to the production of goods not commanding a regular sale, had there not lain a remedy in the very nature of things, to wit, *the different degrees of saleableness* (*Absatzfähigkeit*) *of commodites.* The difference existing in this respect between articles of commerce is of the highest degree of significance for the theory of money, and of the market in general. And the failure to turn it adequately to account in explaining the phenomena of trade, constitutes not only as such a lamentable breach in our science, but also one of the essential causes of the backward state of monetary theory. *The theory of money necessarily presupposes a theory of the saleableness of goods.* If we grasp this, we shall be able to understand how the almost unlimited saleableness of money is only a special case,—presenting only a difference of degree—of a generic phenomenon of economic life—namely, the difference in the saleableness of commodities in general.

IV. Commodities as More or Less Saleable

It is an error in economics, as prevalent as it is patent, that all commodities, at a definite point of time and in a given market, may be assumed to stand to each other in a definite relation of exchange, in other words, may be mutually exchanged in definite quantities at will. It is not true that in any given market 10 cwt. of one article = 2 cwt. of another = 3 lbs. of a third article, and so on. The most cursory observation of market-phenomena teaches us that it does not lie within our power, when we have bought an article for a certain price, to sell it again forthwith at that same price. If we but try to dispose of an article of clothing, a book, or a work of art, which we have just purchased, in the very same market, even though it be at once, before the same juncture of conditions has altered, we shall easily convince ourselves of the fallaciousness of such an assumption. The price at which any one can at pleasure buy a commodity at a given market and a given point of time, and the price at which he can dispose of the same at pleasure, are two essentially different magnitudes.

This holds good of wholesale as well as retail prices. Even such marketable goods as corn, cotton, pig-iron, cannot be voluntarily disposed of for the price at which we have purchased them. Commerce and speculation would be the simplest things in the world, if the theory of the 'objective equivalent in goods' were correct, if it were actually true, that in a given market and at a given moment commodities could be mutually converted at will in definite quantitative relations—could, in short, at a certain price be as easily disposed of as acquired. At any rate there is no such thing as a general saleableness of wares in this sense. The truth is, that even in the best organized markets, while we may be able to purchase when and what we like at a definite price, viz.: the *purchasing price*, we can only dispose of it again when and as we like at a loss, viz.: at the *selling price*.[1]

The loss experienced by any one who is compelled to dispose of an article at a definite moment, as compared with the current purchasing prices, is a highly variable quantity, as a glance at trade and at markets of specific commodities will show. If corn or cotton is to be disposed of at an organised market, the seller will be in a position to do so in practically any quantity, at any time he pleases, at the current price, or at most with a loss of only a few pence on the total sum. If it be a question of disposing, in larger quantities, of cloth or silk-stuffs at will, the seller will regularly have to content himself with a considerable percentage of diminution in the price. Far worse is the case of one who at a certain point of time has to get rid of astronomical instruments, anatomical preparations, Sanskrit writings, and such hardly marketable articles!

If we call any goods or wares *more or less saleable*, according to the greater or less facility with which they can be disposed of at a market at any convenient time at current purchasing prices or with less or more diminution of the same, we can see by what has been said, that an obvious difference exists in this connection between commodities. Nevertheless, and in spite of its great practical significance, it cannot be said that this phenomenon has been much taken into account in economic science. The reason of this is in part the circumstance, that investigation into the phenomena of price has been directed almost exclusively to the *quantities* of the commodities exchanged, and not as well to the greater or less *facility* with which wares may be disposed of at normal prices. In part also the reason is the thorough-going

[1] We must make a distinction between the higher purchasing prices for which the buyer is rendered liable through the wish to purchase at a definite point of time, and the (lower) selling prices, which he, who is obliged to get rid of goods within a definite period, must content himself withal. The smaller the difference between the buying and selling prices of an article, the more saleable it usually proves to be.

abstract method by which the saleableness of goods has been treated, without due regard to all the circumstances of the case.

The man who goes to market with his wares intends as a rule to dispose of them, by no means at any price whatever, but at such as corresponds to the general economic situation. If we are going to inquire into the different degrees of saleableness in goods so as to show its bearing upon practical life, we can only do so by consulting the greater or less facility with which they may be disposed of at prices corresponding to the general economic situation, that is, at *economic* prices.[1] A commodity is more or less saleable according as we are able, with more or less prospect of success, to dispose of it at prices corresponding to the general economic situation, at *economic* prices.

The *interval of time*, moreover, within which the disposal of a commodity at the economic price may be reckoned on, is of great significance in an inquiry into its degree of saleableness. It matters not whether the demand for a commodity be slight, or whether on other grounds its saleableness be small; if its owner can only bide his time, he will finally and in the long run be able to dispose of it at economic prices. Since, however, this condition is often absent in the actual course of business, there arises for practical purposes an important difference between those commodities, on the other hand, which we expect to dispose of at any given time at economic, or at least approximately economic, prices, and such goods, on the other hand, respecting which we have no such prospect, or at least not in the same degree, and to dispose of which at economic prices the owner foresees it will be necessary to wait for a longer or shorter period, or else to put up with a more or less sensible abatement in the price.

Again, account must be taken of the *quantitative* factor in the saleableness of commodities. Some commodities, in consequence of the development of markets and speculation, are able at any time to find a sale in practically any quantity at economic, or approximately economic, prices. Other commodities can only find a sale at economic prices in smaller quantities, commensurate with the gradual growth of an effective demand, fetching a relatively reduced price in the case of a greater supply.

[1] The height of saleableness in a commodity is not revealed by the fact that it may be disposed of at any price whatever, including such as result from distress or accident. In this sense all commodities are pretty well equally saleable. A high rate of saleableness in a commodity consists in the fact that it may at every moment be easily and surely disposed of at a price corresponding to, or at least not discrepant from, the general economic situation—at the economic, or approximately economic, price.

The price of a commodity may be denoted as *uneconomic* on two grounds: (1) in consequence of error, ignorance, caprice, and so forth; (2) in consequence of the circumstances that only a part of the supply is available to the demand, the rest for some reason or other being withheld, and the price in consequence not commensurate with the actually existing economic situation.

V. Concerning the Causes of the Different Degrees of Saleableness in Commodities

The degree to which a commodity is found by experience to command a sale, at a given market, at any time, at prices corresponding to the economic situation (economic prices), depends upon the following circumstances.

1. Upon the number of persons who are still in want of the commodity in question, and upon the extent and intensity of that want, which is unsupplied, or is constantly recurring.

2. Upon the purchasing power of those persons.

3. Upon the available quantity of the commodity in relation to the yet unsupplied (total) want of it.

4. Upon the divisibility of the commodity, and any other ways in which it may be adjusted to the needs of individual customers.

5. Upon the development of the market, and of speculation in particular. And finally,

6. Upon the number and nature of the limitations imposed politically and socially upon exchange and consumption with respect to the commodity in question.

We may proceed, in the same way in which we considered the degree of the saleableness in commodities at definite markets and definite points of time, to set out the *spatial and temporal limits* of their saleableness. In these respects also we observe in our markets some commodities, the saleableness of which is almost unlimited by place or time, and others the sale of which is more or less limited.

The *spatial* limits of the saleableness of commodities are mainly conditioned—

1. By the degree to which the want of the commodities is distributed in space.

2. By the degree to which the goods lend themselves to transport, and the cost of transport incurred in proportion to their value.

3. By the extent to which the means of transport and of commerce generally are developed with respect to different classes of commodities.

4. By the local extension of organized markets and their intercommunication by 'arbitrage.'

5. By the differences in the restrictions imposed upon commercial intercommunication with respect to different goods, in interlocal and, in particular, in international trade.

The time-limits to the saleableness of commodities are mainly conditioned—

1. By permanence in the need of them (their independence of fluctuation in the same).

2. Their durability, *i.e.* their suitableness for preservation.

3. The cost of preserving and storing them.

4. The rate of interest.

5. The periodicity of a market for the same.

6. The development of speculation and in particular of time-bargains in connection with the same.

7. The restrictions imposed politically and socially on their being transferred from one period of time to another.

All these circumstances, on which depend the different degrees of, and the different local and temporal limits to, the saleableness of commodities, explain why it is that certain commodities can be disposed of with ease and certainty in definite markets, *i.e.* within local and temporal limits, at any time and in practically any quantities, at prices corresponding to the general economic situation, while the saleableness of other commodities is confined within narrow spatial, and again, temporal, limits; and even within these the disposal of the commodities in question is difficult, and, in so far as the demand cannot be waited for, is not to be brought about without a more less sensible diminution in price.

VI. On the Genesis of Media of Exchange[1]

It has long been the subject of universal remark in centres of exchange, that for certain commodities there existed a greater, more constant, and more effective demand than for other commodities less desirable in certain respects, the former being such as correspond to a want on the part of those able and willing to traffic, which is at once universal and, by reason of the relative scarcity of the goods in question, always imperfectly satisfied. And further, that the person who wishes to acquire certain definite goods in exchange for his own is in a more favourable position, if he brings commodities of this kind to market, than if he visits the markets with goods which cannot display such advantages, or at least not in the same degree. Thus equipped he has the prospect of acquiring such goods as he finally wishes to obtain, not only with greater ease and security, but also, by reason of the steadier and more prevailing demand for his own commodities, at prices corresponding to the general economic situation—at economic prices. Under

[1] *Cf* my article on 'Money' in the *Handwörterbuch der Staatswissenschaften* (Dictionary of Social Science), Jena, 1891, iii., p 730 *et seq.*

these circumstances, when any one has brought goods not highly saleable to market, the idea uppermost in his mind is to exchange them, not only for such as he happens to be in need of, but, if this cannot be effected directly, for other goods also, which, while he did not want them himself, were nevertheless more saleable than his own. By so doing he certainly does not attain at once the final object of his trafficking, to wit, the acquisition of goods needful to *himself*. Yet he draws nearer to that object. By the devious way of a mediate exchange, he gains the prospect of accomplishing his purpose more surely and economically than if he had confined himself to direct exchange. Now in point of fact this seems everywhere to have been the case. Men have been led, with increasing knowledge of their individual interests, each by his own economic interests, without convention, without legal compulsion, nay, even without any regard to the common interest, to exchange goods destined for exchange (their "wares") for other goods equally destined for exchange, but more saleable.

With the extension of traffic in space and with the expansion over ever longer intervals of time of prevision for satisfying materials needs, each individual would learn, from his own economic interests, to take good heed that he bartered his less saleable goods for those special commodities which displayed, beside the attraction of being highly saleable in the particular locality, a wide range of saleableness both in time and place. These wares would be qualified by their costliness, easy transportability, and fitness for preservation (in connection with the circumstance of their corresponding to a steady and widely distributed demand), to ensure to the possessor a power, not only 'here' and 'now,' but as nearly as possible unlimited in space and time generally, over all other market-goods at economic prices.

And so it has come to pass, that as man became increasingly conversant with these economic advantages, mainly by an insight become traditional, and by the habit of economic action, those commodities, which relatively to both space and time are most saleable, have in every market become the wares, which it is not only in the interest of every one to accept in exchange for his own less saleable goods, but which also are those he actually does readily accept. And their superior saleableness depends only upon the relatively inferior saleableness of every other kind of commodity, by which alone they have been able to become *generally* acceptable media of exchange.

It is obvious how highly significant a factor is habit in the genesis of such generally serviceable means of exchange. It lies in the economic interests of each trafficking individual to exchange less saleable for more saleable commodities. But the willing acceptance of the medium of exchange presupposes already a knowledge of these interests on the part of those economic subjects who are expected to accept in exchange for their wares a commodity which in and by itself is perhaps entirely useless to them. It is certain that this knowledge never arises in every part of a nation at the same time. It is only in the first instance a limited number of economic subjects who will recognise the advantage in such procedure, an advantage which, in and by itself, is independent of the general recognition of a commodity as a medium of exchange, inasmuch as such an exchange, always and under all circumstances, brings the economic unit a good deal nearer to his goal, to the acquisition of useful things of which he really stands in need. But it is admitted, that there is no better method of enlightening any one about his economic interests than that he perceive the economic success of those who use the right means to secure their own. Hence it is also clear that nothing may have been so favourable to the genesis of a medium of exchange as the acceptance, on the part of the most discerning and capable economic subjects, for their economic gain, and over a considerable period of time, of eminently saleable goods in preference to all others. In this way practice and habit have certainly contributed not a little to cause goods, which were most saleable at any time, to be accepted not only by many, but finally by all, economic subjects in exchange for their less saleable goods: and not only so, but to be accepted from the first with the intention of exchanging them away again. Goods which had thus become generally acceptable media of exchange were called by the Germans *Geld*, from *gelten, i.e.* to pay, to perform, while other nations derived their designation for money mainly from the substance used,[1] the shape of the coin,[2] or even from certain kinds of coin.[3]

It is not impossible for media of exchange, serving as they do the commonweal in the most emphatic sense of the word, to be instituted also by way of legislation, like other social institutions. But this is neither the only, nor the primary mode in which money has taken its origin. This is much more to be traced in the process depicted above, notwithstanding the nature of that process would be but very incompletely explained if we were to call it 'organic,' or denote money as something 'primordial,' of 'primœval growth,' and so forth. Putting aside assumptions which are historically unsound, we can only come fully to understand the origin of money by learning to view the establishment of the social procedure, with which we are dealing, as the spontaneous outcome, the unpremeditated resultant, of particular, individual efforts of the members of a society, who have little by little worked their way to a discrimination of the different degrees of saleableness in commodities.[4]

[1] The Hebrew *Keseph*, the Greek *ἀργύριον*, the Latin *argentum*, the French *argent*, &c.

[2] The English *money*, the Spanish *moneda*, the Portuguese *moeda*, the French *monnaie*, the Hebrew *maoth*, the Arabic *fulus*, the Greek *νομισμα*, &c.

[3] The Italian *danaro*, the Russian *dengi*, the Polish *pienondze*, the Bohemian and Slavonian *penize*, the Danish *penge*, the Swedish *penningar*, the Magyar *penze*, &c. (*i.e. denare* = *Pfennige* = *penny*).

[4] *Cf.* on this point my *Grundsätze der Volkswirtschaftslehre*, 1871, p. 250 *et seq*.

VII. The Process of Differentiation Between Commodities Which Have Become Media of Exchange and the Rest

Where the relatively most saleable commodities have become 'money,' the event has in the first place the effect of substantially increasing their originally high saleableness. Every economic subject bringing less saleable wares to market, to acquire goods of another sort, has thenceforth a stronger interest in converting what he has in the first instance into the wares which have become money. For such persons, by the exchange of their less saleable wares for those which as money are most saleable, attain not merely, as heretofore, a higher probability, but the certainty, of being able to acquire forthwith equivalent quantities of every other kind of commodity to be had in the market. And their control over these depends simply upon their pleasure and their choice. *Pecuniam habens, habet omnem rem quem vult habere.*

On the other hand, he who brings other wares than money to market, finds himself at a disadvantage more or less. To gain the same command over what the market affords, he must first convert his exchangeable goods into money. The nature of his economic disability is shown by the fact of his being compelled to overcome a difficulty before he can attain his purpose, which difficulty does not exist for, *i.e.* has already been overcome by, the man who owns a stock of money.

This has all the greater significance for practical life, inasmuch as to overcome this difficulty does not lie unconditionally within reach of him who brings less saleable goods to market, but depends in part upon circumstances over which the individual bargainer has no control. The less saleable are his wares, the more certainly will he have either to suffer the penalty in the economic price, or to content himself with awaiting the moment, when it will be possible for him to effect a conversion at economic prices. He who is desirous, in an era of monetary economy, to exchange goods of any kind whatever, which are not money, for other goods supplied in the market, cannot be certain of attaining this result at once, or within any predetermined interval of time, at economic prices. And the less saleable are the goods brought by an economic subject to market, the more unfavourably, for his own purposes, will his economic position compare with the position of those who bring money to market. Consider, *e.g.*, the owner of a stock of surgical instruments, who is obliged through sudden distress, or through pressure from creditors, to convert it into money. The prices which it will fetch will be highly accidental, nay, the goods being of such limited saleableness, they will be fairly incalculable. And this holds good of all kinds of conversions which in respect of time are compulsory sales.[1] Other is his case who wants at a market to convert the commodity, which has become *money*, forthwith into other goods supplied at that market. He will accomplish his purpose, not only with certainty, but usually also at a price corresponding to the general economic situation. Nay, the habit of economic action has made us so sure of being able to procure in return for money any goods on the market, whenever we wish, at prices corresponding to the economic situation, that we are for the most part unconscious of how many purchases we daily propose to make, which, with respect to our wants and the time of concluding them, are compulsory purchases. Compulsory sales, on the other hand, in consequence of the economic disadvantage which they commonly involve, force themselves upon the attention of the parties implicated in unmistakable fashion. What therefore constitutes the peculiarity of a commodity which has become money is, that the possession of it procures for us at any time, *i.e.* at any moment we think fit, assured control over every commodity to be had on the market, and this usually at prices adjusted to the economic situation of the moment: the control, on the other hand, conferred by other kinds of commodities over market goods is, in respect of time, and in part of price as well, uncertain, relatively if not absolutely.

Thus the effect produced by such goods as are relatively most saleable becoming money is an increasing differentiation between their degree of saleableness and that of all other goods. And this difference in saleableness ceases to be altogether gradual, and must be regarded in a certain aspect as something absolute. The practice of every-day life, as well as jurisprudence, which closely adheres for the most part to the notions prevalent in every-day life, distinguish two categories in the wherewithal of traffic—goods which have become money and goods which have not. And the ground of this distinction, we find, lies essentially in that difference in the saleableness of commodities set forth above—a difference so significant for practical life and which comes to be further emphasized by intervention of the state. This distinction, moreover, finds expression in language in the difference of meaning attaching to 'money' and 'wares,' to 'purchase' and 'exchange.' But it also affords the chief explanation of that superiority of the buyer over the seller, which has found manifold consideration, yet has hitherto been left inadequately explained.

[1] Herein lies the explanation of the circumstances why compulsory sales, and cases of distraint in particular, involve as a rule the economic ruin of the person upon whose estate they are carried out, and that in a greater degree the less the goods in question are saleable. Correct discernment of the uneconomic character of these processes will necessarily lead to a reform in the available legal mechanism.

VIII. How the Precious Metals Became Money

The commodities, which under given local and time relations are most saleable, have become money among the same nations at different times, and among different nations at the same time, and they are diverse in kind. The reason why the *precious metals* have become the generally current medium of exchange among here and there a nation prior to its appearance in history, and in the sequel among all peoples of advanced economic civilisation, is because their saleableness is far and away superior to that of all other commodities, and at the same time because they are found to be specially qualified for the concomitant and subsidiary functions of money.

There is no centre of population, which has not in the very beginnings of civilization come keenly to desire and eagerly to covet the precious metals, in primitive times for their utility and peculiar beauty as in themselves ornamental, subsequently as the choicest materials for plastic and architectural decoration, and especially for ornaments and vessels of every kind. In spite of their natural scarcity, they are well distributed geographically, and, in proportion to most other metals, are easy to extract and elaborate. Further, the ratio of the available quantity of the precious metals to the total requirement is so small, that the number of those whose need of them is unsupplied, or at least insufficiently supplied, together with the extent of this unsupplied need, is always relatively large—larger more or less than in the case of other more important, though more abundantly available, commodities. Again, the class of persons who wish to acquire the precious metals, is, by reason of the kind of wants which by these are satisfied, such as quite specially to include those members of the community who can most efficaciously barter; and thus the desire for the precious metals is as a rule more effective. Nevertheless the limits of the effective desire for the precious metals extend also to those strata of population who can less effectively barter, by reason of the great divisibility of the precious metals, and the enjoyment procured by the expenditure of even very small quantities of them in individual economy. Besides this there are the wide limits in time and space of the saleableness of the precious metals; a consequence, on the one hand, of the almost unlimited distribution in space of the need of them, together with their low cost of transport as compared with their value, and, on the other hand, of their unlimited durability and the relatively slight cost of hoarding them. In no national economy which has advanced beyond the first stages of development are there any commodities, the saleableness of which is so little restricted in such a number of respects—personally, quantitatively, spatially, and temporally—as the precious metals. It cannot be doubted that, long before they had become the generally acknowledged media of exchange, they were, amongst very many peoples, meeting a positive and effective demand at all times and places, and practically in any quantity that found its way to market.

Hence arose a circumstance, which necessarily became of special import for their becoming money. For any one under those conditions, having any of the precious metals at his disposal, there was not only the reasonable prospect of his being able to convert them in all markets at any time and practically in all quantities, but also—and this is after all the criterion of saleableness—the prospect of converting them at prices corresponding at any time to the general economic situation, *at economic prices*. The proportionately strong, persistent, and omnipresent desire on the part of the most effective bargainers has gone farther to exclude prices of the moment, of emergency, of accident, in the case of the precious metals, than in the case of any other goods whatever, especially since these, by reason of their costliness, durability, and easy preservation, had become the most popular vehicle for hoarding as well as the goods most highly favoured in commerce.

Under such circumstances it became the leading idea in the minds of the more intelligent bargainers, and then, as the situation came to be more generally understood, in the mind of every one, that the stock of goods destined to be exchanged for other goods must in the first instance be laid out in precious metals, or must be converted into them, even if the agent in question did not directly need them, or had already supplied his wants in that direction. But in and by this function, the precious metals are already constituted generally current media of exchange. In other words, they hereby function as commodities for which every one seeks to exchange his market-goods, not, as a rule, in order to consumption but entirely because of their special saleableness, in the intention of exchanging them subsequently for other goods directly profitable to him. No accident, nor the consequence of state compulsion, nor voluntary convention of traders effected this. It was the just apprehending of their individual self-interest which brought it to pass, that all the more economically advanced nations accepted the precious metals as money as soon as a sufficient supply of them had been collected and introduced into commerce. The advance from less to more costly money-stuffs depends upon analogous causes.

This development was materially helped forward by the ratio of exchange between the precious metals and other commodities undergoing smaller fluctuations, more or less, than that existing between most other goods,—a stability which is due to the peculiar circumstances attending the production, consumption, and exchange of the precious metals, and is thus connected with the so-called intrinsic grounds determining their exchange value. It constitutes yet another reason why each man, in the first instance (*i.e.* till he invests in goods directly useful to him), should lay in his available exchange-stock in precious metals, or convert it into the latter. Moreover the *homogeneity* of the precious metals, and the consequent facility with which they can serve as *res fungibiles* in relations of obligation, have led to forms of contract by which traffic has been rendered more easy; this too has materially promoted the saleableness of the precious metals, and thereby their adoption as money. Finally the precious metals, in consequence of the peculiarity of their *colour* their *ring*, and partly also of their *specific gravity*, are with some practice not difficult to recognise, and through their taking a durable stamp can be easily controlled as to quality and weight; this too has materially contributed to raise their saleableness and to forward the adoption and diffusion of them as money.

IX. Influence of the Sovereign Power

Money has not been generated by law. In its origin it is a social, and not a state-institution. Sanction by the authority of the state is a notion alien to it. On the other hand, however, by state recognition and state regulation, this social institution of money has been perfected and adjusted to the manifold and varying needs of an evolving commerce, just as customary rights have been perfected and adjusted by statute law. Treated originally by weight, like other commodities, the precious metals have by degrees attained as coins a shape by which their intrinsically high saleableness has experienced a material increase. The fixing of a coinage so as to include all grades of value (*Wertstufen*), and the establishment and maintenance of coined pieces so as to win public confidence and, as far as is possible, to forestall risk concerning their genuineness, weight, and fineness, and above all the ensuring their circulation in general, have been everywhere recognised as important functions of state administration.

The difficulties experienced in the commerce and modes of payment of any country from the competing action of the several commodities serving as currency, and further the circumstance, that concurrent standards induce a manifold insecurity in trade, and render necessary various conversions of the circulating media, have led to the legal recognition of certain commodities as money (to legal standards). And where more than one commodity has been acquiesced in, or admitted, as the legal form of payment, law or some system of appraisement has fixed a definite ratio of value amongst them.

All these measures nevertheless have not first made money of the precious metals, but have only perfected them in their function as money.

Karl Menger.

Translated by Caroline A. Foley, M.A.

SECTION 2

Non-Monetary, Non-Market Trade

8

BILATERAL TRADING PROCESSES, PAIRWISE OPTIMALITY, AND PARETO OPTIMALITY

by Allan M. Feldman

Feldman presents an elegant formalization of Menger's bilateral trade problem, and he carries it in rather a different direction. Starting from an initial endowment, bilateral trade takes place without the use of money or of a price system. Further, traders undertake only those trades that directly result in a preferred allocation. Goods are accepted only when they increase trader satisfaction. They may be retraded subsequently to an even preferable reallocation, but they are not acquired with this aim.

We are then faced with a variety of questions. Does the process converge? If so, what does the limit allocation look like and is it Pareto efficient? Does any role for money develop from the trading process or at the limit allocation?

A technical smoothness condition on utility functions is required to make sure that the trading process does not get snagged on a sharp corner. Assuming this condition, the process converges through a lengthy sequence of trades to a *pairwise optimal* allocation. By this is meant an allocation so that there is no mutually beneficial unexploited reallocation available to any single pair of traders. No two traders, by reallocating their current holdings between them, could make both better off, or one better off and the other no worse.

A pairwise optimal allocation is, however, not necessarily Pareto optimal. This reflects the difficulty of arranging a k-sided ($k > 2$) mutually beneficial reallocation as a sequence of two-sided mutually beneficial trades. The standard example is of three agents-three goods with a cyclic structure of preferences and allocation.

General Equilibrium
Models of
Monetary Economies

ISBN 0-12-663970-1

Let
$$u^1(x_1^1, x_2^1, x_3^1) = 3x_1^1 + 2x_2^1 + x_3^1$$
$$u^2(x_1^2, x_2^2, x_3^2) = x_1^2 + 3x_2^2 + 2x_3^2$$
$$u^3(x_1^3, x_2^3, x_3^3) = 2x_1^3 + x_2^3 + 3x_3^3$$
be the utility functions of agents 1, 2, and 3 repectively. Superscripts denote agents, subscripts denote commodities. Let their allocation be
$$x^1 = (x_1^1, x_2^1, x_3^1) = (1, 1, 0)$$
$$x^2 = (x_1^2, x_2^2, x_3^2) = (0, 1, 1) \quad (1)$$
$$x^3 = (x_1^3, x_2^3, x_3^3) = (1, 0, 1).$$
Each agent holds his most preferred and second most preferred good. A Pareto preferable reallocation would be
$$x^1 = (2, 0, 0),$$
$$x^2 = (0, 2, 0), \quad (2)$$
$$x^3 = (0, 0, 2).$$
There is however no sequence of mutually beneficial bilateral trades that can move the allocation from (1) to (2). (1) is pairwise optimal but not Pareto optimal.

Feldman then states an interesting sufficient condition for equivalence of pairwise and Pareto optimality. Suppose there is (at least) one good that is valued in consumption and is universally held. The presence of such a good at a pairwise optimal allocation—a good such that everyone holds a positive quantity—is a sufficient condition for Pareto optimality of the allocation. It is tempting to think of the universally held good as "money". The proof of sufficiency is simply to note that any failure of Pareto efficiency would show up as a difference between traders in their MRSs of some goods for the universally held good. Then the misallocation would be arbitraged away through trade in the misallocated goods and the universal. Hence the presence of "money" allows this very primitive trading mechanism to achieve a Pareto optimal allocation.

An open question is the extent to which a universally held and valued good would speed the trading process. Not much is known about the speed of convergence of the Feldman barter process. It certainly looks as though it could take a long time, a long succession of meetings where each pair of traders meets to trade and retrade. It would be intriguing to know through analytic solutions or simulations how the speed of convergence would depend (could it be increased?) on the presence of a single good with positive endowment to all, so that no agent's stock is ever depleted to nil during the trading process.

Reprinted from The Review of Economic Studies, Vol. XL (4), October, 1973, Allan M. Feldman, pp. 463-473.

Bilateral Trading Processes, Pairwise Optimality, and Pareto Optimality [1]

ALLAN M. FELDMAN
Brown University

INTRODUCTION

In a world where transferals are costless and multilateral trades can be arranged at no expense, and where utility functions are continuous and depend only on allocations, voluntary trade will lead inevitably to Pareto optimality. However, when transferals are costly and multilateral trades difficult or impossible, optimality is problematical. In this paper we will consider a pure exchange economy in which bilateral trades are costless, but multilateral trades are infinitely costly. We will show that under certain conditions a sequence of bilateral trades will carry the economy to a pairwise optimal allocation, that is, an allocation which cannot be improved upon by bilateral trade. Then we shall prove a theorem which says that, under fairly general conditions, a pairwise optimal allocation is Pareto optimal if it assigns each trader a positive quantity of one good (which we will call " money "), for which each trader has a positive marginal utility. As a corollary, we shall show that certain types of sequences of bilateral trades will always carry an economy to its set of Pareto optimal allocations.

The question of Pareto optimality for a pairwise optimal allocation has been treated before by Rader [8], who showed, essentially, that if there is a trader who can deal in all goods under a given pairwise optimal allocation, that allocation is Pareto optimal. Rader's theorems suggest how important a broker might be in an exchange economy where multilateral trades are impossible. Our theorems, on the other hand, suggest how important a money commodity might be. The role of the money commodity in the model of this paper is different from the role of money in the models of those authors, who, like Niehans [5, 6], view money as something which minimizes transferal (or transport) costs. We will ignore such costs; our analysis is about costly trade only in the sense that all bilateral trades are costless and all multilateral trades prohibitively costly. These are costs associated with the formation of trading groups, irrespective of the nature of the commodities traded.

We are especially interested in bilateral trading processes for two reasons. First, very casual empiricism suggests that bilateral commodity trades are more common than multilateral ones. Second, and much more important, there is good reason to believe that the nontransport costs of effecting trades rise much faster than the size of the groups making those trades. If, for example, information costs are proportional to the number of pairs in a group, they will go up as the square of the size of the group; if they are proportional to the number of subgroups in a group, they will increase exponentially with the size of the group. The assumption that bilateral trades are costless and multilateral trades prohibitively costly is a first approximation in investigating the effects of trading-group-formation costs which rise faster than group size.

Now the connection of bilateral trade and money is not new. Ostroy [7] and Starr [9] have both developed models of bilateral trade in which the introduction of money allows an economy to reach a competitive equilibrium via a finite series of bilateral trades

[1] *First version received July* 1972; *final version received February* 1973 (*Eds.*).

constrained by a *quid pro quo*, or bilateral balance requirement. However, these analyses, unlike the one presented here, assume that equilibrium prices are known by all traders, and they allow trades which may make some parties to them (temporarily) worse off, but which are nonetheless reasonable because of the price information assumed. Our model, on the other hand, is a model of exchange in which no prices are known, and in which traders, having no information or subjective probabilities about trading opportunities, only make trades when they can make themselves better (or no worse) off by so doing. They are truly groping in the dark. Yet, we will show that under general conditions their myopic trading will lead to a pairwise optimal allocation, and that, if there is a universally held money commodity, that pairwise optimal allocation will also be Pareto optimal.

THE MODEL

Consider an n-trader, m-good economy. The goods space is the non-negative orthant of m-dimensional Euclidean space. An *allocation* $x = (x_1, \ldots, x_n)$ is an n-vector of non-negative m-vectors, or a point in R_+^{nm}, whose ith component, x_i, is the *bundle* of goods assigned to trader i. We will let ω_i represent i's initial bundle; $\omega = (\omega_1, \ldots, \omega_n)$ will be a fixed *initial allocation*, and we will let $A(\omega)$ denote society's set of feasible allocations: $A(\omega) \equiv \{x = (x_1, \ldots, x_n) | \, x_i \in R^m, \, x_i \geqq 0$ for all i and $\sum_{i=1}^n x_i = \sum_{i=1}^n \omega_i\}$.[1] We shall assume that all m goods are in positive supply; so $\sum_{i=1}^n \omega_i > 0$.

We will suppose that every trader has preferences which can be represented by a continuous utility function $u_i(x_i)$ which maps R_+^m into R. We will say that the utility function u_i *represents convex preferences* if $u_i(y_i) > u_i(x_i)$ implies $u_i(ty_i + (1-t)x_i) > u_i(x_i)$ whenever $0 < t < 1$. We will say that u_i *represents strictly convex preferences* if

$$u_i(y_i) \geqq u_i(x_i)$$

implies $u_i(ty_i + (1-t)x_i) > u_i(x_i)$ whenever $0 < t < 1$ and $y_i \neq x_i$. The ith individual is said to be *insatiable* if for any bundle x_i there is a bundle y_i such that $u_i(y_i) > u_i(x_i)$.

For any allocation x, $u(x)$ will be the corresponding utility vector; so

$$u(x) \equiv (u_1(x_1), u_2(x_2), \ldots, u_n(x_n)).$$

The set of feasible utility vectors will be called $U(\omega)$; $U(\omega) \equiv \{u \in R^n \mid$ there exists an $x \in A(\omega)$ such that $u = u(x)\}$.

The letter N will represent the set of all n traders in the economy, and we will define as a *coalition* any non-empty subset of N. We will say that a coalition S can *block x from y* is there exist bundles $s_i \geqq 0$, for all $i \in S$, such that

$$\sum_{i \in S} s_i = \sum_{i \in S} y_i,$$

$$u_i(s_i) \geqq u_i(x_i) \quad \text{for all} \quad i \in S, \text{ and}$$

$$u_j(s_j) > u_j(x_j) \quad \text{for some} \quad j \in S.$$

The *core from y*, which we will write $C(y)$, is the set of allocations which cannot be blocked from y by any coalitions. The *core* is $C(\omega)$.

[1] We will use the following (standard) vector inequality notation:
If x and y are two k-dimensional vectors, we define

$$x = y \text{ if } x_i = y_i \text{ for } i = 1, \ldots, k$$
$$x \geqq y \text{ if } x_i \geqq y_i \text{ for } i = 1, \ldots, k$$
$$x \geq y \text{ if } x \geqq y \text{ and } x \neq y$$
$$x > y \text{ if } x_i > y_i \text{ for } i = 1, \ldots, k.$$

We will also use 0 to denote a zero vector of the appropriate dimension.

An allocation x is *Pareto optimal* or *efficient* if it cannot be blocked from ω by N. $P(\omega)$ will denote the set of Pareto optimal allocations. An allocation x will be called *pairwise optimal* if no two-member coalition can block it from x.

An m-vector of prices p, and an allocation y, together form a *competitive equilibrium from* x, if $p \cdot z_i \leqq p \cdot x_i$ implies $u_i(z_i) \leqq u_i(y_i)$ for all i in N and any bundle z_i. If (p, y) is a competitive equilibrium, y is called a *competitive allocation from* x and p is an *equilibrium price vector.*

We can finally define two types of bilateral exchange: We will say that the trade from an allocation x to an allocation y is a *bilateral trade move*, or BTM, if (i) it makes no trader worse off; that is, if $u(y) \geqq u(x)$, and (ii) $x_i = y_i$ for all traders but (at most) two. As a trivial consequence of this definition, if i and j are the two individuals who *are* trading, then $x_i + x_j = y_i + y_j$. Our definition of a BTM does not exclude the possibility that $x_i = y_i$ and $x_j = y_j$, but if $x_i \neq y_i$, then necessarily $x_j \neq y_j$.

If i and j trade to a (sub)allocation which is optimal for them, we will say they are making an optimizing bilateral trade move. More rigorously, let us define, for any allocation x and any given pair of traders $\{i, j\}$, an " optimal with respect to x " set

$O(i, j, x) \equiv \{y \in A(\omega) | \, u(y) \geqq u(x),\ x_l = y_l$ for $l \neq i, j$, and $\{i, j\}$ cannot block y from $x\}$.

($O(i, j, x)$ is non-empty by the continuity of u_i and u_j.)

An *optimizing bilateral trade move between i and j* is a move from an allocation x to an allocation $y \in O(i, j, x)$.

WHERE DOESN'T BILATERAL TRADE LEAD?

Let us imagine that the traders in our economy make a sequence of bilateral trade moves.

Where does that sequence of moves take them? Does it lead to the core, to the set of competitive equilibria, or to the set of Pareto optimal allocations? Does it, at least, bring the economy to the set of pairwise optimal allocations? Or does it lead nowhere?

It is easy to construct an example to show that bilateral trade moves need not lead to the core, even under the severest assumptions on the utility functions and the initial allocation ω. Suppose there are three individuals and two goods in the economy, and all three individuals have utility functions of the form $u_i(x_i) = u_i(x_{i1}, x_{i2}) = x_{i1}x_{i2}$, where x_{ij} is the amount of good j in bundle x_i. Assume that the initial allocation is

$$\omega = (\omega_1, \omega_2, \omega_3) = ((1, 9), (5, 5), (9, 1)).$$

Now consider the move from ω to $y = ((3, 3), (5, 5), (7, 7))$. It is clear that

$$y \in O(1, 3, \omega);$$

that is, the move from ω to y is an optimizing bilateral trade move between 1 and 3. Moreover, y is Pareto optimal, and therefore, no further non-degenerate bilateral trades are possible from y. But y is not in the core, because it can be blocked from ω by the coalition of traders 1 and 2: Take $s_1 = (3, 3)$, $s_2 = (3, 11)$; then

$$s_1 + s_2 = \omega_1 + \omega_2;\ u_1(s_1) = u_1(y_1) \text{ and } u_2(s_2) > u_2(y_2).$$

In the above example, bilateral trade leads to an allocation which is, if not in the core, at least Pareto optimal. However this is not always possible, and the fact that it's not always possible motivates the central theorems of this paper. The following example illustrates the dilemma of an allocation which cannot be improved upon except by multilateral trade, that is, an allocation which is pairwise optimal but not Pareto optimal.

Suppose there are three individuals and three goods, with utility functions and initial bundles given by the table below:

	$u_i(x_i)$	ω_i
Trader 1	$u_1(x_1) = 3x_{11}+2x_{12}+x_{13}$	(0, 1, 0)
Trader 2	$u_2(x_2) = 2x_{21}+x_{22}+3x_{23}$	(1, 0, 0)
Trader 3	$u_3(x_3) = x_{31}+3x_{32}+2x_{33}$	(0, 0, 1)

The initial allocation ω is not efficient because it is dominated by

$$y = ((1, 0, 0), (0, 0, 1), (0, 1, 0)),$$

since $u(y) = (3, 3, 3) > u(\omega) = (2, 2, 2)$. However, it is impossible to move from ω via bilateral trade: individual 1 would be glad to offer some good 2 in exchange for some of 2's good 1, but individual 2 values good 1 twice as highly as he values good 2, and individual 1 is not prepared to make an exchange at such a ratio. Similar considerations prohibit trade between 1 and 3, and 2 and 3. Consequently, no non-degenerate bilateral trades from ω are possible, and the economy cannot reach an optimum, in the sense of Pareto, via bilateral exchange. Moreover, a slight shift of ω into the interior of $A(\omega)$ would not alter the nature of this example. If we started, say, at

$$\omega^* = ((0{\cdot}01, 0{\cdot}98, 0{\cdot}01), (0{\cdot}98, 0{\cdot}01, 0{\cdot}01), (0{\cdot}01, 0{\cdot}01, 0{\cdot}98)),$$

which is *not* pairwise optimal, a sequence of bilateral trades might lead to an allocation like $y^* = ((0{\cdot}03, 0{\cdot}97, 0), (0{\cdot}97, 0, 0{\cdot}03), (0, 0{\cdot}03, 0{\cdot}97))$. Now y^* is pairwise optimal, but it is not Pareto optimal.

Is it possible to construct a sequence of bilateral trade moves which doesn't even lead to the set of pairwise optimal allocations? The answer is obviously yes since we allow for degenerate moves: the sequence of trades from ω to ω to ω... is an example. However, even if we require *optimizing* bilateral trades we aren't through. An example of an infinite sequence of rounds of optimizing bilateral trades which does not lead to a pairwise optimal allocation is given in the concluding section of this paper.

WHERE DOES BILATERAL TRADE LEAD?

In this section, we are going to show that the assumption of a rotating trading pattern, which forces every pair to trade periodically, coupled with an assumption of strictly convex preferences, will ensure that a sequence of optimizing BTM's converges to the set of pairwise optimal allocations. First, however, we will make a definition, motivated by our quite intuitive expectation that bilateral trade *ought* to lead to pairwise optimal allocations.

Consider an infinite sequence $\{b^k\}$ of bilateral trade moves which gives rise to a sequence of allocations $\{x^k\}$. Since the space of allocations $A(\omega)$ is compact, $\{x^k\}$ will have cluster points in $A(\omega)$. We will say that $\{b^k\}$ is *effective* if, whenever x^* is a cluster point of $\{x^k\}$, x^* is pairwise optimal.

In what follows we are going to assume that if b^k is a move from x^k to x^{k+1}, then x^{k+1} is contained in $O(i, j, x^k)$, for some pair $\{i, j\}$. Now for a given pair $\{i, j\}$ and a fixed x, $O(i, j, x)$ is simply a set of allocations, but if we let x vary over $A(\omega)$, $O(i, j, x)$ can be interpreted as a point-to-set correspondence. In the appendix we prove the following proposition, whose usefulness will become obvious as we proceed:

Proposition. *If u_i and u_j are continuous and represent strictly convex preferences, then $O(i, j, x)$ is a continuous correspondence.*

With this result in hand, we can now impose more structure on our as yet loosely defined sequence of bilateral trade moves. It is rather obvious that if one pair of traders is forever prevented from trading, a sequence of bilateral trades will not in general bring an economy to a pairwise optimal allocation. The easiest way to rule out such an occurrence is to assume that the trading pattern is a rotating one; that is, one in which trader 1 trades with trader 2, then with 3, then with 4, ..., then with n, and then 2 trades with 3, then with 4, ..., then with n, and so on, until $n-1$ trades with n, after which the round repeats, *ad infinitum.* If each step b^k of the process involves an optimizing trade, or, for an $i-j$ trade, a move from x to $O(i, j, x)$, we will say that $\{b^k\}$ is a *rotating sequence of optimizing bilateral trade moves.* In Theorem 1 below we will give sufficient conditions for a rotating sequence of optimizing bilateral trade moves to be effective, or to have pairwise optimal cluster points.

Before proceeding with the theorem, we need two preliminary lemmas.

Lemma 1. *Define* $h(i, j, x) \equiv \inf_{y \in O(i, j, x)} [\Delta u(i, j, x, y)]$,

where $\Delta u(i, j, x, y) \equiv \sum_{l=1}^{n} u_l(y_l) - \sum_{l=1}^{n} u_l(x_l) = u_i(y_i) - u_i(x_i) + u_j(y_j) - u_j(x_j)$.

If u_i and u_j are continuous and represent strictly convex preferences, $h(i, j, x)$ is a continuous function.

Proof. By the Proposition, $O(i, j, x)$ is closed for any $x \in A(\omega)$. Since $A(\omega)$ is bounded, $O(i, j, x)$ is compact. $\Delta u(i, j, x, y)$ is continuous by the continuity of u_i and u_j.

Therefore,

$$h(i, j, x) = \min_{y \in O(i, j, x)} [\Delta u(i, j, x, y)].$$

Therefore,

$$-h(i, j, x) = \max_{y \in O(i, j, x)} [-\Delta u(i, j, x, y)].$$

Since $O(i, j, x)$ is a continuous correspondence by the Proposition, the continuity of h follows from 1.8 (4) in [3], or [2, p. 116]. Q.E.D.

Lemma 2. *Suppose all utility functions are continuous and represent strictly convex preferences. Suppose the move from x to y is an optimizing BTM between traders i and j; that is, suppose $y \in O(i, j, x)$. Then for any $\varepsilon > 0$, there exists a $\delta(\varepsilon) > 0$ such that $d(x, y) \geqq \varepsilon$ implies $\Delta u(i, j, x, y) \geqq \delta(\varepsilon)$, where δ is independent of $\{i, j\}$.*[1]

Proof. Consider one pair of traders $\{i, j\}$. By the upper semi-continuity of O, the set $\{(x, y) | \, y \in O(i, j, x)\}$ is closed in $A(\omega) \times A(\omega)$. Given $\varepsilon > 0$ the set $\{(x, y) | \, d(x, y) \geqq \varepsilon\}$ is also closed. Therefore,

$$X \equiv \{(x, y) | \, y \in O(i, j, x)\} \cap \{(x, y) | \, d(x, y) \geqq \varepsilon\}$$

is closed. By the boundedness of $A(\omega)$, X is compact. The function $\Delta u(i, j, x, y)$ is strictly positive on X by the strict convexity assumption. Therefore,

$$\delta(i, j, \varepsilon) \equiv \inf_{(x, y) \in X} \Delta u(i, j, x, y) > 0,$$

[1] If x and y are two allocations, we will let $d(x, y)$ denote the Euclidean distance between x and y. Further, if S is a set of allocations, we will define

$$d(x, S) = \inf_{y \in S} d(x, y).$$

if X is non-empty. If X is empty, define $\delta(i, j, \varepsilon) \equiv 1$. Let $\delta(\varepsilon) \equiv \min_{\{i,j\} \subset N} \delta(i, j, \varepsilon) > 0$, and the lemma follows. Q.E.D.

Now we finally have

Theorem 1. *Suppose all utility functions are continuous and represent strictly convex preferences. Suppose $\{b^k\}$ is a rotating sequence of optimizing bilateral trade moves. Then $\{b^k\}$ is effective.*

Proof. Let $\{x^k\}$ be the sequence of allocations associated with $\{b^k\}$; so b^k is the move from x^k to x^{k+1}. Since $A(\omega)$ is compact, $\{x^k\}$ has cluster points in $A(\omega)$; let x^* be one such point.

First, we claim that $d(x^k, x^{k+1}) \to 0$. If not, there is an $\varepsilon > 0$ such that for an infinite set of indices $\{r\}$, $d(x^r, x^{r+1}) \geqq \varepsilon > 0$. This implies, by Lemma 2, that

$$\sum_{i=1}^{n} [u_i(x^{r+1}) - u_i(x^r)] \geqq \delta(\varepsilon) > 0$$

for all r. But this means $\sum_{i=1}^{n} u_i(x^k) \to \infty$ as $k \to \infty$, which is impossible since $U(\omega)$ is compact, by the compactness of $A(\omega)$ and the continuity of u.

Suppose $\{b^k\}$ is *not* effective. Assume, without loss of generality, that traders 1 and 2 could make a profitable trade from x^*. Therefore, there is a $y \in O(1, 2, x^*)$ such that $\Delta u(1, 2, x^*, y) > 0$. By the upper semi-continuity of O, $O(1, 2, x^*)$ is closed; by the boundedness of $A(\omega)$, $O(1, 2, x^*)$ is compact, and since

$$y \in O(1, 2, x^*) \Rightarrow \Delta u(1, 2, x^*, y) > 0, \; h(1, 2, x^*) > 0.$$

Now consider the subsequence $\{x^s\}$ of allocations which immediately precedes trades between 1 and 2:

$$\{x^s\} = \{x^1, x^{1+\frac{n}{2}(n-1)}, x^{1+2\left[\frac{n}{2}(n-1)\right]}, \ldots\}.$$

We claim that x^* is a cluster point of $\{x^s\}$. This is the case because (i) x^* is a cluster point of $\{x^k\}$; (ii) any element of $\{x^k\}$ is no further than $n(n-1)/2$ places removed from some allocation which is also in $\{x^s\}$; and (iii) $d(x^k, x^{k+l}) \to 0$ for $l \leqq n(n-1)/2$.

Finally, by Lemma 1, $h(1, 2, x)$ is continuous at x^*; therefore, since

$$h(1, 2, x^*) > 0, \; h(1, 2, x^s) \nrightarrow 0.$$

But this implies that $u_1(x_1^k) + u_2(x_2^k)$ grows without bound, contradicting the fact that $U(\omega)$ is compact. Q.E.D.

We might remark at this point that Theorem 1 would still be true under a much broader definition of a rotating sequence of bilateral trade moves. All that is necessary for our proof is that $\{b^k\}$ be a sequence of rounds of a fixed maximum length, and that, in each round, each pair trade at least once. The particular trading pattern $1-2$, $1-3$, ..., $1-n$, $2-3$, ..., $2-n$, ..., $(n-1)-n$, is not essential.

PAIRWISE OPTIMALITY AND PARETO OPTIMALITY

Now we must consider the following question. When is a pairwise optimal allocation also Pareto optimal? This is not a vacuous issue, as we have shown above it is easy to construct a pairwise optimal allocation that is not efficient. Such examples show that bilateral trade moves are not entirely satisfactory for some economies; because of the difficulty, in a barter economy, of multilateral trades, it is important to know how likely it is that bilateral trade will prove unsatisfactory. The theorem below gives relatively simple conditions that ensure that a pairwise optimal allocation is in fact a Pareto optimal allocation.

The proof will turn on the assumption that there is a good for which everyone has a positive marginal utility and of which everyone has a positive quantity. Intuitively, the existence of such a " money " commodity opens up trading possibilities that would otherwise remain closed, as they are in our second example above. We will write $u_{ij}(y_i)$ for the partial derivative of u_i with respect to y_{ij}, that is, the marginal utility of good j for trader i.

Theorem 2. *Suppose u is continuous on $A(\omega)$, u_i represents convex preferences for $i = 1, \ldots, n$, and every u_i has continuous first partial derivatives.*[1]

[1] I am obliged to Harl Ryder for observing that this differentiability assumption is crucial; in fact, the theorem fails without it. (An assumption analogous to differentiability is also essential for Rader's [8] pairwise optimality—Pareto optimality equivalency result.) Consider the following economy:

$$u_1(x_1) = \min\,[100x_{11},\ 3x_{11}+97]+2x_{12}+\ x_{13};\quad \omega_1 = (1, 1, 0);$$
$$u_2(x_2) = \min\,[100x_{21},\ 2x_{21}+98]+\ x_{22}+3x_{23};\quad \omega_2 = (2, 0, 0);$$
$$u_3(x_3) = \min\,[100x_{31},\ x_{31}+99]+3x_{32}+2x_{33};\quad \omega_3 = (1, 0, 1).$$

Now ω is pairwise optimal, all the u_i's are continuous and represent convex preferences, the first good is held in positive quantities by all the traders, and, incidentally, all the utility functions are monotonically increasing in it. But ω is *not* Pareto optimal since it is dominated by ((2, 0, 0), (1, 0, 1), (1, 1, 0)).

If, however, we smooth the kink at $x_{i1} = 1$, our difficulties vanish. Suppose we change the utility functions to

$$u_i^*(x_i) = \begin{cases} \sum_{j=1}^{3} \alpha_{ij}x_{ij}+(2x_{i1}-x_{i1}^2)(100-\alpha_{i1}) & \text{for } x_{i1} \leqq 1 \\ \sum_{j=1}^{3} \alpha_{ij}x_{ij}+(100-\alpha_{i1}) & \text{for } x_{i1}>1, \end{cases}$$

where $\| \alpha_{ij} \| = \begin{bmatrix} 3 & 2 & 1 \\ 2 & 1 & 3 \\ 1 & 3 & 2 \end{bmatrix}$ is the same matrix of constant marginal utilities (for $x_{i1} > 1$) as in the example above. A graph of u_i against x_{i1}, for fixed x_{i2}, x_{i3}, shows what has happened to the utility functions.

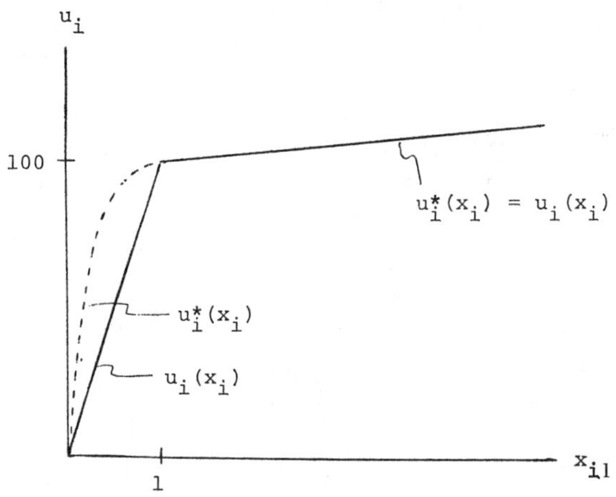

FIGURE 1

Suppose again that we start at $\omega = ((1, 1, 0), (2, 0, 0), (1, 0, 1))$. Now ω is no longer pairwise optimal. For example, traders 1 and 3 can make an exchange to bring the economy to $x^1 = ((1.01, 0.99, 0), (2, 0, 0), (0.99, 0.01, 1))$, and $u(x^1) \geqslant u(\omega)$. The reader can verify that a bilateral trading process in this economy can reach a Pareto optimal allocation.

It is important to observe that any effective bilateral trading sequence in this example will pivot around trader 3's one unit of good one. This is where the differentiability assumption is useful. Trader 3 must take small steps back and forth off the constant slope part of his utility hill: he can do this because the hill is smooth. When his utility function is $u_3(x_3) = \min\,[100x_{31},\ x_{31}+99]+3x_{32}+2x_{33}$, he can't make those small pivoting steps, because there's a cliff behind him!

Suppose y is a pairwise optimal allocation, and for some good, say the first, $u_{i1}(y_i) > 0$ *and* $y_{i1} > 0$, *for all i.*

Then y is a competitive equilibrium allocation, it is in $C(y)$ *and it is Pareto optimal.*

Proof. To lighten the notation, we will drop the y_i in $u_{ij}(y_i)$; it is understood that all the partial derivatives are to be evaluated at y. Our strategy is to define a price vector p with the property that (p, y) is a competitive equilibrium from y. Then we will use Theorem 1 of Debreu and Scarf [4] to establish that y is in the core for y, and is, therefore, Pareto optimal.

Let $p_1 = 1$.

Now choose an individual, say i_2, to whom y assigns a positive amount of good 2, and let

$$p_2 = p_1 u_{i_2 2}/u_{i_2 1} = u_{i_2 2}/u_{i_2 1}.$$

By assumption, $u_{i_2 1}$ is positive.

We claim that p_2 is well defined, in the sense that if j and k are two individuals to whom y assigns positive amounts of good 2, then $u_{j2}/u_{j1} = u_{k2}/u_{k1}$. For if

$$u_{j2}/u_{j1} \neq u_{k2}/u_{k1},\ y_{j1},\ y_{k1},\ y_{j2},\ y_{k2} > 0 \text{ and } u_{j1},\ u_{j2},\ u_{k1},\ u_{k2}$$

are continuous, y is not pairwise optimal, contradicting our assumption.

In general, let $p_k = p_1 u_{i_k k}/u_{i_k 1}$, for $k = 2, 3, \ldots, m$, where i_k is an individual to whom y assigns a positive amount of good k.

Let $p = (p_1, p_2, \ldots, p_m)$. We claim that (p, y) is a competitive equilibrium from y. We must show that, for $i = 1, 2, \ldots, n$, y_i maximizes $u_i(z_i)$, subject to $0 \leqq z_i$ and

$$p \cdot z_i \leqq p \cdot y_i.$$

By the convex preferences assumption, y_i solves this maximization problem if and only if (i) $u_{ij} - \lambda_i p_j \leqq 0$ for all $j = 1, 2, \ldots, m$ and some non-negative λ_i, and (ii) $u_{ij} - \lambda_i p_j = 0$ whenever y_{ij} is positive (see, e.g., [1]). Let $\lambda_i = u_{i1}$, which is, by assumption, positive. Then if y_{ij} is positive, $u_{ij} - \lambda_i p_j = u_{ij} - u_{i1} p_j = u_{ij} - u_{i1}(u_{ij}/u_{i1}) = 0$, so (ii) is satisfied. To establish (i), we must show that if $y_{ij} = 0$, and if k is an individual for whom y_{kj} is positive, then $u_{ij} - u_{i1}(u_{kj}/u_{k1}) \leqq 0$. But if this is not the case, then

$$y_{i1},\ y_{k1} > 0,\ y_{kj} > 0,\ u_{ij}/u_{i1} > u_{kj}/u_{k1},$$

and by the continuity of u_{ij}, u_{i1}, u_{kj}, u_{k1}, y is not pairwise optimal, which is again a contradiction. Therefore, (y, p) is a competitive equilibrium from y.

Because $u_{i1} > 0$ for all i, no i is satiated at y_i. Moreover, all the u_i are continuous and represent convex preferences; therefore, we can apply Theorem 1 of [4]; therefore y is in $C(y)$. Consequently, y is Pareto optimal. Q.E.D.

Theorems 1 and 2 can be combined to provide a set of sufficient conditions under which sequences of bilateral trade moves bring the economy to Pareto optimality.

Theorem 3. *Suppose all utility functions are continuous, have continuous first partial derivatives, represent strictly convex preferences, and are monotonic increasing in at least one common argument.*

Suppose $\{x^k\}$ *is a sequence of allocations which results from a sequence of bilateral trade moves* $\{b^k\}$. *Assume that for some* $\hat{k}$, *the set* $\{x \mid u(x) \geqq u(x^{\hat{k}})\} \subset \mathring{A}(\omega) \equiv$ *the interior of* $A(\omega)$.

Let x^* *be a cluster point of* $\{x^k\}$.

Then if $\{b^k\}$ *is a rotating sequence of optimizing BTM's,* x^* *is Pareto optimal.*

Proof. Since $x^* \in \{x \mid u(x) \geqq u(x^{\hat{k}})\}$, $x^* \in \mathring{A}(\omega)$; i.e., $x^* > 0$. By Theorem 1, x^* is pairwise optimal, and by a trivial application of Theorem 2, x^* is Pareto optimal. Q.E.D.

CONCLUSIONS

In this paper we have treated sequences of bilateral trade moves which are (i) unconstrained by any *quid pro quo* requirements, and (ii) always utility non-decreasing. We think our sequences of moves reflect what is meant by " bilateral barter " in one of its most primitive forms, and we have proved that under the assumptions of continuity and strict convexity of preferences, rotating sequences of optimizing bilateral trade moves lead to pairwise optimal allocations. We further showed that pairwise optimal allocations are Pareto optimal, under rather general conditions, if there is one good which everyone values and possesses in positive amounts.

These theorems tempt us to interpret the real world. Let us consider those primitive economies in which a commodity like a staple food product is used as a medium of exchange. It is probably the case that no household will want to trade away all its yams, or all its cattle, or all of whatever. If the preferences of households are strictly convex, Theorems 1 and 2 suggest that (i) an endless series of bilateral trades will establish pairwise optimality, and (ii), the existence of a commonly held commodity, like yams, or cattle, will guarantee that pairwise optimality is Pareto optimality. Moreover, this is the case even though there are no markets, no well-defined prices, traders are completely ignorant of possible future exchange ratios, and they are dreadfully conservative in the sense that they make no trades which do not directly and immediately gratify them.

We think this a rather striking result. But how general is it? In particular, how important is the stringent assumption of strict convexity? The answer to this question is not yet entirely clear. However, we do know that the correspondence O is not upper semi-continuous if, say, preferences are merely assumed to be convex, rather than strictly convex, and the function h is not necessarily continuous under these conditions.

We also can construct rather perverse examples of optimizing bilateral trading rounds, in which preferences are assumed to be convex, but not strictly convex, which do not establish pairwise optimality. Consider a three-person two-good economy and a trading round described by the following sequence $\{b^k\}$.

	$\omega = x^1$	$\xrightarrow{b^1}$ x^2	$\xrightarrow{b^2}$ x^3	$\xrightarrow{b^3}$ x^4	$\xrightarrow{b^4}$ x^5
$u_1(x_1) = x_{11}$	(1, 0)	(1, 2)	(1, 2)	(1, 0)	(1, 0)
$u_2(x_2) = x_{21}$	(0, 2)	(0, 0)	(0, 0)	(0, 2)	(0, 2)
$u_3(x_3) = x_{31}+x_{32}$	(1, 0)	(1, 0)	(1, 0)	(1, 0)	(1, 0)

Now b^1 is an optimizing trade between 1 and 2, b^2 is a degenerate optimizing trade between 2 and 3, b^3 is again an optimizing trade between 1 and 2, and b^4 is a degenerate optimizing trade between 1 and 3. Suppose after one round the process repeats, *ad infinitum*. Then $x^1 = ((1, 0), (0, 2), (1, 0))$ is a cluster point of $\{x^k\}$. However, it is not pairwise optimal, because traders 2 and 3 can block it. In other words, the process is not effective.

The difficulty here is apparently the perpetually disappearing opportunity of a profitable 2-3 trade; such a difficulty would be ruled out in a strictly convex preferences model, where no pair of players can make an endless sequence of optimizing trades of lengths $\geqq \varepsilon > 0$. Obviously, reasonable assumptions other than strict convexity of preferences might also eliminate such pathological cases. When we say that we are uncertain about the importance of the strict convexity assumption, we simply mean that we have not weighed the significance of perverse cases like this one, and have not weighed the reasonableness of assumptions other than strict convexity which would rule them out.

It would be ideal to have a theorem which gives interesting necessary and sufficient conditions for the effectiveness of bilateral trade move sequences, and it would be ideal to have a much stronger theorem than Theorem 3 for the convergence of such sequences to Pareto optimal allocations. However the ideal is elusive. We hope what little we have done is interesting in itself.

APPENDIX

Proposition. *Suppose u_i and u_j are continuous and represent strictly convex preferences. Then the correspondence $O(i, j, x)$ is continuous.*

Proof. We will show that $O(i, j, x)$ is continuous at any allocation x^0.

Step 1. O is upper semi-continuous. We must show that if $x^q \to x^0$, (where of course $\{x^q\}$ is a sequence of allocations), if $y^q \in O(i, j, x^q)$ for all q and $y^q \to y^0$, then $y^0 \in O(i, j, x^0)$.

Suppose not. It is clear that we must have $y_i^0 + y_j^0 = x_i^0 + x_j^0$, so there must exist a $\hat{y} \in O(i, j, x^0)$ with $(u_i(\hat{y}_i), u_j(\hat{y}_j)) \geqslant (u_i(y_i^0), u_j(y_j^0))$. Because $\hat{y} \in O(i, j, x^0)$,

$$\hat{y}_i + \hat{y}_j = x_i^0 + x_j^0 = y_i^0 + y_j^0,$$

and therefore, since either $\hat{y}_i \neq y_i^0$ or $\hat{y}_j \neq y_j^0$, we must have $\hat{y}_i \neq y_i^0$ and $\hat{y}_j \neq y_j^0$. By the strict convexity assumption, we can choose a $\hat{\hat{y}} \in O(i, j, x^0)$ such that

$$(u_i(\hat{\hat{y}}_i), u_j(\hat{\hat{y}}_j)) > (u_i(y_i^0), u_j(y_j^0)).$$

By the continuity of u_i and u_j, there exists an $\varepsilon > 0$ such that for any $y \in N_{\hat{\hat{y}}}^{\varepsilon}$, where $N_{\hat{\hat{y}}}^{\varepsilon}$ is a closed ε-ball centred on $\hat{\hat{y}}$, and any $y^q \in N_{y^0}^{\varepsilon}$, we have $(u_i(y_i), u_j(y_j)) > (u_i(y_i^q), u_j(y_j^q))$. But since $\hat{\hat{y}}_i + \hat{\hat{y}}_j = x_i^0 + x_j^0$, and since $x_i^q + x_j^q \to x_i^0 + x_j^0$, there exists a Q such that $q \geqq Q$ implies $x_i^q + x_j^q$ can be distributed to i and j in a way which gives an allocation in $N_{\hat{\hat{y}}}^{\varepsilon}$. However, this contradicts the assumption that $y^q \in O(i, j, x^q)$. Therefore, O is upper semi-continuous.

Step 2. O is a lower semi-continuous. Now we must show that if $x^q \to x^0$, and $y^0 \in O(i, j, x^0)$, then there exists a sequence $\{y^q\}$ of allocations, with $y^q \in O(i, j, x^q)$ for all q, such that $y^q \to y^0$.

Step 2*a*. First, we will show that the bilateral trade move correspondence is lower semi-continuous. Let us define

$$B(i, j, x) \equiv \{y \in A(\omega) | \; x \to y \text{ is a BTM between traders } i \text{ and } j\}$$
$$= \{y \in A(\omega) | \; x_l = y_l \text{ for } l \neq i, j, \text{ and } (u_i(y_i), u_j(y_j)) \geqq (u_i(x_i), u_j(x_j))\}.$$

We wish to establish that, under our continuity and strict convexity assumptions, if $\{x^q\}$ is a sequence of allocations satisfying $x^q \to x^0$, and if $y^0 \in B(i, j, x^0)$, then there exists a sequence of allocations $\{y^q\}$, with $y^q \in B(i, j, x^q)$ for all q, such that $y^q \to y^0$.

Case 1. $y^0 = x^0$. Now we can take $y^q = x^q$ for all q, and we are done.

Case 2. $y^0 \neq x^0$. Since $y^0 \in B(u, j, x^0)$, $y_k^0 = x_k^0$ for all $k \neq i, j$, and therefore, $y_i^0 \neq x_i^0$ and $y_j^0 \neq x_j^0$. Now suppose B is *not* lower semi-continuous. Then there is an $\varepsilon > 0$ such that for an infinite number of q's, $B(i, j, x^q) \cap N_{y^0}^{\varepsilon} = \varnothing$, where $N_{y^0}^{\varepsilon}$ is a closed ε-ball centred on y^0. Let $\{x^r\}$ be the subsequence of $\{x^q\}$ for which $B(i, j, x^r) \cap N_{y^0}^{\varepsilon} = \varnothing$.

Consider the allocation $\hat{y} = ty^0 + (1-t)x^0$, where t is chosen so that the distance between $\hat{y}$ and y^0 is exactly $\varepsilon/2$. By the strong convexity of preferences assumption,

$$(u_i(\hat{y}_i), u_j(\hat{y}_j)) > (u_i(x_i^0), u_j(x_j^0)).$$

Since u is continuous, there exists an $\varepsilon' > 0$ which we can choose smaller than or equal to $\varepsilon/2$, such that for any $y \in N_{\hat{y}}^{\varepsilon'}$, and any $x^r \in N_{x^0}^{\varepsilon'}$, $(u_i(y_i), u_j(y_j)) > (u_i(x_i^r), u_j(x_j^r))$. Because $\varepsilon' \leqq \varepsilon/2$, $N_{\hat{y}}^{\varepsilon'} \subset N_{y^0}^{\varepsilon}$.

Now since $x^r \to x^0$, there exists an R_1 such that $r \geqq R_1$ implies $x^r \in N_{x^0}^{\varepsilon'}$, and therefore, $(u_i(y_i), u_j(y_j)) > (u_i(x_i^r), u_j(x_j^r))$ for any $y \in N_{\hat{y}}^{\varepsilon'}$. However, because $x_i^r + x_j^r \to \hat{y}_i + \hat{y}_j$, there must be an R_2 such that $r \geqq R_2$ implies that for some $y \in N_{\hat{y}}^{\varepsilon'}$, $y_i + y_j = x_i^r + x_j^r$. Let $R = \max(R_1, R_2)$. Then $r \geqq R$ implies there exists a $y \in N_{\hat{y}}^{\varepsilon'} \cap B(i, j, x^r) \subset N_{y^0}^{\varepsilon} \cap B(i, j, x^r)$, which contradicts our construction of $\{x_r\}$. Therefore, B must be lower semi-continuous.

Step 2b. To establish the lower semi-continuity of O, we must show that if x^q is a sequence of allocations such that $x^q \to x^0$, and $y^0 \in O(i, j, x^0)$, then there exists a sequence $\{y^q\}$ of allocations, with $y^q \in O(i, j, x^q)$ for all q, such that $y^q \to y^0$.

By the lower semi-continuity of B, there exists a sequence of allocations $\{z^q\}$, with $z^q \in B(i, j, x^q)$ for all q, such that $z^q \to y^0$. Choose $y^q \in O(i, j, z^q)$. Therefore, $y^q \in O(i, j, x^q)$. We claim that $y^q \to y^0$. Let y^* be a cluster point of $\{y^q\}$. Clearly $y^* \in B(i, j, x^0)$. Moreover,

$$(u_i(y_i^*), u_j(y_j^*)) \geqq (u_i(y_i^0), u_j(y_j^0)),$$

since for all q

$$(u_i(y_i^q), u_j(y_j^q)) \geqq (u_i(z_i^q), u_i(z_j^q)), \; z^q \to y^0,$$

and u is continuous.

It must be the case that $(u_i(y_i^*), u_j(y_j^*)) = (u_i(y_i^0), u_j(y_j^0))$, because an inequality would contradict the assumption that $y^0 \in O(i, j, x^0)$. But by the strict convexity assumption, if $(u_i(y_i^*), u_j(y_j^*)) = (u_i(y_i^0), u_j(y_j^0))$, $y^0 \in O(i, j, x^0)$, and $y^* \in B(i, j, x^0)$, then $y^* = y^0$, as claimed. Therefore, O is lower semi-continuous at x^0. Q.E.D.

REFERENCES

[1] Arrow, K. J. and Enthoven, A. C. " Quasi-Concave Programming ", *Econometrica* (1961).

[2] Berge, C. *Topological Spaces* (The Macmillan Co., New York, 1963).

[3] Debreu, G. *Theory of Value* (Cowles Foundation Monograph No. 17, 1959).

[4] Debreu, G. and Scarf, H. " A Limit Theorem on the Core of an Economy ", *International Economic Review* (1963).

[5] Niehans, J. " Money in a Static Theory of Optimal Payments Arrangements ", *Journal of Money, Credit and Banking* (November 1969).

[6] Niehans, J. " Money and Barter in General Equilibrium with Transaction Costs ", *American Economic Review* (December 1971).

[7] Ostroy, J. " The Informational Efficiency of Monetary Exchange ", UCLA Economics Department Working Paper No. 15 (November 1971).

[8] Rader, T. " Pairwise Optimality and Non-Competitive Behavior ", in J. P. Quirk and A. M. Zarley (editors), *Papers in Quantitative Economics* (University Press of Kansas, 1968).

[9] Starr, Ross M. " Exchange in Barter and Monetary Economies ", *Quartery Journal of Economics* (May 1972).

9

PAIRWISE, t-WISE, AND PARETO OPTIMALITIES

by Steven M. Goldman and Ross M. Starr

Goldman and Starr extend Feldman's analysis in two directions while leaving a question mark in a third. Feldman's sufficient condition for equivalence of pairwise to Pareto optimality is weakened. The limitation on trading group size is generalized from pairs to groups of up to size t (a positive integer). The convergence of the trading process when trade takes place in these larger groups is, however, not treated.

Goldman and Starr assume the economy to be in a t-wise optimal allocation—that is, so that no reallocation of current holdings within groups of size t or smaller could result in a preferable allocation for all of those whose holdings were rearranged. For $t = 2$, of course, this includes pairwise optimality as a special case. The main undertaking is then to establish sufficient conditions so that the t-wise optimal allocation be Pareto optimal. Feldman's sufficient condition (and its predecessor, Rader's (1968) sufficient condition that there be a single agent holding positive quantities of all goods) are of course still sufficient. The major weakening consists in formalizing the idea that—though there need be no universally held good—traders' holdings need only overlap sufficiently that through successive chains of t or fewer traders a single set of support prices for the allocation can be established. This condition represents a clarification and weakening of a sufficient condition due to Rader (1976). The overlap condition can be shown to be nearly—but not quite—necessary for t-wise to imply Pareto optimality.

The study leaves unanswered the question of how we are to get to a t-wise optimal allocation. Presumably the answer is very much the way Feldman

General Equilibrium
Models of
Monetary Economies

ISBN 0-12-663970-1

suggests the economy get to a pairwise optimal allocation—through decentralized sequential barter trade, this time in groups of size t. Nevertheless, establishing this result with relatively weak sufficient conditions is a bit of unfinished business.

Econometrica, Vol. 50, No. 3 (May, 1982)

PAIRWISE, t-WISE, AND PARETO OPTIMALITIES

BY STEVEN M. GOLDMAN AND ROSS M. STARR[1]

An allocation is said to be t-wise optimal (for t a positive integer) if for every collection of t traders, there is no reallocation of their current holdings that will make some better off while making none worse off. The allocation is pairwise optimal if it is t-wise optimal for $t = 2$. A t-wise optimal allocation is the outcome of a trading process more decentralized than that of the Walrasian equilibrium. It represents the result of a variety of separate transactions in small groups without the (centralized) coordination provided by a single Walrasian auctioneer.

Necessary conditions and sufficient conditions on allocations for t-wise optimality to imply Pareto optimality are developed. These generally require sufficient overlap in goods holdings among traders to ensure the presence of common support prices. This is formalized as indecomposability of a truncated submatrix of the allocation matrix. A necessary and sufficient condition remains an open question.

0. INTRODUCTION

OUR PRINCIPAL CONCERN in this inquiry is with the decentralization of the trading process. The analysis departs from the familiar Arrow-Debreu general equilibrium framework to examine the efficiency of economies deprived of the coordinating function of the Walrasian price mechanism. The alternative, presented here, is to permit trade to take place only in small groups—say up to t traders in number. We envision an exchange economy wherein groups form and reform in order to barter—as individuals and as small coalitions. If *all* such small groups may form, then such a process might eventually converge to an equilibrium from which no reallocation involving t or fewer traders could result in a Pareto preferable allocation. That is, an allocation which is *t-wise optimal.* The dynamics of pairwise barter trade to achieve a pairwise optimal allocation is thoroughly studied in Feldman [**2**]. The corresponding analysis for trade in larger groups represents an open research topic, though we certainly expect Feldman's analysis to generalize.

It is by no means apparent that such a t-wise optimal allocation would be Pareto optimal. This reflects the difficulty of achieving a reallocation which is preferable for a large group through a sequence of weakly desirable small group trades. Since Pareto optimality is such an essential condition in welfare economics, it is useful to discover under what circumstances the two optimality concepts

[1]The authors are indebted to Andreu Mas-Colell for many helpful conversations about the contributions to an earlier draft, to R. Welch for research assistance, to the editor of this journal, and to an anonymous referee for useful comments. Remaining errors are the authors' responsibility.

This research has been supported by National Science Foundation Grant SOC78-15429 to the University of California, Berkeley, Davis, and San Diego, by a John Simon Guggenheim fellowship, and by the Group for the Applications of Mathematics and Statistics to Economics, University of California, Berkeley.

Any opinions, findings, and conclusions or recommendations expressed in this publication are those of the authors and do not necessarily reflect the views of the supporting groups.

coincide. Below, we investigate necessary and sufficient conditions for the equivalence of t-wise and Pareto optimality.

A simple example can illustrate problems in relating the two optimality concepts. Consider a three-man, three-good economy with allocation

$$x^1 = (x_1^1, x_2^1, x_3^1) = (1, 1, 0),$$

$$x^2 = (x_1^2, x_2^2, x_3^2) = (0, 1, 1),$$

$$x^3 = (x_1^3, x_2^3, x_3^3) = (1, 0, 1),$$

and linear utility functions

$$u^1(x^1) = 2x_1^1 + x_2^1,$$

$$u^2(x^2) = 2x_2^2 + x_3^2,$$

$$u^3(x^3) = x_1^3 + 2x_3^3.$$

We can represent the allocation schematically by the matrix

$$A = \begin{bmatrix} 1 & 1 & 0 \\ 0 & 1 & 1 \\ 1 & 0 & 1 \end{bmatrix}$$

and preferences by the matrix of marginal utilities

$$P = \begin{bmatrix} 2 & 1 & 0 \\ 0 & 2 & 1 \\ 1 & 0 & 2 \end{bmatrix}.$$

Rows represent traders and columns indicate commodities. The allocation is pairwise optimal but not Pareto (3-wise) optimal. Each agent holds one unit of his favorite good and his second most desired good. There is one other holder of the favorite good, and he regards the other good the first agent holds as worthless. Hence, there is no room for pairwise improvement. 3-wise improvement is possible, since each agent can be given more of his favorite in exchange for his second choice. In particular, the reallocation matrix

$$B = \begin{bmatrix} \epsilon & -\epsilon & 0 \\ 0 & \epsilon & -\epsilon \\ -\epsilon & 0 & \epsilon \end{bmatrix}$$

results in the Pareto preferable allocation

$$A + B = \begin{bmatrix} 1+\epsilon & 1-\epsilon & 0 \\ 0 & 1+\epsilon & 1-\epsilon \\ 1-\epsilon & 0 & 1+\epsilon \end{bmatrix}.$$

There is a utility increase of ϵ for each agent resulting from the reallocation.[2]

We are thus led to describe an allocation as pairwise optimal if for every possible pair of traders there is no reallocation of the pair's current holdings, between traders of the pair, that is weakly preferable to both traders with strict preference for at least one. Similarly, for a positive integer t, an allocation is said to be t-wise optimal if, for every group of t individuals, holdings are optimally allocated within the group. In an economy where trade takes place primarily among pairs or t-member groups of agents we expect the resulting allocation to be pairwise or t-wise optimal. It is then of interest to discover when pairwise or t-wise optimal allocations will be Pareto optimal as well.

As the example above suggests, corner solutions, the zeroes of the allocation matrix, play a pivotal role in the analysis. When traders' holdings have much in common with one another (i.e., when several positive entries coincide), the corresponding marginal rates of substitution will be equated across members of trading groups. Since the groups overlap, these MRS's will become common to all traders, hence leading to Pareto optimality. Conversely, if there is little overlap among agents' holdings the assurance of common MRS's is correspondingly weakened. Such a sparse overlap situation is likely to occur when there are many zeroes (corner solutions) in the allocation. This may lead, as in the example, to Pareto nonoptimality despite pairwise or t-wise optimality.

Conversely, sufficient overlap in traders' holdings ensures equivalence of t-wise optimality and Pareto optimality. If there is a universally held good, providing one point of overlap for all traders, then it acts like "money" to ensure the equivalence of pairwise, t-wise, and Pareto optimalities. Similarly, a single trader who holds positive amounts of all goods has complete overlap with all traders. He acts as a universal intermediary resulting again in the equivalence of pairwise, t-wise, and Pareto optimalities. The results are formalized as Theorems 1.1 and 1.2 below.

The focus on corner solutions seems appropriate inasmuch as most individuals do not consume most goods. This is particularly true when we think of commodities as differentiated by date, location, quality, and design.

We have concentrated upon restrictions on the allocation matrix A rather than on the utility functions. This is motivated by the direct observability of allocations (as compared with preferences) and forms the structure for Feldman **[2]** and Rader **[9, 10]** as well. Thus, it might be argued, statements of Pareto

[2] In the example above, the zeroes of the allocation matrix A are essential to the analysis. The zeroes of the marginal utility matrix P are inessential. They could be replaced by small positive numbers so that the optimality properties of the allocation are retained.

optimality based on allocation and trade structure (i.e., t-wise optimality) are grounded in potentially verifiable observations.

1. REPRESENTATION OF ALLOCATIONS AND PREFERENCES

We consider allocations in a pure exchange economy of M consumers and N commodities. An *allocation* is an $M \times N$ nonnegative matrix, $A = (a_{ij})$, where the ijth entry, a_{ij}, represents agent i's holding of good j. (Every row and column of A is assumed to have at least one positive entry.) Let the *utility functions* of the agents be represented by a vector of C^2, quasi-concave functions $u = (u^1, \ldots, u^M)$, where $u^i : R_+^N \to R$. The *linearized utility functions about A* form a vector $\bar{u} = (\bar{u}^1, \ldots, \bar{u}^M)$ where

$$p_{ij} = \frac{\partial u^i(a_{i1}, \ldots, a_{iM})}{\partial a_{ij}} \qquad \text{and} \qquad \bar{u}^i(x) = \sum_{j=1}^{N} p_{ij} x_j.$$

In the case (of considerable interest here) where $a_{ij} = 0$, we shall define

$$p_{ij} = \lim_{k \to 0+} \frac{\partial u^i(a_i + ke_j)}{\partial k}$$

where $a_i = (a_{i1}, \ldots, a_{iN})$ and e_j is the jth unit vector. *Marginal preferences* are then described by the $M \times N$ nonnegative matrix $P = (p_{ij})$. Every row and column of P is assumed to have at least one positive entry.

In what follows, we wish to characterize the efficiency of the economy (A, u) by that of its linear counterpart $(A, \bar{u})$. It is rather straightforward to establish that if $(A, \bar{u})$ is Pareto optimal then so is (A, u), since the optimality of $(A, \bar{u})$ implies the existence of a price vector $\xi \in R_+^N$ where $(A, \bar{u}, \xi)$ must be a competitive equilibrium. Then (A, u, ξ) must be a competitive equilibrium as well given the quasi-concavity and smoothness of u.

But for the Pareto optimality of (A, u) to imply optimality for $(A, \bar{u})$ is equivalent to requiring that (A, u) can be supported by a competitive—not merely compensated—equilibrium. Sufficient conditions for the existence of such a support have been extensively investigated (see McKenzie [7] or Arrow and Hahn [1]) and are generally stated in terms either of a minimum wealth constraint or resource relatedness and irreducibility.

Still an alternative condition deals with a weakened version of monotonicity. For a given consumption bundle if an agent's marginal utility for a good is zero, we shall suppose that reducing his consumption of that good—the remainder of the allocation held fixed—will not reduce utility. That is, a marginal utility of zero is assumed to remain zero after large finite variations in the quantity of the good.[3] Under this hypothesis, each of the following three statements implies the others: (i) (A, u) is Pareto optimal; (ii) $(A, \bar{u})$ is Pareto optimal; (iii) (A, u) can be

[3] Rader [10] assumes that $a_{ij} > 0$ if and only if $u_j^i(a_i) > 0$.

supported by a competitive equilibrium. This argument is present as Lemmas A.1 and A.2 and Theorem A.1 in the Appendix.

We will not specify a particular set of sufficient conditions here. Rather, we shall limit our further discussion to those economies where Pareto optima have competitive supports. Economies (A, u) fulfilling this condition can then be represented, without loss of generality, by their linear counterparts, $(A, \bar{u})$.

A *reallocation* is an $M \times N$ matrix Z so that $A + \epsilon Z$ is an allocation for some $\epsilon > 0$ and $\sum_i z_{ij} = 0$ for each j. A *pairwise reallocation* is a reallocation so that $z_i = 0$ for all but two of $i = 1, \ldots, M$. A *t-wise allocation* $(t = 2, \ldots, N)$ is a reallocation so that $z_i = 0$ for all but t of $i = 1, \ldots, M$. Z is a t-wise improvement if $p_i z_i \geqq 0$ for all $i = 1, \ldots, M$ with strict inequality for at least one i.

A *state* is represented by (A, P). The state is *t-wise* optimal if there is no t-wise reallocation Z constituting a t-wise improvement. The state is said to be *Pareto optimal* if it is M-wise optimal. We wish to investigate the relationship between pairwise, t-wise, and Pareto optimality. In particular we will establish sufficient conditions and necessary conditions for pairwise and t-wise optimality to imply Pareto optimality. The characterization of conditions that are both necessary and sufficient remains an open question.

For a given allocation A, we are interested in the sets of preferences for which (A, P) is t-wise or Pareto optimal. Specifically, let $\Pi^t(A) = \{P \mid (A, P) \text{ is } t\text{-wise optimal}\}$ and $\Pi^*(A) = \{P \mid (A, P) \text{ is Pareto optimal}\}$. $\Pi^t(A)$ is the set of preferences such that an endowment of A would be an allocation unblocked by any coalition of size t or less. For some A, if we have $\Pi^t(A) = \Pi^*(A)$ then for that allocation, preferences consistent with t-wise optimality and Pareto optimality coincide and A is said to exhibit the *t-wise equivalence property*. Hence, if the state (A, P) is pairwise optimal and if we know $\Pi^2(A) = \Pi^*(A)$ then the inference is that (A, P) is also Pareto optimal. We can restate the major straightforward results in this area then as the following theorems.

THEOREM 1.1 (Rader [**9**]): *Let A have a strictly positive row. Then*

$$\Pi^2(A) = \Pi^*(A).$$

THEOREM 1.2 (Feldman [**2**]): *Let A have a strictly positive column. Then*

$$\Pi^2(A) = \Pi^*(A).$$

The intuition for these results is that strict positivity of a row or column allows the immediate introduction of a price system which supports the allocation.

A strictly positive row (Theorem 1.1) represents a trader holding positive quantities of all goods. The corresponding price system is then the vector of this trader's marginal utilities. Pairwise optimality implies that all marginal rates of substitution of goods held in positive quantity coincide with those of the strictly positive row. Hence the price system established will support the allocation.

A strictly positive column represents a universally held good. If the good has positive marginal utility for any trader then pairwise optimality implies a positive marginal utility for all traders. Use the universal good as numeraire and establish prices for all other goods. For any two traders with two goods held by both, equality of their respective MRS's is guaranteed by pairwise optimality. For two goods held separately (one by each of two traders) that there should be a common supporting value of the MRS to use as a price ratio is guaranteed by the presence of the common good. That is, for commodities k and l, traders h and i holding positive quantities of the two goods respectively with good c in common, we have

$$\mathrm{MRS}^h_{k,l} \geqq \mathrm{MRS}^h_{k,c} \cdot \mathrm{MRS}^h_{c,l} \geqq \mathrm{MRS}^i_{k,c} \cdot \mathrm{MRS}^i_{c,l} \geqq \mathrm{MRS}^i_{k,l}.$$

Setting $p_k = \mathrm{MRS}^h_{k,c}$ and $p_l = \mathrm{MRS}^i_{l,c}$ gives the required supporting prices.

2. SYMMETRY

The equivalence, if it occurs, of t-wise (or pairwise) efficiency and Pareto efficiency is symmetric across goods and traders. That is, consider a transpose economy where the names of traders and commodities are substituted for one another. Then t-wise optimality implies Pareto optimality in the original economy if and only if it does so in the transpose economy. In the light of Theorems 1.1 and 1.2 this observation is not surprising. It says that these two separate theorems are really special cases of a single and more general result.

The intuition behind the symmetry argument is that efficient allocation may be considered alternatively as how a trader places his scarce purchasing power (when an efficient allocation is characterized by a market equilibrium) or how supplies of each good are allocated across traders. In the first case the allocation rule is to equate the marginal utility per dollar of expenditure across uses. In the second it is for each good to equate across traders the ratio of marginal utility of income to the marginal utility of that good. Let A' denote the transpose of A. Then we state the following theorem.

THEOREM 2.1: *Let A be an allocation. Then $\Pi^t(A) = \Pi^*(A)$ if, and only if, $\Pi^t(A') = \Pi^*(A')$.*

The proof appears in the Appendix.

3. GENERALIZATION OF THE EARLY RADER/FELDMAN RESULTS

The above cited results by Rader and Feldman may be generalized to the case of t-wise optimality.

THEOREM 3.1: *Let A be an allocation matrix with some row (or column) having $t-2$ or fewer zero entries. Then $\Pi^t(A) = \Pi^*(A)$.*

The proof appears in the Appendix.

Intuitively, if there is a single individual who consumes all but $t-2$ of the commodities then that agent's MRS's form "enough" of a price system to preclude cycles of size $t+1$ or larger. By virtue of Theorem 2.1 this argument is equally applicable to a commodity consumed by all but at most $t-2$ agents. Theorem 3.1 includes as special cases (for $t = 2$) Theorems 1.1 and 1.2.

4. RADER'S CONDITION FOR SUFFICIENCY

Rader **[10]** advances a considerably more general condition for equivalence than found in Theorem 1.1 and Theorem 1.2 above. This gain is offered at the expense however of a further limitation on the allowable space of preferences. Specifically, attention is confined to those cases where each individual has a zero marginal utility for any commodity which does not appear in his allocation bundle. We will denote this restriction as *Condition R*. Essentially, Rader's condition requires that agents may be ordered in such a way that a supporting price system can be constructed from their MRS's by a process of extension. With considerable license, we shall restate these results here.

Let X be a symmetric $N \times N$ matrix $[x_{ij}]$ and $y \subset \{1, \ldots, N\}$, where y has n members. Then define $[X \operatorname{proj} y]$ as the $n \times n$ matrix $[\hat{x}_{ij}]$ where $\forall i, j \in y, \hat{x}_{ij} = x_{ij}$.

Starting from an allocation matrix A we are going to apply this matrix operation to the product matrix $A'A$. A positive ijth entry in $A'A$ indicates that it is possible to find a single agent who holds goods i and j. When $[A'A]_{ij}$ is positive, then pairwise optimality involves a direct determination of a supporting MRS for goods i and j. Now, for an N-vector a, let $a^+ \subset \{1, \ldots, N\}$ denote the set of indices i so that $i \in a^+ \leftrightarrow a_i > 0$. Consider $[A'A \operatorname{proj} a^+]$. A positive ijth entry here indicates that $[A'A]_{ij}$ is positive for some i and j for which the a entries are positive.

Finally, we consider whether $[A'A \operatorname{proj} a^+]$ is reducible (or decomposable), that is, whether by identical rearrangements of rows and columns that matrix can be represented as block diagonal. If not, it is said to be irreducible.

What does the irreducibility of $[(A'A)\operatorname{proj} a^+]$ indicate? For any two goods in a^+ it means that there is a finite sequence of consumers in A so that the first and last elements of the sequence each hold one of the two goods and successive members of the sequence are related to common holdings of other goods in a^+.[4] Hence, if we augment A by a, no independent determination of an MRS would be added to the system.

Conversely, reducibility indicates that there are at least two goods for which there is no implicit determination of an MRS using only goods in a^+.

LEMMA 4.1: *Let A be an allocation matrix such that $\Pi^2(A) = \Pi^*(A)$ and let a be an individual allocation vector such that $[(A'A)\operatorname{proj} a^+]$ is irreducible. Then, if*

[4]The matrix $[(A'A)\operatorname{proj} a^+]$ is analogous to the transition matrix of a Markov process. There, irreducibility allows the transition between two states with positive probability after finitely many steps (see, for example, Kemeny and Snell [5]). Here, irreducibility permits the inference of an implicit MRS between two commodities from a sequence of agents.

preferences are restricted as per condition R above, the allocation A augmented by a, say D, also displays the pairwise equivalence property, i.e., $\Pi^2(D) = \Pi^*(D)$ *and D is called an R-extension of A. The proof is a special case of Lemma* 5.1.

THEOREM 4.2 (Rader [**10**]): *Assuming Condition R, a matrix which may be constructed through successive R-extensions from a single initial row will satisfy the pairwise equivalence property.*

The proof follows immediately from Lemma 4.1.

Below we propose an extension of these results to the case of t-wise efficiency and with the removal of the Condition R. Heuristically, we shall propose a condition for extension such that the new individual will be supported by any price system supporting the previous allocation. Then, observing from the earlier symmetry condition that both rows and columns may be added to an economy, we shall present the appropriate generalization of 4.2. The removal of Condition R is accomplished by modifying the extension rule slightly to provide that new individuals must not desire unconsumed commodities too much.

5. A GENERALIZATION OF RADER'S SUFFICIENCY CONDITION

LEMMA 5.1: *Let A be an allocation matrix such that* $\Pi^t(A) = \Pi^*(A)$ *and let a be an individual allocation vector such that* $[(A'A)^{t-1}\mathrm{proj}\, a^+ \cup \{k\}]$ *for all* $k \leqq N$, *is irreducible. Then A augmented by a, denoted* A^+, *exhibits the t-equivalence property.*

In the above Lemma, the new allocation A^+ is called an extension of A.

The proof is offered in the Appendix.

THEOREM 5.1: *An allocation matrix which may be constructed by successive extensions of the* 1×1 *matrix* $A = (1)$ *by rows and/or columns will satisfy the t-wise equivalence property.*

The proof follows immediately from Lemma 5.1.

Irreducibility of $[(A'A)^{t-1}\mathrm{proj}\, a^+ \cup \{k\}]$ indicates that for any two entries in a^+ or an entry in a^+ and k there is a sequence of traders related by common holdings along the sequence so that the first and last traders have holdings of the specified goods. The common goods relating adjacent members of the sequence are in $a^+ \cup \{k\}$ with the possible exception of subsequences of length no greater than $t-1$. Thus augmentation of A by a^+ will involve no independent determination of an MRS not already implied in A.

6. NECESSITY

All of the results offered thus far have dealt with sufficiency. We shall now direct our attention toward necessary conditions for equivalence. There is a bootstrap property to the relationship between t-wise and Pareto optimality. For an allocation A to exhibit the equivalence property, there must be a coincidence of all intermediate degrees of optimality. Now it is immediately apparent that $\Pi^t(A) \supset \Pi^*(A)$. Indeed, this is a simple consequence of the definition. We will prove that, in essence, if A is not t-equivalent then there exists some preference ordering which is t-wise optimal for A but allows for a Pareto improving trade among $t + 1$ agents.

THEOREM 6.1: $\Pi^t(A) = \Pi^*(A)$ *if, and only if,* $\Pi^t(A) = \Pi^{t+1}(A)$.

The proof is contained in the Appendix.

Theorem 6.1 can be illustrated by a simple example for $t = 2$. If (A, P') is pairwise optimal but not Pareto optimal then the theorem assures us that there is P'' so that (A, P'') is pairwise but not 3-wise optimal. The following example gives us precisely this case:

$$A = \begin{bmatrix} 1 & 1 & 0 & 0 \\ 0 & 1 & 1 & 0 \\ 0 & 0 & 1 & 1 \\ 1 & 0 & 0 & 1 \end{bmatrix}, \quad P' = \begin{bmatrix} 2 & 1 & 0 & 0 \\ 0 & 2 & 1 & 0 \\ 0 & 0 & 2 & 1 \\ 1 & 0 & 0 & 2 \end{bmatrix}, \quad P'' = \begin{bmatrix} 2 & 1 & 0 & 2 \\ 0 & 2 & 1 & 0 \\ 0 & 0 & 2 & 1 \\ 1 & 0 & 0 & 2 \end{bmatrix}.$$

We have shown in Theorem 5.1 that the extension process will always create an allocation with the equivalence property. Further we will argue that a necessary condition for A to have the equivalence property is that A be an extension of the (sub)allocation consisting of A with *any* row or column deleted.

THEOREM 6.2: *Suppose that* $\Pi^t(A) = \Pi^*(A)$ *and that* A^- *denotes* A *with some row vector, say* a *for agent* v, *removed. If* $(A^{-\prime}A^-)$ *is irreducible, then for all* $k \leqq N$, $[(A^{-\prime}A^-)^{t-1}\text{proj}\, a^+ \cup \{k\}]$ *is irreducible.*

The proof is contained in the Appendix.

The necessity of the irreducibility condition posited in Theorem 6.2 can be directly illustrated for $t = 2$. If irreducibility of $[(A^{-\prime}A^-)\text{proj}\, a^+]$ is not fulfilled then, reordering rows and columns, we can represent A as

v	+	+	0
	$\neq 0$	0	$\neq 0$
	0	$\neq 0$	$\neq 0$

.

If we then choose P to look like

2	1	0
1	0	2
0	2	1

,

we have an expanded version of the familiar three-man-three-good example, so that $P \in \Pi^2(A)$ but $P \notin \Pi^*(A)$.

Theorems 5.1 and 6.2 suggest that the irreducibility of $[(A^{-\prime}A^{-})^{t-1}\text{proj}\, a^{+} \cup \{k\}]$ is very nearly a necessary and sufficient condition for t-equivalence. The gap between the necessary and sufficient conditions is those allocation matrices that fulfill the irreducibility property (necessity) but cannot be constructed by the irreducible extension process (sufficiency). Hence a typical counterexample to the conjecture that the condition is both necessary and sufficient would be

$$A = \begin{bmatrix} 1 & 1 & 0 \\ 1 & 1 & 0 \\ 0 & 1 & 1 \\ 0 & 1 & 1 \\ 1 & 0 & 1 \\ 1 & 0 & 1 \end{bmatrix},$$

a multiple version of the three-man-three-good example we started with. $A^{-\prime}A^{-}$ is strictly positive for any deleted row so the irreducibility condition is trivially fulfilled. Nevertheless, as in the original example, pairwise optimality does not imply Pareto optimality.

University of California, Berkeley
and
University of California, San Diego

Manuscript received June, 1980; revision received March, 1981.

APPENDIX: PROOFS

Representation of a Convex Economy by its Linear Counterpart

Lemma A.1: *Suppose* (i) (A, u) *is Pareto optimal, and* (ii) *if* $p_{ij} = 0$ *then* $u^i(a_i) = u^i(b_i)$ $\forall b_i$, $b_{ik} = a_{ik}$, $\forall k \neq j$. *Then* $(A, \bar{u})$ *is Pareto optimal and* $\exists \xi \in R^N_+$ *such that, taking* a_i *as i's endowment,* $(A, \bar{u}, \xi)$ *is a competitive equilibrium.*

Proof of Lemma A.1: We shall first prove, by contradiction, that $\exists \xi$ such that $(A, \bar{u}, \xi)$ is a competitive equilibrium. Suppose not. Then, from Gale [3], there exists a "super self sufficient" subset of agents, S, and complement, S', where (a) $\forall s \in S$, $\forall s' \in S'$, $p_{sj} > 0 \rightarrow a_{s'j} = 0$; (b) $\exists s \in S$, $\exists j \in \{1, \ldots, N\}$, $\forall t \in S$ $a_{sj} > 0$ but $p_{tj} = 0$. Now $p_{sj} = 0$ implies, by hypothesis (ii), that a reduction in a_{sj} will leave agent s unaffected. But since $\exists s' \in S'$ such that $p_{s'j} > 0$, then a small transfer of good j from s to s' would be preferred by s'. Thus (A, u) would not be Pareto optimal. Therefore $\exists \xi$, such that $(A, \bar{u}, \xi)$ is a competitive equilibrium, and then $(A, \bar{u})$ is Pareto optimal. *Q.E.D.*

Lemma A.2: *Suppose* $(A, \bar{u})$ *is Pareto optimal. Then* (A, u) *is also Pareto optimal.*

Proof of Lemma A.2: $\bar{u}$ satisfies condition (ii) in Lemma A.1 above. Therefore, there exists ξ such that $(A, \bar{u}, \xi)$ is a competitive equilibrium.

Then (A, u, ξ) is also a competitive equilibrium. Suppose not. Then $\exists i \in \{1, \ldots, M\}$ and $z_i \in R^N$ such that $\xi z_i \leqq 0$, $u^i(a_i + z) > u^i(a_i)$.

By, quasi-concavity of u^i, $\sum_{j=1}^{N} p_{ij} z_{ij} > 0$ but since $\xi z_i \leqq 0$ this contradicts competitive equilibrium of $(A, \bar{u}, \xi)$ and, as argued above, also the Pareto optimality of $(A, \bar{u})$.

Thus, (A, u, ξ) is a competitive equilibrium and (A, u) is Pareto optimal. *Q.E.D.*

THEOREM A.1: *Let u^i, $i = 1, \ldots, M$, fulfill condition* (ii) *of Lemma A.1. Then (A, u) is a Pareto optimum if and only if $(A, \bar{u})$ is a Pareto optimum. (A, u, ξ) is a competitive equilibrium if and only if $(A, \bar{u}, \xi)$ is a competitive equilibrium.*

PROOF OF THEOREM A.1: The theorem follows directly from Lemmas A.1 and A.2.

PROVING THEOREM 2.1

We will find the following lemma useful:

LEMMA A.3: *Let $U \in \Pi^t(A)$; then $U' \in \Pi^t(A')$.*

PROOF OF LEMMA A.3: Let $U \in \Pi^t(A)$, $V = U'$; suppose contrary to the assertion of the theorem $V \notin \Pi^t(A')$. A proof by contradiction will be used in order to avoid consideration of all t-member subsets. t-optimality of (U, A) means that each t-member subeconomy in (U, A) is Pareto efficient. $V \notin \Pi^t(A')$ implies that there is some t-element subeconomy of (V, A') whose allocation is inefficient and, hence, for which there are no supporting prices. Let the t traders of that subeconomy be $J \subset \{1, \ldots, N\}$. By Lemma A.4 there is a t-good reallocation representing a Pareto improvement for J. Let the t goods be the t-element subset $I \subset \{1, \ldots, M\}$. The contradiction will be established by showing that the presence of supporting prices for I in (U, A) imply support prices for J in (V, A').

Consider the traders I in (U, A). $U \in \Pi^t(A)$ implies that there is $p \in R_+^N$ supporting A.

Let $\lambda_i = \max_{j=1,\ldots,N} u_{ij}/p_j$. We know $u_{ij}/p_j < \lambda_i \Rightarrow a_{ij} = 0$. Or, for all i, j so that $a_{ij} > 0$ we have $u_{ij}/p_j = \lambda_i$ and $u_{ij}/\lambda_i = p_j$.

Now consider the t traders J in (V, A'), and the t goods I which can be advantageously redistributed. We have for each $j \in J$, $v_{ji}/\lambda_i = u_{ij}/\lambda_i = p_j$ for all goods i so that $a_{ij} > 0$. Thus, $\lambda = (\lambda_i)_{i \in I}$ is a vector of support prices for the allocation $(a_{ij})_{j \in J, i \in I}$ of goods I among traders J. But the presence of these prices implies that $(a_{ij})_{j \in J, i \in I}$ is a Pareto efficient allocation, which is a contradiction.

t-wise optimality of (U, A) implies the presence of support prices for the allocation of every t-member subeconomy in (V, A'). Hence (V, A') is t-optimal; $V \in \Pi^t(A')$. *Q.E.D.*

LEMMA A.4: $\Pi^M(A) = \Pi^N(A)$.

PROOF OF LEMMA A.4: Two simple proofs are available. (i) Madden notes that if there is any blocking coalition, there is one of size N (Madden [**6**, Theorem 2]), or equivalently Graham, Jennergen, Peterson, and Weintraub argue that N-wise optimality implies Pareto optimality (Graham, Jennergen, Peterson, and Weintraub [**4**, Corollary 2]).

(ii) Equivalently, Lemma A.5 implies that an allocation that is blocked, is blocked by coalitions of size no greater than N.

LEMMA A.5: *Let Z be a t-improving allocation for (A, P). Then Z can be expressed as the sum of no more than tN t-improving reallocation matrices Z^h where Z^h has no more than one positive entry in each row and column.*

PROOF OF LEMMA A.5: Ostroy-Starr [**8**, Lemma 2].

We now have sufficient machinery to prove Theorem 2.1.

PROOF OF THEOREM 2.1: From Lemma A.4 we have $\Pi^M(A) = \Pi^N(A)$. By Lemma A.1, $U \in \Pi^N(A) = \Pi^M(A)$ if and only if $U' \in \Pi^N(A')$. So $U \in \Pi^M(A)$ if and only if $U' \in \Pi^N(A')$.

By Lemma A.3 $U \in \Pi^t(A)$ if and only if $U' \in \Pi^t(A')$. Thus, $\Pi^t(A) = \Pi^M(A)$ if and only if $\Pi^t(A') = \Pi^N(A')$. But $\Pi^*(A) \equiv \Pi^M(A)$. *Q.E.D.*

PROOF OF THEOREM 3.1: Let A denote those traders who hold m, B denote those who do not. Suppose the theorem is false. Then there is an improving reallocation Z. Without loss of generality (by Theorem 6.1, Lemma A.5) we can take Z to have: (a) precisely $t+1$ non-zero rows; (b) each non-zero row has precisely two non-zero entries; (c) each non-zero column has precisely two non-zero entries (summing to zero). There are at least three elements of A among the rows with non-zero entries in Z, but not all of Z's non-zero rows correspond to elements of A (by Theorem 1.2). Let 1 be an element of A who receives, under Z, a good from some element of B denoted 4. That is, $z_{1n} > 0$, $z_{4n} < 0$; $1 \in A$, $4 \in B$.

Consider the following enumeration procedure in Z. Starting at $z_{1n} > 0$ find the entry in z_1, $z_{1n'} < 0$. Follow this column to its non-zero entry $z_{in'} > 0$, find the other non-zero entry in the row $z_{in''} < 0$, and so forth. This procedure will eventually return to z_{1n}. Before it does so denote as 2 the final element of A in the procedure. $z_{2n^*} < 0$, $z_{3n^*} > 0$ for some element $3 \in B$. Without loss of generality, we may take 4 to be the sole net beneficiary of Z. Denote the set of elements of B between 3 and 4, i.e., 3, 4 and those elements of B not previously enumerated as B^*.

Define λ_j, $j = 1, \ldots, N$, as $\lambda_j = \max_{i \in A}(p_{ij}/p_{im})$. $\lambda \equiv (\lambda_1, \ldots, \lambda_N)$. Note that $\lambda_j = p_{ij}/p_{im}$ for all $i \in A$, $a_{ij} > 0$.

Construct the matrix Y as follows. Let $y_{1m} = z_{1n'}, \lambda_{n'} = -y_{2m}, y_{1n} = z_{1n}, y_{2n^*} = z_{2n^*}$ (N.B.: in the case where n, n^* is in the m and n, n^* entry areas). Let $y_{ij} = 0$ for all $i \in A, i \neq 1, 2$. Let $y_{ij} = z_{ij}$ for $i \in B^*$. Then Y is an improving reallocation and there are only $u \leqq t$ non-zero rows in Y. This is a contradiction. *Q.E.D.*

Proof of Lemma 5.1: If the ijth element of $(A'A)^{t-1}$ is positive, then there is a chain of no more than $t-1$ individuals linking commodities i and j.

If the matrix formed from $(A'A)^{t-1}$ by deleting the rows and columns for which a is zero is irreducible, then for all i and j such that $a_i, a_j > 0$ there exists a chain of individuals linking i and j, which "returns" to the set of commodities for which a is positive at least every $t-1$ steps.

For every $P^+ \in \Pi^t(A^+)$, let P denote P^+ restricted to agents $1, \ldots, M$. (i) $P \in \Pi^t(A)$; (ii) $\exists p$ such that (A, P, p) is a competitive equilibrium. Claim: (A^+, P^+, p) is a C.E.

Since $[(A'A)^{t-1}a^+ \cup \{i\}]$ is irreducible, there is a chain in the first M agents connecting j to i (for all j where $a_{M+1,j} > 0$), which returns to the set of goods that $M+1$ holds every $t-1$ steps or less. Call these links.

In the following argument we will show (a) that $P_{M+1,x}/P_{M+1,y} \geqq p_x/p_y$ for any $x, y \in [1, \ldots, N]$ where $a_{M+1,x} > 0$ and $[(A'A)^{t-1}]_{xy} > 0$, and (b) that $P_{M+1,j}/P_{M+1,i} \geqq p_j/p_i$ for any $i, j \in [1, \ldots, N]$ where $a_{M+1,j} > 0$. (a) Now, if x, y are two commodities with $a_{M+1,x} > 0$ and $[(A'A)^{t-1}]_{xy} > 0$ then there is a sequence of $t-1$ agents, $m_1, \ldots, m_{t-1}$, and a sequence of t goods, $n_1, \ldots, n_t$, where $n_l = x$ and $n_t = y$ such that $\forall l \in [0, t-1]$

$$a_{m_l n_l}, a_{m_l n_{l+1}} > 0.$$

Then $P_{m_l n_l}/P_{m_l, n_{l+1}} = p_{n_l}/p_{n_{l+1}}$, for all $l \in [0, t-1]$. Suppose $P_{M+1,x}/P_{M+1,y} < p_x/p_y$. Then pick Z so that $z_{m_l, n_l} = \epsilon/p_{n_l}$, $z_{m_l, n_{l+1}} = -\epsilon/p_{n_{l+1}}$, and $z_{M+1,x} = -\epsilon/p_x$, $z_{M+1,y} = \epsilon/p_y$.

The change in m_l's utility is given by

$$\epsilon\left[\frac{P_{m_l n_l}}{p_{n_l}} - \frac{P_{m_l n_{l+1}}}{P_{n_{l+1}}}\right] = 0.$$

The change in $M+1$'s utility, however, is

$$\epsilon\left[\frac{P_{M+1,y}}{p_y} - \frac{P_{M+1,x}}{p_x}\right] > 0.$$

Thus the trade vector Z improves a group of size t;

Therefore $P_{M+1,x}/P_{M+1,y} \geqq p_x/p_y$.

(b) Take $i, j \in [1, \ldots, N]$ where $a_{M+1,j} > 0$. Since $[(A'A)^{t-1}\text{proj}\, a^+ \cup \{i\}]$ is irreducible, there exists a sequence $n_1, \ldots, n_Q \in [1, \ldots, N]$ where (i) $(A'A)^{t-1}_{n_q n_{q+1}} > 0$; (ii) $n_1 = j$ and $n_Q = i$; (iii) $a_{M+1,n_q} > 0$ for $q \in [1, \ldots, Q-1]$.

By (1) above,

$$\frac{P_{M+1,n_q}}{P_{M+1,n_{q+1}}} = \frac{p_{n_q}}{p_{n_{q+1}}} \quad \text{and} \quad \frac{P_{M+1,n_{Q-1}}}{P_{M+1,n_Q}} \geqq \frac{p_{n_{Q-1}}}{p_{n_Q}}.$$

Thus $P_{M+1,j}/P_{M+1,i} \geqq p_j/p_i$ and p supports the $M + 1^{st}$ agent as well.

Therefore (A^+, P^+, p) is a competitive equilibrium and $\Pi^t(A^+) = \Pi^*(A^+)$. *Q.E.D.*

PROOF OF THEOREM 6.1: $\Pi^t(A) \neq \Pi^{t+1}(A)$ implies trivially $\Pi^t(A) \neq \Pi^M(A)$. Thus, $\Pi^M(A) = \Pi^t(A) \Rightarrow \Pi^t(A) = \Pi^{t+1}(A)$. We must show

$$\Pi^t(A) = \Pi^{t+1}(A) \Rightarrow \Pi^t(A) = \Pi^M(A).$$

To do this we will prove

$$\Pi^t(A) \neq \Pi^M(A) \Rightarrow \Pi^t(A) \neq \Pi^{t+1}(A).$$

Search $\Pi^t(A) \backslash \Pi^M(A)$ for P^* with the smallest possible blocking coalition S to A. $|S| = t + k$, $k \geqq 1$. If $k = 1$, we are done. Suppose $k > 1$. Let Z be a $t + k$-improving reallocation on S involving $t + k$ goods with no more than one positive entry in each row and column (A can be so restricted without loss of generality by Lemma A.5).

Denote the elements of S by $i_1, i_2, \ldots, i_{t+k}$ and the goods for which they have negative (i.e., supply) entries in Z by $j_1, j_2, \ldots, j_{t+k}$ respectively. For further notational convenience order the elements so that

$$z_{i_1 j_1} < 0, \qquad z_{i_1 j_{t+k}} > 0,$$

$$z_{i_2 j_2} < 0, \qquad z_{i_2 j_1} > 0,$$

$$z_{i_3 j_3} < 0, \qquad z_{i_3 j_2} > 0, \qquad \text{and so forth.}$$

We may, without loss of generality, arrange the magnitudes of the trade so that agent i_1 receives all of the benefits and

(i) $$P_{i_l j_l} z_{i_l j_l} + P^*_{i_l j_{l-1}} z_{i_l j_{l-1}} = 0 \qquad \text{for} \qquad l \neq 1.$$

Consider $P^*_{i_3 j_1}$, i_3's marginal utility for good j_1 (the good that i_2, not i_3, receives under Z). Now if $P^*_{i_3 j_1} z_{i_2 j_1} + P^*_{i_3 j_3} z_{i_3 j_3} \geqq 0$, then let $\bar{Z}$ be identical with Z except for $\bar{z}_{i_3 j_1} = z_{i_2 j_1}$ and $\bar{z}_{i_2 j_1} = \bar{z}_{i_2 j_2} = 0$.

But then $\bar{Z}$ is a $t + k - 1$ improving reallocation for P^*, a contradiction. Therefore $P^*_{i_3 j_1} z_{i_2 j_1} + P^*_{i_3 j_3} z_{i_3 j_3} < 0$.

Let $\bar{P}$ be P^* with $\bar{P}_{i_3 j_1}$ replacing $P^*_{i_3 j_1}$, where

(ii) $$\bar{P}_{i_3 j_1} z_{i_2 j_1} + P^*_{i_3 j_3} z_{i_3 j_3} = 0.$$

Since $\bar{Z}$ would be a $t + k - 1$ improving reallocation for $\bar{P}$—a contradiction—then $\bar{P} \notin \Pi^t(A)$. Thus, there is Y a t-improving reallocation for $(\bar{P}, A)$, where $y_{i_3 j_1} > 0$, and for some other good j'_3, $y_{i_3 j'_3} < 0$.

Without loss of generality, we may scale Y so that

(iii) $$y_{i_3 j_1} = z_{i_2 j_1}$$

and arrange the trade so that

(iv) $$\bar{P}_{i_3 j_1} y_{i_3 j_1} + P^*_{i_3 j'_3} y_{i_3 j'_3} = 0.$$

Consider $\bar{Y}$ identical to Y except that $\bar{y}_{i_3 j_1} = 0$,

$$\bar{y}_{i_3 j_2} = z_{i_3 j_2} = -\bar{y}_{i_2 j_2} = -z_{i_2 j_2}, \qquad \bar{y}_{i_2 j_1} = y_{i_3 j_1} = z_{i_2 j_1}.$$

Now, from (i) (for $l = 3$) and (ii)

(v) $$P^*_{i_3 j_2} z_{i_3 j_2} = \bar{P}_{i_3 j_1} z_{i_2 i_1}$$

and by (v) and (iii)

(vi) $$P^*_{i_3j_2}z_{i_3j_2} = \bar{P}_{i_3j_1}y_{i_3j_1}$$

and by (vi) and (iv)

$$P^*_{i_3j_2}z_{i_3j_2} + P^*_{i_3j_3'}y_{i_3j_3'} = 0.$$

Since $\bar{y}_{i_3j_2} = z_{i_3j_2}$ and $\bar{y}_{i_3j_3'} = y_{i_3j_3'}$, then

$$P^*_{i_3j_2}\bar{y}_{i_3j_2} + P^*_{i_3j_3'}\bar{y}_{i_3j_3'} = 0,$$

so i_3 neither benefits nor loses by $\bar{Y}$.

Since $\bar{y}_{i_2j_1} = y_{i_3j_1} = z_{i_2j_1}$ and

$$\bar{y}_{i_2j_2} = z_{i_2j_2},$$

then by (i) for $l = 2$

$$P^*_{i_2j_1}\bar{y}_{i_2j_1} + P^*_{i_2j_2}\bar{y}_{i_2j_2} = 0$$

and i_2 neither benefits nor loses by $\bar{Y}$.

The remaining trades of $\bar{Y}$ are the same as Y, a t-improving reallocation for $(\bar{P}, A)$. But P^* and $\bar{P}$ are the same except for $P_{i_3j_1}$ and $\bar{y}_{i_3j_1} = 0$. Therefore, $\bar{Y}$ is a $t + 1$ improving reallocation for (P^*, A). This is a contradiction and implies $k = 1$. *Q.E.D.*

PROOF OF THEOREM 6.2: Suppose not. Then there are two commodities i and j at least one of which is positive in a (say j) such that the ijth element of $[(A^{-\prime}A^{-})^{t-1}\text{proj}\, a^{+} \cup \{i\}]^{x}$ equals zero for all $x > 0$. Assign utility weights as follows. Marginal utilities equal 1 for all agents other than v and all commodities. For agent v, marginal utility equals 2 for good i and any other good k which v nolds for which there exists some x such that the ikth element of $[(A^{-\prime}A^{-})^{t-1}\text{proj}\, a^{+} \cup \{i\}]^{x} > 0$. Consider a chain of agents (not v) connecting i and j (possible by assumption that A^{-} is irreducible). The chain involves at least t agents since $[(A^{-\prime}A^{-})^{t-1}\text{proj}\, a^{+} \cup \{i\}]_{ij} = 0$. Consider a transfer around the chain from commodity j. Transfer a unit of i from the last one in the chain to v and a unit of j from v to the first in the chain. The trade is Pareto improving involving at least $t + 1$ traders. *Q.E.D.*

REFERENCES

[1] ARROW, KENNETH J., AND FRANK H. HAHN: *General Competitive Analysis*. San Francisco: Holden-Day, Inc., 1971.

[2] FELDMAN, ALLAN: "Bilateral Trading Processes, Pairwise Optimality, and Pareto Optimality," *Review of Economic Studies*, 40(1973), 463–473.

[3] GALE, DAVID: "The Linear Exchange Model," *Journal of Mathematical Economics*, 3(1976), 205–209.

[4] GRAHAM, DANIEL A., L. PETER JENNERGEN, DAVID W. PETERSON, AND E. ROY WEINTRAUB: "Trader-Commodity Parity Theorems," *Journal of Economic Theory*, 12(1976), 443–454.

[5] KEMENY, JOHN G., AND J. LAURIE SNELL: *Finite Markov Chains*. Princeton, N.J.: D. Van Nostrand Co., Inc.

[6] MADDEN, PAUL: "Efficient Sequences of Non-Monetary Exchange," *Review of Economic Studies*, 42(1975), 581–596.

[7] MCKENZIE, LIONEL W.: "The Classical Theorem on Existence of Competitive Equilibrium," Presidential Address to the Econometric Society, Vienna, 1977; mimeo, July, 1980 version.

[8] OSTROY, JOSEPH M., AND ROSS M. STARR: "Money and the Decentralization of Exchange," *Econometrica*, 42(1974), 1073–1113.

[9] RADER, TROUT: "Pairwise Optimality and Non-Competitive Behavior," in *Papers in Quantitative Economics*, ed. by J. P. Quirk and A. M. Zarley. Lawrence, Kansas: University Press of Kansas, 1968.

[10] ———: "Pairwise Optimality, Multilateral Optimality and Efficiency with and without Externalities," in *Theory and Measurement of Economic Externalities*, ed. by Steven A. Y. Lin. New York: Academic Press, 1976.

SECTION 3

Bilateral Market Trade

10

THE INFORMATIONAL EFFICIENCY OF MONETARY EXCHANGE

by Joseph M. Ostroy

Starting from an initial endowment in a pure exchange economy where equilibrium prices have already been determined, this paper and those of Starr (selection 11) and Ostroy-Starr (selection 12) consider the function of money in the process of bilateral trade to the equilibrium allocation. These papers start where the Walrasian model concludes. Equilibrium prices have been established, and all traders know what trades they wish to make. The apparently trivial problem remaining is to formulate means for implementing these plans.

The first difficulty comes from the recognition that the reallocation required to implement the equilibrium allocation is multilateral but trade is bilateral. This implies a limitation on the possible reallocation in each bilateral trade, a minimum time (number of bilateral trades) for execution of the reallocation to equilibrium, and a need for a mechanism to coordinate trading decisions among isolated trading pairs so that they are consistent with the general equilibrium reallocation. There are actually two difficulties associated with the coordination problem: information and motivation (incentive compatibility). In particular, Ostroy argues that a bilateral trading procedure should make sense in terms of representing optimizing behavior of the agents at each stage of the trading process as well as at the end point. This results in a strategic foundation for the *budget balance* or *quid pro quo* constraint on bilateral trade, which requires agents at each stage of the trading process to deliver, to those they trade with, goods of value equal to those they receive. Absent such a requirement there would be an incentive (without penalty) to exceed budget in the reallocation. The *quid pro quo* or budget balance

General Equilibrium
Models of
Monetary Economies

ISBN 0-12-663970-1

requirement is an additional restriction imposed on bilateral trade to make individual incentives and the overall budget constraint compatible. It is striking that the budget balance requirement can be derived from more elementary considerations. This additional constraint then implies a restriction on the class of acceptable bilateral trades and precludes some of the most expeditious in effecting the equilibrium allocation. Money is introduced in the form of a central accounting authority (essentially a check-clearing system) with the power to penalize overdrafts at the end of trade. Once introduced, money alleviates the restriction on trade imposed by the budget balance (*quid pro quo*) constraint while retaining the overall budget constraint.

The paper is distinctive for the focus on the trading pair as an elementary unit of the exchange process at equilibrium prices. The result is a formal rationale for the budget balance (*quid pro quo*) restriction in bilateral trade and the development of a detailed formal trade model.

The Informational Efficiency of Monetary Exchange

By JOSEPH M. OSTROY*

The gains from exchange may be extended if individuals are not required at each trade to balance the value of purchases and sales. But self-interest, the motive force of trade, does not move individuals to realize these gains. Suppose that X has an excess demand for ten apples and an excess supply of ten oranges. It may be efficient for X to receive the ten apples from Y, who has an excess supply, and later give his ten oranges to Z, who has an excess demand. In the actual execution, what is to prevent X from asking for eleven apples from Y, justifying his claim by saying he will supply an equal number of oranges, or give up only nine oranges to Z, saying that he took only nine apples? The purpose of this paper is to show that the essential property of money is to discourage the making of such inconsistent claims without also discouraging efficient patterns of trade.

This is "old stuff"; but it cannot be incorporated int^ the standard theory of value.[1] To illustrate, consider a paradox contained in Robert Clower's (1967) proposal to introduce money into the standard theory. His suggestion was to add to the existing budget constraint the injunction that current purchases be financed by sale of money only, not by current supplies of other commodities. This modification contradicts the belief that the introduction of money improves the allocation of resources. Because it is an additional constraint, it is at best not binding; and if binding, it will narrow the set of permissible exchanges compared to its barter counterpart. Clower's constraint makes no sense in the Walrasian model of exchange, but for a perfectly sensible reason. It does no good to append what is a trading constraint to a model which ignores trade.

In the standard theory, equilibrium is said to exist when (W) the sum of individual excess demands is zero for each commodity. What (W) defines is a Walrasian equilibrium of prices. Nevertheless, from the individuals' points of view, they are in disequilibrium as long as we do not have (A) all individual excess demands are zero for each commodity.

Should the economy reach the state defined by (W), will it then go to (A)? Interpretations of the standard theory say that the Walrasian auctioneer, after announcing equilibrium prices, expedites demands and supplies. If there is one theme which distinguishes the present treatment from the standard theory, it is that exchange is a do-it-yourself affair. Individuals will not exchange with "the market"; they will exchange with each other. This elementary logistical consideration is the basis upon which I shall construct an argument for monetary exchange.[2]

* Assistant professor of economics, University of California, Los Angeles. I have benefited from discussions with Ronald Britto, Jack Hirschleifer, Ben Klein, Axel Leijonhufvud, Louis Makowski, Richard Sweeney, Earl Thompson, and Joseph Wharton. Bryan Ellickson, Peter Howitt, and Ross Starr made many improvements in the formulation and presentation. My introduction to the topic came through the research of Robert Clower whose continued advice and encouragement were invaluable.

[1] By this phrase I mean the model of general equilibrium first proposed by Walras and recast into its definitive mathematical form by such contributors as Arrow and Debreu.

[2] Recently, formal notice has been taken of the fact that the valuable exchange services rendered by the

I. Summary

I shall assume that trade occurs between pairs of individuals so that the advantages of multilateral exchange must be obtained through a sequence of bilateral trades. During a unit interval of time, an individual meets with only one other so that during the interval an individual's trades are limited by his own and his trading partner's current endowments. When one pair meets, other pairs are also making contact, so that exchange occurs as a sequence of *simultaneous* bilateral trades.[3]

In the comparison of money and barter trading arrangements, no explicit account is taken of the physical or psychic costs of exchange. The single criterion is the number of periods it takes to accomplish the task of going from (W) to (A). Any decrease in the number is good and any increase is bad. Obviously a crude picture of the costs of exchange, it may be tolerated because the object is only an exposition of the role of money, not a general theory of trade.[4]

In the analysis of the problem of going from (W) to (A), I shall focus on the following three properties of trading sequences: (i) their technical feasibility, (ii) their informational feasibility, and (iii) their equilibrium properties, or what might be called their "behavioral feasibility." Property (i) defines the restrictions on a sequence of exchanges imposed by the fact that trade occurs between pairs. Property (ii) requires (i) and the restriction that a pair cannot base its trading decision on information available only to other pairs. For example, a pair cannot make its decisions depend on the full details of excess demands among all other pairs. Property (iii) requires (ii) and the restriction that each individual have no incentive to depart from the sequence. In a barter economy, if trades leading from (W) to (A) do not satisfy bilateral balance (BB)—where the value of purchases and sales are equated at each bilateral encounter—those trades will not form an equilibrium sequence.

We shall see that those trades which are technically and/or informationally feasible and which also minimize the number of periods in going from (W) to (A) will not satisfy BB. Imposition of BB does not preclude equilibrium in the sense of (A); it only means that it will take longer. But this time is not well spent because there is no technical or informational constraint underlying it. Additional time is required because individuals do not feel constrained to balance their budgets over a sequence of trades if they are not so compelled at each

auctioneer are costly to provide. Much of the motivation for these studies has been a desire to fit monetary exchange into the standard theory. We may learn from some of them that costly exchange can be introduced without giving up the assumption that exchange is coordinated by a central agency—an auctioneer who charges for his services. See Frank Hahn (1971), Mordecai Kurz, Jürg Niehans (1971), K. C. Sontheimer and N. Wallace. According to the present treatment, however, it is only when the exchange process is decentralized that the role of money can be understood. See Clower (1971). We may learn from Niehans (1969) that even when exchange is restricted to pairs it need not be completely decentralized. The selection of a least cost bilateral trading network can be made by a central planner who solves a complicated programming problem. A similar difficulty occurs in Starr (1970) where individuals choose optimal *sets* of bilateral transactions but require a central agency to hook them together. Roy Radner and Karl Brunner and Allan Meltzer have approached monetary exchange as a reflection of imperfect information. Radner has suggested that money might arise from the unpredictability of future spot prices and Brunner and Meltzer have indicated that money arises because of the need for a commonly recognizable asset. I shall discuss these points in Section IV. The present treatment is related to the work of Hicks, Starr (1972), and E. C. H. Veendorp.

[3] It is this simultaneity—while one pair is exchanging other pairs are not standing still—which contributes to the informational demands on trade.

[4] It would have been possible to formulate a model in which the costs of exchange varied with the amounts of commodities and the number of individuals with whom one traded per unit time. Ignoring the resulting complexities, the outcome must concede that not everyone exchanges everything at once if it is to gain insight into monetary exchange.

trade. Any device which would encourage such constraint could be substituted for the added time. Money is such a device.

I shall assume throughout that individuals know equilibrium exchange rates. Because we are accustomed to thinking of equilibrium in the sense of (W), this assumption may appear to be disquietingly strong. In general, it is; but *not* for the purposes of understanding monetary exchange. The line of reasoning adopted here permits me to assert that if we cannot find a role for money when equilibrium prices are known, we shall not find one when they are unknown. There can hardly be a speculative demand for the medium of exchange without a transactions demand and this transactions demand does not depend on price uncertainty.

II. A Model of a Trading Economy

There are three components of the model: (i) the set of possible tastes and endowments and their corresponding competitive equilibrium allocations; (ii) the logistical description of the trading arrangement; and (iii) the pattern of information describing what individuals know and do not know at each trading opportunity.

A Family of Exchange Economies

Individual i is initially endowed with a nonnegative quantity w_{ic} of commodity $c=1, \ldots, m$. The complete list of his initial endowments is the m-vector $w_i = (w_{i1}, \ldots, w_{im})$. If i, whose tastes are represented by $u_i(\cdot)$, were asked to exchange his initial endowment for any other (m-vector) x_i satisfying the constraint $p \cdot x_i = p \cdot w_i$, where $p=(p_1, \ldots, p_m)$ is the vector of prices, let his answer be the bundle $a_i=(a_{i1}, \ldots, a_{im})$, $a_{ic} \geq 0$, $c=1, \ldots, m$ and

$$(1) \qquad u_i(a_i) = \max u_i(x_i), \quad p \cdot a_i = p \cdot x_i = p \cdot w_i{}^{5}$$

[5] $p \cdot w_i \equiv \Sigma_c p_c w_{ic}$ is the dot product of p and w_i.

At prices p, let i be described by the pair of vectors (a_i, w_i) and let the collection of individuals $i=1, \ldots, n$ be described by the pair of matrices (A, W), where a_i and w_i are the ith rows of the nxm matrices A and W, respectively. The pair (A, W) forms a competitive equilibrium (CE) if the aggregate demand for each commodity is equal to the aggregate supply,

$$(2) \qquad \sum_i a_{ic} = \sum_i w_{ic}, \qquad c = 1, \ldots, m$$

The matrix A *is the CE allocation* for the CE price vector p and matrix of initial endowments W. The problem of going from equilibrium in the sense of (W) to equilibrium in the sense of (A) is now reduced to the problem of going from the matrix W to the matrix A.

I shall deal only with collections of individuals described by nonnegative matrices (A, W) satisfying

$$(3) \qquad n = m$$

and

$$(4) \qquad \sum_i a_{ic} = \sum_c a_{ic} = \sum_i w_{ic} = \sum_c w_{ic} = 1$$

The set of all such pairs of nxn matrices whose row and column sums are unity, call $\mathcal{U}$. If (4) is to satisfy (1) for every member of $\mathcal{U}$, any $p=(r, r, \ldots, r)$, $r>0$, must be a CE price vector. This will mean that if i knows he is in an economy belonging to $\mathcal{U}$, he knows equilibrium exchange rates.

In the space of all possible economies, the set $\mathcal{U}$ occupies only a small corner. I choose to deal with it because $\mathcal{U}$ exhibits the salient features of the general case. The assumption in (3) that the number of commodities is equal to the number of individuals is, strictly speaking, not essential to our results and can be shown to follow a fortiori if $m>n$. However, the trading arrangement I shall postulate allows each individual's trading opportunities to increase with the size of the population so that as n/m increases the logistical problems of exchange disappear.

The assumption that individual endowments are of the same size ($\sum_c w_{ic}=1$, $i=1,\ldots,n$) is significant only insofar as it makes clear that there is no individual whose initial endowment is, for *all* $(A, W)\in\mathfrak{U}$, large enough for him to act as a central distributor supplying everyone else's excess demands.[6] The set $\mathfrak{U}$ exhibits a similar feature with respect to the insufficiency of endowments to permit a medium of exchange.

About the origin and use of money, Adam Smith said:

> In order to avoid the inconvenience of such situations, every prudent man in every period of society, after the first establishment of the division of labour, must naturally have endeavoured to manage his affairs in such a manner, as to have at all times by him besides the peculiar produce of his own industry, a certain quantity of some one commodity or other, such as he imagined few people would be likely to refuse in exchange for the produce of their industry. [p. 22]

The purpose of this paper is to isolate the function of a medium of exchange and I shall proceed by analyzing the difficulties when one does not have "a certain quantity of some one commodity." There is no commodity whose initial value is, for *all* $(A, W)\in\mathfrak{U}$, a significant fraction of the value of each individual's planned purchases.[7] This will allow me to bring out more clearly that the essential feature of monetary exchange has its origin in the trading arrangement and not in the nature of the money commodity.[8]

The first result, which serves as an introduction to the problem, is

PROPOSITION 1: *For almost all $(A, W)\in\mathfrak{U}$, if the collection of n individuals is divided into any two groups consisting of k and $n-k$ individuals, $1\leq k\leq n-1$, who cannot trade with each other, the CE allocation cannot be obtained.*[9]

If $n>2$, there is little hope of finding a double coincidence of wants. In fact, everyone will have to depend on everyone else if the *CE* allocation is to be realized.

How Traders Meet

I shall assume that the sequence of pairwise meetings is parametric rather than a subject for choice. From his point of view, each individual seems to collide every so often with someone else.

Let $\pi=\{\pi^t\}$, $t=1,\ldots,\tau$ be a sequence of permutations of the integers $i=1,\ldots,n$ such that for all i and t,

$$\pi^t(i) = j \tag{5}$$

if and only if $\pi^t(j)=i$

The permutation π^t determines who meets whom at t; i.e., $\pi^t(i)=j$ means i and j are trading partners at t. The final period, after which all trading ceases, is $t=\tau$.

Let $\{W^t\}$, $t=1,\ldots,\tau+1$, τ be a sequence of matrices with nonnegative elements where $W^t=(w^t_{ic})$ is the matrix of endowments at the beginning of t. Suppose $\pi=\{\pi^t\}$ describes the sequence of meetings; then $\{W^t\}$ *is technically feasible for* π, if for all i and t and $\pi^t(i)=j$,

$$\overset{t+1}{w_i} + \overset{t+1}{w_j} = \overset{t}{w_i} + \overset{t}{w_j} \tag{6}$$

[6] For example, individual j could be a central distributor for (A, W) if $w_{jc}>\delta$, $c=1,\ldots,m$, and if max $|a_{ic}-w_{ic}|$ over all c and $i\neq j$ were less than δ/n.

[7] For example, commodity d could be used as a medium of exchange for (A, W) if $w_{id}>\delta$, $i=1,\ldots,n$, and if max $|a_{ic}-w_{ic}|$ over all i and $c\neq d$ were less than δ/m.

[8] These qualifications as well as their consequences are more fully discussed in Ostroy and Starr.

[9] PROOF: Suppose the contrary; then it would require that for some subset, T, consisting of fewer than n individuals, $\Sigma_{i\in T}(a_i-w_i)=0$. This defines a less than full dimensional class of economies in $\mathfrak{U}$.

This says that an individual can add to his current endowment only by subtracting from the current endowment of his current trading partner and that commodity totals are not changed in the process of trade, just redistributed.

If the sequence $\{W^t\}$ *also* satisfies

$$p \cdot (w_i^{t+1} - w_i^t) = 0 \tag{7}$$

for all i and t, where p is the *CE* price vector, then *bilateral balance* (*BB*) obtains. At every bilateral encounter, the value of what is given up is equal to the value of what is received. Clearly, *BB restricts the set of trades beyond the demands of technical feasibility.*

Let us agree to say that the *CE allocation is technically feasible for* π if, for *all* $(A, W) \in \mathfrak{U}$, there exists a sequence $\{W^t\}$, technically feasible for π, with $W^1 = W$ and $W^{\tau+1} = A$. This means that the sequence π is not biased; it permits all possible *CE* configurations to be realized. Denote by Π_τ the set of all such π of length τ.

What is the minimum value of τ for which the *CE* allocation is technically feasible? Proposition 1 tells us that everyone must be "connected" to everyone else but this connection need not be direct since (6) permits indirect or middleman trade.

PROPOSITION 2: *If* $n = 2^k$, $k = 1, 2, \ldots,$ *the minimum number of periods for which the CE allocation is technically feasible is*[10]

$$\tau = k(\tau = \log_2 n)$$

To demonstrate, note that it is true for $k=1$, and assume it is true for $k=q$. This means that any group consisting of 2^q individuals can be connected in q periods so that two groups each consisting of 2^q individuals can be connected in period $q+1$ if every member of the one group is assigned to a member of the other. Since $2 \cdot 2^q = 2^{q+1}$, Proposition 2 is proved.

Call such a π which satisfies Proposition 2 an *indirect trading sequence* and a trading economy which makes use of it an *indirect exchange model.* It should be pointed out that

PROPOSITION 3: *If trades must satisfy BB, the CE allocation is not technically feasible for the indirect exchange model.*[11]

Suppose every individual is permitted to meet every other directly. Obviously, the *CE* allocation will be technically feasible. This will require $n(n-1)/2$ bilateral meetings and assuming n is even, will take, at a minimum, $\tau = n-1$ periods. Call such a sequence which allows everyone to meet everyone else in a minimum number of periods a *direct exchange sequence* and a trading economy which makes use of it a *direct exchange model.* An interesting feature of this model is

PROPOSITION 4: *If trades must satisfy BB, the CE allocation is technically feasible for the direct exchange model.*[12]

Propositions 3 and 4 say that it takes longer to reach the *CE* allocation if *BB* is imposed. Alternatively, the temporal advantages of the indirect exchange model are incompatible with *BB*. This will not, by itself, offer a basis for monetary exchange. Other considerations intrude.

How Trades Are Made

I shall make a distinction between (a)

[10] The following was obtained in correspondence with Lloyd Shapley: To complete the solution to minimizing the number of time periods for $n \neq 2^k$, let m be the largest integral power of two such that $m = 2^k < n$. Then, $\tau = (\log_2 m) + 1$ if n is even and $n \neq 2^k$ and $\tau = (\log_2 m) + 2$ if n is odd.

[11] Proposition 3 holds for all $n \geq 4$, the smallest number for which the advantages of indirect trade appear. See the *Remark* following Proposition 5 for a demonstration in the case $n=4$.

[12] Proofs of Proposition 4 are in Ostroy and Starr, and G. Bradley.

the decision a pair of traders make based on the information they reveal to each other and (b) the decision as to what information to reveal. It will be assumed that (a) is taken out of the hands of the pair and given to a fictional third party, a broker, who makes the trading decision solely on the basis of what each member of the pair tells him. We may suppose that the broker uses his unlimited ingenuity and computational capacity to help the pair reach their *CE* allocations. His only constraint is that he knows no more than what the pair tells him. Until Section IV, the decision (b) will be ignored by assuming that there is no distinction between what individuals know and what they reveal.[13]

At the beginning of period t, those features of the economy which cannot be changed constitute the state of the economy. They are the initial configuration of tastes and endowments, the order in which pairs will meet, and the trades which have been made up to t. Denote a typical state by $\hat{S}^t=(\hat{A}, \hat{W}^1, \ldots, \hat{W}^t; \hat{\pi})$. The set of all possible states at t is

$$(8) \quad \mathcal{S}^t = \{\hat{S}^t : (A, \hat{W}^1) \in \mathcal{U} \text{ and } \{\hat{W}^k\}, k = 1, \ldots, t \text{ is technically feasible for some } \hat{\pi} \in \Pi_\tau\}$$

Suppose the actual state is $S^t=(A, W^1, \ldots, W^t; \pi)$. Let $I_i^t(S^t)$ be the information i has at t about the actual state. It will be assumed throughout that

$$(9) \quad I_i^t(S^t) = \{\hat{S}^t \in \mathcal{S}^t : \hat{a}_i = a_i, \hat{w}_i^k = w_i^k, \hat{\pi}^k(i) = \pi^k(i), k = 1, \ldots, t\}$$

If you were to ask i what he knows about the state of the economy, according to (9) he would say: "I have no idea. All I know is that it belongs to the set of possible states, and I can therefore tell you what *CE* prices are, and what I would want if I had to balance my budget at those prices, and that I have made certain trades as indicated by $\{w_i^k\}$, $k=1, \ldots, t-1$, leading to my current position w_i^t."[14]

Each member of a pair of trading partners tells what he knows to the broker who then decides what trades they should make. The different trading pairs have different brokers who cannot communicate so the situation is much the same as if the pair themselves decided what to trade.

As a formalization of this story, let $\rho_i^t(I_1^t(S^t), \ldots, I_n^t(S^t)) = w_i^{t+1}$, $i=1, \ldots, n$, be a trading rule, changing w_i^t into w_i^{t+1}, which depends on the actual state of the economy and what individuals know about it. I shall say that $\rho = \{\rho_i^t\}$ *is an informationally feasible trading rule* if for all i and t, and $\pi^t(i)=j$,

$$(10) \quad \rho_i^t + \rho_j^t = w_i^t + w_j^t$$

and, for all $\hat{S}^t \in I_i^t(S^t) \cap I_j^t(S^t)$,

$$(11) \quad \rho_i^t(I_1^t(\hat{S}^t), \ldots, I_n^t(\hat{S}^t)) = \rho_i^t(I_1^t(S^t), \ldots, I_n^t(S^t))$$

Condition (10) says the rule must be technically feasible. If the pair (i, j) were to share their information they could determine that the actual state was in the set $I_i^t \cap I_j^t$ and nothing more. Condition (11) says that the trading decision must respect this ignorance, which is to say that each pair's trading decision cannot be made contingent on the tastes and trading histories of other pairs.[15]

[13] Getting individuals to reveal what they know, for example, their tastes, has been recognized as the principal difficulty in allocating collective goods (see Paul Samuelson). We shall see that there are similar strategic issues in a barter economy.

[14] This is the game-theoretic method for describing imperfect information. J. C. Harsanyi has shown how this may be applied to the case of players in a game who do not know each others' payoffs. The treatment above was developed independently in Ostroy (1970).

[15] The less one knows the smaller is his set of possible strategies. See Radner for a restriction similar to (11).

Once a trading rule is selected, the course of the economy is uniquely determined by its initial state. Given $S^1=(A, W^1; \pi)$, (9) determines $\{I_i^1(S^1)\}$, the input into the trading rule $\{\rho_i^1\}$, which determines W^2 and therefore $S^2=(A, W^1, W^2; \pi), \ldots$, etc. To summarize this recursive relation, let us say that if the initial state is $(A, W; \pi)$ and the trading rule is ρ, the end result is $g_i[\rho|(A, W; \pi)] = w_i^{\tau+1}$, $i=1, \ldots, n$.

Now, *the CE allocation is informationally feasible* if there exists an informationally feasible trading rule $\rho=\{\rho_i^t\}$ such that for *all* $(A, W)\in\mathfrak{U}$ and $\pi\in\Pi_\tau$, $g_i[\rho|(A, W; \pi)] = a_i$, $i=1, \ldots, n$. To illustrate this definition, consider the first period trading decision for any pair (i,j). If the *CE* allocation is informationally feasible, their broker has a sure-fire method for putting them on a path leading to their *CE* allocation no matter what the values of a_k and w_k, $k\neq i, j$.

III. Informational Aspects of Trade

In this section, the consequences of informational feasibility are explored. First, we have

PROPOSITION 5: *The CE allocation is not informationally feasible in the indirect exchange model.*

To demonstrate, take $n=4$. Let the trading partners be assigned as follows: individual 1's trading partners in the first and second periods are $\pi^1(1)=2$ and $\pi^2(1)=3$ while 4 is the partner of 3 in the first period and of 2 in the second $-\pi^1(3) = \pi^2(2)=4$. It is readily verified that this sequence allows each individual to trade directly or indirectly with everyone else. From Proposition 2, this is the minimum number of periods since $\tau=log_2 4=2$. Assume that initial endowments are given by the identity matrix; i.e., $w_{ic}=1$, if $i=c$, and $w_{ic}=0$ if $i\neq c$, where i, $c=1$, 2, 3, 4. This will simplify the demonstration, but it is not essential.

To go from W to A it is necessary that the exchange between individuals 1 and 2 be such that 1 begin the second period with $w_1^2=(w_{11}^2, w_{12}^2, w_{13}^2, w_{14}^2)$ where

$$(12)\quad w_{1c}^2 = \begin{cases} 1-(a_{2c}+a_{4c}), & \text{if } c=1 \\ (a_{1c}+a_{3c}), & \text{if } c=2 \\ 0, & \text{otherwise} \end{cases}$$

Individuals 1 and 2 do not know the tastes of 3 and 4, given by the vectors a_3 and a_4. According to (11), this means that for all possible values of a_3 and a_4, 1 and 2 must make the same trade. Now, whatever trade they make, they will have made the right decision for at most one pair (a_3, a_4) and will have made the wrong decision in all other cases. Therefore, the *CE* allocation is not informationally feasible.

Remark. The rule (12) is compatible with *BB* only if the configuration of tastes satisfies $a_{21}+a_{41}=a_{12}+a_{32}$; i.e., almost never.

I have assumed that individuals know only equilibrium prices and their own tastes and endowments. They do not know each other's excess demands and trading decisions are bound by this ignorance. But, to take advantage of indirect exchange, individuals must act as middlemen passing excess supplies in just the right sequence of intermediary trading to the final demander. What is the right sequence depends on the entire configuration of excess demands as well as on the order in which all pairs will meet. Proposition 5 brings out an obvious and basic point: *the informational requirements for indirect trade go beyond a knowledge of prices.*

Of course, the restrictions imposed on $\{I_i^t\}$ are rather harsh. I have taken the information available to an individual in the standard theory where he does not have to do his own trading and inquired as to its sufficiency where he does. From here, it would be possible to go on to find the minimum information compatible with the result that the *CE* allocation is informationally feasible in the indirect exchange model. It has already been determined from Propositions 3 and 4 that the required trades will not satisfy *BB*. Therefore, the argument could be made that only with money would the individuals reveal what they knew. I shall not follow this course because the informational demands for the indirect exchange model appear to be complicated and are certainly exorbitant. The same argument can be more easily elaborated with the direct exchange model.[16]

PROPOSITION 6: *If trades must satisfy BB, the CE allocation is not informationally feasible in the direct exchange model.*[17]

The reasons for Proposition 6 are similar to those underlying Proposition 5. In the class of economies $\mathfrak{U}$, no commodity is in sufficient supply to serve merely as a balancing item; and it will not do to pay one's debts in just any commodity or commodities. If the *CE* allocation is to be achieved under *BB*, commodities used as payment by i in his trade with j must also be those which j can pass on to $k, \ldots$, etc., so that they pass in just the right sequence and end up in just the right hands. But this involves the individuals in indirect trade whose informational demands they cannot meet.

Proposition 6 points to a feature of the medium of exchange distinguishing it from a standard I.O.U. *When money is used, the parties to the transaction are admitting their inability to predict with whom and how the account will be settled.*

Proposition 6 is important because of its relation to

PROPOSITION 7: *When BB is not imposed, the CE allocation is informationally feasible in the direct exchange model.*

The trading rule which demonstrates Proposition 6 is: for all i and t, $\pi^t(i)=j$, and $\rho_i^t=(\rho_{i1}^t, \ldots, \rho_{im}^t)$, let ρ_{ic}^t, $c=1, \ldots, m$ be such that

(13)

$$\rho_{ic}^t=\begin{cases} w_{ic}^t+\min\left[\,|a_{ic}-w_{ic}^t|,\ |a_{jc}-w_{jc}^t|\,\right] & \text{if } (a_{ic}-w_{ic}^t)\geq 0 \text{ and } (a_{jc}-w_{jc}^t)<0 \\ w_{ic}^t-\min\left[\,|a_{ic}-w_{ic}^t|,\ |a_{jc}-w_{jc}^t|\,\right] & \text{if } (a_{ic}-w_{ic}^t)<0 \text{ and } (a_{jc}-w_{jc}^t)\geq 0 \\ w_{ic}^t, & \text{otherwise} \end{cases}$$

The rule described by (13) is an example of what Ross Starr (1972) has called excess demand diminishing (*EDD*) trades. They follow the prescription "never engage in any trade which changes the sign of your excess demand." If you start out as a buyer of a commodity, do not accept more than you planned to purchase; and, if you start out as a seller of a commodity, do not give more than you planned to sell. The prescription is designed to prevent indirect or middleman trade.

It is clear that (13) satisfies the technical feasibility condition (6) and is informationally feasible since it requires only a knowledge of the trading pair's current excess demands, $(a_i-w_i^t)$ and $(a_j-w_j^t)$. It is a straightforward matter to show that (13) must always result in the *CE* alloca-

[16] The indirect exchange sequence, by explicitly denying the informational sufficiency of prices, provides the kind of environment hospitable to the activities of specialists in exchange. See Ostroy (1970). All of this is of a piece with money. Nevertheless, when our interest is just monetary exchange, we may use the direct exchange model to isolate the essential aspects of the problem in the context of a neater solution.

[17] Proofs of Proposition 6 follow along the lines of the demonstration of Proposition 5. Clearly, for $n=1$ and 2, it is false. It is also false for $n=3$. The reason is that once any two information sets $\{I_i^t\}$, $i=1, 2, 3$, are known the other may be inferred so there is effectively perfect information. Unless the additional assumption is made that individuals do not know their own trading histories, Proposition 6 is false for $n=4$. See Ostroy and Starr for a proof when $n\geq 5$.

tion if everyone is able to meet everyone else.

The merits of *EDD* trades are substantial. In terms of information, they are extremely economical and they lead, in the direct exchange (but not the indirect exchange!) model, to the *CE* allocation. They have demerits as well.

1. *EDD trades do not satisfy BB*. This is to be expected in light of Proposition 6. For emphasis, I shall add that they almost never satisfy *BB* (if $n>2$). To illustrate, consider the case of $W=I$, the identity matrix. Then, for all $(A, I)\in\mathfrak{U}$, *EDD* trades satisfy *BB* if, and only if, A is symmetric.[18]

2. *EDD trades do not form a utility increasing sequence.* Whenever $p\cdot(w_i^{t+1}-w_i^t)<0$, so that sales exceed purchases, we must admit the possibility that $u_i(w_i^{t+1})<u_i^t(w_i^t)$. Similarly, whenever $p\cdot(w_i^{t+1}-w_i^t)>0$, so that purchases exceed sales, we may have $u_i(w_i^{t+1})>u_i(w_i^t)$; and, if some of one's purchases are made before any of one's sales, we may have $u_i(w_i^t)>u_i(a_i)$! This agrees with everday experience. If you did not have to pay for your purchases your utility would be above what it otherwise is.

3. *EDD trades are unpredictable.* If an individual has a positive (negative) excess demand at the start of t, he cannot tell how much of it will be fulfilled (taken) during the period. To know this, he would have to know the entire configuration of initial excess demands as well as who met whom before t. This means that during the course of trade, an individual cannot determine whether he is on a path leading to his *CE* allocation or some other point. Only at $t=\tau+1$ does he know where he ends up. Suppose i does not end up at a_i because, to jump ahead, someone other than i misrepresented himself. Now, i knowns this was not his fault, but he cannot determine from his trading positions, $w_i^1, w_i^2, \ldots, w_i^{\tau+1}$, who was responsible. He cannot, for example, surmise that if $\pi^t(i)=j$, and $p\cdot(w_i^{t+1}-w_i^t)<0$, that j overstated his demands. It may have been that at period s, when $\pi^s(i)=k$, and $p\cdot(w_i^s-w_i^s)>0$, that individual k understated his supplies.

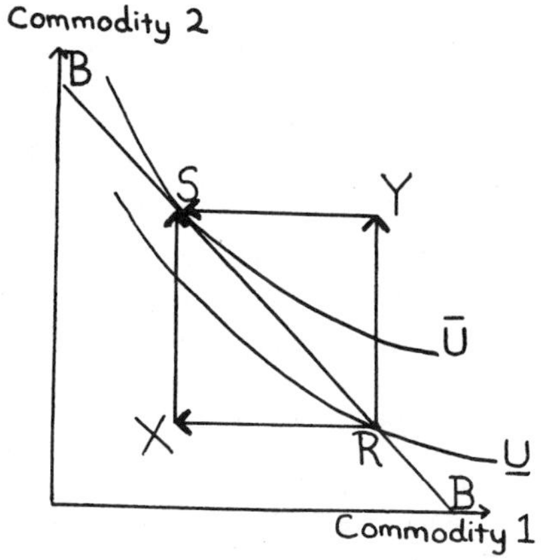

FIGURE 1

The above three features of *EDD* trades are illustrated in Figure 1. The straight line, *BB*, is the budget line. It goes through the initial endowment, point *R*, and the *CE* allocation, point *S*. The *EDD* trades begin and end on the budget line but in the interim they depart from it. The path $R\rightarrow X\rightarrow S$ indicates a trading sequence in which sale preceded purchase while the path $R\rightarrow Y\rightarrow S$ indicates the reverse. There is no guarantee that the intermediate posi-

[18] Applying (13) when $W=I$, we have that for any i and $\pi^t(i)=j$,

$$\overset{t}{\rho}_{ic}=\begin{cases}\overset{t}{w}_{ic}+a_{ic}, & \text{if } c=j\\ \overset{t}{w}_{ic}-a_{jc}, & \text{if } c=i\\ 0, & \text{otherwise}\end{cases}$$

Therefore, when $p=(r, r, \ldots, r), r>0, p\cdot(w_i^{t+1}-w_i^t)=0$ if, and only if, $a_{ij}=a_{ji}$.

tions, indicated here by the points X and Y, will lie within the region whose lower bound is $\underline{U}$, the indifference curve passing through the initial endowment, and whose upper bound is $\overline{U}$, the indifference curve passing through the CE allocation.

IV. Equilibrium

Recall that in defining the trading rule, $\rho=\{\rho_i^t\}$, it was assumed that individuals had no choice. Each revealed what he knew to the best of his knowledge. However, the trading rule does not require this accuracy. All that is required and all I shall assume is that no one says he has more of a commodity than he knows he has, although he may say he has less.

Let $h_i^t(I_i^t)=\hat{I}_i^t$ be the information i conveys to the broker. It is his decision whether or not to misrepresent what he knows. A strategy for i is a system $h_i=\{h_i^t(I_i^t)\}$, detailing what he will say he knows given what he actually knows at each trading opportunity. Therefore, $\{h_i^t\}$ rather than $\{I_i^t\}$ will be the informational inputs determining the course of trade.

Suppose a trading rule $\rho=\{\rho_i^t\}$ and strategies h_i^t, $i=1, \ldots, n$ have been selected. The outcome is uniquely determined by the initial state. If $S^1=(A, W^1; \pi)$, this determines $\{I_i^1(S^1)\}$ and therefore $\{h_i^1(I_i^1)\}$, and then $\{\rho_i^1(h_1^1, \ldots, h_n^1)\}$ which determines W^2 and therefore $S^2=(A, W^1, W^2; \pi), \ldots,$ etc. We may summarize this recursive relation by saying that if the initial state is $(A, W; \pi)$ and the trading rule is given by $\rho=\{\rho_i^t\}$ and individual strategies are given by $h_1, \ldots, h_n$, the end result is

$$g_i[\rho, h_1, \ldots, h_n \mid (A, W; \pi)] = w_i^{\tau+1}, \qquad i = 1, \ldots, n$$

Now, we may say that *the CE allocation is an equilibrium* if for *all* $(A, W)\in\mathfrak{U}$ and $\pi\in\Pi_\tau$ there exists a trading rule $\rho^*=\{\rho_i^{*t}\}$ and strategies $h_1^*, \ldots, h_n^*$ such that for all $i=1, \ldots, n$,

$$(14) \quad g_i[\overset{*}{\rho}, \overset{*}{h}_1, \ldots, \overset{*}{h}_n \mid (A, W; \pi)] = a_i$$

and

$$(15) \quad u_i(a_i) = \max_{h_i} u_i(g_i[\overset{*}{\rho}, \overset{*}{h}_1, \ldots, h_i, \ldots, \overset{*}{h}_n \mid (A, W; \pi)])$$

The CE allocation is an equilibrium if the CE allocation is informationally feasible (14) and if it is in no individual's interest to depart from his strategy given the trading rule and strategies of the others (15).[19]

Underlying the question of the equilibrium of the CE allocation is the necessary condition of budget balance (BUB),

$$(16) \quad p\cdot(w_i^{\tau+1} - w_i^1) = 0, \qquad i = 1, \ldots, n$$

Over the course of trade, if not at each trade, (16) says the purchases and sales balance.

Supposing individuals to have no choice so that they are compelled to satisfy BUB, it follows immediately from the definition of the CE allocation (see (1)) that

PROPOSITION 8: *If the CE allocation is informationally feasible and if BUB is imposed, the CE allocation is an equilibrium.*

If BUB were not imposed from outside, would individuals voluntarily choose strategies leading to it; i.e., would they choose to reveal what they know? If not, the CE allocation is not an equilibrium.

The only means the individuals have of imposing BUB amongst themselves is through BB. Suppose that all $i\neq j$ give instructions to their brokers that they will refuse to partake in any trade for which $p\cdot(w_i^{t+1}-w_i^t)<0$; then j cannot do other than satisfy BUB over the course of trade. If some i does not adhere to this, j is not

[19] Condition (15) is the definition of a noncooperative equilibrium proposed by John Nash.

constrained by *BUB*. It has already been determined (Proposition 6) that *BB* precludes the informational feasibility of the *CE* allocation in the direct exchange model. But to give up *BB* is to give up the incentive to reveal what one knows. The summary conclusion is

PROPOSITION 9: *The CE allocation is not an equilibrium for the direct exchange model.*[20]

Of course, if the individuals are willing and able to allow more time for trade, the opposite conclusion may be drawn. Consider the following "turn-taking" routine: Individual 1 goes to each of the others in turn asking for commodities to fulfill his (positive) excess demands and paying for them with his excess supplies so that *BB* is maintained. After $(n-1)$ periods he will reach his *CE* allocation. Next, 2 takes his with 3, . . . , n in the same manner, . . . , etc., so that after $n(n-1)/2$ periods the *CE* allocation is achieved.[21]

V. Money as a Record-Keeping Device

How to enforce *BUB* without imposing *BB*? Rather than ask how this enforcement is actually effected, I shall focus on the conditions which must precede enforcement. Again, it is a matter of information.

Consider the direct exchange model and assume that if an individual who has "over-balanced" his budget—$p\cdot(w_i^{\tau+1}-w_i^1)>0$—is found out, he will be made to give up more than will put him back in balance; but if he is not found out, he may keep what he has. This represents a shortcut to the conclusions derived from a more extensive version (see Ostroy (1971)) which supposed that individuals were in an economy consisting of a large number of repetitions of the above direct exchange model.

At the completion of trade, we may ask i whether j balanced his budget. Recall from the definition of $I_i^{\tau+1}$, what he knows at the completion of trade, that i cannot say. Individual i knows only his own trading history and this will not suffice to infer what j has done. However, he does know one fact about j's trading history. At t, when $\pi^t(i)=j$, $p\cdot(w_j^{t+1}-w_j^t)=-p\cdot(w_i^{t+1}+w_i^t)$. If the information possessed by all $i\neq j$ were added together, we could compute $\sum_{t=1}^{t=\tau} p\cdot(w_j^{t+1}-w_j^t)=p\cdot(w_j^{\tau+1}-w_j^1)$. As it stands, however, this information is scattered among the individuals with no one other than j, himself, able to determine whether he has balanced his budget.

As a monetary version of the model of a trading economy, introduce a central receiving station called a monetary authority. Its function is to collect and collate the bits of information individuals have about each others' trading histories. Each will require his trading partner to write a signed statement, a check, indicating the amount by which the partner's purchases exceed his sales. This record is forwarded to the monetary authority who revises individual accounts on the basis of this new information. *Sellers, by requiring payment in money, are guaranteeing a steady flow of information such that the monetary authority, and it alone, is able to monitor trading behavior.* Of course, there is every incentive to require and deposit this information with the monetary authority; otherwise, one would not receive credit for sales and so have to cut back on purchases. Therefore,

[20] This result does not hold when $n<5$ (see fn. 17).

[21] This is an upper bound and not necessarily a minimum estimate of the number of periods required to make the *CE* allocation informationally feasible with *BB*. This result demonstrates that to achieve the same end additional time can be substituted for lack of information. The tradeoff may be pushed further. Allan Feldman has shown that when individuals know nothing but their own tastes and endowments but have an unlimited number of bilateral trading opportunities, if they accept only utility-increasing trades they will, under certain assumptions, eventually reach a Pareto optimal allocation.

PROPOSITION 10: *In the monetary version of the direct exchange model, the CE allocation is an equilibrium.*[22,23]

There is a small slip. We have seen that for any $(A, W) \in \mathfrak{U}$, any vector $p = (r, r, \ldots, r), r > 0$, is a *CE* price vector. If the monetary authority is to be able to make trades between different individuals commensurable, they must all agree to the same value of r; i.e., we require a common unit of account. While this convention is essential to the operation of the record-keeping system, it is not identical to it. Money is not simply a unit of account.

VI. Conclusion: Integrating Monetary and Value Theory

In the Walras-Hicks-Patinkin tradition, the goal of monetary theory has been to present a picture of a money economy which would be a logical extension of the standard theory of value. Walras brought the equation of the offer and demand for money into line with the rest of his system by making a distinction between the stock of money, assumed to be without any utility of its own, and the "services of availability" of the stock which does contribute to one's well-being. Just as no inquiry is made into the sources of satisfaction from other goods, the services of availability are similarly unquestioned.

Recently, several theorists have suggested that it might be useful to dig a little more deeply.[24] While the traditional approach could be readily applied to determine why individuals might hold more or less money given that they valued it in certain ways in the first place, perhaps, just perhaps, it might clarify some contemporary monetary muddles if we asked why money is held at all.

This poses a dilemma. How to make money appear without making the standard theory disappear? Normal research strategy says that for a theory to be complete and consistent it must be derivable from the standard theory. But the standard theory has been cultivated to its present high level as a model of exchange in which money does not appear. Unlike the Walras-Hicks-Patinkin approach which left the standard theory intact and relied on conceptual appendages to introduce money, the recent approach forces us to look for modifications within the body of the theory. The following are some suppositions as to where to look on which I have not relied. I shall argue that they are superseded by the conclusions obtained from the above model of a trading economy.

1. *Money enlarges the set of feasible transactions.*[25] In the standard theory, any redistribution of commodities which preserves their totals is feasible. Into this model we can introduce the problems of exchange as a kind of transport cost of getting from one bundle of goods to another. We may then reason that monetary exchange represents a least cost network, so that without the money commodity the set of feasible transactions must shrink. While this may be adequate metaphorically, it misses the point. It is fairly well

[22] PROOF: Let h_i^* be such that $h_i^{*t}(I_i^t) = I_i^t$, $i = 1, \ldots, n$ and let ρ^* be the *EDD* trades given by (13). These verify the first condition, (14), that the *CE* allocation is technically and informationally feasible.

The *assumed* informational and enforcement powers of the monetary authority make it clear to each individual that he cannot spend more than he earns so that besides the technical and informational restrictions, he must obey $p \cdot (w_i^{\tau+1} - w_i^1) \leq 0$. Therefore, if $h_j^t(I_j^t) \neq I_j^t$ for some j and t, then $u_j(w_j^{\tau+1}) \leq u_j(a_j)$. Since it is in each individual's interest to reveal accurately his excess demands, the remaining equilibrium condition, (15), is satisfied.

[23] I have avoided use of the term "transactions costs" because its meaning varies from writer to writer. However, the present treatment seems consistent with the the usage of my colleague, Earl Thompson, who defines transactions costs as those losses arising from differences in information. With his definition, we may say: Money reduces transactions costs.

[24] Compare fn. 2. That we recognize there is a problem at all is due largely to the important papers of Don Patinkin, Jacob Marschak, Hahn (1965), and Clower (1967).

[25] See Hahn (1971), Kurz, Niehans (1971) and Sontheimer.

established that the term "feasible" denotes what *could* happen, ignoring individual behavior, not what *would* happen. Monetary exchange does not enlarge the set of feasible transactions; it merely enables trades, which must be feasible in the first place to be realized.

2. *Money is held because we do not know what prices will be.*[26] Price uncertainty is neither necessary nor sufficient to explain the presence of a medium of exchange. The above model of a trading economy assumed that exchange rates were known; yet it required a record-keeping device. Suppose, however, that exchange rates were unknown but that individuals voluntarily agreed to keep accurate records of their transactions (in terms of a common unit of account) in order to balance their budgets. There would be no need for a medium of exchange.[27]

3. *The advantages of money have their origin in the properties of the money commodity.*[28] In the above model of a trading economy, all commodities are perfectly portable, durable, divisible, and recognizable, yet there is a need for money. The origin of this need is the decentralized trading arrangement. I chose to introduce a monetary authority and bookkeeping entries as a kind of ideal monetary arrangement because the record-keeping function of money is conceptually distinct from the properties of the commodities traded. Of course, to understand a particular monetary arrangement, it becomes a matter of recognizing a minimum cost method of imposing budget balance and in a society unfamiliar with double entry bookkeeping, the monetary version of the model of a trading economy would not be ideal. Then, bilateral balance might be the only means of insuring that individuals keep accurate records and balance their accounts and we would have to look for a minimum cost method of imposing bilateral balance. In such a situation, the principle would not change but the practice might well be to choose as a method of enforcing budget balance a commodity which is most portable, durable, divisible, and recognizable.

To the standard theory of value, the phenomenon of monetary exchange is surprising and distressing; surprising because the phenomenon is inexplicable and distressing because the phenomenon would seem to be one of the most elemental conclusions to be derived from any theory of exchange. Once we give up the standard theory framework which allows the execution of exchange to be the province of a centralized agency and concentrate on the logistics of more disaggregated trading arrangements, monetary exchange becomes explicable as a matter of course. It follows that these logistical considerations are worthy of attention by general equilibrium theorists.[29]

[26] See Radner.

[27] When individuals are groping for equilibrium exchange rates in a world where such voluntary restraint is lacking, monetary exchange would be essential. Imagine how much more difficult would be the approach to equilibrium if payment for one commodity were made in an arbitrary collection of other commodities. On this issue of price dynamics, I have benefited from reading Peter Howitt's study of stability in a decentralized regime of monetary exchange.

[28] See Brunner and Meltzer.

[29] See Donald Walker for a similar conclusion on the deficiencies of Walras' theory of exchange. Any reader familiar with the work of George Stigler and the contributors to Edmund Phelps et. al. will recognize that these logistical considerations have already received some attention as determinants of search unemployment in labor markets.

REFERENCES

K. J. Arrow and G. Debreu, "Existence of an Equilibrium for a Competitive Economy," *Econometrica,* July 1954, *22,* 265–90.

G. Bradley, "Trading Rules for a Decentralized Exchange Economy," rep. no. 55,

Yale Department of Administrative Sciences, May 1972.

K. Brunner and A. H. Meltzer, "The Uses of Money: Money in the Theory of an Exchange Economy," *Amer. Econ. Rev.*, Dec. 1971, *61*, 784–805.

R. W. Clower, "A Reconsideration of the Microfoundations of Monetary Theory," *Western Econ. J.*, Dec. 1967, *5*, 1–8.

———, "Theoretical Foundation of Monetary Policy," in G. Clayton et al., eds., *Monetary Theory and Monetary Policy in the 1970's*, London 1971, 15–28.

A. M. Feldman, "Non-Recontracting, Recontracting, and Equitable Trading Processes," unpublished doctoral dissertation, Johns Hopkins Univ. 1972.

F. H. Hahn, "On Some Problems of Proving the Existence of Equilibrium in a Money Economy," in Hahn and F. Brechling, eds., *The Theory of Interest Rates*, London 1965, 126–35.

———, "Equilibrium with Transactions Costs," *Econometrica*, May 1971, *39*, 417–40.

J. C. Harsanyi, "Games with Incomplete Information Played by Bayesian Players, I," *Manage. Sci.*, Nov. 1967, *14*, 159–82.

J. Hicks, "The Two Triads. Lecture I," in Hicks, ed., *Critical Essays in Monetary Theory*, London 1967, 1–16.

P. W. Howitt, "Stability and the Quantity Theory," unpublished, 1971.

M. Kurz, "Equilibrium with Transaction Cost and Money in a Single-Market Exchange Economy," tech. rep. no. 51, Institute of Mathematical Studies in the Social Sciences, Stanford Univ., Jan. 1972.

J. Marschak, "The Rationale of Money Demand and of 'Money Illusion'," *Metroeconomica*, Aug. 1950, *2*, 71–100.

J. F. Nash, "Non-cooperative Games," *Annals of Mathematics*, 1951, *54*, 155–62.

J. Niehans, "Money in a Static Theory of Optimal Payments Arrangements," *J. Money, Credit, Banking*, Nov. 1969, *1*, 796–26.

———, "Money and Barter in General Equilibrium with Transactions Costs," *Amer. Econ. Rev.*, Dec. 1971, *61*, 773–83.

J. M. Ostroy, "Exchange as an Economic Activity," unpublished doctoral dissertation, Northwestern Univ. 1970.

———, "The Informational Efficiency of Monetary Exchange," disc. pap. no. 15, UCLA Department of Economics, Nov. 1971.

——— **and R. M. Starr,** "Money and the Decentralization of Exchange," forthcoming.

D. Patinkin, "The Indeterminacy of Absolute Prices in Classical Economic Theory," *Econometrica*, Jan. 1949, *17*, 1–27.

E. S. Phelps et. al., *Microeconomic Foundations of Employment and Inflation Theory*, New York 1970.

R. Radner, "Competitive Equilibrium under Uncertainty," *Econometrica*, Jan. 1968, *38*, 31–58.

P. A. Samuelson, "The Pure Theory of Public Expenditure," *Rev. Econ. Statist.*, Nov. 1954, *36*, 387–89.

A. Smith, *The Wealth of Nations*, New York 1937.

K. C. Sontheimer, "On the Determination of Money Prices," *J. Money, Credit, Banking*, forthcoming.

R. M. Starr, "Equilibrium and the Demand for Media of Exchange in a Pure Exchange Economy with Transactions Costs," Cowles Foundation disc. pap. no. 300, Oct. 1970.

———, "Exchange in Barter and Money Economies," *Quart. J. Econ.*, May 1972, *86*, 290–302.

G. J. Stigler, "Information in the Labor Market," *J. Polit. Econ.*, Oct. 1962, *70*, 94–105.

E. C. H. Veendorp, "General Equilibrium Theory for a Barter Economy," *Western Econ. J.*, Mar. 1970, *8*, 1–23.

N. Wallace, "An Approach to the Study of Money and Nomoney Exchange Structures," disc. pap. no. 6, Center for Economic Research, Univ. of Minnesota, June 1971.

D. A. Walker, "Leon Walras in Light of His Correspondence and Related Papers," *J. Polit. Econ.*, July/Aug. 1970, *78*, 685–701.

L. Walras, *Elements d'Economie Politique Pure*, trans. W. Jaffe, *Elements of Pure Economics*, Homewood 1954.

11

THE STRUCTURE OF EXCHANGE IN BARTER AND MONETARY ECONOMIES

by Ross M. Starr

This model starts by assuming Ostroy's conclusion that the bilateral budget balance rule will be imposed. Trade takes place pairwise. Three restrictions on trade are considered. The first is a *quid pro quo* requirement; at each trade agents are required to deliver goods of value equal to those they receive. Next, *monotone excess demand diminution*, is an attempt to formalize Jevons' double coincidence of wants condition. At each transaction, traders are required to deliver only goods of which they have initial excess demands. Further, these excess demand/supply positions are not to be overfulfilled. Finally the requirement of excess demand fulfillment, that is, that all excess demands and supplies be reduced to nil in the course of trade, is introduced.

Initial excess demands and supplies are arbitrary except that they are required to sum to the zero vector. Starting from the arbitrary excess demand/supply vector it can be shown that it is generally possible to find trades fulfilling any two of the three restrictions but not generally all three. This is the "difficulty of barter." Thus, for example, in general if we seek a scheme to achieve excess demand fulfillment with *quid pro quo*, we must accept some non-monotonic trades. Some traders will be required to accept goods in payment that they do not themselves want and subsequently to retrade them for goods they do want.

Money is introduced as an $N+1^{\text{st}}$ good. The efficacy of monetary trade comes from the convention that the monotonicity requirement need not apply to money. Money can be accepted though undesired or delivered though not in excess supply. In a monetary economy then, all three conditions, *quid pro quo*, monotonicity, and excess demand fulfillment, can be fulfilled.

ISBN 0-12-663970-1

Relaxation of the monotonicity condition for a single good allows it to be fulfilled for all other goods and not conflict with *quid pro quo* or excess demand fulfillment. This is the superiority of monetary trade.

THE STRUCTURE OF EXCHANGE IN BARTER AND MONETARY ECONOMIES *

Ross M. Starr

I. Transactions and Money in General Equilibrium Models

In a Walrasian pure exchange general equilibrium model,[1] trade takes place between individual households and "the market." Households do not trade directly with each other. This aspect makes it difficult to study transactions and money in this family of models. The analysis below sets up a framework with a general equilibrium viewpoint in which transactions and money enter essentially. The focus is on the structure — and presumed awkwardness — of barter and the resultant superiority of monetary exchange. Ineffectiveness of barter is supposed to arise inasmuch as, unlike monetary exchange, barter requires "double coincidence of wants." [2]

The most precise statement of the problem can be found in Jevons:

> The earliest form of exchange must have consisted in giving what was not wanted directly for that which was wanted. This simple traffic we call *barter* . . . , and distinguish it from sale and purchase in which one of the articles exchanged is intended to be held only for a short time, until it is parted with a second act of exchange. The object which thus temporarily intervenes in sale and purchase is money.
>
> The first difficulty of barter is to find two persons whose disposable possessions mutually suit each other's wants. There may be many people wanting, and many possessed those things wanted; but to allow an act of barter, there must be a double coincidence which will rarely happen.[3]

* It is a pleasure to acknowledge the advice and criticism of K. J. Arrow. I have had helpful discussions and correspondence with D. Foley, W. P. Heller, J. Ostroy, E. Thompson, and J. Tobin. Any errors are the author's responsibility. The research described in this paper was carried out under grants from the National Science Foundation and from the Ford Foundation.

1. G. Debreu, *Theory of Value* (New York: John Wiley and Sons, 1959).

2. W. S. Jevons, *Money and the Mechanism of Exchange* (London: D. Appleton and Co., 1875), and N. Wallace, "An Approach to the Study of Barter and Money Market Structures," unpublished manuscript, University of Minnesota.

3. Jevons, *op. cit.*, p. 3.

Thus, for Jevons, barter is not merely the exchange of goods against goods, but rather the exchange of reciprocally desired goods. A barter transaction is one in which, for each trader, excess demand is not increased for any commodity and excess supply is not increased for any commodity.[4]

The concept of double coincidence has two parts. The first is that all trade in a barter economy satisfies some ultimate want. When goats are traded for apples it is because the owner of the goats has an excess supply of goats and an excess demand for apples; the owner of the apples has an excess supply of apples and an excess demand for goats. The second part of the double coincidence condition is the idea that the only compensation a trader receives for supplying a second trader's wants is received from the second trader. One would suppose that this condition is obvious except that it is somewhat at variance with the spirit and form of most general equilibrium models.

The double coincidence of wants requirement is a severe restriction on the trades that can take place. Indeed, it is very easy to generate examples of economies where trade is necessary to reach efficient allocations and yet in which no trade can take place because there is no trade satisfying the "double coincidence of wants" condition. This is the substance of Theorem 1 and the three-man, three-good example, below.

Some considerable prestidigitation is required to make difficulties arising from the absence of a double coincidence of wants a reason for the introduction of money. If we agree that to operate a system of exchange under such restrictive rules is awkward or ineffective, that hardly seems reason to complicate the system further by the introduction of another commodity. However, when money is introduced to this family of models, it is defined to be *the* commodity to which the standard restrictions on desirability of commodities traded do not apply. Money is the only commodity that can be accepted in trade though the recipient has no excess demand for it; money is the only commodity that can be given in trade though the donor has no excess supply of it. The effect of introducing money is seen in Theorem 2.

But instead of introducing a single extra commodity for which the double coincidence condition need not hold, why not simply eliminate the double coincidence condition? This would allow all commodities to change hands without necessarily satisfying ultimate

4. An alternative interpretation is that in barter each trade (weakly) increases each trader's utility.

wants. All goods would act as "money." This is the argument of Lemma 1. The answer is not clear. There is a definite feeling in the monetary literature that the number of media of exchange, "moneys," should be small. In particular, not every commodity should be accepted in exchange, like money, only soon to be traded again.

It is very difficult in a general equilibrium model to discover why any commodity should be unacceptable in trade as a medium of exchange. In a general equilibrium model all prices are known to all traders, thus eliminating price uncertainty as a rationale for unacceptability. We generally abstract from transactions costs, which if they differed among commodities might make one commodity preferred over another as a medium of exchange. And in general equilibrium models all commodities have those other properties that are supposed to make them peculiarly suited to function as media of exchange: divisibility and cognizability. I do not think that the analysis below resolves this problem, but it should serve to put it in relief.

II. Representation of Equilibrium and Exchange

I will consider a model of two closely related economies. The focus is not on the existence and determination of equilibrium prices, the initial concern of most general equilibrium analysis, but rather on the nature of the transactions that take place once the prices have been determined and are taken as given. One economy is a traditional pure exchange barter economy. The second is an identical economy except that an additional commodity is introduced. This $N+1^{st}$ good is thought to behave like "money." The intention is to compare the two economies, and in some cases to see to what extent quantities determined in one economy can be adequately substituted into the other.

Such substitution is designed as a use of the concept of the "classical dichotomy" between money and value theory. Working on the assumption that meaningful relative price determination is the result solely of real variables, we can take a price vector p determined as an equilibrium for the barter economy and attach an arbitrary price of money p^m so that $p^M = (p, p^m)$ is an equilibrium for the corresponding monetary economy. Notations will be defined as needed. Generally, a notation of the form x^B indicates that x is a monetary quantity and x^B is its barter counterpart. A notation of the form x^M indicates that x is a barter quantity and x^M

is the monetary counterpart of x. The process of converting a quantity to its barter or monetary counterpart will usually consist simply in the deletion or insertion, respectively, of an $N+1^{st}$ coordinate.

Trades are described as a quantity of goods going from trader j to trader i, a_{ij}. In the barter economy a_{ij} will be an N dimensional vector; in the monetary economy a_{ij} will be an $N+1$ dimensional vector. a_{ij}^n then denotes the amount of commodity n going from trader j to trader i. An array of a_{ij} for all possible pairs of traders i, j, then describes all trades taking place.

III. The Barter Economy

The economy consists of a finite set of traders T. A commodity bundle is an element of the nonnegative orthant of E^N. A transaction is an element of E^N; a transaction is not generally nonnegative. A price system, usually denoted p, is an element of the nonnegative orthant of E^N. For each $t \epsilon T$, there is an excess demand correspondence $d_t(p)$. Note that for any $x \epsilon d_t(p)$, $p \cdot x = 0$.

The notation $| T |$ denotes the number of elements in the set T. A complex of transactions in the economy is represented as a rectangular array, a $| T |^2 \times N$ matrix.[5] Each row of the matrix corresponds to a pair of traders. The N column entries of each row represent amounts of various goods being exchanged between the two traders. Each row of the matrix will be denoted by two indices. Each index indicates a trader. Thus we write that A is an exchange, $A = || a_{ij} ||$, where $i, j \epsilon T$, and a_{ij} is the transaction between i and j, an N dimensional vector.

Definition. *An exchange,* $\mathrm{A} = || \mathrm{a}_{\mathrm{ij}}{}^{\mathrm{k}} ||$, *is a* $| T |^2 \times N$ *matrix such that* $\mathrm{a}_{\mathrm{ij}} = -\mathrm{a}_{\mathrm{ji}} \cdot \mathrm{a}_{\mathrm{ij}}$ *is called transaction* ij.

The restriction that $a_{ij} = -a_{ji}$ ensures that goods sent from i to j are received by j and understood to be from i. The sign convention indicates the direction in which the goods are going. A commodity whose component in a_{ij} is positive is going from j to i; commodities with negative entries in a_{ij} are going from i to j.

Definition. *An exchange* A *is said to be price consistent at (price vector)* p, *if for each row of* A, a_{ij}, $\mathrm{p} \cdot \mathrm{a}_{\mathrm{ij}} = 0$.

Price consistency is a concept fundamental to the transactions analysis of a monetary economy. Because it applies to transactions and not directly to excess demands or consumptions, it is a condi-

5. Since the number of pairs of traders in the economy is $| T | (| T | - 1)/2$, this is a larger array than we need, but it makes for easier bookkeeping.

tion that does not appear in the general equilibrium literature. What price consistency requires is that all goods acquired must be paid for by sending goods of equal value from the trader acquiring the purchased goods to the trader supplying them. Price consistency is fulfilled whenever an exchange of goods involves a quid pro quo of equal value at the prices quoted. This is, of course, a considerably more stringent requirement than the usual condition on demand functions that the value of goods supplied to the market should equal the value of goods demanded from the market. Price consistency requires that the value of goods supplied to another trader equal the value of goods received from him. Without some requirement of this sort there is no point in discussing media of exchange, inasmuch as there is no need to pay the seller for goods purchased.

The price consistency condition is merely the abstraction of the fact verified by casual empiricism that when one buys something, one pays the seller for it. Payment for goods purchased seems a concept almost absent from general equilibrium theory. It is required there that the value of goods demanded equal the value of goods supplied, but there is no requirement that the supplier of goods demanded be the recipient of goods supplied. If transactions are actually supposed to take place in a general equilibrium model, then one might conclude that when a trader seeks to purchase goods from their owner he says to the owner, "I wish to acquire from you k units of good n, of which I understand you have an excess supply. I assure you that this acquisition will not cause a violation of my budget constraint at prevailing prices. You may of course consider that by supplying me with k units of n, your budget is enhanced by kp^n." Exchanges consisting of transactions like this are studied in Lemma 2. Since the world of general equilibrium theory is one of certainty, of honest men making binding contracts in good faith with no possibility of default, the seller agrees to the above sale and delivery is made. The only payment for the goods consists in an addition to the seller's budget and a subtraction from the buyer's. These budgets seem to exist mainly in the memories or records of the agents in question. Such a system is unsatisfactory in a world of deceit, forgetfulness, and (honest) mistakes in arithmetic.

The following definition seeks to formulate part of the concept of double coincidence of wants in a market economy.

DEFINITION. *Let* A *be an exchange, and let* p *be a price vector.* A *is said to be monotonically excess demand diminishing at prices* p *if for each* $i \in T$ *there is* $w_i \epsilon d_i(p)$ *so that*

(i) *sign* $a_{ij}^k = $ *sign* w_i^k *or* $a_{ij}^k = 0$, *for* $j \epsilon T$, $k = 1, \ldots, N$,

and

(ii) $|\sum_{j \epsilon T} a_{ij}^k| \leqslant |w_i^k|$.

The sign restriction (i) says that each transaction of an exchange satisfying the definition reduces, or does not increase, the magnitude of excess demands and supplies of each commodity for both parties to the transaction. Condition (ii) ensures that a trader does not overfulfill his excess demands, acquiring more than his demand for some good, delivering more than his excess supply.

One should note that monotone excess demand diminution is only half of Jevons' "double coincidence" of wants. Fulfillment of the former implies that goods are supplied by traders with excess supplies to traders with excess demands. It does not imply that the latter have excess supplies of goods for which the former have excess demands. If an exchange is price consistent and monotonically excess demand diminishing, then I think it fulfills Jevons' concept of "double coincidence" of wants. In such a case each trader supplies others with goods of which he has an excess supply and receives from them each individually goods of an equal value of which they have an excess supply and for which he has an excess demand.

Definition. *Let* A *be an exchange.* A *is said to be excess demand fulfilling at prices* p *if, for each* $t \epsilon T$, $(\sum_{i \epsilon T} a_{ti}) \epsilon d_t(p)$.

Definition. *Let* $p \epsilon E^N$, $p \geqslant 0$. p *is said to be an equilibrium price vector if for each* $t \epsilon T$ *there is* $x_t \epsilon d_t(p)$ *so that* $\sum_{t \epsilon T} x_t = 0$.

Lemma 1. *Let* p *be an equilibrium price vector. There is an exchange* A *that is price consistent and excess demand fulfilling.*

Proof. Choose $x_t \epsilon d_t(p)$ for each $t \epsilon T$ so that $\sum_{t \epsilon T} x_t = 0$. Let $a_{1i} = -x_i$, $i \epsilon T$, $i \neq 1$, $a_{ij} = 0$ for $i \neq 1 \neq j$. Then we have $p \cdot a_{ij} = 0$ all i, j. $\sum_{j \epsilon T} a_{ij} = x_i$, all $i \neq 1$. $\sum_{j \epsilon T} a_{1j} = \sum_{i \epsilon T,\, i \neq 1} -x_i = \sum_{i \epsilon T} -x_i + x_1 = 0 + x_1 = x_1$. Thus A is price consistent and excess demand fulfilling. QED

Lemma 1 makes the reasonably obvious statement that at equilibrium prices there is an exchange that fulfills all traders' excess demands and relieves them of their excess supplies. Further, the exchange is price consistent; for every delivery of goods there is a quid pro quo of equal value. How is this achieved? In the proof, this is achieved by having all traders give their excess supplies to trader 1 and accept from trader 1 their excess demands. A single trader performs the function of a market clearinghouse familiar from general equilibrium theory; we might just as well have several such traders. There is a clearinghouse function that will usually have to be performed. Clearly such an exchange will usually lack the monotone excess demand diminution property; there are large flows of goods through traders with neither excess demands nor supplies for them.

LEMMA 2. *Let* p *be an equilibrium price vector. There is an exchange* A *that is monotonically excess demand diminishing and excess demand fulfilling at* p.

Proof. For each $t \epsilon T$ choose $x_t \epsilon d_t(p)$ so that $\sum_{t \epsilon T} x_t = 0$. The proof proceeds by distributing excess supplies of a commodity among traders with excess demands for the commodity. Such an operation performed over all traders and all commodities yields an exchange satisfying the two conditions. Without loss of generality let $x_1^i < 0$. That is, trader 1 has an excess supply of commodity i. Survey traders 2, 3, . . . , $|T|$ in order; if $x_2^i > 0$ let $a_{21}^i = \min(|x_1^i|, |x_2^i|)$; if not, let $a_{21}^i = 0$. If $x_3^i > 0$, let $a_{31}^i = \min(|x_3^i|, |x_1^i - x_{21}^i|)$; if not, let $a_{31}^i = 0$ and so on for all commodities i and all trading pairs $(1, t)$, $t \epsilon T$. For all i so that $x_1^i < 0$, $a_{t1}^i = \min(|x_t^i|, |x_1^i - \sum_{r \epsilon T, r<t} a_{r1}^i|)$ if $x_t^i > 0$, and $a_{t1}^i = 0$ if $x_t^i \leqslant 0$. Let $x_2^i < 0$ some i. Then if $x_1^i > 0$ set $a_{12}^i = \min(|x_2^i|, |x_1^i|)$; if not, set $a_{12}^i = 0$. If $x_{3i} > 0$ set $a_{32}^i = \min(|x_2^i - x_{12}^i|, |x_3^i - x_{31}^i|)$, $a_{32}^i = 0$ otherwise . . . . Since $\sum_{t \epsilon T} x_t = 0$ this distribution will exhaust all excess supplies and fill all excess demands. QED

According to Lemma 2, for any equilibrium price vector there is an exchange that satisfies all traders' excess demands, involves them in no transaction that would increase the magnitude of any excess demand or supply, but does not involve payment directly to the supplier by the recipient for goods received. I think it is just such exchanges that are at the back of one's mind in most general equilibrium analysis.

LEMMA 3. *Let* p *be a price vector (not necessarily an equilibrium price vector). There is an exchange* A *that is price consistent and monotonically excess demand diminishing.*

Proof. Let A be the exchange all of whose elements are zero.

QED

THEOREM 1. *Let* p *be an equilibrium price vector. For any two of the three conditions:*

(i) *price consistency,*

(ii) *monotone excess demand diminution,*

(iii) *excess demand fulfillment,*

there is an exchange satisfying those two conditions at p.

Proof. Lemmas 1, 2, 3. QED

The three conditions of Theorem 1 cannot generally all be satisfied by the same exchange. A useful example of this is the case of three goods and three traders. Let prices be (1, 1, 1) and suppose $d_1(p) = (1, 0, -1)$, $d_2(p) = (-1, 1, 0)$, $d_3(p) = (0, -1, 1)$. This is typical of the cases where, though equilibrating trades are obvious, there is no transaction between any pair of traders that diminishes excess demands, increases no excess supplies, and gives payment of equal value for all goods received.

The relation of the three concepts adduced to the double coincidence of wants now becomes clear. Double coincidence holds at equilibrium prices p if there is an exchange A such that:

(i) Goods delivered to trader i from trader j are paid for with goods of equal value sent from i to j. That is, the exchange is price consistent.

(ii) Only goods for which trader i has an excess demand and of which trader j has an excess supply are sent from j to i. That is, the exchange is monotone excess demand diminishing.

(iii) Trade proceeds to equilibrium; all excess demands are satisfied. Thus, the exchange is excess demand fulfilling.

(i) is implicit in Jevons. If (i) were not required there would be no point to the insistence on a double coincidence; a single coincidence of demand and supply would be sufficient for trade to take place. (ii) is explicit. (iii) brings us into a meaningful general equilibrium framework.

IV. The Money Economy

I am about to perform a bit of sleight of hand that has unfortunately fallen into disrepute of late, the trick of converting a barter economy to a monetary economy by the introduction of an $N+1^{st}$ good. The difference between the monetary and barter economies is the interpretation of excess demand diminution. In the monetary economy, the constraints of that definition are not applied to the $N+1^{st}$ good.

Definition. *A monetary exchange is a* $|T|^2 \times (N+1)$ *matrix,* $||a_{ij}^k||$, *such that* $a_{ij} = -a_{ji}$, a_{ij} *is called transaction* ij.

In keeping with the classical dichotomy approach to monetary economies, we arbitrarily set the price of money, $p^{N+1} \equiv 1$. Also, all traders' excess demands and supplies of the $N+1^{st}$ good are taken to be zero.

DEFINITION. *Let* A $= \|a_{ij}^k\|$, $k=1, \ldots, N+1$, *be a monetary exchange. The real counterpart of* A, *denoted* A^B, *is* $\|a_{ij}^k\|$, $k=1, \ldots, N$. *That is, the real counterpart of a monetary exchange is the same exchange with all* N+1st *elements of the monetary exchange deleted.*

Let p be a price vector for the barter economy. Then $p^M \equiv (p, 1)$ is a price vector for the monetary economy. Let $p = (p^1, p^2, \ldots, p^{N-1}, p^N, 1)$ be a price vector for the monetary economy. Then $p^B = (p^1, p^2, \ldots, p^{N-1}, p^N)$ is a price vector for the barter economy.

The following definition embodies the special status of the $N+1$[st] good.

DEFINITION. *Let* A *be a monetary exchange and* p *be a monetary price vector.* A *is said to be monotone excess demand diminishing at* p *if* A^B *is monotone excess demand diminishing at* p^B.

The implication here is that, unlike most goods, money will be accepted in exchange whether it is desired or not.

DEFINITION. *Let* A *be a monetary exchange and* p *be a price system for the monetary economy.* A *is said to be excess demand fulfilling at* p *if* A^B *is excess demand fulfilling at* p^B.

The following theorem, Theorem 2, constitutes the fundamental reason for the introduction of money in this family of models. Theorem 2 asserts the existence in the monetary economy of exchanges having characteristics discussed as desirable earlier in this essay. As shown in the three-man, three-good example, such exchanges do not generally exist for the barter economy.

THEOREM 2. *Let* p *be an equilibrium price vector for the monetary economy. There is a monetary exchange* A *that, at* p, *is price consistent, monotonically excess demand diminishing, and excess demand fulfilling.*

Proof. Choose $x_t \epsilon d_t(p)$ for each $t \epsilon T$ so that

$$(1) \qquad \sum_{t \epsilon T} x_t = 0.$$

For $k=1, \ldots, N$, choose a_{ij}^k so that sign $a_{ij}^k =$ sign $x_i^k = -$sign x_j^k or $a_{ij}^k = 0$ and so that

$$(2) \qquad \sum_{j \epsilon T} a_{ij}^k = x_i^k \text{ all } i \epsilon T,\ k=1, \ldots, N.$$

(1) ensures the existence of such a_{ij}^k. Let

$$(3) \qquad a_{ij}^{N+1} = -\sum_{k=1}^{N} p^k a_{ij}^k.$$

(3) gives price consistency. Sign restrictions on a_{ij}^k imply excess demand diminution. (2) implies excess demand fulfillment. QED

Theorem 2 reiterates the fundamental point discussed earlier. In a monetary economy all excess demands can be fulfilled by trades each of which satisfies some excess demand of the trader accepting goods, alleviates an excess supply of the trader furnishing same, and includes direct payment in full to the supplier for goods received. This is not generally true of a barter economy.

V. Relation of Monetary to Barter Exchange

In a classical dichotomy world, money may facilitate commerce, and certainly does not impede it. One can show this by the ingenuous approach of describing a barter exchange and simply noting that a monetary exchange identical to the barter exchange except that there is an appropriate $N+1^{st}$ element in each row is a monetary exchange that has all the qualities (e.g., price consistency, excess demand fulfillment) of the barter exchange from which it was derived.[6] Since for every acceptable barter exchange there is a corresponding acceptable monetary exchange and the converse is false, there are more acceptable monetary exchanges. This suggests that if one is seeking an extremum of some function over exchanges — minimizing search or transactions costs, for example — the extremum over the monetary exchanges will be at least as good as that over barter exchanges.

Theorem 3. *Let* A *be a barter exchange that is monotonically excess demand diminishing and excess demand fulfilling at prices* p. *Then there is a monetary exchange* B *that is price consistent, monotonically excess demand diminishing, and excess demand fulfilling at* p^M *such that* $B^B = A$.

Proof. Let $B = \| b_{ij}^k \|$. For $k=1, 2, \ldots, N$ let $a_{ij}^k \equiv b_{ij}^k$. Let $b_{ij}^{N+1} = -p \cdot a_{ij}$.

Then

$$p^M \cdot b_{ij} = p \cdot b^B{}_{ij} + b_{ij}^{N+1} = p \cdot a_{ij} - p \cdot a_{ij} = 0.$$

Thus, B is price consistent. Since A is excess demand fulfilling and monotonically excess demand diminishing, so is B. QED

Corollary 1 to Theorem 3. *Let* A *be a barter exchange that is monotonically excess demand diminishing, excess demand fulfilling, and price consistent at prices* p. *Then there is a monetary exchange* B *with the same properties at* p^M *so that* $b_{ij}^{N+1} = 0$ *for all* $i, j \epsilon T$.

6. This argument enters essentially in F. H. Hahn, "On Some Problems of Proving the Existence of an Equilibrium in a Monetary Economy," in F. H. Hahn and F. P. R. Brechling, eds., *The Theory of Interest Rates* (London: Macmillan; New York: St. Martin's Press, 1965).

Proof. Let B be as in the proof of the theorem. $b_{ij}^{N+1} = -p \cdot a_{ij}$. By price consistency of A, $b_{ij}^{N+1} = -p \cdot a_{ij} = 0$. QED

COROLLARY 2 TO THEOREM 3. *Let* $M(p)$ *be the class of all barter exchanges,* A, *that are monotonically excess demand diminishing, excess demand fulfilling, and price consistent at prices* p. *Let* $N(p)$ *be the family of* B^B *where* B *is a monetary exchange having those properties at* p^M. *Then* $M(p) \subseteq N(p)$.

Proof. Let $B = A^M$ be as constructed in the proof of Corollary 1, then $A \in M(p)$ implies $A \in N(p)$. QED

COROLLARY 3 TO THEOREM 3. *Let* g *be a real valued function defined on barter exchanges. Then*

$$\min_{A \in N(p)} g(A) \leqslant \min_{A \in M(p)} g(A)$$

$$\max_{A \in N(p)} g(A) \geqslant \max_{A \in M(p)} g(A).$$

Proof. Follows directly from Corollary 2. QED

One might note that Corollaries 2 and 3 are of somewhat limited interest inasmuch as $M(p)$ is nonempty only if the economy fulfills double coincidence of wants at p.

VI. BEHAVIOR OF MONEY BALANCES

Returning now to a starting point of this essay, we can analyze part of the classical dichotomy. As an assumption the thesis has been built into the analysis mainly by assuming that demand for goods depends only on the relative prices of goods (definition of excess demand fulfillment in the monetary economy). What does the classical dichotomy mean in this family of models? Clearly it does not mean that transactions are unaffected by the introduction of money. The emphasis of this study is money's effect on transactions. Rather, the classical dichotomy means that the introduction of money does not affect the total net trade (i.e., final consumption) achieved by any trader. That is,

DEFINITION. *Let* A *be a monetary exchange.* A *is said to fulfill the classical dichotomy at prices* p, *if*

$$\sum_{j \in T} a_{tj}^B \in d_t(p^B) \quad \textit{for all} \quad t \in T.$$

DEFINITION. *Let* $A = \| a_{ij}^k \|$ *be a monetary exchange.* A *is said to be money clear if for each* $t \in T$ $\sum_{i \in T} a_{ti}^{N+1} = 0$.

LEMMA 4. *Let* A *be a monetary exchange. At prices* p, A *fulfills the classical dichotomy if and only if* A *is excess demand fulfilling.*

Proof. Compare definitions of excess demand fulfillment in the monetary economy and classical dichotomy. QED

THEOREM 4. *Let* p *be an equilibrium price vector for the monetary economy. Let* A *be a monetary exchange that is price consistent and excess demand fulfilling at* p. *Then* A *is money clear.*

COROLLARY 1. *Let* p *be an equilibrium price vector for the monetary economy. Let* A *be a monetary exchange that is price consistent and fulfills the classical dichotomy. Then* A *is money clear.*

COROLLARY 2. *Let* p *be an equilibrium price vector for the monetary economy. There is a monetary exchange that, at* p, *is price consistent, monotonically excess demand diminishing, excess demand fulfilling, classical dichotomy fulfilling, and money clear.*

Proof of Theorem 4 and Corollaries. Corollary 1 follows from the theorem immediately by application of Lemma 4. Corollary 2 follows by applying the theorem and Lemma 4 to the exchange shown to exist in Theorem 2.

Price consistency gives

(1) $p \cdot a_{ij} = 0$, all i, $j \epsilon T$.

By the definition of excess demand fulfillment in the monetary economy,

(2) $(\sum_{j \epsilon T} a_{ij}{}^{B}) \epsilon d_i(p^B)$ all $i \epsilon T$.

By (1) $\sum_{j \epsilon T} p \cdot a_{ij} = 0$ all i, but

(3) $\sum_{j \epsilon T} p \cdot a_{ij} = p \cdot \sum_{j \epsilon T} a_{ij} = p^B \cdot \sum_{j \epsilon T} a_{ij}{}^{B} + \sum_{j \epsilon T} a_{ij}{}^{N+1}$.

By (2) $p^B \cdot \sum_{j \epsilon T} a_{ij}{}^{B} = 0$ so by (1) and (3)

$$0 = \sum_{j \epsilon T} p \cdot a_{ij} = p^B \cdot \sum_{j \epsilon T} a_{ij}{}^{B} + \sum_{j \epsilon T} a_{ij}{}^{N+1} = 0 + \sum_{j \epsilon T} a_{ij}{}^{N+1}$$

so $\sum_{j \epsilon T} a_{ij}{}^{N+1} = 0$ for all $i \epsilon T$. QED

Theorem 4 makes the reasonably elementary point that in an economy where no trader has an excess supply or demand for money holdings, exchanges that fulfill excess demands and are consistent with prices will make no change in money holdings.

VII. CONCLUSION

This essay seeks to analyze the structure of transactions and the use of money in an economy with emphasis on coincidence of wants as a condition for barter exchange. Stating this family of questions in a form susceptible of a rigorous abstract analysis is itself a substantial innovation. Theorems 1 and 2 and the discussion surrounding them emphasize that three conditions on exchange are closely related to the desirability of money in the economy. Of the conditions on exchange — monotone excess demand diminution, price consistency, excess demand fulfillment — there is always a barter exchange satisfying any two, but only if there is double coincidence of all wants will there be a barter exchange satisfying all three. Theorem 2 makes the fundamental point that in a monetary economy all three conditions can always be satisfied. Theorem 3 and its corollaries assert — roughly — that anything a barter economy can do a monetary economy can do better (or as well), at least in the case where the monetary system itself is costless.

The broader intention of the essay is to help make a start at filling Hicks's prescription for making a rigorous microeconomic theory of money.[7] As such it joins a small but growing literature.[8]

YALE UNIVERSITY

7. J. Hicks, "A Suggestion for Simplifying the Theory of Money," *Economica*, 1935; reprinted in Hicks's *Critical Essays in Monetary Theory* (Oxford: Oxford University Press, 1967).

8. Some of the elements of the literature are R. Clower, "Micro-Foundations of Monetary Theory," *Western Economic Journal*, V (1967); D. K. Foley, "Economic Equilibrium with Costly Marketing," Working Paper No. 52, Department of Economics, Massachusetts Institute of Technology, Feb. 1970; F. Hahn, "Equilibrium with Transactions Costs," Walras-Bowley Lecture, Econometric Society Meeting, Dec. 1969, mimeographed; J. Niehans, "Money and Barter in General Equilibrium with Transactions Costs," unpublished manuscript; J. Ostroy, "Exchange as an Economic Activity," Ph. D. thesis, Northwestern University, 1970; E. C. H. Veendorp, "General Equilibrium Theory for a Barter Economy," *Western Economic Journal*, VIII (March 1970); and Wallace, *op. cit.*

12

MONEY AND THE DECENTRALIZATION OF EXCHANGE

by Joseph M. Ostroy and Ross M. Starr

Just as Ostroy (selection 10) represents an inquiry into the origins of the *quid pro quo*[1] requirement on trade, the present study investigates the idea of double coincidence of wants and the use of money. The focus is the organizational difficulties of coordination in trade. These difficulties arise from overdeterminacy in demand for goods resulting from their use as media of exchange to fulfill *quid pro quo* in addition to consumption demands. It is found that trading procedures using a sufficiently abundant medium of exchange successfully relax the overdeterminacy. The conclusion is that the use of money allows decentralization of the trading process; alternative trading procedures require more time or more coordination.

Suppose trade to take place pairwise sequentially subject to a *quid pro quo* (bilateral budget balance) restriction and a nonnegativity condition (traders can only deliver goods they actually hold—no IOUs). These two requirements and the desire to move to an equilibrium allocation overdetermine the demand for goods in trade. Goods are needed to fulfill final demands but they are also needed to act as media of exchange. If trade is to take place in limited time, then some means is required of ensuring that goods go expeditiously to those with excess demands for them. Without some means to ensure this, goods may spend so much trading time as media of exchange that they cannot in the end get to those who require them for consumption.

[1] The phrase 'quid pro quo' is used to indicate the restriction that when two traders meet to trade, they deliver to one another goods and money of equal value.

ISBN 0-12-663970-1

Money provides a solution to the difficulty by allowing *quid pro quo* requirements to be fulfilled by a specialized good. It can do this if available in sufficiently large quantity to avoid violating nonnegativity restrictions. The use of a specialized good has two implications. Most important, it reduces the coordination required to decide what good to use in settling up accounts to fulfill *quid pro quo*—everyone knows the good will be money. This eliminates the overdeterminacy in the demand for other goods. Second, a single specialized medium of exchange allows achievement of the equilibrium allocation in that good as an algebraic consequence of its achievement in the others. A system of multiple media of exchange does not possess this helpful simplification.

Money is used to overcome the great organizational complexity of nonmonetary trade. In order to formalize this view, a concept of decentralization of the trading process is presented. Trade is said to be decentralized if the decision on what goods to trade between two agents depends only on their own excess supplies and demands. If the trading decision depends on others' excess supplies and demands then this represents sufficient complexity that the process is thought to be centralized. The major results then are that (*i*) there is a centralized trading procedure that achieves the equilibrium allocation; (*ii*) there does not generally exist a decentralized procedure to achieve the equilibrium allocation; (*iii*) in a monetary economy (i.e., where there is a sufficiently large stock of a single good to be used as money) there is a decentralized procedure that achieves the equilibrium allocation. The use of money achieves a reallocation simply that would otherwise require the greater complexity of a centralized trading procedure, or greater time devoted to trade.

The proof of (*i*), existence of a centralized procedure, is by construction and comes in two parts. First it is shown that the complex of excess demands and supplies can always be decomposed into a finite number of elementary configurations, chains, so that each agent in the chain has an excess demand for one good, excess supply of another and, for each good, supply equals demand across the chain. A centralized trading procedure is developed for trades in chains. The centralized procedure for the economy then is for each pair of traders, when they meet to trade, to perform the sum of the trades appropriate to the chains they have in common.

Once the complex of excess demands and supplies can be represented as the sum of a finite number of primitive chains, it remains to show that each chain can have its demands fulfilled in a single sequence of trades. The trading procedure that achieves this requires sufficient information and coordination to allocate traders to chains and let them know what chains they have in common. Hence it does not qualify as decentralized. When two traders meet, if they are members of a common chain they exchange excess supplies corresponding to the chain. This breaks the chain into two smaller disjoint chains. The process continues until all chains are of unit length, i.e., excess demands are fulfilled. This can be illustrated diagrammatically; a chain can be represented as

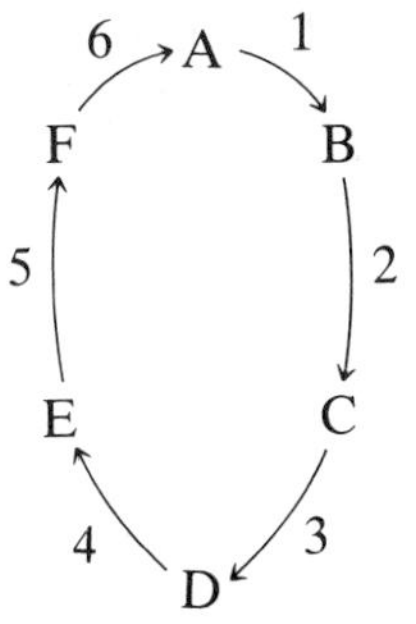

This is read "A has an excess supply of 1 for which B has an excess demand; B has an excess supply of 2 for which C has an excess demand; . . . 6 for which A has an excess demand." Suppose A and C are the first elements of the chain to meet. They exchange excess supplies. The resulting array is

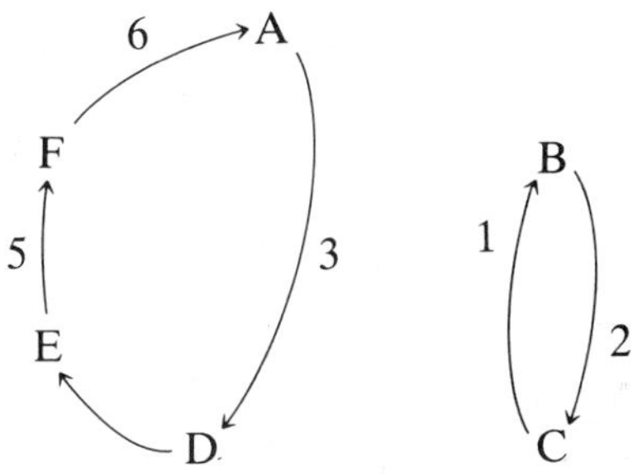

two smaller disjoint chains. The process is repeated for each chain separately until each excess demand is fulfilled.

Ostroy-Starr further argues that this complexity is unavoidable. Theorem 2 says that it is not generally possible to find a decentralized trading rule that moves in limited time to the equilibrium allocation. The proof consists of presenting two different economies with some traders identical in each. The example is set up so that the trades these traders must make in one economy to achieve equilibrium consistent with other traders' demands would preclude achievement of equilibrium in the other. Under a decentralized rule however, the traders cannot distinguish between the two economies for purposes of deciding on their trades, since the difference is not in their own excess demands but in others'.

The use of money overcomes these difficulties by substituting decentralized monetary trade for either centralized trade or much more time-consuming decentralized trade (Starr, selection 13). The decentralized monetary trading procedure, designed to represent trade in actual monetary economies, is simply that traders scan their excess supplies and demands; when they find a match, goods go from the supplier to the demander; accounts are then settled in the monetary commodity to fulfill *quid pro quo*.

Econometrica, Vol. 42, No. 6 (November, 1974)

MONEY AND THE DECENTRALIZATION OF EXCHANGE

BY JOSEPH M. OSTROY AND ROSS M. STARR[1]

A pairwise trading process is formulated subject to conditions of non-negativity of traders' holdings, *quid pro quo*, and a limited number of trading opportunities. The following points are made: (i) there is a *centralized* procedure that achieves the equilibrium allocation for an arbitrary economy; (ii) it is not in general possible to find a *decentralized* procedure that achieves the equilibrium allocation for an arbitrary economy; and (iii) in a monetary economy there is a decentralized procedure that achieves the equilibrium allocation. The usefulness of money is that it allows decentralization of the trading process.

1. THE PROCESS OF TRADE

AN EMINENT SCHOLAR has related to us an anecdote elaborating the "inconveniences of barter:"

> Consider the eminent scholar travelling far from home. He stops at a hotel and asks for lodging for the night. The clerk replies, "That will be fifteen dollars (unit of account)." E.S. agrees and extracts from the trunk of his car a copy of his latest textbook. "Here's a copy of my latest textbook. It sells for fifteen dollars (unit of account)." "Good, here's your room key. Have a pleasant stay." The hotel keeper trades the book for fifteen dollars' worth of soap. The soap distributor sends the book as payment for detergent, to a detergent manufacturer. The latter pays the book, as dividend, to a stockholder. The stockholder sends the book, as allowance to his son, studying at a major university where E.S.'s text is used in a large lecture course. The boy trades the book to a student in the course in exchange for fifteen dollars' worth of contraband, which he consumes.

That is how trade would take place in an ideally coordinated barter economy. The need for such coordination arises from the restriction that goods when received must be paid for by a corresponding opposite delivery of goods of equal value, *quid pro quo*. The origins of this restriction are strategic. Without a *quid pro quo* constraint, agents would not be effectively prevented from violating their budget constraints.

The inconveniences of barter consist in the information and coordination implicit in the story at each stage of trade. Only if the hotel keeper knows that his distributor's supplier will accept textbooks in trade is he likely to accept E.S.'s book in exchange for lodging. To make a substantial number of transactions depend on trading partners' demands, trading partners' trading partners' demands, trading partners' trading partners' . . . trading partners' demands, would make even the simplest trade depend on the communication of massive

[1] The research described in this paper was supported by grants from the Ford Foundation, the National Science Foundation, and the University of California Board of Regents. Collaboration was initiated while Professor Starr was consultant to the Western Management Science Institute, UCLA, whose support and that of its director, Jacob Marschak, is gratefully acknowledged. We are deeply indebted to Gordon Bradley for providing the essential step in the proof of Lemma 1. We have also benefited from discussions with Robert Clower, Peter Howitt, Herbert Scarf, and James Tobin. Errors are the authors' responsibility.

amounts of data about who trades with whom, when, and what they want. As long as there is a generally acceptable, universally held medium of exchange, no such communication is necessary. Each trade merely consists in the exchange of a desired commodity for the medium of exchange. All one need know about one's trading partners' trading partners is that, like everyone else, they accept the medium of exchange. The informational requirements of barter imply the need for a central coordination of trade; *the function of a common medium of exchange is to allow decentralization of the trading process.*

2. A MODEL OF THE TRADING PROCESS

Let there be N commodities indexed by $n = 1, \ldots, N$ and a set of J traders, I, indexed by $i = 1, \ldots, J$. Let each trader have an endowment bundle $b_i \in R^N_+$.[2] Trader i's net trade vector is z_i. The complex of initial endowments will be represented by the $J \times N$ matrix $B = \|b_{in}\|$. Similarly, let $Z = \|z_{in}\|$.

For the purposes of this paper, an exchange economy will be characterized by a price vector $p = (p_1, \ldots, p_N)$, a matrix of excess demands, and a matrix of initial endowments, (p, Z, B), which satisfy the following, and only the following restrictions:

(U.1) $Zp = 0$, where $p_n > 0$ $(n = 1, \ldots, N)$,

(U.2) $\sum z_i = 0$, and

(U.3) $Z \geqslant -B$ (the inequality holds entry-wise).

Condition (U.1) says that at the (strictly positive) prices p, the value of a trader's supplies and demands are equal. Conditions (U.2) and (U.3) guarantee that aggregate trades and individual trades, respectively, are feasible.

A competitive equilibrium of an exchange economy is the most interesting case of (p, Z, B) fulfilling (U). A competitive equilibrium must satisfy (U) *and*, for all i, z_i must be maximal for his preferences among all allowable excess demands. However, because the problem addressed here is the implementation, not the existence, of a competitive equilibrium and because any (p, Z, B) is a competitive equilibrium for some pattern of preferences, the qualification that z_i be maximal can be ignored.[3]

No theory of price formation is advanced here. It is assumed that the process of price formation occurs prior to the process of exchange to be discussed below. A supporting hypothesis is as follows: the Walrasian auctioneer announces equilibrium prices but leaves the expedition of trades to the individuals themselves. This common knowledge of prices will be used to define *quid pro quo* in

[2] R^N_+ is the non-negative orthant of N-dimensional Euclidean space.

[3] If p is an equilibrium price vector, there may be many distinct Z's such that z_i is an element of i's excess demand correspondence and (p, Z, B) fulfills (U). Since the focus of this study is the implementation of an allocation, Z, it is necessary first to specify which of a multiplicity of possible allocations is to be implemented. Hence the use of a specific Z rather than a correspondence. This represents, of course, an indeterminancy that recurs throughout general equilibrium theory.

exchange, a standard of behavior traders will impose on each other. Elsewhere, it has been shown that if any one trader does not enforce *quid pro quo* and accepts an exchange which decreases the value of his endowment at these prices while the other traders refused to make such trades, his final trading position will suffer.[4]

Trade is supposed to take place between one trader and another, in pairs. If we adopt the convention that a trader can be a member of only one pair at a time, it requires τ periods for each trader to form a pair with every other trader, once and only once, where

$$\tau = \begin{cases} J - 1 & \text{if } J \text{ is even,} \\ J & \text{if } J \text{ is odd.}^5 \end{cases}$$

In the analysis below, we take the order in which pairs meet to be arbitrary. The order of meetings is described by $\{\pi^t\}$, $t = 1, \ldots, \tau$, a sequence of permutations of the set I, so that (i) $\pi^t(i) = j$ if and only if $\pi^t(j) = i$, all $i \in I$ and $t = 1, \ldots, \tau$; (ii) $\pi^t(i) \neq i$, all i and t if J is even, and $\pi^t(i) = i$ for exactly one t, each $i \in I$, if J is odd; and (iii) $\pi^t(i) \neq \pi^s(i)$, all $i \in I$ and $s \neq t$. These three conditions guarantee that for all $i, j \in I$, there is precisely one t, $1 \leqslant t \leqslant \tau$, such that $\pi^t(i) = j$. Call such a sequence, $\{\pi^t\}$, *a round*. Any such sequence will do in that none of our results depend on more than (i), (ii), and (iii).

At the start of the tth period, trader i's holdings will be represented by w_i^t with $w_i^1 = b_i$. The change in i's holdings between t and $t + 1$, $a_i^t = w_i^{t+1} - w_i^t$, is the trade i performs in period t. The matrix of trades in t is $A^t = \|a_{in}^t\| = \|w_{in}^{t+1}\| - \|w_{in}^t\| = W^{t+1} - W^t$. Trader i's hitherto unsatisfied excess demands on entering period t are $v_i^t = v_i^1 - \Sigma_{T=1}^{T=t-1} a_i^T$, with $v_i^1 = z_i$.

Let $\pi^t(i) = j$. Consider the meeting and trade between i and j. Each brings his holdings, w_i^t and w_j^t, to the pair. Positive entries in the vector a_i^t indicate goods going from j to i and negative entries, goods going from i to j. After trading, i's holdings will be $w_i^{t+1} = w_i^t + a_i^t$ and j's will be $w_j^{t+1} = w_j^t + a_j^t$. We place the following three restrictions on a_i^t and a_j^t:

(A.1) $\quad w_i^t + a_i^t \geqslant 0, \quad w_j^t + a_j^t \geqslant 0 \quad$ (non-negativity of holdings).

(A.2) $\quad a_i^t = -a_j^t \quad$ (conservation of commodities).

(A.3) $\quad p \cdot a_i^t = 0 = p \cdot a_j^t \quad$ (*quid pro quo*).

Should trades fulfill (A) for all $i, j \in I$ and $t = 1, \ldots, \tau$, we shall say that *the sequence of trades is admissible.*

The non-negativity requirement, (A.1), says that a trader can at no time have a negative holding of any commodity. A trader cannot deliver to his partner more of a commodity than he currently holds. This may be interpreted as a prohibition on the issue of I.O.U.'s.[6]

[4] See [**9**, Section IV].

[5] See [**9**] for some properties of a model of bilateral exchange where each trader meets with only a fraction of the other traders.

[6] In a model including futures markets, (A.1) does not prevent a trader from selling futures contracts for goods which do not yet exist, but to which he has title.

The conservation condition, (A.2), says that in the process of trade, commodities are neither created nor destroyed. Goods delivered are received and *vice versa*.

The *quid pro quo* condition, (A.3), requires that in the trade between i and j each delivers to the other goods of equal value. Full payment is made for value received where goods are evaluated at equilibrium prices.

Conditions (A.1) and (A.2) are feasibility restrictions defining bilateral exchange. The origins of (A.3) are behavioral; if A^t were proposed such that $p \cdot a_i^t < 0$ for some i, then i would refuse to trade.

Given prices, an order of meetings for the pairs of traders, and an admissible sequence of trades, the outcome can be described as the resulting allocation of goods among traders. At the end of one round the outcome is $W^{\tau+1} = B + \Sigma_{t=1}^{\tau} A^t$. We will say that *full execution* of excess demands Z has been achieved in one round if

$$\text{(E)} \qquad \sum_{t=1}^{t=\tau} A^t = Z.$$

Should time run out ($t = \tau$) before all demands are fulfilled and supplies delivered, (E) will not be satisfied.

To illustrate, let the order of meetings in a four-person economy be $(\overline{12}, \overline{34})$, $(\overline{14}, \overline{23})$, and $(\overline{13}, \overline{24})$ in periods 1, 2, and 3, respectively, where $\overline{ij}$ indicates that i and j form a pair. Then if $p = (1, 1, 1, 1)$ and initial excess demands and endowments are given by the matrices Z and B, where rows denote traders and columns denote commodities,

$$Z = \begin{bmatrix} 1 & -1 & 0 & 0 \\ 0 & 1 & -1 & 0 \\ 0 & 0 & 1 & -1 \\ -1 & 0 & 0 & 1 \end{bmatrix}, \qquad B = \begin{bmatrix} 0 & 1 & 0 & 0 \\ 0 & 0 & 1 & 0 \\ 0 & 0 & 0 & 1 \\ 1 & 0 & 0 & 0 \end{bmatrix},$$

trades fulfilling (A) and (E) may be found. If the last period is dropped, either (A) or (E) may be satisfied, but not both.

Will (E) be fulfilled without violating (A)? To answer this we must specify what information traders have at each trading opportunity.

A trading rule is a function that tells each pair what trade to make. The inputs for the decision are not only what they have on hand—which defines what they can do—but what they know. Indeed, what they have on hand is just a part of what they know. There is a substantial variety of alternative assumptions and out of these we choose to examine extreme cases. Define a trading rule as a function

$$\rho(w_i^t, w_j^t | L^t) = (a_i^t, a_j^t)$$

where $\pi^t(i) = j$ and L^t is the set of information, beyond their current holdings, available to the pair at date t.

A rule is thought of as *decentralized* if it does not require more information than i,j are likely to possess. More precisely, varying degrees of modest informational requirements are characterized as follows:

(D.1) $$L^t = \{(v_i^t, v_j^t)\},$$

(D.2) $$L^t = \{(v_i^t, v_j^t), (i, j)\},$$

(D.3) $$L^t = \{(v_i^t, v_i^{t-1}, \ldots, v_i^1 ; v_j^t, v_j^{t-1}, \ldots, v_j^1), (i, j)\}.$$

(D.1) says that the decision on what i and j trade depends on i and j's currently unsatisfied excess demands and supplies. Equation (D.2) says that the decision may depend not only on current excess demands and supplies, but on who i and j are, their names, as well. Equation (D.3) says that in addition the decision may depend on i's and j's trading histories.

The notion of decentralization advanced here is a suitable extension of that concept to the problem under consideration. An economic arrangement is generally described as decentralized if it involves individual agents making decisions based on a fairly small body of universally communicated information (e.g., prices) and on information which the agents themselves may be supposed to possess (e.g., individual tastes and endowments and, in this case, the pair's trading history). (D) applies these restrictions to trading rules for pairs of agents.[7]

A trading rule is centralized if it requires more information than (D.1), (D.2), or (D.3) can provide. It will suffice to represent the informational requirements of a centralized rule by

(C) $$L^t = \{(v_1^t, v_1^{t-1}, \ldots, v_1^1;\ \ v_2^t, \ldots, ;\ \ v_J^t, v_J^{t-1}, \ldots, v_J^1),\ \ (i, j)\}.$$

If ρ requires (C), then i and j's trading decision depends on the trading histories of everyone in the economy, not only those of i and j.

The role of money as a medium of exchange consists in allowing full execution to be achieved in one round by a decentralized rule, whereas, in the absence of money, full execution requires more time, or a centralized rule, or sufficient quantities of non-money commodities.[8] These contentions are embodied in the following results.

THEOREM 1: *There is a trading rule which, for all (p, Z, B) satisfying (U), satisfies (A), (C), and (E).*

[7] According to (D.3), traders know or remember only part of the trading histories they may previously have known and used to make trading decisions. A rule making full use of trading history data (precluded by (D.3)) would allow traders to make their trading decisions not only on the basis of their previous trades, their current partner's previous trades, but as well on their previous partners' previous trades, . . . , etc. With this information each trader would be able to make more precise estimates of the probable excess demands of future partners and this would certainly allow the traders to come closer to full execution. But the record-keeping and complexity that such a rule would require appears to be so great as to be unfeasible, or at least very costly.

[8] The role of inventories of non-money commodities was brought to our attention by R. W. Clower, who pointed out Theorem 3 below.

THEOREM 2: *There is no trading rule which, for all (p, Z, B) satisfying (U), satisfies (A), $(D.3)$, and (E).*

THEOREM 3: *Let (p, Z, B) satisfy (U); further let there be a trader $j \in I$ with $b_j \geqslant \Sigma_{i \neq j} [z_i]^+$.*[9] *Then there is a trading rule which satisfies (A), $(D.2)$, and (E).*

THEOREM 4: *Let (p, Z, B) satisfy (U); further let there be a commodity m, $1 \leqslant m \leqslant N$, so that $p_m b_{im} \geqslant p \cdot [z_i]^+ - p_m[z_{im}]^+$ for all $i \in I$. Then there is a trading rule which satisfies (A), $(D.1)$, and (E).*

Theorems 1 and 2 demonstrate the trade-off between full execution and the limited information. Together, they say that although there exists a rule which makes (A) and (E) compatible for every competitive equilibrium (p, Z, B), that rule must be centralized. Theorems 3 and 4 demonstrate the trade-off between full execution and the presence of inventories. They say that if there is enough slack in initial endowments—either a trader whose endowments are sufficient to fulfill all others' excess demands (Theorem 3), or a commodity such that the value of each trader's holdings of it is at least equal to the value of his planned purchases of all other commodities (Theorem 4)—decentralized trading is compatible with full execution. In particular, the commodity m in Theorem 4 is regarded as money, and it behaves as money in the trading rule used to prove that theorem.

These results are conditional on bilateral trading opportunities being limited to precisely one round. Extending the model to include additional rounds, e.g., as many as there are traders, it can be shown that neither inventories nor information beyond that contained in (D), are necessary to make (A) and (E) compatible. Thus, there is a trade-off between time and information or inventories in achieving full execution.

3. IDEAL COORDINATION IN A BARTER ECONOMY

This section is devoted to a proof of Theorem 1. The strategy for the proof is as follows: (i) define a *chain* as an elementary configuration of excess demands, (ii) show that there is a centralized rule which achieves full execution of a chain in one round, (iii) show that *any* equilibrium configuration of excess demands may be represented as the sum of a finite number of chains, and (iv) apply the rule developed in (ii) to the chains in (iii) and show that the trade consisting of the sum of the trades prescribed for each of the chains is admissible and achieves full execution.

Let $\{i_1, i_2, \ldots, i_s\}$ be a subset of the traders called the members of the chain, $\{n_1, n_2, \ldots, n_s\}$ a subset of the commodities, and let δ be a positive scalar. Denote by $[(i_1 n_1 i_2 n_2 \ldots i_s n_s i_1), p, \delta]$ that configuration of excess demands where (i) i_1 has excess supply of n_1 for which i_2 has excess demand, i_2 has excess supply of n_2

[9] For a vector $x = (x_1, \ldots, x_N)$, $[x]^- \equiv (\min(x_1, 0), \ldots, \min(x_N, 0))$ and $[x]^+ \equiv (\max(x_1, 0), \ldots, \max(x_N, 0))$.

for which $i_3 \ldots$, and i_s has excess supply of n_s for which i_1 has excess demand; and (ii) the value of the commodity each individual demands is equal at the prices, p, to the value of the commodity he supplies, and is equal to δ.

Call $[(i_1 n_1 i_2 \ldots i_s n_s i_1), p, \delta]$ a *chain of length* s and *width* δ. By definition $2 \leqslant s \leqslant \min(J, N)$ when J is the number of traders and N is the number of commodities.

A matrix representation of the chain $[(i_1 n_1 i_2 \ldots i_s n_s i_1), p, \delta]$ will be denoted by the $J \times N$ matrix $\tilde{Z} = \|\tilde{z}_{in}\|$ where

$$\tilde{z}_{in} = \begin{cases} -\delta/p_n & \text{if } (i, n) = (i_r, n_r) \quad (r = 1, \ldots, s), \\ \delta/p_n & \text{if } (i, n) = (i_r, n_{r-1}) \quad (r = 2, \ldots, s \text{ or } (i, n) = (i_1, n_s)), \\ 0 & \text{otherwise.} \end{cases}$$

A positive entry indicates demand and a negative entry supply of a commodity. An example of a matrix representation of a chain of length 4 and width 1 is given by the numerical illustration of Z in Section 2, above. There, $i_r = r$, $r = 1, \ldots, 4$ and $n_r = r + 1$, $r = 1, 2, 3$, and $n_4 = 1$.

There is an equivalence between chains and cyclic permutations. By relabelling the indices on traders and commodities in the chain $[(i_1 n_1 i_2 \ldots i_s n_s i_1), p, \delta]$ we may obtain $i_h = n_h = h, h = 1, \ldots, s$. Then, ignoring p and δ, the interdependencies among the members of a chain of length s may be represented by the cyclic permutation

$$\alpha = \begin{pmatrix} 1 & 2 & \ldots & s \\ 2 & 3 & \ldots & 1 \end{pmatrix}.$$ [10]

The first line lists the "names" of the traders in the chain, and the second line contains the same list in a different order. The appearance of "2" under "1" denotes that trader 1 gives commodity 1 to trader 2, ..., and "1" under "s" that trader s gives commodity s to trader 1.

Suppose trader 1 and r, $1 < r \leqslant s$, meet and exchange their excess supplies. What change in the pattern of interdependence occurs as a result of this trade? The exchange is a transposition of the excess supplies of traders 1 and r and is represented by the permutation

$$\beta = \begin{pmatrix} 1 & 2 & \ldots & r & \ldots & s \\ r & 2 & \ldots & 1 & \ldots & s \end{pmatrix}.$$

The effect of this trade on the original chain is given by premultiplying α by β:

$$\beta \cdot \alpha = \begin{pmatrix} 1 & 2 & \ldots & r-1 & r & r+1 & \ldots & s \\ 2 & 3 & \ldots & 1 & r+1 & r+2 & \ldots & r \end{pmatrix}.$$

To verify, for example, the last column, note that $\alpha(s) = 1$ and $\beta(1) = r$, so $\beta \cdot \alpha(s) = r$. Notice that $\beta \cdot \alpha$ consists of two disjoint chains (disjoint cyclic permutations).

[10] The definition of a cyclic permutation and the above double-rowed method of representing it is contained in most introductory texts on algebra. A standard reference is [7].

One is of the first $r-1$ traders, and the other is of the last $s-(r-1)$ traders. This result provides us with an elementary proof of the following lemma:

LEMMA 1: *Let* $(p, \tilde{Z}, B)$ *satisfy* (U) *and suppose* $\tilde{Z}$ *is the matrix representation of the chain* $[(i_1 n_1 i_2 \ldots i_s n_s i_1), p, \delta]$. *Then there is a trading rule satisfying* (A), (C), *and* (E).

PROOF: It suffices to prove the existence of a rule satisfying (A) and (E) since such a rule, if it exists, can require no more than complete information which is (C).

The proof is by induction on the length of the chain, now denoted by k. For $k = 2$, (A) and (E) follow if the pair exchange excess supplies when they meet.

Suppose there is a rule satisfying (A) and (E) for all k, $k \leqslant s-1 < \min(J, N)$. From the demonstration of the relation between chains and cyclic permutations we may denote a typical chain of length s by α, above.

Let $\bar{t}$ be the first period in which any pair of traders from $\{1, \ldots, s\}$ meet. Without loss of generality, assume $\pi^{\bar{t}}(1) = r$, $1 < r \leqslant s$. Let this pair exchange their excess supplies. The result is to transform the original chain into two smaller disjoint chains of lengths $(r-1)$ and $(s-(r-1))$. Since $\bar{t}$ is the first period in which any of the set $\{1, \ldots, s\}$ meet and since $\{\pi^t\}$ permits all pairs to meet, there is a t, $\bar{t} \leqslant t \leqslant \tau$ such that every pair within each disjoint chain meet. Apply the induction hypothesis to each of these chains, whose lengths are less than or equal to $s-1$, to obtain the desired conclusion.[11] *Q.E.D.*

Not every non-zero matrix of excess demands in (U) is a chain. However, every such matrix can be written as a sum of chains. We shall show that any exchange economy represented by (p, Z, B) satisfying (U) can be broken down into components $(p, \tilde{Z}^k, B^k)$ each of which satisfy (U) and $\Sigma\tilde{Z}^k = Z$, $\Sigma B^k = B$.

As a simple illustration, suppose $p = (1, 1, 1)$ and

$$Z = \begin{pmatrix} 8 & -7 & -1 \\ -3 & 9 & -6 \\ -5 & -2 & 7 \end{pmatrix}, \qquad B = \begin{pmatrix} 0 & -7 & -1 \\ -3 & 0 & -6 \\ -5 & -2 & 0 \end{pmatrix}.$$

Note that Z is not itself a chain. However,

$$\tilde{Z}^1 = \begin{pmatrix} 1 & 0 & -1 \\ 0 & 0 & 0 \\ -1 & 0 & 1 \end{pmatrix}, \qquad \tilde{Z}^2 = \begin{pmatrix} 4 & -4 & 0 \\ 0 & 4 & -4 \\ -4 & 0 & 4 \end{pmatrix},$$

$$\tilde{Z}^3 = \begin{pmatrix} 0 & 0 & 0 \\ 0 & 2 & -2 \\ 0 & -2 & 2 \end{pmatrix}, \qquad \tilde{Z}^4 = \begin{pmatrix} 3 & -3 & 0 \\ -3 & 3 & 0 \\ 0 & 0 & 0 \end{pmatrix},$$

[11] Lemma 1 is simply a slight refinement of an elementary result in the theory of groups that every cyclic permutation (called here a chain) can be represented as a product of transpositions (called here bilateral trades). See [7, p. 94]. The refinement amounts to showing that any permutation can be represented as the product of a *fixed* list of cycles, where each cycle is used at most once.

are matrix representations of chains and $\tilde{Z}^1 + \tilde{Z}^2 + \tilde{Z}^3 + \tilde{Z}^4 = Z$. If we set $B^k = -[\tilde{Z}^k]^-$, then $\Sigma B^k = B$ and $(p, \tilde{Z}^k, B^k), k = 1, 2, 3, 4$ is the desired decomposition.

The general proposition is as follows:

LEMMA 2: *Let (p, Z, B) satisfy (U) and $Z \neq 0$. Then there exist $(p, \tilde{Z}^k, B^k)$, $k = 1, \ldots, K$ satisfying (U) and,* (i) *$\tilde{Z}^k$ is the matrix representation of a chain at prices p, all k;* (ii) *$Z = \tilde{Z}^k, B = \Sigma B^k$.*

PROOF: Since $Z \neq 0$ satisfies (U.2), there are traders, i_1 and i_2, and a commodity, n_1, such that $z_{i_1 n_1} < 0$ and $z_{i_2 n_1} > 0$. Since (U.1) holds, there must be a commodity n_2 such that $z_{i_2 n_2} < 0$. Continue in this manner to order traders and commodities such that $z_{i_s n_s} < 0$ and $z_{i_s n_{s-1}} > 0$ as long as $i_s \neq i_r, r = 1, \ldots, s-1$ and/or $n_s \neq n_{r-1}, r = 2, \ldots, s-1$. However, (U.1) and (U.2) insure that there is some $s \leqslant \min(J, N)$ with $i_s = i_r$ or $n_s = n_{r-1}$.

(i) If $i_s = i_r$, then we have

$$(p^{n_r})(z_{i_r n_r}) < 0, \qquad (p^{n_r})(z_{i_{r+1} n_r}) > 0, \qquad \ldots, \qquad (p^{n_{s-1}})(z_{i_{s-1} n_{s-1}}) < 0,$$

and

$$(p^{n_{s-1}})(z_{i_r n_{s-1}}) > 0.$$

Let δ be the minimum of the absolute values of these amounts. Then we may form the chain $[(i_r n_r i_{r+1} \ldots i_{s-1} n_{s-1} i_r), p, \delta]$.

(ii) If $n_s = n_{r-1}$, then we have

$$(p^{n_r})(z_{i_r n_r}) < 0, \qquad (p^{n_r})(z_{i_{r+1} n_r}) > 0, \qquad \ldots, \qquad (p^{n_{r-1}})(z_{i_s n_{r-1}}) < 0,$$

and

$$(p^{n_{r-1}})(z_{i_r n_{r-1}}) > 0.$$

Let δ be the minimum of the absolute values of these amounts. Then we may form the chain $[(i_r n_r i_{r+1} \ldots i_s n_{r-1} i_s), p, \delta]$.

In either case let $\tilde{Z}^1$ be the matrix representation of the resulting chain. By construction, $\operatorname{sign} \tilde{z}^1_{in} = \operatorname{sign} z_{in}$. Further, $Z - \tilde{Z}^1$ satisfies (U.1) and (U.2) and has at least one fewer non-zero entry than Z. To find $\tilde{Z}^2$ apply to $Z - \tilde{Z}^1$ the procedure used to derive $\tilde{Z}^1$. To find $\tilde{Z}^l$, apply the procedure to $Z - \Sigma_{k=1}^{k=l-1} \tilde{Z}^k$. This will guarantee that $\operatorname{sign} z^l_{in} = \operatorname{sign} z_{in}$ and that $Z - \Sigma_{k=1}^{k=l} \tilde{Z}^k$ has at least one fewer non-zero entry than $Z - \Sigma_{k=1}^{k=l-1} \tilde{Z}^k$. Since Z has at most JN non-zero entries, the procedure must terminate—i.e., $Z - \Sigma_{k=1}^{k=K} \tilde{Z}^k = 0$—for some $K \leqslant JN$.

It only remains for us to find B^k such that $(p, \tilde{Z}^k, B^k)$ satisfy (U.3) and $\Sigma B^k = B$. This may be done by setting $B^k = -[\tilde{Z}^k]^-$, which implies $\tilde{Z}^k \geqslant -B^k$, $k = 1, \ldots, K-1$, and by setting $B^K = B - \Sigma_{k=1}^{k=K-1}(-[\tilde{Z}^k]^-) = B + Z - \tilde{Z}^K$. Since $B + Z \geqslant 0$, $\tilde{Z}^K \geqslant -B^K$, and therefore, $\Sigma_{k=1}^{k=K} B^k = B$. *Q.E.D.*

Lemma 2 permits the extension of the trading rule shown to exist in Lemma 1 to any equilibrium matrix of excess demands which may now be viewed as a sum of chains. It has already been shown that for any chain $\tilde{Z}^k$ there is a sequence of admissible trades, denoted by $\{A^{kt}\}$, $t = 1, \ldots, \tau$ guaranteeing full execution.

THEOREM 1: *Let (p, Z, B) satisfy (U). There is a trading rule satisfying (A), (C), and (E).*

PROOF: Let $\{A^{kt}\}$ be the trades prescribed by the trading rule shown to exist in Lemma 1 for $(p, \tilde{Z}^k, B^k)$ and let $\Sigma_t A^{kt} = \tilde{Z}_k$, $\Sigma_k B^k = B$ where $\tilde{Z}^k$ and Z, B^k and B, satisfy the conditions of Lemma 2. To execute the matrix Z, prescribe trades in period t to be

$$A^t = \Sigma_k A^{kt}.$$

By inspection the information contained in (C) is sufficient to allow this to be implemented. By Lemma 1, $\tilde{Z}^k = \Sigma_t A^{kt}$. By hypothesis and Lemma 2, $Z = \Sigma_k \tilde{Z}^k$. Therefore, $Z = \Sigma_t \Sigma_k A^{kt}$ and (E) is satisfied. To establish (A), note that $Z \geqslant -B$ and sign $\tilde{z}^k_{in} = z_{in}$. From Lemma 1, it is known that for $\pi^t(i) = j$, the trading rule prescribes $a_i^{kt} = -a_j^{kt}$ and $p \cdot a_i^{kt} = 0$ for all t. Therefore $\Sigma_k a_i^{kt} = -\Sigma_k a_j^{kt}$ [(A.2)] and $p \cdot \Sigma_k a_i^{kt} = 0$ [(A.3)]. It only remains for us to show (A.1) to prove the theorem.

By hypothesis, $\tilde{Z}^k$ is a chain, sign $\tilde{z}^k_{in} =$ sign z_{in} and $Z = \Sigma_k \tilde{Z}^k$. Choose B^k as in Lemma 2. From Lemma 1, we know that the trading rule applied to $(p, \tilde{Z}^k, B^k)$ satisfies (A.1) and, therefore, so does this procedure applied to $(p, \Sigma_k \tilde{Z}^k, \Sigma_k B^k)$. *Q.E.D.*

Theorem 1 asserts that a rather complicated procedure can be used to achieve full execution of a competitive equilibrium in one round of trade in a barter economy, while fulfilling the conditions of *quid pro quo*, conservation, and non-negativity. To summarize the procedure:

(i) The matrix of excess demands is decomposed into a sum of chains. This decomposition is both complex and arbitrary. Without some central direction and notification there is no reason why a trader should have any idea about the chains to which he is assigned and who the other members are.

(ii) Trades are assigned on the basis of (i). At any meeting a pair engages in trade depending on all chains in that period of which both elements of the pair are members. These may be numerous, generating correspondingly complex trades. Assigned trades may include such non-obvious actions as passing up mutually beneficial trading opportunities (when traders meeting are not members of the same chain) and often exchanging for each other goods which neither party to the trade desires. These latter trades are made in anticipation of future trades for desired goods or future trades for goods which, in future trades, will be traded for desired goods, or future trades for goods which in future trades will be traded for goods which in future trades will be traded....

Of course, we have only shown that this complex trading rule is sufficient for (A) and (E) but not that it is necessary. The following section shows that these complications are unavoidable.

4. THE IMPOSSIBILITY OF DECENTRALIZING EXCHANGE IN A BARTER ECONOMY

In this section we shall demonstrate the impossibility of (A), (D), and (E) within a particular class of exchange economies, and this will, of course, suffice to prove Theorem 2. Note that this theorem does not merely say there exists no "plausible" trading rule—e.g., a rule which places limits on the ingenuity or computational capacity of traders or even satisfies some mild continuity condition. It says that within the class of all functions (rules) whose domain is what the traders know and whose range is their sets of feasible trades, there is none which satisfies the stated conditions. It will require that we construct two economies which fulfill the following conditions: (i) under (D) a pair of traders will not be able to determine in which one of the economies they are, and (ii) the necessary conditions for full execution in the two economies are disjoint for the pair of traders (no matter what the other pairs do).[12]

It is desirable to choose the "smallest" example for which (i) and (ii) obtain. Simple calculations show that there will have to be at least three commodities and three traders, and it is not difficult to show that the case of three traders is also too small, no matter what the number of commodities. We shall show that the following trading rule satisfies (A), (D), and (E) for all (p, Z, B) fulfilling (U) if $J \leqslant 3$:

Trading rule γ: For $\pi^t(i) = j$, let $a_i^t = x_i^t + y_i^t$ and $a_j^t = x_j^t + y_j^t$ where

$$(1)\qquad x_{in}^t = -x_{jn}^t = \begin{cases} 0 & \text{if } v_{in}^t v_{jn}^t \geqslant 0, \\ \min(|v_{in}^t|, |v_{jn}^t|) & \text{if } v_{in}^t > 0 \quad \text{and} \quad v_{jn}^t < 0, \\ -\min(|v_{in}^t|, |v_{jn}^t|) & \text{if } v_{in}^t < 0 \quad \text{and} \quad v_{jn}^t > 0, \end{cases}$$

and $y_i^t = -y_j^t$ is constructed according to

$$(2)\qquad \begin{aligned} &[v_i^t - x_i^t]^- < y_i^t < 0 \quad \text{and} \quad p \cdot (x_i^t + y_i^t) = 0, \quad \text{if } p \cdot x_i^t > 0, \\ &[v_j^t - x_j^t]^- < y_j^t < 0 \quad \text{and} \quad p \cdot (x_j^t + y_j^t) = 0, \quad \text{if } p \cdot x_j^t > 0. \end{aligned}$$

Part (1) of rule γ says, for example, that if i has an excess demand of one unit for a commodity for which j has an excess supply of two units, j is to give one unit to i. Trades are made so as to reduce the partners' excess demands to the maximum extent consistent with the dictum "never change the sign of your excess demand."

In the likely event that $p \cdot x_i^t \neq 0$, say $p \cdot x_i^t > 0$, part (2) says that i may choose from among *any* commodities for which he still has an excess supply ($v_{in}^t - x_{in}^t < 0$) and give to j *any* bundle of those commodities whose value will allow him to maintain *quid pro quo*. The fact that payment is made in *any* of the selected set of bundles shows that the rule is compatible with (D) and also accounts for its failure to satisfy (E) when $J \geqslant 4$.[13]

[12] See [**9**, Proposition 5], for an impossibility result similar to Theorem 2.

[13] However, a modification of rule γ, which introduces a convention as to how to redistribute excess supplies, can be made such that (A), (D), and (E) appear to be compatible for all (p, Z, B) in (U) if $J \leqslant 4$ so that we shall have to admit economies having at least five traders.

An important consequence of rule γ is that if $y_{in}^t > 0$, then j may be required to more than fulfill his excess demand for commodity n in order to allow i to maintain *quid pro quo*—i.e., j must be willing to convert an excess demand into an excess supply. To formalize the opposite, we shall say that *a trading rule satisfies* (*P*) *at date t*, if for all i and n,

$$\text{(P)} \qquad \begin{aligned} v_{in}^t &\geqslant v_{in}^{t+1} \geqslant 0 \qquad \text{if } v_{in}^t \geqslant 0, \\ v_{in}^t &\leqslant v_{in}^{t+1} \leqslant 0 \qquad \text{if } v_{in}^t \leqslant 0. \end{aligned}$$

Property (P) specifies that for each commodity trade should not change the sign or increase the absolute value of any excess demand.[14]

The relation between γ and (P) is as follows:

LEMMA 3: *For trading rule γ to satisfy property (P) at date t, it is necessary and sufficient that $a_i^t = x_i^t$ (i.e., $y_i^t = 0$), $i = 1, \ldots, J$.*

PROOF: *Sufficiency*: By inspection if $v_{in}^t \geqslant 0$, then $v_{in}^t \geqslant x_{in}^t \geqslant 0$ and $v_{in}^t \geqslant v_{in}^{t+1} = v_{in}^t - a_{in}^t = v_{in}^t - x_{in}^t \geqslant 0$. Similarly, if $v_{in}^t < 0$, $v_{in}^t \leqslant x_{in}^t \leqslant 0$ and $v_{in}^t \leqslant v_{in}^{t+1} = v_{in}^t - x_{in}^t \leqslant 0$.

Necessity: If $a_i^t \neq x_i^t$, there is a $y_{in}^t \neq 0$, say $y_{in}^t < 0$. From (2) of rule γ, $y_{in}^t < 0$ implies $p \cdot x_i^t > 0$ and $v_{in}^t < x_{in}^t \leqslant 0$. Since $a_{jn}^t = -a_{in}^t = -(x_{in}^t + y_{in}^t)$, either $v_{jn}^t \leqslant 0$, in which case $v_{jn}^{t+1} = v_{jn}^t + (x_{in}^t + y_{in}^t) = v_{in}^t + y_{jn}^t < v_{jn}^t$; or $v_{jn}^t > 0$, in which case $-x_{in}^t = v_{jn}^t$ and $v_{jn}^{t+1} = v_{jn}^t + (x_{in}^t + y_{in}^t) < 0$. In both cases, (P) is contradicted. *Q.E.D.*

It is to be expected that a demonstration of Theorem 2 will involve economies—unlike those of Theorems 3 and 4—admitting very little slack in their endowments. For a matrix of excess demands Z, call the matrix of initial endowments B *minimally sufficient* for Z if $[Z]^- = -B$. If B is minimally sufficient for Z, then each trader will want to sell all of his initial endowments in exchange for commodities of which he has none to start.

Rule γ will be a basic ingredient in the proof of Theorem 2 because it is the essentially unique method of guaranteeing full execution in economies with three traders whenever endowments are minimally sufficient.

LEMMA 4: *For all (p, Z, B) fulfilling (U) such that initial endowments are minimally sufficient ($b_i = -[z_i]^-$, $i = 1, \ldots, J$) and $z \neq 0$ for at most three traders, trading rule γ is necessary and sufficient for (A) and (E).*

PROOF: *Necessity*: The result is trivial when all $z_i = 0$ and is readily verified for exactly two $z_i \neq 0$, in which case there is a perfect double coincidence of wants. When there are three non-zero vectors z_i, we can without loss of generality denote them by $i = 1, 2, 3$ and assume that they meet in the sequence $\overline{12}$, $\overline{13}$, and $\overline{23}$ in periods 1, 2, and 3, respectively.

[14] In an atemporal context trades satisfying (P) are called excess-demand-diminishing in [**11**]. Their properties in the present model of a trading economy are studied in [**9**].

For any trading pair $\overline{ij}$, the set of trades consistent with rule γ are defined by the restrictions (i) $a_i^t = -a_j^t$, (ii) $p \cdot a_i^t = 0$, and for all n, (iii) $(v_{in}^t - a_{in}^t)(v_{jn}^t - a_{jn}^t) \geqslant 0$. Condition (iii) says that after i and j perform trades according to γ, there is no commodity such that i has an unsatisfied excess demand for the commodity and j has an undelivered excess supply. Since (i) and (ii) hold for any admissible trade, γ is violated if and only if (iii) is not satisfied. If (iii) is not satisfied by the pair $\overline{12}$ at $t = 1$, there must be at least one n such that (a) $v_{1n}^2 (= v_{1n}^1 - a_{1n}^1) > 0$ and $v_{2n}^2 < 0$ or (b) $v_{1n}^2 < 0$ and $v_{2n}^2 > 0$. Suppose (a); then by the hypothesis that endowments are minimally sufficient and $\Sigma_i v_{in}^t = 0$, $[v_{1n}^2]^+ = -[v_{2n}^2]^- - [v_{3n}^2]^- > -[v_{3n}^2]^- = -[v_{3n}^1]^- = b_{3n}$. Since $t = 2$ is 1's last opportunity to trade and 3 cannot possibly fulfill all of 1's excess demand for commodity n, (A) and (E) are contradicted. Supposing (b), a similar conclusion follows. This shows that γ is necessary at $t = 1$, and the same arguments may be applied to the trading pair $\overline{13}$ at $t = 2$ to show that if γ (condition (iii), above) is violated, (A) and (E) will be contradicted. Finally, at $t = 3$, (E) implies $v_2^3 = -v_3^3$ which requires $a_2^3 = v_2^3 - v_3^3$, exactly what γ prescribes.

Sufficiency: This may be constructed directly from the above. However, since γ is necessary and by Theorem 1 there always exist trading rules satisfying (A) and (E), it must be sufficient. *Q.E.D.*

The informational restrictions imposed by (D.3) will be shown to imply that any pair of traders will not be able to determine whether they are or are not in a three-trader economy. That is, (D.3) requires that they perform the same trade independent of the economy in which they are located. When this is coupled with Lemma 3, the result is a sweeping limitation on the "degrees of freedom" in any successful, decentralized rule. If the rule is to work it must satisfy γ and we shall see that except in special cases this will mean that it must violate (P). To prove Theorem 2, it only remains to construct economies where if (P) is violated, full execution is precluded.

Bradley [**1**] has found an example showing that (A), (D), and (E) are inconsistent for $J \geqslant 5$ if the trading rule satisfies the additional assumption that it is insensitive to a relabelling of commodities—i.e., it is only the amounts of commodities, not their names, which matter. Theorem 4 with its monetary trading rule, below, contradicts Bradley's assumption. The money commodity is definitely in an asymmetric position compared to all other commodities. This could be interpreted as showing the advantages of having at least one commonly recognizable commodity to be used by all traders in settling their accounts. However, suppose, as we have in (D), that all commodities are recognizable. Theorem 2 shows that even when they are, this is not sufficient to guarantee full execution.

An Example that Proves Theorem 2

Throughout the remainder of this section we shall consider only those economies (p, Z, B) satisfying (U) such that (i) there are five traders and four commodities, (ii) initial endowments are minimally sufficient so that $b_i = -[z_i]^-$, $i = 1, \ldots, 5$, and (iii) equilibrium prices are the same for all commodities, e.g., $p = (1, 1, 1, 1)$. Under conditions (i)–(iii), any economy fulfilling (U) can be completely described by a 5×4 matrix (of initial excess demands), Z, whose row and column sums are zero. Denote by $\mathscr{U}$ the set of all such Z.

Also throughout, let the sequence of trading partners in a five-trader economy be $(\overline{12}, \overline{35}, \overline{4})$, $(\overline{13}, \overline{24}, \overline{5})$, $(\overline{14}, \overline{25}, \overline{3})$, $(\overline{1}, \overline{23}, \overline{45})$, and $(\overline{15}, \overline{34}, \overline{2})$ in periods 1–5 consecutively. This constitutes a round.

Let $\mathscr{L} \subset \mathscr{U}$ be the class of economies representable by matrices of the form

$$Z = \begin{bmatrix} a & 1-a & -b & b-1 \\ 0 & 0 & e & -e \\ -a & a-1 & b-e & 1-b+e \\ 0 & 0 & 0 & 0 \\ 0 & 0 & 0 & 0 \end{bmatrix}$$

where $0 \leqslant a, b \leqslant 1$ and $b - e \geqslant 0$ if $e \geqslant 0$ and $1 - b + e \geqslant 0$ if $e \leqslant 0$.[15]

PROPOSITION 1: *If $Z(=V^1) \in \mathscr{L}$, a necessary condition for (A) and (E) is that $v_2^2 = 0$.*

PROOF: By Lemma 3, γ is necessary. By inspection, its application leads to $V_2^2 = 0$.

Let $\mathscr{M} \subset \mathscr{U}$ be the class of economies representable by matrices of the form,

$$Z = \begin{bmatrix} a & 1-a & -b & b-1 \\ 0 & 0 & e & -e \\ -c & c-1 & d & 1-d \\ c-a & a-c & b-d-e & d+e-b \\ 0 & 0 & 0 & 0 \end{bmatrix}$$

where $0 \leqslant a, b, c, d \leqslant 1$ and again $b - e \geqslant 0$ if $e \geqslant 0$ and $1 - b + e \geqslant 0$ if $e \leqslant 0$.

The classes $\mathscr{L}$ and $\mathscr{M}$ have been constructed so that by the hypothesis of (D) the pair $\overline{12}$ cannot determine at $t = 1$ whether Z belongs to $\mathscr{L}$ or $\mathscr{M}$. The pair must make the same initial trade in each. From Proposition 1, rule γ is necessary if $Z \in \mathscr{L}$. Therefore, if (A), (D), and (E) are to hold for all $Z \in \mathscr{U}$, the pair $\overline{12}$ must adopt it for all $Z \in \mathscr{L} \cup \mathscr{M}$. Since the other traders must be inactive, it follows that γ is necessary at $t = 1$. The following says that γ is necessary for all t.

[15] Traders 4 and 5 are "dummies" having no endowments and thus no demands. Their presence in this and the following constructions is a device for minimizing the difficulty in describing the set of admissible trades satisfying (E). When it is recognized that a dummy is a special case of a trader who has already fulfilled his excess demands before trade begins, it will be seen that the overall results would follow a fortiori if we replaced these dummies by "real" traders.

PROPOSITION 2: *A necessary condition for (A), (D), and (E) to hold for all $Z \in \mathscr{U}$ is that if $Z \in \mathscr{M}$, trades must satisfy trading rule γ.*[16]

Each of the classes $\mathscr{L}$ and $\mathscr{M}$ provided a necessary condition for (A), (D), and (E) to be satisfied for all $Z \in \mathscr{U}$. Next, we introduce another class of economies and with it an additional necessary condition which will be shown to be inconsistent with the above requirements and will, therefore, confirm Theorem 2.

Let $\mathscr{N} \subset \mathscr{U}$ be the class of economies representable by matrices of the following form:

$$Z = \begin{bmatrix} a & 1-a & -b & b-1 \\ 1-a & a & b-1 & -b \\ -c & c-1 & d & 1-d \\ c-1 & -c & 1-d & d \\ 0 & 0 & 0 & 0 \end{bmatrix}$$

where $0 \leqslant a, b, c, d \leqslant 1$.

PROPOSITION 3: *For any $Z \in \mathscr{N}$, a necessary condition for (A) and (E) is that trades satisfy (P) at $t = 2$.*

So far, it has been established that if $Z \in \mathscr{M}$, trades must satisfy rule γ in every period (Proposition 2), and that if $Z \in \mathscr{N}$, trades must satisfy property (P) at $t = 2$ (Proposition 3). These two necessary conditions do not, by the next result, coincide.

PROPOSITION 4: *There exists no trading rule satisfying (A) such that for all $Z \in \mathscr{M} \cup \mathscr{N}$, the application of trading rule γ at $t = 2$ will exhibit property (P).*

Since a trading rule cannot satisfy (A) and (E) for all $Z \in \mathscr{U}$ while remaining invariant for all $Z \in \mathscr{M} \cup \mathscr{N}$, it only remains for us to show that (D) requires such invariance.

Whether $Z \in \mathscr{M}$ or $\mathscr{N}$, $z_1 (= v_1^1)$ is defined by the parameters (a, b). The possible changes in trader 1's excess demands and their implications are stated as the following proposition:

PROPOSITION 5: (i) *For all $Z \in \mathscr{M} \cup \mathscr{N}$, if z_1 is defined by (a, b) and trades satisfy (A), then v_1^2 is of the same form as $v_1^1 (= z_1)$ and is defined by $(a, b'), 0 \leqslant b' \leqslant 1$;* and (ii) *if (A), (D), and (E) are to hold for all $Z \in \mathscr{U}$, the trading pair $\overline{13}$ will not be able to determine at $t = 2$ whether $Z \in \mathscr{M}$ or $\mathscr{N}$.*

Propositions 1–5 are now combined to prove Theorem 2.

PROOF: From Proposition 5, the trading pair $\overline{13}$ will not be able to determine at $t = 2$ whether $Z \in \mathscr{M}$ or $\mathscr{N}$. From Proposition 2, if $\mathscr{M}$, trading rule γ must be followed; and, from Proposition 3, if $\mathscr{N}$, the trading rule must satisfy (P). From

[16] Propositions 2 through 5 are proved in the Appendix.

Proposition 4, there will exist economies in both $\mathcal{M}$ and $\mathcal{N}$ in which the application of rule γ will fail to satisfy (P). Since (D) requires that the same trading decision must be made in all such cases, whichever of the mutually exclusive alternatives—γ or (P)—is chosen, it will fail to achieve (A) and (E) in either $\mathcal{M}$ or $\mathcal{N}$. *Q.E.D.*

5. MONEY AND COMMODITY INVENTORIES

The difficulties of barter exchange may be traced to an over-determinacy in the demand for commodities. They are wanted both for final consumption and as a means of payment. Without a double coincidence of wants, these two functions cannot be easily satisfied and each unit of a commodity supplied may have to serve both as a means of payment to one's present trading partner and as an exchange which will satisfy the demands of one's present trading partner's future partners, . . . , etc.

Assuming that information beyond that given by (D) is simply not available, some slack in initial endowment is essential to guarantee full execution. When endowments are large, relative to what is minimally sufficient, there are trading rules permitting these two conflicting demands for commodities to be separated in a straightforward, decentralized manner. The very presence of a medium of exchange implies a slackness, that B is not minimally sufficient. Imagine a money economy, with m the money commodity, in a position of equilibrium where traders have no desire to increase or decrease their money balances ($z_{im} = 0$). If endowments were minimally sufficient, this would imply $b_{im} = 0$, hardly a description of a money economy. Although the levels of inventories may remain constant on the average, fluctuations from period to period should be regarded as a valuable input in the process of exchange. (Of course, inventories cannot fluctuate if their initial levels are zero.) This is the view taken by R. W. Clower [**2**], who has emphasized that it is not only inventories of money, but of all commodities, which facilitates exchange. In this section, Theorems 3 and 4 support this contention.

Suppose trader 1's initial endowments are so large that he may fulfill all other traders' excess demands—$b_1 \geqslant \Sigma_{i \neq 1}[z_i]^+$. Consider the following:

Trading rule σ: For $\pi^t(i) = j$, let

$$a_i^t = 0 = -a_j^t \qquad \text{if } i, j \neq 1,$$

$$a_i^t = v_i^t = -a_j^t \qquad \text{if } i \neq j = 1.$$

It is clear that we have the following theorem:

THEOREM 3: *If* $b_1 \geqslant \Sigma_{i \neq 1}[z_i]^+$, *trading rule* σ *satisfies* (*A*), (*D*.2), *and* (*E*).

Trading rule σ specifies that trader 1 acts as a clearinghouse. He is the hub of commodity exchange. Other traders look to him and only to him, to purchase their demands and sell their supplies (cf. [**11**, Lemma 1], though [**11**] lacks the nonnegativity constraint).

In order to function as a medium of exchange, money must have a positive value in exchange, a positive price. It has been suggested by some that the major aim in the integration of monetary and value theory is to construct a model in which money has a positive equilibrium price.[17] This paper represents another tack. For a commodity with positive value, are there any conditions under which it could be usefully employed as a medium of exchange? In this model Theorem 4 answers affirmatively. Suppose there is a commodity, m, such that the value of each trader's endowment of it is at least as large as the value of his desired purchases of commodities other than m—$p_m b_{im} \geqslant \Sigma_{n \neq m} p_n [z_{in}]^+$, $i \in I$. Then consider the following:

Trading rule μ: For $\pi^t(i) = j$, let

$$a_i^t = x_i^t + y_i^t \qquad \text{and} \qquad a_j^t = x_j^t + y_j^t$$

where

$$(1) \qquad x_{in}^t = -x_{jn}^t = \begin{cases} 0 & \text{if } v_{in}^t v_{jn}^t \geqslant 0, \quad \text{or if } n = m, \\ \min(|v_{in}^t|, |v_{jn}^t|) & \text{if } v_{in}^t > 0 \quad \text{and} \quad v_{jn}^t < 0, \\ -\min(|v_{in}^t|, |v_{jn}^t|) & \text{if } v_{in}^t < 0 \quad \text{and} \quad v_{jn}^t > 0, \end{cases}$$

and

$$(2) \qquad y_{in}^t = -y_{jn}^t = \begin{cases} 0 & \text{if } n \neq m, \\ q \text{ where } p \cdot x_i^t + p_m q = 0 & \text{if } n = m. \end{cases}$$

Trading rule μ assigns a unique, asymmetric role to the commodity m.[18] The rule says that when traders i and j meet, they should make trades that diminish one's excess supplies and reduce the other's excess demands. Any failure of *quid pro quo* should be made up in m, the commodity which acts as money. Rule μ should be compared with rule γ of Section 4. Parts (1) of each rule are identical except in the treatment of commodity m. Part (2) of γ says that payment can be made in any assortment of commodities in which the trader has an excess supply, whereas part (2) of μ narrows the choice of means of payment to commodity m without, however, imposing the restriction that m be in excess supply before it is given up.

THEOREM 4: *If* $p_m b_{im} \geqslant \Sigma_{n \neq m} p_n [z_{in}]^+$, $i \in I$, *trading rule* μ *satisfies* (*A*), (*D*.1), *and* (*E*).

PROOF: The rule requires only a knowledge of the pairs' excess demands and the convention that payment be made in commodity m. It satisfies (D.1). (A.3)

[17] It seems fairly clear that such a conclusion cannot be obtained from the model of an exchange economy without additional assumptions on the backing or utility of money (Cf. Hahn [**4**], Kurz [**6**], Marschak [**8**], Sontheimer [**10**], and Starr [**12**]). The ad hoc nature of these constructs suggest that the problem of integrating monetary and value theory is not equivalent to the demonstration of a positive price for money.

[18] Cf. Clower [**3**]. Trading rule μ appears also in [**9** and **11**].

follows from the definition of trading rule μ, part (2). For goods other than m, it will be shown that the rule consisting only of (1), above, satisfies (A.1), (A.2), and (E) and then it will be shown that (2) never contradicts the trades prescribed in (1).

According to (1), if $v_{in}^1 \geqslant 0$, $v_{in}^t \geqslant x_{in}^t \geqslant 0$, and if $v_{in}^1 < 0$, $v_{in}^t \leqslant x_{in}^t \leqslant 0$, all t. Since $V^t \geqslant -W^t$, (A.1) is satisfied. (A.2) holds by definition. There is also the implication that if

$$\begin{aligned} &v_{in}^1 \geqslant 0, \qquad \text{then } v_{in}^t \geqslant v_{in}^{t'} \geqslant 0, \qquad \text{and if} \\ &v_{in}^1 < 0, \qquad \text{then } v_{in}^t \leqslant v_{in}^{t'} \leqslant 0 \end{aligned} \tag{3}$$

for $t' > t$ and $n \neq m$.

Suppose $v_{in}^{\tau+1} \neq 0$ for $n \neq m$. Then there is at least one commodity, $n \neq m$, and two traders, i and j, such that $v_{in}^{\tau+1} > 0$ and $v_{jn}^{\tau+1} < 0$. By hypothesis, there is exactly one period, s, when $\pi^s(i) = j$. By (3), $v_{in}^s \geqslant v_{in}^{\tau+1}$ and $v_{jn}^s \leqslant v_{jn}^{\tau+1}$. If the traders followed (1), either $|v_{jn}^s| \geqslant |v_{in}^s|$, in which case $v_{in}^{s+1} = 0$ or $|v_{jn}^s| < |v_{in}^s|$, in which case $v_{jn}^{s+1} = 0$. They cannot both be non-zero, contradicting the assertion that $v_{in}^{\tau+1} \neq 0$. From (U.1) $p \cdot z_i = 0$ so $v_{in}^{\tau+1} = 0$, for all $n \neq m$, implies $v_{im}^{\tau+1} = 0$, as well. Thus (E) is fulfilled for all n.

By hypothesis

$$p_m b_{im} = p_m w_{im}^1 \geqslant p \cdot [z_i]^+ - p_m[z_{im}]^+ = p \cdot [v_i^1]^+ - p_m[v_{im}^1]^+$$

and from (3)

$$[v_i^1]^+ \geqslant \sum_{t=1}^{t=s} [x_i^t]^+ \qquad (s = 1, \ldots, \tau)$$

Therefore

$$\begin{aligned} p_m w_{im}^s &= p_m w_{im}^1 - p \cdot \left(\sum_{t=1}^{t=s-1} x_i^t \right) \geqslant p_m w_{im}^1 - p \cdot \left(\sum_{t=1}^{t=s-1} [x_i^t]^+ \right) \\ &\geqslant p_m w_{im}^1 - p \cdot [v_i^1]^+ \geqslant 0 \qquad (s = 1, \ldots, \tau + 1). \end{aligned}$$

Q.E.D.

Between the two trading rules, σ and μ, and the slack conditions they impose, can we point to one as more efficient than the other? Within the confines of the model, we cannot. Nevertheless, it should be recognized that these qualifying conditions on initial endowments are fundamentally different. One rule requires that the slack be "real" and concentrated in a single agent; the other requires that the slack be in value, concentrated in a single commodity. With trading rule σ, trader 1 acts as a clearinghouse for excess supplies and demands. But there is a crucial difficulty. Trader 1 cannot perform his function without having, to start, substantial quantities of his own commodities. There is no way of getting around this requirement if trades are to satisfy (A) and (E).[19]

[19] With only a modest endowment to start, trader 1 could act as the unique redistributor by accepting all commodities offered for sale and filling purchase orders from previously received supplies. Clearly, if *quid pro quo* is to be maintained in every exchange, full execution will require many more periods than are contained on one round.

In trading rule μ, the amounts b_{im} are unimportant as long as they are positive and p_m is sufficiently large. These features are peculiar to commodity m only. In trading rule μ, the proof of Theorem 4 shows that part (1) of the rule almost suffices to guarantee (A), (D), and (E). It fails only in not satisfying *quid pro quo*. The sole purpose of trade in commodity m is to establish a counting device to insure that the sum of additions to and subtractions from the value of one's holdings during the course of trade is zero. That the device is embodied in a tangible commodity is clearly inessential.[20]

6. CONCLUSION

Jevons writes that difficulties of barter arise because of the absence of double coincidence of wants.[21]

> The earliest form of exchange must have consisted in giving what was not wanted directly for that which was wanted. This simple traffic we call *barter*..., and distinguish it from sale and purchase in which one of the articles exchanged is intended to be held only for a short time until it is parted with in a second act of exchange. The object which thus temporarily intervenes in sale and purchase is money.
>
> The first difficulty of barter is to find two persons whose disposable possessions mutually suit each others wants. There may be many people wanting, and many possessing those things wanted; but to allow an act of barter, there must be a double coincidence which will rarely happen [**5**, p. 3].

Monetary exchange requires only single coincidence: a demander of a commodity encountering a supplier of the commodity and paying the supplier in money. Why should a trader refuse to exchange one excess supply for another? Why is double coincidence regarded as necessary for non-monetary exchange?

In the presence of double coincidence, barter exchange can take place in a fully decentralized way. Given double coincidence, execution of a given redistribution of goods requires traders to consult only their own and their current trading partner's excess supplies and demands and then trade so as to yield up their excess supplies and fulfill their excess demands. In the absence of double coincidence such a trading rule will achieve an inefficient allocation far from competitive equilibrium [**9, 11**]. If the trading rule is relaxed to permit sellers to accept payment in commodities for which they have no excess demand, there is always a centralized rule but, in general, no decentralized rule which guarantees full execution in a limited number of trades. Full and decentralized execution is achieved through monetary exchange.

University of California at Los Angeles
and
Yale University

Manuscript received November, 1973.

[20] If it were, it is hard to see how we could have advanced from the abacus to the pencil-and-paper method of doing sums. See [**9**]. The structure of the present model suggests approaches for further research: introducing specialization in production and exchange, making monetary exchange even more essential; allowing the order of trade to be a matter of choice so that by selling before buying one may choose to reduce the required amount of initial money balances.

[21] Other classical writers including Smith and Mill make virtually the same argument.

APPENDIX

Propositions 2 through 5 are restated and proved. Notation and definitions are found in Section 4.

PROPOSITION 2: *A necessary condition for* (A), (D), *and* (E) *to hold for all* $Z \in \mathscr{U}$ *is that if* $Z \in \mathscr{M}$, *trades must satisfy trading rule* γ.

PROOF: It is demonstrated in the text that rule γ is necessary at $t = 1$. Following γ at $t = 1$ implies $v_2^2 = 0$. If at $t = 2$ we ignore the presence of trader 2 whose excess demands are zero, we may apply Lemma 4 to obtain the desired result. It only remains to show that if trader 2 does exchange at any date $t > 1$, (A) and (E) are contradicted. Trader 2 is precluded from exchange at $t = 3$ when he meets the dummy trader 5 and at $t = 5$, when he meets no one. Clearly, if his first non-zero trade is at $t = 4$, (A) and (E) are impossible, since he would then acquire an excess demand which he could not fulfill in the subsequent period of no trade. This leaves $a_2^2 \neq 0$ as the remaining possibility. There appear to be numerous ways of showing a contradiction. One is as follows: assume e, $(a - c)$, and $(d + e - b)$ all greater than zero. Since $v_2^2 = 0$ and endowments are minimally sufficient, $w_2^2 = (0, 0, e, 0)$. Thus if $a_2^2 \neq 0$, 2 must give up some amount, δ, of commodity 3 to 4, his partner at $t = 2$. Since $w_4^2 = w_4^1 = (a - c, 0, d + e - b, 0)$, the only way for 4 to satisfy *quid pro quo* is to give up δ of commodity 1, so $0 < \delta \leqslant \min(e, a - c)$.

Now, $v_{11}^1 = a$ and by non-negativity $v_{11}^2 = v_{11}^1$ and $v_{11}^3 = v_{11}^4 = a - c$ and 1's last opportunity to exchange is at $t = 3$ when he meets trader 4. However, because 4 gave up δ of commodity 1 at $t = 2$, $v_{11}^4 > a - c > w_{41}^4 = a - c - \delta$. So 1's demand for commodity 1 will remain unfulfilled. *Q.E.D.*

PROPOSITION 3: *For any* $Z \in \mathscr{N}$, *a necessary condition for (A) and (E) is that trades satisfy (P) at* $t = 2$.

PROOF: $Z \in \mathscr{N}$ is defined by the parameters (a, b, c, d), and since trade at $t = 1$ takes place only between traders 1 and 2 redistributing their excess supplies of commodities 3 and 4, V^2 will belong to the class $\mathscr{N}$ with $w_i^2 = -[v_i^2]^-$ and will be defined by the parameters (a, b', c, d), $0 \leqslant b' \leqslant 1$. For any $V^2 \in \mathscr{N}$, we shall examine some necessary conditions for (A) and (E).

Let r_n be the absolute value of the amount of commodity n exchanged at $t = 2$ between $\overline{13}$ and let s_n be analogously defined for the pair $\overline{24}$. Trader 3 cannot give up more of commodity 1 than $w_{31}^2 = w_{31}^1 = c$. If $c > a$ and $c \geqslant r_1 > a$, trader 3 will have on hand at the start of the fourth period only $c - r_1$ of commodity 1 to meet trader 2's excess demand which, at the very least, is $1 - a - (1 - c) = c - a$. Since $c \geqslant r_1 > a$, and $t = 4$ is 2's last trading opportunity, (A) and (E) are contradicted. Therefore, $r_1 \leqslant \min(a, c)$ which implies that trader 1 should not take more of commodity 1 than will fulfill his excess demand. Reasoning along the same lines yields $s_2 \leqslant \min(a, c)$; $r_2, s_1 \leqslant \min(1 - a, 1 - c)$; $r_3, s_4 \leqslant \min(b', d)$; and $r_4, s_3 \leqslant \min(1 - b', 1 - d)$.

The above inequalities on r_n and s_n prohibit a positive excess demand from being increased or converted into a negative. Also shown above was that if $Z \in \mathscr{N}$, endowments at $t = 2$ would be minimally sufficient for excess demands which makes it impossible by (A) for a negative excess demand to be increased (in absolute value) or converted into a positive. These conditions define (P). *Q.E.D.*

PROPOSITION 4: *There exists no trading rule satisfying (A) such that for all* $Z \in \mathscr{M} \cup \mathscr{N}$, *the application of trading rule* γ *at* $t = 2$ *will exhibit property (P).*

PROOF: For all $Z \in \mathscr{M} \cup \mathscr{N}$, if trades at $t = 1$ satisfy (A), then v_1^2 must be of the form $(a, 1 - a, -b', b' - 1)$, $0 \leqslant b' \leqslant 1$, and $v_3^2 = v_3^1$ must be $(-c, c - 1, d, 1 - d)$. Since $\overline{13}$ are trading partners at $t = 2$, apply the results of Lemma 3 to exhibit the necessary and sufficient conditions under which rule γ and property (P) will overlap. They are as follows:

$$(*) \qquad \min(a, c) + \min(1 - a, 1 - c) = \min(b', d) + \min(1 - b', 1 - d)$$

which describes that coincidence where excess demands can be reduced to the maximum extent (satisfying part (1) of γ) without additional trade to maintain *quid pro quo* (not violating (P)). Such an exact state cannot always obtain.

Suppose the contrary. Then, it must be true that for all $0 \leqslant a, b, c, d \leqslant 1$, there exists b', $0 \leqslant b' \leqslant 1$, satisfying (*) above. But, for all b', $0 \leqslant b' \leqslant 1$,

$$\min(b', d) + \min(1 - b', 1 - d) \geqslant \min(d, 1 - d);$$

and, for any δ, $0 \leqslant \delta \leqslant 1$, there exist values of a and c, $0 \leqslant a, c \leqslant 1$, such that

$$\delta \geqslant \min(a, c) + \min(1 - a, 1 - c).$$

Since a, c, and d are independent, they may be chosen such that $\min(d, 1 - d) > \delta$, and condition (*) is not satisfied. *Q.E.D.*

PROPOSITION 5: *(i) For all $Z \in \mathcal{M} \cup \mathcal{N}$, if z_1 is defined by (a, b) and trades satisfy (A), then $\overline{v}_1^2$ is defined by (a, b'), $0 \leqslant b' \leqslant 1$; and (ii) if (A), (D), and (E) are to hold for all $Z \in \mathcal{U}$, the trading pair $\overline{13}$ will not be able to determine at $t = 2$ whether $Z \in \mathcal{M}$ or $\mathcal{N}$.*

PROOF: (i) For trader 1, whether $\mathcal{M}$ or $\mathcal{N}$, at $t = 1$ he can only trade in commodities 3 and 4. If $\mathcal{M}$, then $a_1^1 = (0, 0, x, -x)$ where $\min(e, 0) \leqslant x \leqslant \max(e, 0)$. Since $v_1^2 = v_1^1 - a_1^1$, set $b' = b - x$ and obtain $0 \leqslant b' \leqslant 1$. If $\mathcal{N}$, then $a_1^1 = (0, 0, x, -x)$ where $-b \leqslant x \leqslant 1 - b$. Again, set $b' = b - x$ to get $0 \leqslant b' \leqslant 1$.

(ii) From Proposition 2, it has been shown that if $Z \in \mathcal{M}$, trader 1 must set $b' = b - e$. Therefore, if $Z \in \mathcal{N}$, and trader 1 changes from b to any $\bar{b}$, $0 \leqslant \bar{b} \leqslant 1$, there exists $Z \in \mathcal{M}$ with e such that $\bar{b} = b - e$. For trader 3, $a_3^1 = 0$ for all $Z \in \mathcal{M} \cup \mathcal{N}$. Since traders can only recall their previous trades and not their previous partners' excess demands, the observations made by 1 and 3 in $\mathcal{M}$ or $\mathcal{N}$ are indistinguishable at $t = 2$. *Q.E.D.*

In the proofs of Propositions 1–5, care has been taken to show that the results hold when the parameters satisfy inequality rather than equality conditions. This suggests that Theorem 2 holds for a positive fraction of all $Z \in \mathcal{U}$. It would be interesting to inquire whether the fraction of economies for which there exists no decentralized rule leading to full execution increases with the number of individuals and commodities.

REFERENCES

[1] BRADLEY, GORDON: "Trading Rules for a Decentralized Exchange Economy," in *Symposium on the Theory of Scheduling and its Applications*, ed. S. E. Elmaghrabig. New York: Springer-Verlag, 1973.

[2] CLOWER, ROBERT W.: "Is There an Optimal Money Supply?" *The Journal of Finance*, 25 (1970), 425–433.

[3] ———: "A Reconsideration of the Microfoundations of Monetary Theory," *Western Economic Journal*, 5 (1967), 1–8.

[4] HAHN, FRANK: "On Some Problems of Proving the Existence of Equilibrium in a Money Economy," in *The Theory of Interest Rates*, ed. F. H. Hahn and F. P. R. Brechling. London: Macmillan, 1965.

[5] JEVONS, WILLIAM S.: *Money and the Mechanism of Exchange*. London: D. Appleton and Co., 1875.

[6] KURZ, MORDECAI: "Equilibrium with Transactions Cost and Money in a Single-Market Exchange Economy," Technical Report No. 51, Institute for Mathematical Studies in the Social Sciences, Stanford University, January, 1972.

[7] MACLANE, SAUNDERS, AND GARRETT BIRKHOFF: *Algebra*. New York: Macmillan, 1967.

[8] MARSCHAK, JACOB: "The Rationale of Money Demand and of 'Money Illusion'," *Metroeconomica*, 2 (1950), 71–100.

[9] OSTROY, JOSEPH M.: "The Informational Efficiency of Monetary Exchange," *American Economic Review*, 63 (1973), 597–610.

[10] SONTHEIMER, KEVIN: "On the Determination of Money Prices," *Journal of Money, Credit, and Banking*, 4 (1972), 489–508.

[11] STARR, ROSS M.: "The Structure of Exchange in Barter and Monetary Economies," *Quarterly Journal of Economics*, 88 (1972), 290–302.

[12] ———: "The Price of Money in a Pure Exchange Monetary Economy with Taxation," *Econometrica*, 42 (1974), 45–54.

13

DECENTRALIZED NON-MONETARY TRADE

by Ross M. Starr

It was shown in Ostroy-Starr (selection 12) that the availability of a monetary commodity allowed a simple informationally decentralized trading procedure to implement the equilibrium allocation in limited time. It was shown that the use of money economizes on organizational complexity. The alternative, presented in this section, is to retain the organizational simplicity of monetary trade but to allow all goods to act as media of exchange. This process does not generally fully implement the equilibrium allocation in a fixed finite time, but it does converge over time to full implementation. Hence, we conclude that a specialized monetary commodity allows achievement simply in limited time of a reallocation that could be achieved in its absence equally simply over a longer period. Ostroy-Starr (selection 12) showed that money saves on organizational complexity. This selection demonstrates an alternative interpretation: that money saves trading time.

The following is reprinted with permission from *Econometrica,* vol. 44, No. 5, 1976. © 1976, The Econometric Society.

ISBN 0-12-663970-1

Econometrica, Vol. 44, No. 5 (September, 1976)

DECENTRALIZED NONMONETARY TRADE

BY ROSS M. STARR[1]

"[Money] is a machine for doing quickly and commodiously, what would be done, though less quickly and commodiously, without it."
J. S. Mill, *Principles of Political Economy* (III: VII 3)

IT IS SHOWN in [**2**] that the use of money in trade allows the achievement of an equilibrium allocation of commodities in fixed trading time; the allocation could otherwise be achieved without the use of money in a fashion requiring more elaborate organization of the trading process. This confirms Mill's contention on the "commodious" nature of monetary trade. This note investigates a nonmonetary trading procedure with organization no more elaborate than monetary trade but requiring more trading time for achievement of an equilibrium allocation. Once again Mill's contention is verified. The nonmonetary process is equally commodious (simple in its organization) but a good deal slower.

The theorem below, in conjunction with Theorems 2 and 4 of [**2**], develops the trade-off between time required to achieve equilibrium allocation and the use of money. The restrictions on bilateral trade implied by constraints of nonnegativity, quid pro quo, and informational decentralization are investigated in [**1** and **2**]. It is argued [**2**, Theorem 4] that a medium of exchange universally held in quantity sufficient to finance intended net purchases allows trade to an equilibrium allocation to be achieved in a single sequence of meetings (one for each pair) among the traders of an economy. Consider trade similarly restricted in the absence of a universally held medium of exchange. Theorem 2 in [**2**] says that, in this case, it will not generally be possible to achieve the equilibrium allocation in a single round of decentralized trade. The analysis of nonmonetary trade below shows that if the time available for trade is extended, a decentralized process converges geometrically to the equilibrium allocation.

The trading process represents a barter procedure without a restriction of double coincidence of wants; it may be viewed as a "monetary" procedure where all goods act as "money". The analysis of [**2**] suggested that the use of money economizes on information (with respect to individual traders' excess supplies and demands) and coordination. The theorem below says alternatively that the use of money economizes on trading time. Barter mechanisms can succeed as quickly as monetary trade if coordination and sufficient market information are freely available [**2**, Theorem 2]. In their absence, successful barter may require much longer.

All notation and conventions are taken from [**2**].

DECENTRALIZED NONMONETARY TRADE, RULE γ

An anarchic, intuitive, and informationally decentralized approach is for traders to trade in all goods such that one agent has an excess supply and the other an excess demand, until the smaller of the two is exhausted. Quid pro quo is then maintained by payment from the debtor to the creditor in goods of which the debtor has an excess supply. This is rule γ of [**2**] and it works essentially as the monetary trade rule (rule μ of [**2**]) with all goods indiscriminately acting as media of exchange. If rule γ is followed for several rounds the value of unsatisfied excess demand remaining at the end of round v converges to 0 as $(1/2)^v$. I have not been able

[1] I am indebted to Joseph Ostroy for collaboration in an earlier essay. Errors are my own. The hospitality of the London School of Economics and the Institute for Mathematical Studies in the Social Sciences, Stanford University was very helpful. The support of the Cowles Foundation for Research in Economics at Yale University is gratefully acknowledged. The research described in this paper was undertaken by grants from the National Science Foundation and from the Ford Foundation.

to show that full execution will be achieved in finite time, nor have I been able to discover an example where trading rule γ continues indefinitely without achieving full execution.

Recall that v_{in}^t is i's unsatisfied excess demand or supply of commodity n.

TRADING RULE γ: For $\pi^t(i) = j$, let $a_i^t = x_i^t + y_i^t$ and $a_j^t = x_j^t + y_j^t$ where

$$(1) \qquad x_{in}^t = -x_{jn}^t = \begin{cases} 0 & \text{if } v_{in}^t v_{jn}^t \geqslant 0, \\ \min(|v_{in}^t|, |v_{jn}^t|) & \text{if } v_{in}^t > 0 \text{ and } v_{jn}^t < 0, \\ -\min(|v_{in}^t|, |v_{jn}^t|) & \text{if } v_{in}^t < 0 \text{ and } v_{jn}^t > 0, \end{cases}$$

and $y_i^t = -y_j^t$ is constructed according to

$$(2) \qquad \begin{cases} [v_i^t - x_i^t]^- < y_i^t < 0 & \text{and} \quad p \cdot (x_i^t + y_i^t) = 0, \quad \text{if } p \cdot x_i^t > 0, \\ [v_j^t - x_j^t]^- < y_j^t < 0 & \text{and} \quad p \cdot (x_j^t + y_j^t) = 0, \quad \text{if } p \cdot x_j^t > 0. \end{cases}$$

Part (1) says that when i and j meet to trade they scan their respective excess supplies and demands to see if i has an excess supply in a good of which j has an excess demand or if j has an excess supply of a good for which i has an excess demand. If so, the goods go from the supplier to the demander in quantity sufficient to exhaust the excess supply or fulfill the excess demand, whichever is smaller. This trade will usually leave one of the traders a net debtor to the other. Part (2) specifies that the debtor settle accounts by sending to the creditor goods of sufficient value from his excess supplies.

Rule γ fulfills all the conditions of [**2**]. It is decentralized [**2**, D.1] requiring of i and j that they base their trading decision only on their own current excess demands and supplies. Rule γ is even less informationally demanding than the monetary trade rule μ of [**2**] since γ does not require that one distinguish a specific universally-agreed-upon commodity as "money". Nonnegativity [**2**, A.1] follows since traders deliver only their excess supplies. Pairwiseness [**2**, A.2] is definitional. Quid pro quo [**2**, A.3], that traders pay for what they get, comes directly from (2) in the specification of γ.

Rule γ implies a lower bound on the volume of trade. In the course of one round all outstanding excess supplies must be traded at least once (see Lemma 2, below). But no more than half (in value terms) of an exchange can be for maintenance of quid pro quo. The remainder according to rule γ must be for fulfillment of excess demands. Thus, in the course of each round, at least half of the excess demands outstanding at the start of the round are fulfilled (Lemma 3). Geometric convergence to the equilibrium allocation then follows by iteration.

LEMMA 1: *Let trade proceed by rule γ. Then $k \geqslant 0$, $v_{in}^t \leqslant 0$ imply $v_{in}^{t+k} \leqslant 0$.*

Lemma 1 notes that rule γ will never allow an excess supply to be changed to an excess demand.

LEMMA 2:[2] *Let trade proceed by rule γ. Then for each i, n, $|\Sigma_{T=1}^{\tau} [a_{in}^{t+T}]^-| \geqslant |[v_{in}^t]^-|$.*

Lemma 2 says that during one round, each trader must engage in transactions in each commodity at least as great as the excess supplies of the commodity he held at the start of the round. The argument for this is simple. For each such excess supply, either the holder will trade it when he meets a demander or he will have already spent it in paying for a desired acquisition. By Lemma 1, he will confront during one round demanders for all the excess supplies with which he started the round. Hence, the result is established.

[2] Recall the following notations from [**2**]. τ is the number of trading periods in one round. In τ periods each trader meets each other trader precisely once. $[x]^- \equiv \min[0, x]$; $[x]^+ = \max[0, x]$. If x is a vector, $[x]^+ = ([x_1]^+, [x_2]^+, \ldots, [x_N]^+)$.

LEMMA 3: *Let trade proceed by rule* γ. $\Sigma_i p \cdot [v_i^{t+\tau}]^+ \leqslant \frac{1}{2} \Sigma_i p \cdot [v_i^t]^+$.

Lemma 3 says that in one round of trade (τ trading periods) the value at p of unsatisfied demand remaining at the end of the round must be no more than half what it was at the start of the round. From Lemma 2 we know that the value of the total volume of trade in the round evaluated at p must be at least as large as the value of excess demands at the beginning of the round. Trade is either to satisfy demands or fulfill quid pro quo. But, by the specification of γ, no more than half of the trade can be for quid pro quo because to each of the latter corresponds a demand fulfilling trade. Further, by Lemma 1, supplies are not converted to demands. Thus, in one round of trade the value of unsatisfied demands is reduced to, at most, half of its previous level. The theorem then follows merely by iteration of Lemma 3.

THEOREM: *Let trade proceed by rule* γ. *For* $v = 1, 2, \ldots, \Sigma_i p \cdot [v_i^{1+v\tau}]^+ \leqslant (\frac{1}{2})^v \Sigma_i p \cdot [z_i]^+$.

PROOF OF LEMMA 1: $v_{in}^t \leqslant 0$ implies $v_{in}^t \leqslant x_{in}^t \leqslant 0$.

Case 1:

$$0 \geqslant y_{in}^t \geqslant v_{in}^t - x_{in}^t,$$
$$v_{in}^{t+1} = v_{in}^t - (x_{in}^t + y_{in}^t),$$
$$0 \geqslant v_{in}^t - x_{in}^t - y_{in}^t = v_{in}^{t+1}.$$

Case 2:

$$y_{in} \geqslant 0,$$
$$v_{in}^t - x_{in}^t \leqslant 0, \qquad v_{in}^{t+1} = v_{in}^t - (x_{in}^t + y_{in}^t),$$
$$v_{in}^{t+1} = v_{in}^t - x_{in}^t - y_{in}^t \leqslant 0.$$

Thus, $v_{in}^{t+1} \leqslant 0$. By k-fold replication of the same argument $v_{in}^{t+k} \leqslant 0$. *Q.E.D.*

PROOF OF LEMMA 2: If $v_{in}^t = 0$ the result follows trivially. Consider i, n so that $v_{in}^t < 0$. Let i and j meet in $t + T_j$. For each commodity n, define $l(n) \subset I$ so that $j \in l(n)$ if and only if $v_{jn}^t > 0$. Consider $\Sigma_{j \in l(n)} v_{jn}^{t+T_j}$.

Case 1: $\Sigma_{j \in l(n)} v_{jn}^{t+T_j} = 0$. By Lemma 1, under rule γ this can occur only if $|\Sigma_{T=1}^{\tau} [a_{in}^{t+T}]^-| \geqslant |v_{in}^t|$ and we are done.

Case 2: $\Sigma_{j \in l(n)} v_{jn}^{t+T_j} > 0$. For each $j \in l(n)$ either $v_{in}^{t+T_j} = 0$ and we are done, or $v_{in}^{t+T_j} < 0$ and $a_{in}^{t+T_j} = -\min(|v_{jn}^{t+T_j}|, |v_{in}^{t+T_j}|)$. Then either $a_{in}^{t+T_j} = v_{in}^{t+T_j}$ and we are done or $v_{in}^{t+T_j} - a_{in}^{t+T_j} < 0$. But if this inequality holds for all $j \in l(n)$, then $\Sigma_{j \in l(n)} v_{jn}^{t+T_j+1} = 0$ and $\Sigma_{T=1}^{\tau} |[a_{in}^{t+T}]^-| \geqslant |[v_{in}^t]^-|$. *Q.E.D.*

PROOF OF LEMMA 3: By Lemma 2 we have $p \cdot [\Sigma_{T=1}^{\tau} (x_i^{t+T} + y_i^{t+T})]^+ \geqslant p \cdot [v_i^t]^+$. But $\Sigma_i p \cdot [x_i^{t+T}]^+ \geqslant \Sigma_i p \cdot [y_i^{t+T}]^+$ so $\Sigma_i p \cdot [\Sigma_{T=1}^{\tau} x_i^{t+T}]^+ \geqslant \frac{1}{2} \Sigma_i p \cdot [v_i^t]^+$ and $[v_i^{t+\tau}]^+ = [v_i^t]^+ - [\Sigma_{T=1}^{\tau} x_i^{t+T}]^+$. Hence, $\Sigma_i p \cdot [v_i^{t+\tau}]^+ \leqslant \frac{1}{2} \Sigma_i p \cdot [v_i^t]^+$. *Q.E.D.*

PROOF OF THEOREM: By iteration of Lemma 3.

University of California, Davis

Manuscript received June, 1975.

REFERENCES

[1] OSTROY, JOSEPH M.: "The Informational Efficiency of Monetary Exchange," *American Economic Review*, 63 (1973), 597–610.

[2] OSTROY, JOSEPH M., AND ROSS M. STARR: "Money and the Decentralization of Exchange," *Econometrica*, 42 (1974), 1093–1113.

Part III

Transaction Costs and Intertemporal Allocation

14

TRANSACTION COSTS AND INTERTEMPORAL ALLOCATIONS: MONEY AS A STORE OF VALUE

Modelling the foundations of the role of money as a store of value requires modelling the market implementation of the intertemporal allocation of consumption and production. An allocation plan can be arranged on futures markets as in the Arrow-Debreu model. Alternatively, assets can be carried intertemporally and liquidated on spot markets to finance expenditure.

The Arrow-Debreu Walrasian general equilibrium model positively denies a role for money as a store of value. Fortunately, in doing so it clarifies the role of a store of value and necessary conditions for money's usefulness. In the Arrow-Debreu model, all trade takes place at a single instant prior to actual production and consumption of goods. Goods are described by their characteristics, location, and date of delivery. A household's endowment consists of goods (including labor) available at a variety of dates. Its budget is simply the value of this endowment plus the present discounted value of its share of the streams of future business profits. The budget is in the nature of a lifetime budget constraint. The presence of the futures markets eliminates the distinction between income and wealth. Given this lifetime budget constraint, the household allocates its wealth to the purchase of present and future consumption. It acquires a portfolio (of present goods and of contracts for future delivery) sufficient to exhaust its budget constraint. Firms buy contracts for present and future inputs, and sell contracts for present and future output, to maximize the present discounted value of profits. Once these contracts are fully arranged, the balance of economic activity consists of their

ISBN 0-12-663970-1

fulfillment. There is no need for markets to reopen in the future—all desirable trades have already been arranged. But without reopening of markets, there is no function for money as a store of value. Hence the Arrow-Debreu theory establishes sufficient conditions for money to be useless and positively denies it any intertemporal allocative function.

Though striking, this conclusion is unsurprising; money has no job to perform here because its job is being done by futures markets. The Arrow-Debreu futures markets are designed to perform the two principal intertemporal allocative functions: price and output determination at each date and intertemporal reallocation of purchasing power. The first function could be performed by spot markets (with intertemporal perfect foresight). The second function is a capital market function. The futures markets allow sales of current output to finance purchases for future delivery, hence supplanting the savings role of money. Futures markets allow sales of future output to finance current purchases, hence fulfilling the role of a debt market. With a full set of futures markets, separate debt instruments are otiose. The equilibrium allocation of lifetime consumption plans and intertemporal production plans is Pareto efficient. Hence the model provides sufficient conditions for the uselessness of money as a store of value and for the uselessness of capital markets.

Conversely, if the conditions that allow the futures markets so fully to exercise their functions are absent, we may expect a role for money and for futures markets in money (debt instruments). In actual economies, the Arrow-Debreu conditions are seldom fulfilled. Futures markets for most goods are generally inactive (loosely speaking, do not exist). The reason for this is the structure of transaction costs, which favors spot over futures transactions. In the presence of differential transaction costs on spot and future transactions, the Arrow-Debreu model becomes inapplicable and we are led to the sequence economy models of Radner (1972), Hahn (selection 16), and Starrett (selection 17).

Differential transaction costs on spot and futures markets (in particular, higher costs on futures) imply that markets may reopen over time and agents will face a budget constraint at each date. For a given agent, the time pattern of the value of planned consumption may differ from that of endowment. In order to implement such plans consistent with the sequence of budget constraints, futures markets may be used or real assets held intertemporally as stores of value. Both approaches imply incurring real resource costs needed only for fulfillment of budget constraints and technically unnecessary to implementing the allocation. These costs, and any reallocation of consumption plans undertaken to avoid them, represent an efficiency loss. Introduction of fiat money—assumed to be transaction costless—results in a move to a Pareto efficient allocation. Hence the role of money as a store of value is confirmed in the sequence economy model as an essential element in achieving an efficient allocation over time in the presence of transaction costs.

Just as in the case of bilateral trade models, the budget constraint faced by individual agents takes a significantly different form in a sequence economy from the single lifetime budget constraint of the Arrow-Debreu world. The single lifetime budget constraint is replaced by a sequence of budget balance constraints over time. At each date, the value of goods and contracts for future delivery that an agent sells to the market must be at least as large as the value of goods and contracts he accepts from the market. Replacement of the single lifetime budget constraint by a sequence of periodic budget constraints imposes a transaction timing problem on the individual agent. He may be endowed primarily with current period goods, but wish to consume in the present and at a variety of future periods. In the presence of sufficient futures markets he could implement this plan by spot sales in the present, and simultaneous futures purchases for planned consumption. However, transaction costs in the futures markets may be higher than in spot markets. The only reason for using futures markets rather than spot markets is the sequential budget constraint, forcing the transaction dates of his sales and purchases to coincide. Hence the institutional constraint imposes real resource costs on the economy, and an efficiency loss results. Alternatively he could rely on spot markets and carry assets intertemporally to be sold to provide purchasing power. Any durable good, ownership claim, or futures contract can perform the function of shifting purchasing power forward or back in time, but transaction and storage costs associated with some instruments will be prohibitive. Once again, an efficiency loss results. A distinguishing feature of money is assumed to be its low transaction and storage costs as compared to goods and futures contracts. Households may transfer purchasing power over time by accumulating and depleting their money balances and by the use of money futures contracts (loans). If desired timing of purchase and sale transactions do not coincide, money acts as a carrier of purchasing power between the two transaction dates. Money as a store of value restores allocative efficiency by allowing both fulfillment of the sequential budget constraints and the use of spot goods transactions only, without distortion of the lifetime consumption plan.

Transaction costs are not a source of inefficiency in themselves. Part of economic activity is the reallocation of goods and resources. If that reallocation process is a resource-using activity, then resources devoted to it are engaged productively. The institutional setting of the non-monetary sequence economy may cause agents in equilibrium to undertake individually rational transactions, incurring consequent transaction costs, that are not technically necessary to the reallocation. Such an unnecessary resource expenditure is inefficient. In a model where futures markets have higher transaction costs than spot markets, use of futures markets is generally inconsistent with Pareto efficiency. Nevertheless, in a non-monetary economy, futures market transactions may be the only way simultaneously to fulfill budget constraints at each date and to achieve an intertemporal reallocation of consumption and production plans, (Hahn, selection 16). Money is then introduced (Starrett, selection 17) as an intertemporal asset that allows, in equilibrium, the reallocation to be achieved without the use of the costly futures markets. Goods will be traded on spot markets only and the intertemporal reallocation of purchasing power will take place through carrying of money from one date to the next. Pareto efficiency is described taking account of the minimum transaction costs necessary to achieve a proposed reallocation.

Transaction costs, like prices, are correctly computed as present discounted values. Hence one reason that transaction costs may be higher on futures markets than on spot markets is the timing with which the costs are actually incurred. Costs are incurred at the transaction date and at the delivery date. In the case of spot transactions these dates coincide. If the delivery date is in the distant future, then at a positive discount rate, the present discounted value of the transaction cost for a distant spot transaction will be small. In contrast, the transaction cost on a futures transaction conducted in the present, but with the same distant delivery date, may be substantial. Hence, time discounting notably strengthens the argument for reliance on spot rather than futures markets. Under uncertainty, the argument for spot markets as a low-cost device is again strengthened by considering Arrow-Debreu contingent commodity futures or Arrow securities markets as the alternatives. Because of the multiplicity of contingencies, many contingent futures contracts will be written that will not be executed by delivery. Subject to a different, possibly Pareto inefficient, allocation of risk-bearing, a reduction in the number of transactions and a corresponding reduction in transactions costs is achieved by reliance on spot rather than futures markets.

The studies here present three views on an economy with transaction costs. A descriptive approach (Foley selection 15, Kurz, selection 18) is concerned with the formal presentation of the concept of transaction costs and with the existence of general equilibrium in a model with these costs. The next, and most ambitious, is to use a transaction cost analysis to formalize and explain the role of money as a store of value (Hahn, selection 16; Starrett, selection 17). The intertemporal holding of money, or money-denominated financial instruments, is shown to represent a low transaction cost method of intertemporal reallocation. Finally we touch on a recurrent theme in monetary economics, the transaction demand for money as a stock in the presence of other financial assets (possibly with higher yield) (Heller-Starr, selection 19). Transactions are treated here in approximately the way production is treated in a conventional general equilibrium model. A transactions technology with inputs and outputs is posited. Transaction costs enter directly into individual agents' opportunity sets either as a differential between buying and selling prices or as a physical input requirement of the household transaction technology.

In Foley's elegant paper the transaction technology is a single price-taking profit maximizer for the economy as a whole. For any good, individual transactors face a buying price and a selling price. That is, if they wish to sell the good they receive a lower price than they would have to pay if they wished to buy. This wedge between buying and selling prices simply represents the cost of resources used in the transaction process by the specialized transacting firm. Geometrically it is to be represented as a household budget constraint kinked at the endowment point. Assuming continuity, convexity and a positive income (net of transactions costs), equilibrium exists.

The intertemporal models of Hahn and Starrett emphasize strongly the choice of trading date in agents' trading plans. This emphasis allows a distinct role in the Starrett paper for an intertemporal carrier of purchasing power of low transaction cost, money. Each good in the sequence economy models is distinguished by its transaction date and its delivery date. For spot transactions, the ones we usually see, these dates are the same. But for futures transactions, the transaction date precedes the delivery date. There is a single unified transaction technology operating as a profit-maximizing price taker. The technology is linear so a zero-profit condition is fulfilled. Individual transactors face different buying and selling prices.

Hahn (selection 16) sets up the formal structure of a sequence economy model with transaction costs and recognizes the possible inefficiency. Further, a strong sufficient condition for the sequence economy allocation to be efficient is developed. The sufficient condition, the "Debreu property," is that price ratios be the same for a given pair of goods at given delivery dates independent of the transaction date. This is a sufficient condition in equilibrium but it is not necessary, and we would not generally expect it to be fulfilled. After all, part of the information that prices should convey is the transaction cost. If transaction costs differ between spot and futures transactions, prices with the Debreu property would fail to reflect that information. Starrett (selection 17) then fully characterizes the inefficiency of the equilibrium allocation in a sequence economy and formulates the function of money as a transaction-costless store of value in overcoming the inefficiency.

The Kurz model individualizes the transaction technology. Each household faces its own transaction technology, incurs its own costs and provides its own resources (or those it purchases) to the transaction process. The market has a single price for each good, but the resources required to get goods to and from the market may be substantial. This formulation makes explicit the optimizing behavior of agents with regard to incurrring resource costs for transaction purposes.

The Heller-Starr model emphasizes the possibility of set-up costs or other non-convexity in transactions, while retaining the Kurz viewpoint that transaction technology and decision making are at the level of the individual transactor. Thus, households and firms may find it useful to concentrate their transactions at a particular time in order to take advantage of the scale economy. Scale economies at the household level pose a technical problem of discontinuity or non-convexity in behavior, which seems to preclude the possibility of market equilibrium. A now standard technique allows the discontinuities to be averaged out across individuals so that aggregate behavior is nearly continuous or nearly convex and an approximate equilibrium is achieved. Scale economies in transactions are a classic reason for the holding of inventories of goods and of money (Baumol, 1952; Tobin, 1956). A monetary economy is usually characterized by positive quantities of the monetary commodity held as a stock even when money's yield is dominated by other assets. Hence it is a useful step to establish an equilibrium with a demand for inventories of money.

The sequence economy model with transaction costs provides a rationale for the use of money in transactions and for holding money and money-denominated instruments over time in general equilibrium. No utility or taste for money is posited. Rather, the demand for money as a stock is derived from more fundamental assumptions.

SECTION 1

Transaction Costs in a One-Period Model

15

ECONOMIC EQUILIBRIUM WITH COSTLY MARKETING

by Duncan K. Foley

An essential step in modelling monetary behavior of the economy is to formalize the idea of transaction cost. Money and financial intermediaries are designed to reduce the real resource requirements of the trading process. In order to make this idea clear we must start by precisely stating those resource requirements. Foley does this by suggesting that households face two sets of prices—buying prices at which they can purchase goods, and (lower) selling prices at which they can sell endowment. The wedge between buying and selling prices reflects the real resource inputs used in the transaction process by firms engaging therein. The typical household budget frontier then is two half-hyperplanes meeting in a kink at the endowment point. Since the angle is (weakly) less than 180° the budget set is convex.

Given convexity of production and transaction technology (ruling out set-up costs on transactions) and other conventional assumptions, the existence of a general equilibrium is established. A significant outcome of the study is the characterization of sufficient conditions for the positive activity (loosely speaking, the "existence") of markets. A market for a good will exist when the difference between the lowest reservation price and highest opportunity cost exceeds the transactions cost.

The particular virtue of the present article is the crisp clarity it brings to formalizing the problem. It was among the earliest, along with Hahn's article (selection 16), to do so. All of the very effective structure of the Walrasian model is retained. The next step—from subsequent authors—is a treatment of money, finance, and intertemporal allocation.

The following is reprinted with permission from *Journal of Economic Theory*, N.2, © 1970.

ISBN 0-12-663970-1

Reprinted from JOURNAL OF ECONOMIC THEORY
Vol. 2, No. 3, September 1970

Economic Equilibrium with Costly Marketing

DUNCAN K. FOLEY*

Massachusetts Institute of Technology, Cambridge, Massachusetts 02139

1. INTRODUCTION

The traditional theory of general market equilibrium, the most famous rigorous presentation of which can be found in Debreu [1], remains the deepest scientific resource of economists, and is the basis of the most sophisticated attempts to study a wide range of economic problems. It is therefore disturbing that this theory, when applied to the complete problem of economic interaction over time, space, and in the presence of chance, predicts the formation of numerous markets in timedated, place-tagged, contingent commodities which do not actually exist. Corollary to this embarrassment is the prediction by the theory that economic agents will choose one plan of action good for all time and all contingencies, which they clearly do not.

The embarrassment does not come from the fact that the theory is too weak, but because it is too strong. Its assumptions are general and unexceptional but its conclusions awesomely specific. Confronted by this problem, which has become acute only as an aftermath of the rigorous mathematical formulation of the theory, economists have tried to find weak links in the underlying assumptions. One such weakness is the absence from the theory of any real resource costs in information gathering and processing, or in the operation of "markets."

It is my purpose here to outline a very simple modification of the traditional model in which it is possible to analyze the consequences of costs in the operation of "markets." I believe this modification sacrifices none of the generality and rigor which make the theory of general equilibrium so splendid. The modification does, however, drastically alter the stylized picture the theory yields. In particular, markets will not generally exist in unlikely contingencies or for deliveries in the distant future, nor will economic agents find it useful or even possible to bind themselves to a single unchanging plan.

* While writing this paper, I was a Ford Faculty Research Fellow.

The key aspect of the modification I propose is an alteration in the notion of "price." In the present model there are two prices in each market: a buyer's price and a lower seller's price. The difference between these yields an income which compensates the real resources used up in the operation of the markets.

2. Consumers and Demands

Each of n consumers has a consumption set $X^i \subset E^m$ (since there are m commodities) which defines the consumer's biologically and technically feasible consumption plans. A point $x^i \in X^i$ includes provision of services and resources which the consumer owns as negative numbers. On the set X^i there is a preference ordering $\succcurlyeq_i$.

The set $X = \Sigma_i X^i$ is the aggregate consumption set. $\hat{X}^i$ is the "attainable" consumption set for each consumer, the set of consumption plans for the consumer that the whole economy has resources and technical knowledge to provide.

I will make the following assumptions about X^i and $\succcurlyeq_i$:

(a.1) The aggregate consumption set X has a lower bound. (This implies that each X^i also has a lower bound.)

(a.2) For each i, X^i is closed and convex.

(b.1) For every consumption $\hat{x}^i \in \hat{X}^i$ there exists $x^i \in X^i$ with $x^i \succ \hat{x}^i$. (This assumption asserts that the full productive capacity of the economy is not sufficient to satiate any consumer completely.)

(b.2) For every $x^i \in X^i$ the sets

$$\{\bar{x}^i \in X^i \mid \bar{x}^i \succcurlyeq_i x^i\} \qquad \text{and} \qquad \{\bar{x}^i \in X^i \mid \bar{x}^i \preccurlyeq_i x^i\}$$

are closed in X^i.

(b.3) For every $x^i \in X^i$ the set

$$\{\bar{x}^i \in X^i \mid \bar{x}^i \succcurlyeq_i x^i\}$$

is convex.

(c.1) $0 \in X^i$ for all i.

The consumer faces two sets of prices, p^S and p^B. (I will very often write $\pi = p^B - p^S$ to denote the difference between these.) The cost of any consumption plan x^i will depend on the two vectors x^{iB} and x^{iS} defined by

$$x_j^{iB} = \max[x_j^{\,i}, 0]$$

and

$$x_j^{iS} = \min[x_j^i, 0].$$

x^{iB} is the vector of purchases and x^{iS} is the vector of sales. The value of a plan x^i is $p^B x^{iB} + p^S x^{iS}$.

For any wealth w^i, the consumer is restricted to the set $B^i(p^S, p^B, w^i) = \{x^i \in X^i / x^i = x^{iB} + x^{iS}$, where $p^B x^{iB} + p^S x^{iS} \leqslant w^i\}$.

It is easy to see that if $p_j^B < p_j^S$ for some commodity j the set B^i is unbounded because any consumer can buy and sell commodity j at a profit. In what follows I assume always that $p^B \geqslant p^S$, i.e., $\pi \geqslant 0$, and that $p^S \geqslant 0$.

In two dimensions, the consumer's budget set is the intersection of two price lines (see Fig. 1).

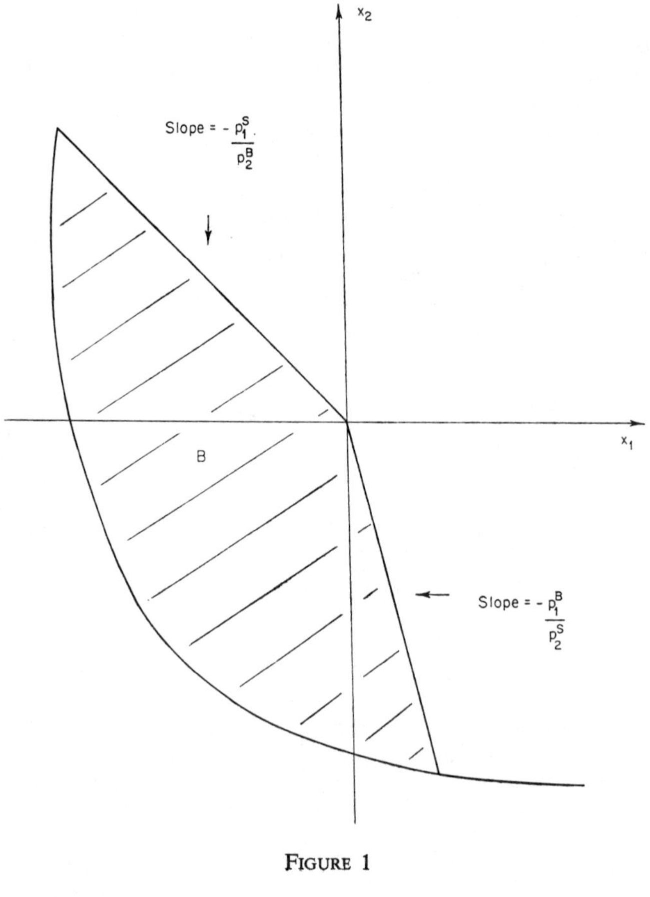

FIGURE 1

If every consumer has $w^i = 0$ and chooses a point x^i with $p^B x^{iB} + p^S x^{iS} = 0$, then in the aggregate $p^B x^B + p^S x^S = 0$, where $x^B = \Sigma_i x^{iB}$ and $x^S = \Sigma_i x^{iS}$, or writing $z = x^B + x^S$, $(p^B - p^S)x^B = -p^S z$.

This observation is analogous to Walras' Law, but has an interesting interpretation. The vector z is a vector of net consumer supplies and demands to producers. At any p^B, p^S pair, consumers are willing to release resources just equal in value to the total premium they pay through higher buying prices. In a pure exchange economy without production, the vector z represents resources used up in the operation of the markets.

It is possible to show that the budget set B^i is convex and then go on to prove that consumer demands in the two-price environment have the same continuity and convexity properties that hold in the one-price environment. I prefer to proceed by a shortcut, and to show that the consumer I have described is mathematically equivalent to another consumer in a one-price economy who satisfies the assumptions made above.

This useful way of describing consumer choice in the two-price environment is suggested by writing the budget constraint as

$$p^S \cdot x + (p^B - p^S)x^B = p^S \cdot x + \pi \cdot x^B \leqslant w.$$

The selling prices are applied to the entire bundle, with a premium for transactions at the buying prices. In fact, it is possible to define a new consumption set $\bar{X}^i \subset E^{2m}$ and new preferences on this set $\succcurlyeq_i'$ by the relations

(a) $\bar{X}^i = \{(x, z) \mid x \in x^i, z_j \geqslant \max[x_j, 0] \quad \text{for} \quad j = 1, ..., m\}$;

(b) if (x, z) and $(\bar{x}, \bar{z}) \in \bar{X}^i$, then $(x, z) \succcurlyeq_i' (\bar{x}, \bar{z})$ if $x \succcurlyeq_i \bar{x}$ in X^i.

It is easy to verify that if X^i and $\succcurlyeq_i$ satisfy assumptions (a.1), (a.2), (b.1), (b.2), and (b.3), then $\bar{X}^i$ and $\succcurlyeq_i'$ will satisfy them as well. The indifference curves in $\bar{X}^i$ will not exhibit strict monotonicity, since the commodities z do not make the consumer any better off. Fortunately equilibrium analysis is sophisticated enough to handle this situation (cf. Debreu [2]).

The key to proving that $\bar{X}^i$ and $\succcurlyeq_i'$ satisfy the other assumptions made above is to show that $\bar{X}^i$ is convex and closed if X^i is.

THEOREM 2.1. *If X^i is convex and closed, then $\bar{X}^i$ is convex and closed.*

Proof. First, take closure. Let $\{(x^q, z^q)\} \to (\hat{x}, \hat{z})$ be a sequence of points such that $(x^q, z^q) \in \bar{X}^i$ for all q. Since X^i is closed, $\hat{x} \in X^i$, being the limit of a sequence contained in X^i. The only other condition is that $\hat{z}_j \geqslant \max[\hat{x}_j, 0]$. Suppose that for some j, $\max[\hat{x}_j, 0] - \hat{z}_j > \epsilon$. For large

q, $|x_j^q - \hat{x}_j| < \epsilon/4$, $|z_j^q - \hat{z}_j| < \epsilon/4$, so that $\max[x_j^q, 0] - z_j^q > \epsilon/2$, which contradicts the assumption that $(x^q, z^q) \in \bar{X}^i$.

Next consider convexity. If $(\bar{x}, \bar{z})$ and $(\hat{x}, \hat{z}) \in \bar{X}^i$, and $(\tilde{x}, \tilde{z}) = \alpha(\bar{x}, \bar{z}) + (1 - \alpha)(\hat{x}, \hat{z})$ $(0 < \alpha < 1)$, convexity of X^i implies that $\tilde{x} \in X^i$. The problem is to check that $\tilde{z}_j \geqslant \max[\tilde{x}_j, 0]$ for $j = 1,..., m$.

$$\begin{aligned}\tilde{z}_j &= \alpha\bar{z}_j + (1 - \alpha)\hat{z}_j \geqslant \alpha \max[\bar{x}_j, 0] + (1 - \alpha)\max[\hat{x}_j, 0]\\ &= \max[\alpha\bar{x}_j, 0] + \max[(1 - \alpha)\hat{x}_j, 0]\\ &\geqslant \max[\alpha\bar{x}_j + (1 - \alpha)\hat{x}_j, 0]\\ &\geqslant \tilde{x}_j \qquad \text{Q.E.D.}\end{aligned}$$

The proofs that the $\bar{X}^i$ and $\succcurlyeq_i'$ also satisfy the other assumptions follow easily from this theorem.

It is also true that if the new consumer chooses (x^{i*}, z^*) and prices (p^{S*}, π^*) then the old consumer will choose x^{i*} at p^{S*} and $p^{B*} = p^{S*} + \pi^*$.

THEOREM 2.2. *Suppose* $(x^{i*}, z^*) \in \bar{X}^i$ *satisfies for* $p^{S*}, p^{B*} \geqslant 0$, $\pi^* = p^{B*} - p^{S*} \geqslant 0$,

(a) $p^{S*}x^{i*} + \pi^* z^* \leqslant w^i$;

(b) $(x^{i*}, z^*) \succcurlyeq_i' (x^i, z)$ *for all* $(x^i, z) \in \bar{X}^i$ *with* $p^{S*}x^i + \pi^* z \leqslant w^i$;

(c) $x^{i*} \in \hat{X}^i$.

Then $x^{i*} \in X^i$ *will satisfy*

(a¹) $p^{S*}x^{i*S} + p^{B*}x^{i*B} \leqslant w^i$;

(b¹) $x^{i*} \succcurlyeq_i x^i$ *for all* $x^i \in X^i$ *with* $p^{S*}x^{iS} + p^{B*}x^{iB} \leqslant w^i$.

Proof. Since $z_j^* \geqslant x_j^{i*B} = \max[x_j^{i*}, 0]$ and $p_j^B \geqslant 0$, part (a¹) follows immediately from (a).

Suppose there existed $\hat{x}^i \in X^i$ with $p^{S*}\hat{x}^{iS} + p^{B*}\hat{x}^{iB} \leqslant w^i$ and $\hat{x}^i \succ_i x^{i*}$. Then $(\hat{x}^i, \hat{x}^{iB}) \in \bar{X}^i$ by definition of $\bar{X}^i$, $p^{S*}\hat{x}^i + \pi^*\hat{x}^{iB} \leqslant w^i$, and $(\hat{x}^i, \hat{x}^{iB}) \succ_i' (x^{i*}, z^*)$, which is a contradiction. Q.E.D.

All the usual results of demand theory based on the assumptions (a.1), (a.2), (b.1), (b.2), (b.3), and (c.1) can be applied to the consumer with consumption set $\bar{X}^i$ and preferences $\succcurlyeq_i'$ and through him to an ordinary consumer in a two-price environment.

If the consumer's preferences can be represented by a utility function $u(x)$, his demand problem is the constrained maximization problem

$$\text{maximize } u(x) \text{ subject to } p^B x^B + p^S x^S \leqslant w.$$

The first order conditions are

$$\partial u/\partial x_j - \lambda p_j{}^B = 0 \qquad \text{if} \quad x_j > 0$$

and

$$\partial u/\partial x_j - \lambda p_j{}^S = 0 \qquad \text{if} \quad x_j < 0,$$

where λ is the Lagrangean shadow price corresponding to the wealth constraint, which depends on the prices.

Since $p_j{}^B \geqslant p_j{}^S$, these conditions can be written $p_j{}^S \leqslant (1/\lambda)(\partial u/\partial x_j) \leqslant p_j{}^B$, $j = 1,..., m$ where the left equality holds for $x_j < 0$ and the right equality for $x_j > 0$.

3. Production and Marketing

While consumers have no choice but to buy at the buying price and sell at the selling price in a market, at least some producers can involve themselves in marketing activities, at a cost in real resources. For producers, the terms "buying" and "selling" prices might better be replaced by the terms "retail" and "wholesale" prices. A firm can buy at the lower wholesale price or sell at the higher retail price if it expends real resources in marketing activities. Some firms may specialize in marketing activities, some in transformation, some may mix the two. One firm may buy a service or good wholesale and sell it to another firm retail. The production plan of a producer can be written (y^j, y^{Bj}), where y^j is the total net transaction the producer makes, and y^{Bj} is the vector of purchases and sales subject to the premium buying price.

The y^{Bj} vector may include both inputs or outputs. A firm that hires labor through an employment agency, for instance, will write its labor input in y^{Bj}. The profit arising from such a plan at prices (p^S, p^B) will be

$$\pi^j(p^S, \pi) = p^S y^j + \pi y^{Bj} \qquad \text{where} \quad \pi = p^B - p^S.$$

Some producers will do no marketing of their own, hiring resources at the buying price and selling their product at the selling price. Other producers may do all their marketing in all markets, hiring resources at the selling price and selling their output at the buying price. The second procedure, of course, will require more resources than the first, even if the total output is the same, if marketing is costly. Other producers may do some transactions at buying prices and others at selling prices.

What determines how much marketing a producer does for himself? The producer will market if the spread between buying and selling prices is large enough to make it profitable for him. If the spread is small a producer will prefer to leave the marketing to other producers.

If marketing activities were costless, there would be no spread between buying and selling prices and the economy would be the same as in the traditional models.

What are the costs involved in marketing activities? They include the effort required to inform buyers or sellers of the existence of a supply or demand for a commodity, and of the price. This may include advertising, costs of holding stocks for wide distribution, spoilage, breaking down commodities for retail sale, and product standardization and certification. The important feature of these costs is that they expend real resources without altering the characteristics of the delivered product.[1]

I assume that the set of feasible production plans for each producer, Y^j, has the following properties:

(d.1) $0 \in Y^j$ for all j. (This assumption, together with (c.1), assures that there are feasible allocations for the economy.)

(d.2) There is no $(y^j, y^{jB}) \in Y^j$ with $(y^j, y^{jB}) > 0$. (This rules out the possibility of free production or free marketing.)

(d.3) Y^j is a convex cone for all j If $(\bar{y}^j, \bar{y}^B) \in Y^j$ and $(\hat{y}^j, \hat{Y}^{jB}) \in Y^j$, then $(\alpha\bar{y}^j + \beta\hat{y}^j, \alpha\bar{y}^{jB} + \beta\hat{y}^{jB}) \in Y^j$ for $\alpha, \beta \geqslant 0$.)

(d.4) $Y = \sum_j Y^j$ is closed.

Assumption (d.3) rules out any set-up costs or indivisibilities in marketing activities. Many economists have argued that indivisibilities are characteristic of marketing activities.

4. Equilibrium

It is easy to generalize the notion of general competitive equilibrium to an economy with marketing costs.

Definition. A market equilibrium is a vector of prices (p^{S*}, π^*), a vector $x^{i*} \in X^i$ for each consumer, and a vector $(y^{j*}, y^{jB*}) \in Y^j$ for each producer such that

(a) x^{i*} is maximal with respect to $\succcurlyeq_i$ in $B^i(p^{S*}, \pi^*, 0)$;

(b) $p^{S*}y^{j*} + \pi^* y^{jB*} \geqslant p^{S*}y^j + \pi^* y^{jB}$ for all $(y^j, y^{jB}) \in Y^j$, $j = 1,..., k$;

(c) $\sum_i (x^{i*}, x^{i*B}) - \sum_j (y^{j*}, y^{jB*}) = 0$;

(d) $p^{S*} \neq 0, \pi^* \geqslant 0$.

[1] This is a copout.

In equilibrium, consumers are maximizing according to their preferences subject to the budget constraint, producers are maximizing profit both in ordinary production and in marketing activity, and all markets clear.

The equilibrium determines a distribution of marketing activities among producers, according to their various technologies and relative prices. Some firms will find it advantageous to specialize in marketing, that is, buying wholesale and selling retail without other transformations. Others may find it profitable to combine marketing and production; a large manufacturer in a city may open storefront employment offices, for example. In equilibrium the market balance condition (c) assures that whatever someone is selling wholesale, someone else is buying wholesale, and whatever someone buys retail, someone is selling retail. Some factors may never be marketed at all. The labor hired wholesale by the large manufacture is used by the firm directly and never resold at retail prices.

The easiest way to show the existence of such an equilibrium is to study an extended economy with $2m$ commodities, and apply to the extended economy known existence theorems. The best existence theorem for my purpose is contained in Debreu [2]. I paraphrase that result here.

THEOREM 4.1 (Existence of Quasiequilibrium). *An economy $\mathscr{E}$ defined by consumption sets X^i, preferences $\succcurlyeq_i$, production sets Y^j, and a vector $\{\Theta_{ij}\}$ indicating the i-th consumer's share of the profits of the j-th producer (if any) which satisfies assumptions* (a.1), (a.2), (b.1), (b.2), (b.3), (c.1), (d.1), (d.2), *and* (d.3) *has a* quasiequilibrium; *that is, there exists* $((x^{i*}), (y^{j*}), p^*) \subset ((X^i), (Y^j), E^m)$ *such that*

(a) x^{i*} *is maximal with respect to* $\succcurlyeq_i$ *in*

$$\left\{x^i \in X^i \,\middle|\, p^*x^{i*} \leqslant \sum_j \Theta_{ij} p^* y^{j*}\right\}, \quad \textit{or} \quad p^*x^{i*} = \min p^*X^i, \quad \textit{for every} \quad i;$$

(b) $p^*y^{j*} = \max p^*Y^j$ *for every* j;

(c) $\sum_i x^{i*} - \sum_j y^{j*} = 0$;

(d) $p^* \neq 0$.

I want to apply this theorem to the economy with consumption sets $\overline{X}^i$, preferences $\succcurlyeq_i'$, production sets Y^j, and an arbitrary vector (Θ_{ij}) with $\Theta_{ij} \geqslant 0$, $\sum_i \sum_j \Theta_{ij} = 1$.

This yields a set of consumption and production plans $((x^{i*}, z^{i*}), (y^{j*}, y^{Bj*}), (p^{S*}, \pi^*))$ with the properties

(a) $(x^{i*}, z^{i*}) \in \overline{X}^i$ is maximal with respect to $\succcurlyeq_i'$ in

$$\left\{(x^i, z^i) \in \overline{X}^i \,\middle|\, p^{S*}x^i + \pi^* z^i \leqslant \sum_j \Theta_{ij}(p^{S*}y^{j*} + \pi^* y^{Bj*})\right\},$$

or

$$p^{S*}x^{i*} + \pi^* z^{i*} = \min(p^{S*}, \pi^*)\,\overline{X}^i;$$

(b) $p^{S*}y^{j*} + \pi^* y^{Bj*} = \max(p^{S*}, \pi^*)\,Y^j$;

(c) $\sum_i (x^{i*}, z^{i*}) - \sum_j (y^{j*}, y^{Bj*}) = 0$;

(d) $(p^{S*}, \pi^*) \neq 0$.

This is practically equivalent to the definition of market equilibrium given above. To establish complete equivalence I need to show that $\pi^* \geqslant 0$, and that the profits of all producers are zero. The latter proposition follows from profit maximization and the assumption that production sets are cones. $\pi^* \geqslant 0$ follows from the unboundedness of $\overline{X}^i$ in the z^i components and assumption (b.1), since if $\pi_j^* < 0$, a consumer could increase z_j^i without limit and achieve a consumption outside $\hat{X}^i$ and preferred to X^{i*}.

This argument proves that a quasiequilibrium exists with market costs under the assumptions of traditional equilibrium analysis. The most important restriction involving market costs is the assumption that marketing, like other productive activities, is not subject to increasing returns to scale or indivisibilities.

The difficulty that some consumers may in fact be at a minimum wealth point in their consumption set and not at a preference maximizing point remains. Debreu [2] notes that existence of a true equilibrium, in which this situation occurs for no consumer, can be assured by requiring that (a) the production set intersect the interior of the aggregate consumption set, and that (b) if any consumer is at the minimum-wealth point in a quasiequilibrium, all are. This theorem carries over to the economy with marketing costs, because this model is mathematically identical to the model studied by Debreu.

In some situations there may be difficulties in showing that the requirement (b) above is met, because of the existence of the new artificial retail commodities. For example, Debreu defines an "always desired" commodity as one such that every consumer can reach a preferred point *in his consumption* set by increasing his consumption of that commodity only. This will not be possible for bought commodities in the marketing costs model because increasing only that component of the consumption bundle takes the consumer out of his consumption set, unless the corresponding retail component is also increased.

With the assumptions that each consumer can dispose of a finite amount of all commodities, and that there are production activities which produce every commodity retail using only wholesale inputs, it is possible to show that a quasiequilibrium is a true equilibrium. If any consumer is at the minimum wealth point in quasiequilibrium, all selling prices must be zero. But at least one buying premium is therefore positive. However, this situation contradicts the property of profit maximization in quasiequilibrium, because there exists an activity with positive retail output of the commodity with a positive buying premium, and wholesale inputs, which would give positive profits. Because I assume production and marketing sets to be cones, a positive profit in any activity is not compatible with profit maximization.

A stronger result than this is desirable and presumably discoverable.[2]

5. Pareto Optimum and the Core

In a formal sense the traditional analysis of Pareto optima and the core[3] can be applied to the extended economy used above to study the existence problem. But I think to do this would be to travel too fast.

The essential notion in studies of Pareto optimal and core allocations is the set of allocations achievable in some purely technological sense by a group of economic agents. In a pure exchange economy, for example, feasible allocations for any coalition (or for the economy) are those which sum to the total endowment of the coalition (zero in the present model since I measure all trades from the endowment point). The introduction of market cost is intended to reflect information costs involved in sustaining an allocation, but the assumptions made implicitly refer to the institutional environment, i.e., to markets. It is not obvious that radically different organizations of exchange would have the same type or magnitude of resource costs in the exchange process. A deeper and more satisfactory study of the core and Pareto optima would begin from a fundamental account of information costs of exchange without references to institutions and derive "markets" as one of a number of possible organizations of exchange. Only in such a theory could the "efficiency" of the equilibrium proposed here be studied other than trivially.

[2] Frank Hahn brought this difficulty to my attention.

[3] See Debreu [1] and Debreu and Scarf [3].

6. The Existence of Markets

Under what circumstances will there be trade in a given market at equilibrium with market costs? Put another way, when will the addition or elimination of a given market make no difference to equilibrium prices or to any consumer's demand in any other market?

I will treat this problem for a market in a commodity which is not an input or output of production. Producers are not either buyers or sellers of the commodity, but provide market services in the market if it pays them.

In describing consumer equilibrium in Section 2, I showed that at the equilibrium trade to each consumer there corresponded a number λ^i (in the case where consumer's preferences can be described by a differentiable utility function) such that

$$p_j{}^S \leqslant (1/\lambda^i) \quad (\partial u^i/\partial x_j) \leqslant p_j{}^B, \qquad j = 1,\dots, m.$$

If another market opens in a good not previously traded (but represented in utility functions), an individual will not trade if the prices p^S_{m+1}, p^B_{m+1} in the new market satisfy

$$p^S_{m+1} \leqslant (1/\lambda^i)(\partial u^i/\partial x_{m+1}) \leqslant p^B_{m+1} \tag{1}$$

at the original equilibrium demands. A large spread between buying and selling prices ensures that no consumer will trade.

Producers, on the other hand, will be induced by a large spread between prices to expend real resources in providing market services in the $(m + 1)$-st market. Suppose that Δ is the marginal cost at equilibrium prices of expanding trading in the $(m + 1)$-st market. Producers will be content with the previous equilibrium only if

$$p^B_{m+1} \leqslant p^S_{m+1} + \Delta. \tag{2}$$

If (1) holds simultaneously for all consumers, then

$$p^S_{m+1} \leqslant \min_i[(1/\lambda^i)(\partial u^i/\partial x_{m+1})] \tag{3}$$

and

$$p^B_{m+1} \geqslant \max_i[(1/\lambda^i)(\partial u^i/\partial x_{m+1})]. \tag{4}$$

It will be possible to find p^S_{m+1} and p^B_{m+1} satisfying (2), (3), and (4) if and only if

$$\Delta \geqslant \max_i[(1/\lambda^i)(\partial u^i/\partial x_{m+1})] - \min_i[(1/\lambda^i)(\partial u^i/\partial x_{m+1})]. \tag{5}$$

This, put in common sense language, means that the difference between the highest price at which any consumer would be willing to buy and the lowest price at which any consumer would be willing to sell is smaller than the cost of bringing about the transaction. If the $(m + 1)$-st commodity were an input or output in production these conditions would be modified to exclude producers' trade as well. The highest price at which a producer is willing to buy the commodity is the maximum of the values of its marginal product to the producers; the lowest price at which a producer will sell is the minimum of the marginal costs of production.

In the case where the $(m + 1)$-st commodity is traded only by consumers, a sufficient condition for no trade is

$$\Delta \geqslant \max_i[(1/\lambda^i)(\partial u^i/\partial x_{m+1})]. \tag{6}$$

If the $(m + 1)$-st market is in a commodity dated in the far distant future or a commodity in a contingency with low probability, its marginal utility will be small because of time preference in one case, and the small contribution it makes to expected utility in the other. The important idea here is that current actual resources are required to market futures or contingent commodities. If the consumers value these commodities little in relation to current actual resources, it will not pay anyone to set up a market to trade them.

7. An Example

A simple numerical example may help to clarify the notion of equilibrium proposed above. Suppose an economy exists in which the only goods are consumption dated at successive future dates, and suppose that there are two types of consumers with similar utility functions who discount utility 100% per period:

$$u^i(c_0, c_1, \ldots, c_m) = \sum_{j=0}^{m} [\ln(c_j + w_j^i)]/2^j,$$

where w_j^i is the endowment of the i-th consumer in the period j and c_j is his net purchase or sale of consumption in period j.

The demand functions for this utility function are well-known. The problem is to

$$\text{maximize} \sum_j^m [\ln(c_j + w_j)]/2^j \text{ subject to} \sum_j^m p_j c_j = 0.$$

The first order conditions are:

$$1/[2^j(c_j + w_j)] - \lambda p_j = 0, \qquad j = 0,\ldots, m,$$

or,

$$1/[\lambda(2^j)] = (p_j c_j + p_j w_j), \qquad j = 0,\ldots, m.$$

Adding these for all j,

$$\left[\sum_{j=0}^{m} (1/2^j)\right][1/\lambda] = \sum_{j=0}^{m} p_j w_j\,, \quad \text{or} \quad 1/\lambda = \left[\sum_{j=0}^{m} p_j w_j\right] \Big/ \left[\sum_{j=0}^{m} (1/2^j)\right].$$

This gives the demand functions

$$c_{j'} = \left[(1/2^{j'}) \Big/ \sum_j (1/2^j)\right]\left[\sum_{j=0}^{m} p_j w_j\right] / p_{j'} - w_{j'}, \qquad j' = 0,\ldots, m.$$

For the case of two markets ($m = 1$) the equilibrium price vector $p = (1, 1/2)$, and the equilibrium demands are

$$c_0^1 = 1/3, \quad c_1^1 = -2/3 \quad \text{when} \quad w^1 = (1, 2),$$
$$c_0^2 = -1/3, \quad c_1^2 = 2/3 \quad \text{when} \quad w^2 = (2, 1).$$

If a market in period 2 is added the equilibrium price vector is (1, 1/2, 1/4), and if $w^1 = (1, 2, 1.4)$ and $w^2 = (1, 2, 1.6)$, then equilibrium demands are

$$c_0^1 = 0.34, \quad c_1^1 = -0.66, \quad c_2^1 = -0.06,$$
$$c_0^2 = -0.34, \quad c_1^2 = 0.66, \quad c_2^2 = 0.06.$$

The existence of the extra market changes each type of consumer's demand for goods in other periods.

Suppose now that trading a unit of any good costs 0.1 units of consumption in period 0. The production set is a cone containing the vectors $(-0.1, 0; 1, 0)$ and $(-0.1, 0; 0, 1)$. In the case $m = 2$, the cone contains the three vectors $(-0.1, 0, 0; 1, 0, 0)$, $(-0.1, 0, 0; 0, 1, 0)$, and $(-0.1, 0, 0; 0, 0, 1)$.

The consumer problem becomes

$$\text{maximize} \sum_{j=0}^{m} [\ln(c_j + w_j)]/2^j \text{ subject to} \sum_{j=0}^{m} p_j^S c_j^S + \sum_{j=0}^{m} p_j^B c_j^B = 0,$$

where

$$c_j^S = \min[c_j\,, 0] \qquad \text{and} \qquad c_j^B = \max[c_j\,, 0].$$

The first-order conditions become

$$1/[2^j(c_j + w_j)] - \lambda p_j{}^S = 0 \qquad \text{if} \quad c_j < 0$$

and

$$1/[2^j(c_j + w_j)] - \lambda p_j{}^B = 0 \qquad \text{if} \quad c_j > 0.$$

These can be written

$$(1/2^j)(1/\lambda) = p_j{}^S c_j + p_j{}^S w_j \qquad \text{if} \quad c_j < 0$$

and

$$(1/2^j)(1/\lambda) = p_j{}^B c_j + p_j{}^B w_j \qquad \text{if} \quad c_j > 0.$$

Adding up the terms which apply,

$$(1/\lambda) \sum_j (1/2^j) = \sum_{j=0}^m p_j{}^S c_j{}^S + \sum_{j=0}^m p_j{}^B c_j{}^B + \sum_{j=0}^m \binom{p_j{}^B}{p_j{}^S} w_j ,$$

where $\binom{p_j{}^B}{p_j{}^S}$ is $p_j{}^B$ or $p_j{}^S$ depending on whether $c_j \gtrless 0$.

The demand functions can be written

$$c_{j'} = \left[(1/2^{j'})\Big/\sum_j (1/2^j)\right]\left[\sum_j \binom{p_j{}^B}{p_j{}^S} w_j\right]\Big/p_{j'}^B - w_{j'} \text{ if } c_{j'} > 0$$

$$= \left[(1/2^{j'})\Big/\sum_j (1/2^j)\right]\left[\sum_j \binom{p_j{}^B}{p_j{}^S} w_j\right]\Big/p_{j'}^S - w_{j'} \text{ if } c_{j'} < 0.$$

In searching for an equilibrium with marketing costs I assume that it will be sufficiently near the regular equilibrium that type 1 will be a buyer in period 0 and a seller in period 1 and vice versa for type 2. The problem is to clear the two markets. Clearly the relation between buying and selling price in each market must be $p_j{}^B = p_j{}^S + 0.1 p_0{}^S$. Taking $p_0{}^S = 1$, $p_0{}^B = 1.1$, and $p_1{}^B = p_0{}^S + 0.1$, the problem reduces to finding $p_0{}^S$ that will clear the period 1 market. Adding the demand functions where $w^1 = (1, 2)$ and $w^2 = (2, 1)$,

$$c_1{}^1 + c_1{}^2 = [1/3(1.1 + 2p_1{}^S)/p_1{}^S] - 2$$
$$+ [1/3[2 + (p_1{}^S + 0.1)]/p_1{}^S + 0.1] - 1 = 0.$$

This gives a quadratic equation in $p_1{}^S$,

$$6p_1^{S^2} - 2.5p_1{}^S - 0.11 = 0.$$

with a positive root $p_1{}^S = 0.457$, implying $p_1{}^B = 0.557$.

The demands are

$$c_0^1 = 0.22, \qquad c_1^1 = -0.53,$$
$$c_0^2 = -0.30, \qquad c_0^2 = 0.53.$$

It is instructive to compare this equilibrium with the one where there was no trading cost. In the usual case the interest rate for both borrowers and lenders implied by the prices in 100%. With transaction costs, type 1 people, who are borrowers, face an interest rate equal to

$$(p_0^B/p_1^S) - 1 = (1.1/0.457) - 1 = 1.41,$$

i.e., 141%. The type 2 lenders, on the other hand, are receiving an interest rate of only

$$(p_0^S/p_1^B) - 1 = 1/0.557 - 1 = 0.79,$$

i.e., 79%.

To illustrate the point made in Section 6, consider adding another market in period 2 consumption, with $w^1 = (1, 2, 1.4)$ and $w^2 = (2, 1, 1.6)$.

The λ multipliers implied by the previous equilibrium are $\lambda^1 = 0.745$, $\lambda^2 = 0.588$, and $(1/\lambda^1)(\partial u^1/\partial c_2) = 0.242$, $(1/\lambda^2)(\partial u^2/\partial c_2) = 0.251$. In this case $\Delta = 0.1$, obviously, and the condition

$$\Delta \geqslant \max_i[(1/\lambda^i)(\partial u^i/\partial x_{m+1})] - \min_i[(1/\lambda^i)(\partial u^i/\partial x_{m+1})]$$

is met since $\Delta = 0.1 \geqslant 0.251 - 0.242 = 0.009$.

If in the new market the selling price is established at 0.2 and the buying price at 0.3 neither consumer will want to trade and the price differential will not be sufficient to draw resources into setting up a market.

The implied two-period borrowing and lending rates can be found by solving $(1 + r_B)^2 = (p_0^S/p_2^B)$ and $(1 + r_2)^2 = (p_0^B/p_2^S)$.

For the prices suggested above, the borrowing rate is 144% and the lending rate 83%, in contrast to the equilibrium without market costs where both rates are equal to 100%.

8. Conclusions

Although the model described above is logically consistent, it is not as satisfactory in one important respect as the traditional model of equilibrium with futures and contingency markets. Consumers and producers in the traditional model have all the information they need to make once and for all a complete consumption plan. There is no reason why they should not simply exploit to the limit their trading opportunities at equilibrium prices, then rest content and simply carry out their predetermined plan. If markets were reopened no trade would take place; the equilibrium price system would remain the same. Given the environment of the traditional model with full contingency and futures markets, there is no reason why a sensible consumer should not behave as the model predicts.

In the present model, however, prices will change when markets reopen and consumers know it. The reason is that the production sets change with time in a particular way: It is not possible to use period *m* resources in operating markets until period *m* actually arrives. In the next period, new markets will open and price spreads in other markets will change. The consumer, then, has reason not to behave in the way I have postulated. He may choose not to exploit fully his trading opportunities at this moment, but to defer some trades to the future when other markets will exist and price spreads may be more favorable to him.[4]

Thus consideration of marketing costs in this simple model leads directly to the study of sequential trading. In these models there will be both futures and spot markets, and the interaction of prices in these various markets becomes the focus of interest.

Acknowledgments

I would like to thank Ross Starr for numerous helpful conversations on this subject. Frank Hahn has independently developed a model very similar in structure to the one presented here.

References

1. G. Debreu, "Theory of Value," John Wiley and Sons, Inc., New York, 1959.
2. G. Debreu, New concepts and techniques for equilibrium analysis, *Int. Econ. Rev.* **3** (September 1962), 257–273.
3. G. Debreu and H. Scarf, A limit theorem on the core of an economy, *Int. Econ. Rev.* **4** (September 1963), 235–246.
4. R. Radner, Competitive equilibrium under uncertainty, *Econometrica* **36** (January 1968), 31–58.

[4] Another reason for changing prices is that some contingency which everyone judged very unlikely may come to pass. Since no trade was done in that contingency or any subset of it, the price spreads will be large, initially. A somewhat similar problem of reopened markets arises in Radner [4], where the problem is that new information changes consumption and production sets.

PRINTED IN BELGIUM BY THE ST. CATHERINE PRESS, TEMPELHOF, 37, BRUGES, LTD.

SECTION 2

Efficient Intertemporal Allocation

16

EQUILIBRIUM WITH TRANSACTION COSTS

by Frank H. Hahn

In December, 1969, Prof. Frank Hahn delivered the Walras-Bowley lecture at the Econometric Society meeting in New York. This was an important event for the general equilibrium analysis of monetary economies. His was the most visible presentation of what soon became a large variety of models of equilibrium with transaction costs.

A slightly cumbersome device is used to formalize the idea of a transaction technology. The dimension of the commodity space is doubled to allow labelling each unit of a good as "named" or "anonymous". All goods start out as named but only anonymous goods may be purchased. The process of transforming a named good to anonymous is a resource-using activity intended to represent the transactions process.

Sufficient conditions are developed for the existence of equilibrium, but the most important results of the study are those dealing with allocative efficiency. The major contribution of this article is the discovery of the possible inefficiency of equilibrium in a sequence economy over time with transaction costs. The temporal and financial structure of the model is essential to this observation. There is a sequence of periods, and a budget constraint applies in each period. This contrasts with the single lifetime budget constraint of the Arrow-Debreu model. At each date the value of goods and futures contracts delivered to market must equal the value of those received from the market. Since the value of endowment available at each date may not equal the value of planned consumption, futures market transactions are required to finance current consumption through sale of future (or past) goods. If there is a higher transaction cost on futures transactions than spot, then their use to fulfill a budget constraint implies an efficiency loss. Origins of the higher

ISBN 0-12-663970-1

futures transaction cost are elementary. Futures transactions may be more complex than spot. Costs are incurred at the time of contracting as well as at delivery. In the presence of time discounting, the present discounted value of a futures market transaction cost incurred long before delivery is likely to exceed its later spot market counterpart.

A very strong sufficient condition for efficiency—which will not generally prevail—is identified. If price ratios for all goods in equilibrium are invariant with the transaction date—i.e., if it doesn't matter whether you trade futures or wait to trade spot—then the equilibrium is easily shown to be efficient. However this condition—called the *Debreu property*—will seldom prevail. Markets where it does are uninteresting in the sense that transaction costs there have no real effect.

Hahn discusses in a preliminary way the implications of this model for the theory of a monetary economy. The problem recognized here is then treated and resolved in Starrett (selection 17).

ECONOMETRICA

VOLUME 39 May, 1971 NUMBER 3

EQUILIBRIUM WITH TRANSACTION COSTS[1]

BY F. H. HAHN[2]

This paper examines some of the modifications required in well known propositions of general equilibrium theory when transactions require resources. Some preliminary remarks on the analysis of money in such economies are also offered.

INTRODUCTION

IT IS USUAL to describe an Arrow-Debreu economy as one in which all markets, including all contingent futures markets, exist. This is rather ambiguous since a market may be feasible but inactive. It is more useful to say that an economy is Arrow-Debreu (A-D), if we may interpret it in equilibrium as one where all transactions are carried out at a single date. In such an economy money can play no essential role.

In the economies we know, there are transactions at every date. It is also not the case that at any date and for every good agents have a choice of transacting forward or spot on terms which leave them indifferent as to which they do. This suggests that one wants to study markets as activities in order to have a theory to account for the presence of active spot markets at every date. This allows one to treat as an unknown in the analysis the markets which are active in an equilibrium. Such a study leads one to an equilibrium of a sequence of markets. It is pretty plain from general considerations that such a construct is required as a preliminary to a satisfactory monetary theory.

This paper is concerned with this preliminary undertaking and it goes only part of the way. By far the larger part of the study is concerned with economies in which all prices are announced and there is certainty. Only in the last section do I offer some remarks on some of the problems encountered in a less restrictive framework. For the most part also I am concerned with a pure exchange economy and I need some fairly restrictive technical assumptions. The paper must be regarded as a first step.

Even so the result is not perhaps easy nor pleasant reading, and I take this opportunity to note some of the more important conclusions.

[1] This paper was originally presented in New York as the Walras Lecture, December, 1969. Mr. Duncan Foley has also studied the problem of transactions in general equilibrium. However, he seems to be concerned with single-period models.

[2] I should like to acknowledge the debt I owe to the writings of Roy Radner on sequence economies and to discussions which I have had with him. He has also kindly and usefully commented on this paper.

If one regards transactions as using resources of goods available at the transaction date, then one has an immediate reason for the fact that there are normally spot markets at every date. Suppose, for instance, that labour is a required input into a market activity. It would then be odd for an economy to choose, provided it were feasible, to supply labour in the initial period only and none at all thereafter. This in itself is sufficiently strong ground for expecting spot markets at every date.

In formalising the notion of markets as activities, I distinguish between *named* and *anonymous* goods. This serves to distinguish a given physical good at a particular time and place owned by an agent from the same good when it is being bought by another agent. It has of course the consequence that the buying and selling price of the same physical good at the same time and place may differ.

The single most important consequence of this is that, in general, households face a sequence of budget constraints and there may be no unique set of discount rates applicable to all households which allows one to "amalgamate" all those constraints into a single present value budget constraint. The inter-temporal transfers open to a household depend on whether at each of the two dates it is a seller or buyer of the good in terms of which such a transfer is most advantageous. Not only will the borrowing and lending rates differ, in general, but each of these rates may be different for different households.

The fact that one has to deal with a sequence of constraints poses certain technical difficulties. But this is not the important point. More interesting is the fact that equilibria need not be efficient. Care must of course be taken with the definition of efficiency. For the set of feasible allocations, unlike that of the usual theory, must for sense be taken relative to a given *distribution* of endowment. In particular the question whether every efficient allocation may be decentralised may make no sense if endowment reallocations require resources.

But of course the most important consequence of the whole approach is that since it leads to a sequence of spot markets one cannot in practice take the prices at future dates as known to the agents at an earlier date. I shall discuss some of these issues, albeit very briefly. In an Arrow-Debreu world all the future is collapsible into the present—in this sort of world the future unfolds. This of course has important consequences to one's views on the allocative efficiency of a perfectly competitive world.

I shall also offer some reflections, as they are best called, on money in the kind of model I have been discussing. The attempt to arrive at a model of the economy as satisfying as Debreu's, but which can accommodate money, is the motivation of this whole enquiry. In execution, the preparatory work has taken most of my time and intellectual energy, and I hope to pursue this problem further at another occasion. But I shall argue here that at least the pure transaction theory of money seems to require in an essential way that the set of marketing activities exhibits a certain kind of increasing returns. I have not been able to formulate this to my full satisfaction. But if the argument is correct, difficulties present themselves in the study of equilibrium. More importantly still, we should not be surprised to find a monetary equilibrium inefficient in a certain sense quite different from Friedman's. It is just possible that, abstract as this research is, it might in due course lead one to formulate public policies designed to create markets or to abolish some. Adam Smith started on a study of markets and their relation to the division of labour—formal economics has not gotten much further since and indeed has ignored the Smithian analysis.

A Note on Notation: In what follows if a and b are two vectors, $a \gg b$ means $a_i > b_i$ for all i, $a > b$ means $a_i \geqslant b_i$, $a_i > b_i$ for some i. Also a^+ is the vector with components $\max(0, a_i)$, a^- is the vector with components $\min(0, a_i)$.

1. GOODS AND PRICES

One of the aims of this paper is to make the existence or non-existence of markets an economic question. The natural procedure is to regard a market as an activity which uses resources. To make this precise I shall enlarge the usual commodity space.

Let only one state of the economy be possible and say that a good is of type (i, t) if, when time is measured in discrete intervals, it has the locational and physical characteristics i and is available at t. I let $i = 0, \ldots, n - 1$, $t = 1, \ldots, T$ and call the non-negative orthant, Ω^{nT}, the space of anonymous goods. This nomenclature is designed to underline that these goods can be specified without using the name of any agent.

Let there be H households. I shall call a good of type (i, t) owned by household h, a *named* good (i, h, t). There can be HnT named goods. But in most of what follows while I shall take it to be of economic significance whether a good of a given type has a name or not, I shall suppose it to be of no significance what the name is. In that case I refer to a named good of type (i, t) as (i, H, t) and the dimension of the commodity space is $2nT$.

At a later stage I shall wish to single out special goods of type (n, t), $t = 1, \ldots, T$, which have the characteristic that they are not subject to the ordering of households or the distinction between named and anonymous. These goods will be called money (of different dates) and when they are included in the analysis the commodity space is $\Omega^{(2n+1)T}$.

A market (i, t) will be regarded as an activity which transforms (i, H, t) into (i, t). It is described in Section 3.

The commodity space, however, will have to be further enlarged. To understand this, a matter of considerable significance, it is best first to consider the prices of the goods so far specified.

Let $p, q \in \Omega^{2nT}$ represent the price vectors of anonymous and named goods. Note that (p, q) is "a price system at an unspecified location at an unspecified instant." [**2**]. If $q_{rt} > 0$, say, then $(p^t, q^t) = (1/q_{rt})(p, q)$ is the price system viewed from t in terms of the numeraire (r, H, t). If $t' > t$ let us interpret $p^t_{it'}$ as the forward price at t of (i, t'). If $t' = t$ interpret it as the spot price (at t') of (i, t').

With this interpretation, where the ratios are defined, the relative spot prices of a named and anonymous good of any type are the same as the relative forward prices. That is

$$\frac{p_{it'}^{t'}}{q_{it'}^{t'}} = \frac{p_{it'}^{t}}{q_{it'}^{t}}.$$

This at once suggests that our construction is not yet rich enough in goods to allow us to study an economy where markets are activities using resources. For at present, the transaction date is inessential and the interpretation of $p_{it'}^{t}$ as spot or forward is a purely formal one. For instance, the analysis could proceed just as well if $t > 1$, $t' < t$, so that we would be dealing with "backwards" prices and markets. When, however, one is concerned with actual market activities one cannot suppose in advance that a particular relation exists between the anonymous and named price of a good of a given type at any date. Nor is it possible to neglect the direction of time.

This point is of considerable significance since it shows that a study of transactions will involve more than a trivial modification of the familiar model. Indeed it will lead us to study sequence economies. The next section will serve to clarify this matter further.

If one then further distinguishes goods by the date of their trading but does not allow any good of type (i, t) to be traded at $t' > t$, then the number of possible goods will be $N = 2nT(T + 1/2)$. The number of possible prices will be larger than that. If we take our viewpoint at $t = 1$, then prices of goods traded at $t' > t$ will in practice be the subject of the expectations of households and these of course may be different. For the first part of this study, however, I shall take all prices as announced, so that there are also N prices.

2. HOUSEHOLDS

I shall employ the following notation. A household's activities are indexed $h = 1, \ldots, H$. I write $C^h \subset \Omega^{nT}$ as the set of possible consumptions of h with typical element c^h. The vectors c^{hh} and c^h have as components named and anonymous goods respectively and $\tilde{c}^h = c^{hh} + c^h$. The subvectors $\tilde{c}^h(t)$, $c^{hh}(t)$, and $c^h(t)$ have as components goods of type (i, t), $i = 0, \ldots, n - 1$. Note that with this definition C^h is the usual Debreu set of possible consumptions, which also includes leisure of various dates. The vector $\bar{c}^{hh} \in \Omega^{nT}$ is the vector of named goods representing the endowment of h. Also $\bar{c}^{hh}(t)$ is the subvector whose components are named goods available at t, i.e., of type (i, t), $i = 0, \ldots, n - 1$.

Let $N^* = nT(T - 1)/2$ and let x^{hh} be a vector with $-x^{hh} \in \Omega^{N^*}$. Then x^{hh} is the vector of forward sales, all components of which are named. The vector $x^h \in \Omega^{N^*}$ is the vector of forward purchases with only anonymous components. One defines $\tilde{x}^h = x^{hh} + x^h$. The vectors $\tilde{x}^h(t)$, $x^{hh}(t)$, $x^h(t)$ have as components goods of type (i, t') with $t' > t$, for which the transaction date is t. Thus $x_{it'}^{hh}(t)$, a member of $x^{hh}(t)$, represents the sale at t of named good of type (i, t'), and $\tilde{x}_{it'}^h(t)$ represents the net commitment (positive or negative) made at t with respect to good of type (i, t'). The vector $\tilde{\tilde{x}}(t)$ is the vector of net commitments at t from past contracts.

If $\tilde{\tilde{x}}_i(t)$ is the ith component, then

$$\tilde{\tilde{x}}_i(t) = \sum_{t'<t} \tilde{x}^h_{it}(t').$$

One defines S^h as the set of storage activities available to h. A typical element $\tilde{s}^h$ of S^h has as positive components storage outputs and, as negative components, storage inputs. I write $\tilde{s}^{h+}(t)$ as the vector of storage outputs of named goods type $(i, t), i = 0, \ldots, n-1$, and $\tilde{s}^{h-}(t)$ as the vector of storage inputs of goods of this type. Also

$$\tilde{s}^{h-}(t) = s^{hh-}(t) + s^{h-}(t)$$

where all components of $s^{hh-}(t)$ are named and all those of $s^{h-}(t)$ are anonymous.

The vector $w^h(t)$ is defined by

$$w^h(t) = \bar{c}^{hh}(t) + s^{h+}(t) + \tilde{\tilde{x}}^h(t).$$

A typical component $w^h_i(t)$ is the sum of the endowment of named good (i, t), the amount of that good coming out of storage, and the net commitment to receive or deliver (i, t). Clearly $w^h_i(t) < 0$ is possible, in which case I shall say that the household has a net endowment of anonymous good type (i, t). If $w^h_i(t) \geqslant 0$ the household is said to have a net endowment of named good of type (i, t). The vector $w^{h+}(t)$ is the net endowment vector of named goods available at t and the vector $w^{h-}(t)$ is the net endowment vector of anonymous goods available at t.

I write $p \in \Omega^N$ and $q \in \Omega^N$ as the price vectors of anonymous and named goods; p^t and q^t are subvectors of prices of goods traded at t. I write $p^t = (p^t(t), p^t(t'), \ldots)$, $q^t = (q^t(t), q^t(t'), \ldots)$ where $t' > t$, etc., and $p^t(t')$, for instance, is the vector of prices of anonymous goods type (i, t') traded at t.

Lastly the household receives profits in unit of account from its shares in marketing activities. I write $\pi^h(t)$ as the profits received at t and π^h as the vector of these profits. Because of the assumptions of the next section we may take $\pi^h(t) \geqslant 0$.

I shall make the following assumptions concerning households.

ASSUMPTION (H.1): (i) *C^h is closed and convex;* (ii) *the ordering of the household can be represented by a continuous, quasi-concave utility function $u^h(\tilde{c}^h)$ from C^h; and* (iii) *there is no $\tilde{c}^{*h} \in C^h$ such that $u^h(\tilde{c}^{*h}) > u^h(\tilde{c}^h)$ for all $\tilde{c}^h \in C^h$.*

These assumptions are sufficiently familiar. It is worth re-emphasizing that the household's ordering is on C^h so that it is only concerned with the type of a good and not with its name or trading date. This seems sensible.

ASSUMPTION (H.2): (i) *S^h is convex and compact with $0 \in S^h$;* (ii) *$\tilde{s}^h > 0$ implies $\tilde{s}^h \notin S^h$; and* (iii) *the components of $\tilde{s}^{h-}(t)$ are goods of type $(i, t), i = 0, \ldots, n-1$.*

Once again there is nothing special about Assumption (H.2). I am stipulating decreasing returns to storage. Also the inputs at t are all goods available at t.

A plan of a household is the triple $(\tilde{c}^h, \tilde{s}^h, \tilde{x}^h)$ with $\tilde{c}^h \in C^h$, $\tilde{s}^h \in S^h$, $\tilde{x}^h \in E^{N^*}$. It is said to be *feasible* if it also satisfies the following constraints.

Constraint (C.1): The household cannot buy named goods of type (i, t) at t:

$$c^{hh}(t) - s^{hh-}(t) \leqslant \bar{c}^{hh}(t) + s^{h+}(t) + \tilde{\bar{x}}^{h+}(t).$$

Constraint (C.2): The household's assets at T must be nonnegative:

$$q^T w^{h+}(T) + p^T w^{h-}(T) + \pi^h(T) \geqslant 0; \qquad x^h(T) = x^{hh}(T) = 0.$$

Constraint (C.3): The household must satisfy the budget constraints

$$p^t(c^h(t) - s^{h-}(t), x^h(t)) + q^t(c^{hh}(t) - s^{hh-}(t), x^{hh}(t))$$
$$\leqslant p^t(t)w^{h-}(t) + q^t(t)w^{h+}(t) + \pi^h(t) \qquad (t = 1 \ldots T).$$

Constraint (C.1) formalises the notion of named goods. A household cannot use more of a good of a given type than it has without acquiring anonymous goods of that type. On the other hand when a household buys a good forward it is ensuring that it will have quantities of that good bearing its name. The Constraint (C.2) is one of "financial probity," which prevents a household from making arbitrarily large forward sales. In its present form it is somewhat unnatural in giving all households the horizon T.

It may be worthwhile to spell out Constraint (C.3) for a given t. The first term on the left of the inequality represents the value of all purchases at t, spot and forward. The second term is the sum of spot purchases at t the household makes from itself $(q^t(t)(c^{hh}(t) - s^{hh-}(t)))$, and the value of all forward sales at t. The first term on the right represents the value of the net obligation to buy anonymous goods at t undertaken prior to t. The second term is the value of the household's net endowment of named goods. The last term is the value of profits at t.

Consider (C.1) again. It certainly allows h to consume a named good of type (i, t) even though its net endowment of this good is negative. If it indeed does this, it will have to buy that much more anonymous good of that type to meet its forward commitment. Since its utility depends on $c_{it}^{hh} + c_{it}^{h}$, it clearly would have been just as well off if it had consumed more of the anonymous good (i, t) and less of the named. Accordingly we may modify the Constraint (C.1) to read as follows.

Constraint (C*.1): $c^{hh}(t) - s^{hh-}(t) \leqslant w^{h+}(t)$.

The set of choices open to the household is thereby modified but the utility attainable is not.

It is clear that for some $(p, q, c^{-hh}) > 0$, no feasible plan may exist; then I shall say that h is *bankrupt*. This can only be the case if at $t < 1$ the household undertook commitments for $t \geqslant 1$. However at the moment when all expectational matters are excluded, bankruptcy is unnatural and I stipulate the next assumption.

Assumption (H.3): $\tilde{x}^h(t) = 0$ *for* $t < 1$.

One may interpret Assumption (H.3) to mean that the household did not exist before $t = 1$. When I come to consider expectational matters this assumption will turn out not to save one from embarrassment.

Next I shall use the following definition.

DEFINITION (D.1): A feasible plan $(\tilde{c}^h, \tilde{x}^h, \tilde{s}^h)$ is *weakly efficient* at $(p, q, \pi^h, \bar{c}^{hh})$ if any other plan $(\tilde{c}^h, \tilde{x}^{h'}, \tilde{s}^{h'})$ with $\tilde{c}^{h'} \gg \tilde{c}^h$ is not feasible at $(p, q, \bar{c}^{hh})$.

It is clear that a weakly efficient plan may not exist. Thus $(p, q) > 0$ is consistent with $p^1 = q^1 = 0$ in which case it is easily verified that plans with the desired property do not exist. (The household plans are in fact undefined.) Or again, (p, q) might be such that the implied borrowing rates of interest, in unit of account, are below the lending rates, in which case again there may be no weakly efficient plans. I wish to exclude these cases.

This leads me to the definition of an admissible price set $\mathscr{P}$. In formulating this set one writes $(\bar{p}^t, \bar{q}^t)$ as the set of forward prices at t and also e as the unit row vector which is always conformable with the column vector which it premultiplies. Also $\varepsilon > 0$ is a small, and $B > 0$ a large, scalar.

DEFINITION (D.2): The prices $(p, q) \in \mathscr{P}$ if (i) $(p, q) > 0$, $e(p, q) = 1$; (ii) $p \geqslant q$; (iii) there exist numbers $\alpha(t), \beta(t), \alpha(t) \geqslant \varepsilon, 0 \leqslant \beta(t) \leqslant B$, such that $\bar{p}^t \geqslant \alpha(t+1)p^{t+1}$, $\bar{q}^t \leqslant \beta(t+1)q^{t+1}$, $t = 1, \ldots, T-1$; and (iv) letting $\alpha(\bar{p}^t, p^{t+1}) \leqslant +\infty$ be the largest $\alpha(t+1)$ satisfying (iii) for $(\bar{p}^t, p^{t+1})$ and letting $\beta(\bar{q}^t, q^{t+1})$ be the smallest $\beta(t+1)$ satisfying (iii) for $(\bar{q}^t, q^{t+1})$, then

$$\alpha(\bar{p}^t, p^{t+1}) \geqslant \beta(\bar{q}^t, q^{t+1}) \qquad (t = 1 \ldots T-1).$$

The economics of (D.2) will be discussed presently. First I prove the following lemma.

LEMMA 1: (i) *For all* $(p, q) \in \mathscr{P}$, $(p^1, q^1) > 0$; *and* (ii) $\mathscr{P}$ *is convex and compact.*

PROOF: (i) If not, then in view of (D.2(i)) and (D.2(ii)) there must be some t' and (i, t) with $t \geqslant t' + 1$, such that $p_{it}^{t'+1} > 0$. Then by (D.2 (iii)), $p_{it}^{t'} > 0$ and by (D.2(iii)) again, $p_{it}^{t'-1} > 0$. Proceeding, one finds $p_{it}^1 > 0$ contrary to assumption.

(ii) It is immediate that $\mathscr{P}$ is convex and bounded. Let (p^v, q^v) be a sequence in $\mathscr{P}$ approaching (p^0, q^0). One shows in the familiar way that (p^0, q^0) satisfies (D.2(i)) and (D.2(ii)). If it does not satisfy (D.2 (iii)), then for some t' and $t \geqslant t'$, either $\bar{p}_{it}^{0t'} = 0$, $p_{it}^{0(t'+1)} > 0$ for some i, or $\bar{q}_{jt}^{0t'} > 0$, $q_{jt}^{0(t'+1)} = 0$. Then for v large enough, $\bar{p}^{vt'}(t) > 0$, $p^{v(t'+1)}(t) > 0$, and

$$\alpha^v(t'+1) \leqslant \frac{\bar{p}_{it}^{vt'}}{p_{it}^{vt'+1}} < \varepsilon,$$

and by a similar argument,

$$\beta^v(t'+1) \geqslant \frac{\bar{q}_{jt}^{vt'}}{q_{jt}^{vt'+1}} > B.$$

In either case for v large enough, $(p^v, q^v) \notin \mathscr{P}$.

From their definitions, $\alpha(\bar{p}^t, p^{t+1})$, $\beta(\bar{q}^t, q^{t+1})$ are continuous in their arguments so that (p^0, q^0) satisfies (D.2(iv)).

LEMMA 2: *For all* $(p, q) \in \mathscr{P}$ *a weakly efficient plan exists when* $\pi^h(t)$ *and* $\bar{c}^{hh}(t)$ *are finite, all* t.

PROOF: (i) Suppose $q^1 = 0$. Then by Lemma 1 $p^1 > 0$ and the proposition follows from (C.3) with $t = 1$. So from now on take $q^1 \neq 0$.

(ii) Let

$$z^h(t) = c^h(t) - s^{h-}(t) - w^{h-}(t), \qquad z^{hh}(t) = c^{hh}(t) - s^{hh-}(t) - w^{h+}(t).$$

By (C.1) the consumption of named goods at $t = 1$ is certainly bounded. If the Lemma is false with (C.1) it must be false with (C*.1). Hence I use the latter constraint so that

$$(1) \qquad z^{hh}(t) \leqslant 0 \quad \text{for all } t.$$

(iii) Let the vectors $\bar{x}^h(t)$ and $\bar{x}^{hh}(t)$ have the components

$$\bar{x}^h_{it}(t) = \sum_{t'<t} x^h_{it}(t'), \qquad \bar{x}^{hh}_{it} = \sum_{t'<t} x^{hh}_{it}(t')$$

so that $\bar{x}^h(t) + \bar{x}^{hh}(t) - \bar{\bar{x}}^h(t) = 0$, $t > 1$. Also let $\alpha^*(t) = \alpha(\bar{p}^t, p^{t+1})$, $\beta^*(t) = \beta(\bar{q}^t, q^{t+1})$, $\hat{\alpha}(t) = \alpha^*(1) \ldots \alpha^*(t)$, $\hat{B}(t) = \beta^*(1) \ldots \beta^*(t)$, with $\hat{\alpha}(1) = \hat{\beta}(1) = 1$. Also write $\bar{q}^1(t)$, $\bar{p}^1(t)$ for the price vectors in period 1 for goods dated $t' > t$. From (D.2) one has for $t > 1$,

$$\hat{\alpha}(t)p^t \geqslant \hat{\alpha}(t)q^t \geqslant \hat{\beta}(t)q^t \geqslant (q^1(t), \bar{q}^1(t)),$$

$$\hat{\alpha}(t)q^t \leqslant \alpha(t)p^t \leqslant (p^1(t), \bar{p}^1(t)).$$

(iv) Multiplying the budget constraint for t by $\hat{\alpha}(t)$ and adding gives

$$G = \sum \hat{\alpha}(t)p^t(z^h(t), x^h(t)) + \sum \hat{\alpha}(t)q^t(z^{hh}(t), x^{hh}(t)) \leqslant \sum \hat{\alpha}(t)\pi^h(t).$$

By (1) and the inequalities in (iii) one has, using (C.2), i.e., $x^h(T) = x^{hh}(T) = 0$,

$$(2) \qquad G \geqslant \sum_{t=1} q^1(t)z^h(t) + \sum_{t=1} p^1(t)z^{hh}(t) + \sum_{t=1} \bar{q}^1(t)\bar{x}^h(t) + \sum_{t=1} \bar{p}^1(t)\bar{x}^{hh}(t).$$

By (D.2(i)) and the definitions one verifies that

$$\begin{aligned} q^1(t)(\bar{x}^h(t) - w^{h-}(t)) + p^1(t)(\bar{x}^{hh} - w^{h+}(t)) \\ \leqslant q^1(t)(\bar{x}^h(t) + x^{hh}(t) - \bar{\bar{x}}^h(t)) - q^1(t)(\bar{c}^{hh}(t) - s^{h+}(t)) \\ = -q^1(t)(\bar{c}^{hh}(t) + s^{h+}(t)). \end{aligned}$$

From the definitions of $z^h(t)$ and $z^{hh}(t)$ therefore,

$$G \geqslant q^1c^h + p^1c^{hh} - q^1\bar{c}^{hh} - q^1s^{h-} - p^1s^{hh-} - q^1s^{h+}.$$

But $q^1s^{h-} + p^1s^{hh-} + q^1s^{h+} \leqslant q^1\tilde{s}^h$, whence

$$(3) \qquad q^1c^h + p^1c^{hh} \leqslant q^1\bar{c}^{hh} + q^1\tilde{s}^h + \sum \hat{\alpha}(t)\pi^h(t).$$

Since by (H.2), $q^1\tilde{s}^h$ is bounded and since $q^1 > 0$ and $p^1 > 0$, this inequality establishes the Lemma.

Let me now discuss (D.2). There is nothing new in (D.2(i)) and I pass it by. Definition (D.2(ii)) will, in the next section, be justified with reference to the market technology. This, because it uses resources, will ensure that in searching for an equilibrium one need not consider price situations where the price of a named good exceeds that of an anonymous one. The conditions (D.2(iii)) and (D.2(iv)) are more interesting.

Suppose a household wishes to lend a unit of account at t for repayment at $t + 1$. Then the gain from this operation depends on the good which it buys forward at t, and on whether in its plan, it is a buyer or seller of this good at $t + 1$. Thus suppose it buys $(1/p^t_{it+1})$ units of good $(i, t + 1)$. If, in its plan, it was a purchaser of $(i, t + 1)$ at $t + 1$, it will now save $(p^{t+1}_{it+1}/p^t_{it+1})$ units of account at $t + 1$. If it was a seller of the good it will sell more of it and receive $(q^{t+1}_{it+1}/q^t_{it+1})$ units of account. (If it was neither seller nor buyer, the gain is between the sums calculated on the above basis.) Naturally we may define the lending rate of interest, $r^h_L(t, t + 1)$ as the largest one of all the possible rates obtainable by forward purchases. If that involves trading in good $(r, t + 1)$, one has, from what has just been said,

$$r^h_L(t, t + 1)p^t_{rt+1} \geqslant p^{t+1}_{rt+1} - p^t_{rt+1},$$

and from (D.2(iii)) and (D.2(iv)),

$$\frac{1 - \alpha^*(t)}{\alpha^*(t)} p^t_{rt+1} \geqslant p^{t+1}_{rt+1} - p^t_{rt+1}$$

whence

$$r^h_L(t, t + 1) \leqslant \frac{1 - \alpha^*(t)}{\alpha^*(t)}.$$

By an exactly similar argument, if $b^h(t, t + 1)$ is the household's borrowing rate attained by selling forward at t and either buying spot at $t + 1$ or selling less spot at $t + 1$, one has

$$r^h_B(t, t + 1)q^t_{st+1} \geqslant q^{t+1}_{st+1} - q^t_{st+1}$$

and from (D.2(iii)) and (D.2(iv)),

$$\frac{1 - \beta^*(t)}{\beta^*(t)} q^t_{st+1} \leqslant q^{t+1}_{st+1} - q^t_{st+1},$$

whence

$$r^h_B(t, t + 1) \geqslant \frac{1 - \beta^*(t)}{\beta^*(t)}.$$

So by (D.2(iv))

$$r_B^h(t, t + 1) \geqslant \frac{1 - \beta^*(t)}{\beta^*(t)} \geqslant \frac{1 - \alpha^*(t)}{\alpha^*(t)} \geqslant r_L^h(t, t + 1).$$

The borrowing rate implied by any $(p, q) \in A$ is therefore not less than the implied lending rate. Although I have shown this for adjacent intervals only, the reader can easily verify this relationship for any length of interval (by using $\hat{\alpha}(t)$ and $\hat{\beta}(t)$).

It is now of some importance to understand that $\alpha^*(t)$ and $\beta^*(t)$ need not be the discount factor appropriate to any one household. In particular the rate appropriate for h for any time interval depends on that household's plans. Not only is it important whether that household borrows or lends, but also whether the most favorable terms open to it involve a purchase (or a reduction in planned purchase), or a sale (or a reduction in planned sale), at the delivery date. It is because of this that we must deal with sequences of budget constraints (and the richer commodity space), and this is one of the more interesting consequences of paying explicit attention to transactions.

Indeed let us say that (p, q) has the Debreu property if there are numbers $\lambda(t, t') > 0$ such that for $t' > t$

$$p^{t'} = \lambda(t, t')\bar{p}^t, \quad q^{t'} = \lambda(t, t')\bar{q}^t$$

(where of course $\bar{p}^t$ and $\bar{q}^t$ contain prices of only those goods that are in $p^{t'}$ and $q^{t'}$). Then one can prove the first theorem.

THEOREM 1: *For every* $\bar{c}^{hh} > 0$ *and* $u^h(\tilde{c}^h)$ *satisfying* (H.1) *a household will be indifferent between making all transactions at* $t = 1$ *or engaging in a sequence of transactions, if and only if* (p, q) *has the Debreu property.*

PROOF: Multiplying the budget constraint for t' by $\mu(1, t') = 1/\lambda(1, t')$ and adding, one obtains, if (p, q) has the Debreu property,

$$p^1c^h + q^1c^{hh} \leqslant q^1\bar{c}^{hh} + \sum \mu(1, t')\pi^h(t') + \sigma^h \tag{4}$$

where σ^h is the net profit (positive or negative) from storage calculated at (p^1, q^1). But then the set of $\tilde{c}^h$ satisfying (4) is exactly the same as the set of $\tilde{c}^h$ satisfying the sequence of budget constraints. Hence the sufficiency part of the proposition follows.

If (p, q) does not have the Debreu property, then for some t', $r_B^h(1, t') \neq r_L^h(1, t')$. But then (4) cannot be obtained by adding suitably multiplied budget constraints. There will be $\tilde{c}^h$ feasible under the sequence that are not feasible under (4). An appropriate choice of $\bar{c}^{hh}$ and $u^h(\tilde{c}^h)$ then establishes necessity.

Since (p, q) which satisfies the Debreu property is a subset of $\mathscr{P}$, our formulation is capable, in principle, of exhibiting a Debreu equilibrium. I return to this below.

I shall now suppose that among feasible plans, h picks the one that maximises $u^h(\tilde{c}^h)$. In doing this I shall take the familiar step of confining the household's choices to $\bar{C}^h \subset C^h$, a closed, convex, and bounded subset. I do not change the notation for plans for this artificial problem since one suspects in advance that these fictitious constraints, suitably chosen, will in any equilibrium be inoperative.

Let $a^h = (c^h, x^h, c^{hh}, x^{hh}, \tilde{s}^h)$, a $2N$ vector, be a plan or activity of household h. Then I define $F^h(p, q, \bar{c}^{hh})$ by

$$F^h(p, q, \bar{c}^{hh}) = \{a^h | c^h + c^{hh} \in \bar{C}^h,\ \tilde{s}^h \in S^h \text{ and (C.1) to (C.3) hold}\}.$$

Hence $F^h(p, q, \bar{c}^{hh})$ is the set of feasible activities for household h. I now prove the following lemma.

LEMMA 3: *The set of feasible activities* $F^h(p, q, \bar{c}^{hh})$ *is convex for* $(p, q) \in \mathscr{P}$.

PROOF: Let $w^h(a^h, t)$ be the net endowment vector of h at t under the plan a^h. If a^h and $a^{h'}$ are two plans, write $a^h(\alpha) = \alpha a^h + (1 - \alpha)a^h$, $\alpha \in (0, 1)$. Certainly also:

$$(5) \qquad w^{h-}(a^h(\alpha), t) \geqslant \alpha w^{h-}(a^h, t) + (1 - \alpha)w^{h-}(a^{h'}, t).$$

Write (C.3) as

$$(6) \qquad \begin{aligned} &p^t(c^h(t) - s^{h-}(t), x^h(t)) + q^t(c^{hh}(t) - s^{hh-}(t), x^{hh}(t)) \\ &\qquad \leqslant q^t(t)w^h(a^h, t) + (p^t(t) - q^t(t))w^{h-}(a^h(t), t) + \pi^h(t). \end{aligned}$$

Then if a^h and $a^{h'}$ satisfy these constraints, since $w^h(a^h(\alpha), t) = \alpha w^h(a^h, t) + (1 - \alpha)w^h(a^{h'}, t)$, it follows from (5) and (H.2) that $a^h(\alpha)$ will also satisfy the constraints since by (D.2(ii)) $(p^t(t) - q^t(t)) \geqslant 0$. By the same argument $a^h(\alpha)$ satisfies (C.2) and it is obvious that it satisfies (C.1). Lastly $\bar{C}^h$ is convex.

It would be useful if F^h always had a non-empty interior. The rather strong postulate $\bar{c}^{hh} \gg 0$ is not enough for this since there is $(p, q) \in \mathscr{P}$ with $q = 0$. This is a mildly interesting by-product of this analysis, to which I return below. For the moment I sidestep this difficulty by making the following assumption.

ASSUMPTION (H.4): (*i*) *for each* h, $\bar{c}^{hh} \gg 0$; (*ii*) *for each* h, $\pi^h(t) > 0$ *if* $\pi(t) > 0$ $(\pi(t) = \Sigma_h \pi^h(t))$.

Both assumptions are of course silly. Assumption (H.4(ii)) in fact postulates that each household owns a strictly positive share in every marketing activity.

To establish the next theorem, I need to prove a preliminary result. Let $y^h = (c^h(1), x^h(1), c^{hh}(1), x^{hh}(1))$ and $W^h = q^1\bar{c}^{hh} + \pi^h(1)$.

LEMMA 4: (*i*) *For every* y^h *such that* $(p^1, q^1)y^h \leqslant W^h > 0$ *there is a plan* $a^h \in F^h(p, q, \bar{c}^{hh})$; (*ii*) *if* $a^h \in F^h(p, q, \bar{c}^{hh})$ *and* $W^h(p, q) > 0$, *then there exists* y^h *such that* $(p^1, q^1)y^h \leqslant W^h(p, q)$ *and* $c^{hh}(1), c^h(1) \geqslant 0$.

PROOF: (i) Set $\tilde{s}^h = 0$ and also $\tilde{x}^h(t), c^h(t) = 0$ for $t > 1$. Let $c^{hh}(t) = \max(0, \bar{c}^{hh}(t) + \tilde{\bar{x}}^h(t))$, $t > 1$. Then a^h with these components and y^h is a member of F^h.

(ii) If $a^h \in F^h(p, q, \bar{c}^{hh})$ then from (C.3) there is some y^h such that $W^h \geqslant (p^1, q^1)y^h - p^1(1)s^{h-}(1) - q^1(1)s^{hh-}(1) \geqslant (p^1, q^1)y^h$.

One can now prove the next theorem.

THEOREM 4: *The correspondence $F^h(p, q, \bar{c}^{hh})$ is continuous at $(p^0, q^0) \in \mathscr{P}$, when $W^h(p, q) > 0$, all (p, q)*

PROOF: (i) The set (p, q, a^h) satisfying (C.1)–(C.3), $\tilde{c}^h \in \bar{C}^h$, $\tilde{s}^h \in S^h$, is closed; hence F^h is upper semicontinuous at (p^0, q^0).

(ii) Let $(p^v, q^v) \in \mathscr{P}$ be a sequence approaching (p^0, q^0) and let $a^{h0} \in F^h(p^0, q^0, \bar{c}^{hh})$. By Lemma 4(ii) there then exists y^{h0} such that $(p^{10}, q^{10})y^{h0} \leqslant W^h(p^0, q^0)$. But we may choose a sequence y^{hv} such that $(p^{1v}, q^{1v})y^{hv} \leqslant W^h(p^v, q^v)$, $y^{hv} \to y^{h0}$, by the well known method of Debreu [**2**] since there is y^{h*} such that $(p^{10}, q^{10})y^* < W^h(p^0, q^0)$. By Lemma 4(i) to every y^{hv} in this sequence there is $a^{hv} \in F^h(p^v, q^v, \bar{c}^{hh})$. Hence there exists a sequence $a^{hv} \in F^h(p^v, q^v, \bar{c}^{hh})$ which converges on a^{h0} and so F^h is lower semicontinuous.

Now let $a^h(p, q, \bar{c}^{hh})$ be the set a^h in$F^h(p, q, \bar{c}^{hh})$ which maximises $u^h(\tilde{c}^h)$. I state without proof (since it is familiar territory) the following theorem.

THEOREM 3: *$a^h(p, q, \bar{c}^{hh})$ is convex and an upper semicontinuous correspondence if $W^h(p, q) > 0$ for all (p, q).*

This is all that I require concerning households.

3. THE MARKET TECHNOLOGY

For reasons of brevity I shall take all market activities at t to be fully integrated, that is, discuss them as if they were under the control of a single firm. I write M^t as the set of market activities that are technologically feasible at t. A member of M^t is a vector $\tilde{m}^t = (m^t, m^{Ht})$. Here m^t is the vector of net outputs of anonymous goods at t. One takes $m^{Ht} \leqslant 0$ and regards it as the vector of inputs of named goods at t. If $m^{Ht}_{it'}$ is a component of m^{Ht}, then $m^{Ht}_{it'}$ is the input of named good type (it') summed over h. That is, the actual name of the input is irrelevant in specifying the market technology. I shall write $\tilde{m}^t(t) = (m^t(t), m^{Ht}(t))$ as the sub-vector of $\tilde{m}^t$ whose components are goods of the type dated t and $\bar{\tilde{m}}^t = (\bar{m}^t, \bar{m}^{Ht})$ as the subvector whose components are goods dated $t' > t$. I postulate the following assumption.

ASSUMPTION (M.1): *(i) For all t, M^t is convex and closed; (ii) $M^t \cap (-M^t) = 0$ (irreversibility); (iii) $M^t \supset (-\Omega)$ (free disposal); (iv) $\tilde{m}^t \neq 0$, $\tilde{m}^t \in M^t$ implies $m^t(t) + m^{Ht}(t) < 0$ and $\bar{m}^t + \bar{m}^{Ht} = 0$; (v) there is $\tilde{m}^1 \in M^1$ with $m^1 \gg 0$.*

Some of these assumptions are pretty terrible. Assumption (M.1(i)) rules out increasing returns when casual observation suggests that set up costs are an important feature in transaction technologies. The assumptions are made because at present I do not see how to proceed without them. (M.1(iv)) is interpreted as follows. If $\tilde{m}t$ is feasible at t, then, provided $\tilde{m}t \neq 0$, (a) it must use more of some good of the type dated t as named input than it produces as anonymous output, and use not less of any such good as named input than it produces as output; (b) the activity transforms quantities of named goods of type dated $t' > t$ equal to the quantities of inputs of named goods of this type. This assumption ensures that a market activity dated t uses some resources dated t but uses no resources dated $t' > t$. For instance, to transact forward butter today uses some good available today but no good, other than the named forward butter, available after today.

There is a further serious assumption embedded in the definitions: the vector $\tilde{m}^t$ has no components bearing the name of the marketing firm. This is tantamount to ruling out durable inputs. The reason this unpalatable assumption is used is that I do not know what to postulate as a proper motive for marketing firms when present values cannot be unambiguously calculated. Recall that the shareholders, that is households, may have different discount factors. One way of overcoming this is to postulate a utility function for firms. I do not do this because it does not seem helpful to sidestep these difficulties so formally. For the same reason I do not allow any firm to engage in storage.

Let $M = \times M^t$; $\overline{M}$ is a bounded subset of M. Then I define $\tilde{m}(p, q)$, the market correspondence, where

$$\tilde{m}(p, q) = \{\tilde{m} | (p, q)\tilde{m} \geqslant (p, q)\tilde{m}', \text{ all } \tilde{m}' \in \overline{M}, \tilde{m} \in \overline{M}\}.$$

It is easy to see that if $\tilde{m} \in \tilde{m}(p, q)$, then

$$\tilde{m}^t \in \{\tilde{m}^t | (p^t, q^t)\tilde{m}^t \geqslant (p^t, q^t)\tilde{m}'^t, \text{ all } \tilde{m}'^t \in \overline{M}^t, \tilde{m}^t \in \overline{M}^t\}.$$

Since all this is closely related to well known production theory, I state without proof the next theorem.

THEOREM 4: *$\tilde{m}(p, q)$ is an upper semicontinuous correspondence from $\mathscr{P}$.*

The following lemma will be useful later.

LEMMA 5: *For $p^1 > 0$, $0 \notin \tilde{m}^1(p^1, 0)$.*

PROOF: By (M.1(v)) there is $\tilde{m}^1 \in M^1$, $\tilde{m}^1 \gg 0$, from which $(p^1, 0)\tilde{m}^1 > (p^1, 0)0$.

4. EQUILIBRIUM

I define

$$z^t(t) = \sum_h (c^h(t) - s^{h-}(t) - w^{h-}(t)) - m^t(t),$$

$$z^{Ht}(t) = \sum (c^{hh}(t) + s^{hh-}(t) - \bar{c}^{hh}(t) - s^{h+}(t)) - m^{Ht}(t),$$

$$\bar{z}^t = \sum x^h(t) - \bar{m}^t, \qquad \bar{z}^{Ht} = \sum x^{hh}(t) - \bar{m}^{Ht}(t),$$

$$z^t = (z^t(t), z^{Ht}(t), \bar{z}^t, \bar{z}^{Ht}) \qquad (z = z^1, \ldots, z^T).$$

Then I use the following definition.

DEFINITION (D.3): An equilibrium of a pure exchange economy with transactions is a price vector (p^*, q^*), a vector of household plans $a^* = (a^{*1} \ldots a^{*H})$, and a market activity vector $\tilde{m}^*$ such that (i) $a^{*h} \in a^h(p^*, q^*, \bar{c}^{hh})$ for all h, (ii) $\tilde{m}^* \in \tilde{m}(p^*, q^*)$, (iii) $z^* \leqslant 0$.

All this is straightforward and requires no comment. From what has already been established in earlier sections we suspect that by now traditional methods will show that an equilibrium exists. However, these methods take the price-simplex as the set to be mapped into itself while we have been concerned with the set $\mathscr{P}$.

Let $(p, q) \in \mathscr{P}$. By Lemma 1(i), $p^1 > 0$. If $q^1 > 0$, then by (H.4) $W^h(p, q) > 0$. If $q^1 = 0$, then by Lemma 5 $\pi(1) > 0$, whence by (H.4) $\pi^h(1) > 0$ and so $W^h(p, q) > 0$. Hence each household has positive wealth for all $(p, q) \in \mathscr{P}$ and so from Theorems 3 and 4, $z(p, q)$, the excess demand correspondence for the economy (i.e., a satisfies (D.3(i)) and $\tilde{m}$, (D.3(ii))), is upper semicontinuous and convex at all $(p, q) \in \mathscr{P}$.

From $\pi = (p, q)\tilde{m}$, (6), and (H.1), one easily verifies for $z \in z(p, q)$:

$$(7) \qquad \sum_t (p^t(t) - q^t(t), q^t(t), \bar{p}^t, \bar{q}^t)\hat{z}^t = 0$$

where $\hat{z}^t = (z^t(t), z^{Ht}(t) + z^t(t), \bar{z}^t, \bar{z}^{Ht})$, $\hat{z} = (\hat{z}^1 \ldots \hat{z}^T)$.

One may now proceed as in Debreu [**2**]. That is, we let $\mu(\hat{z})$ be the set of $(p, q) \in \mathscr{P}$ which maximises (7) given $\hat{z} \in \bar{E}^N$. Since $\mathscr{P}$ is compact, $(p - q) > 0$, this is a well defined problem and $\mu(\hat{z})$ is convex and upper semicontinuous. The mapping $\mu(\hat{z}) \times z(p, q)$ of $\mathscr{P} \times \bar{E}^N$ into itself has a fixed point (p^*, q^*, z^*). Using (7) one verifies from the definition of $\mu(\hat{z})$ that this is an equilibrium for the bounded economy. One then shows that by a suitable choice of bounds this is also the equilibrium for the actual economy. Here the procedure is no different from the usual one and I simply state the next theorem.

THEOREM 5: *The pure exchange economy with transactions has at least one equilibrium, with* $(p^*, q^*) \in \mathscr{P}$.

There is one comment I should like to make on this now. In establishing the existence of an equilibrium one need only be concerned with (7) even though a sequence of "Walras' laws" holds for the economy. When we come to discuss efficiency in the next section, matters will be different.

One would expect that many markets will be inactive in an equilibrium. Some anonymous goods will not be "produced" or demanded and the corresponding named goods not supplied or demanded. The analysis here is exactly analogous to that of non-produced goods in the conventional model. The abstraction becomes particularly irksome here, however, since one is asked to suppose that prices are established for all possible markets, active or not.

Consider an equilibrium in which all markets after $t = 1$ are inactive and suppose that all market activities require the input of leisure, and that households cannot consume more leisure than they are endowed with. (This last assumption causes no difficulty for Theorem 5.) Then since by (M.1(iv)) market firms will demand only leisure dated $t = 1$, it must be that in this economy the optimum plan of households involves the consumption of all their leisure after $t = 1$ (since the demand for leisure from other sources is zero). On the other hand, of course, the market activities at $t = 1$ must not use more leisure than there is. It is easy to see that such an equilibrium will be rather special and it is easy by some choice of Cobb-Douglas utility and market activity functions and endowments to construct a large class of examples where this equilibrium is impossible.

The point is, of course, simple: the economy may have active markets at various dates, because this is a sensible intertemporal use of resources. One is accustomed to saying that Debreu assumed all future markets to exist or at least that this is how his system can be interpreted. In the present construction this of course makes no sense. The Debreu economy results when only markets of a given date are active.

5. EFFICIENCY

I am interested in the question of whether an equilibrium for the economy is efficient.

In the present economy the distinction between named and anonymous goods is fundamental. One must therefore expect that in the definition of the set of feasible allocations, or transactions, the distribution of named goods between households and so the distribution of endowment between them will be essential. This is an important departure from the usual procedure where only aggregate endowments matter. We must also take account of transaction dates. A definition of efficiency will have to be relative to the given endowment matrix, denoted by $\hat{\bar{c}}$, and of course relative to the given market and storage technologies.

Let

$$A^h(\bar{c}^{hh}) = \{a^h | c^{hh} \leqslant \bar{c}^{hh} + s^{h+} + \tilde{\tilde{x}}^{h+}, w^h(T) \nless 0, \tilde{s}^h \in S^h, c^{hh}, c^h \geqslant 0\}.$$

Then $A^h(\bar{c}^{hh})$ is the set of activities of h which, given its endowment and storage technology, will not lead it to consume more of a named good of any type than it has, and will not lead it to a net endowment vector at T with every component negative. The set is not empty since $a^h = (0, 0, \bar{c}^{hh}, 0, 0)$ is a member. The set is convex, since S^h is. Write

$$A(\hat{\bar{c}}) = \mathop{\times}_h A^h(\bar{c}^{hh}),$$

a an element of $A(\hat{\bar{c}})$. For any a^h, let $v^h(a^h)$ be the vector with components

$$v^h_{it} = (\bar{c}^{hh}_{it} + s^h_{it} + \tilde{\tilde{x}}^h_{it} - c^{hh}_{it} + s^{h-}_{it})$$

and as usual $v^{h-}(a^h)$ has the components $\min(0, v_{it}^h)$. Also

$$v^-(a) = \sum v^{h-}(a^h).$$

The components of $v^-(a)$ measure the quantities of the anonymous good of the given type which must be bought if households are to fulfill their forward commitments.

Now let $\hat{a}^h$ be the vector a^h without the components $\tilde{s}^h$ and define

$$b(a) = \sum_h (\hat{a}^h - \tilde{s}^h) - (v^-(a), 0, \bar{c}, 0).$$

Then a positive element of $b(a)$ is the requirement of anonymous good of given type for the economy with plan a and endowment $\hat{c}$. A negative element is the available quantity of named good of given type.

I now write the set of feasible transactions b as

$$B = \{b | b = b(a) \text{ for some } a \in A(\hat{c}), b \leqslant \tilde{m} \text{ for some } \tilde{m} \in M\},$$

but I shall postpone discussion of this set until a little later.

Let a^* be an allocation of household activities, $b^* = b(a^*) \in B$ with $\tilde{m} = \tilde{m}^*$. Every activity a^h defines a unique consumption vector

$$\tilde{c}^h(a^h) = c^{hh} + c^h$$

and so one may write the set of activities h prefers to a^{h*} as

$$P^h(a^{h*}) = \{a^h | u^h(\tilde{c}^h(a^h)) > u^h(\tilde{c}^h(a^{h*}))\}$$

and also

$$P(a^*) = \bigtimes_h P^h(a^{h*}).$$

Definition (D.4): The set of transactions strictly Pareto superior to b^* is

$$\hat{B}(b^*) = \{b | b = b(a) \text{ for some } a \in P(a^*)\}$$

and $(b^*, \tilde{m}^*)$ is strictly efficient if

$$\hat{B}(b^*) \cap B = \varnothing.$$

It is not hard to show, given Assumption (H.4) [**1**], that there is no real loss of generality in considering strictly efficient rather than efficient transactions.

Now let $(a^*, \tilde{m}^*, p^*, q^*)$ be an equilibrium. Let

$$\hat{P}^h = P^h(a^{h*}) \cap A^h(\bar{c}^{hh}).$$

It is easy to see that $\hat{P}^h$ is not empty. Let $\hat{P} = \bigtimes_h \hat{P}^h$ and consider $a \in \hat{P}$, $b = b(a)$. By the definition of an equilibrium a^h cannot be feasible for h under his budget constraints. Since in general h faces a sequence of budget constraints, this does not, however, imply that the budget constraint for every t must be violated.

To be more precise, first note that by the usual arguments

$$(p^*, q^*)\tilde{m}^* \geqslant (p, q)\tilde{m}, \quad \text{all } \tilde{m} \in M,$$

whence on our assumptions $\pi^{h*} \geqslant \pi^h$, where π^{h*} is the profit received by h in equilibrium and π^h is the profit for any other transactions.

Also for each h there must be some t such that

$$(8) \qquad (p^{*t}(t) - q^{*t}(t), q^{*t}(t), \bar{p}^{*t}, \bar{q}^{*t})(z^h(t), z^h(t) + z^{hh}(t), x^h(t), x^{hh}(t)) > \pi^h(t).$$

But there may be $t' \neq t$ where the reverse inequality holds. Since this is true for all h, summing over h for every t may give

$$(p^{*t}(t) - q^{*t}(t), q^{*t}(t), \bar{p}^{*t}, \bar{q}^{*t})\hat{z}^t \leqslant 0, \quad \text{all } t.$$

But then we cannot show that $\hat{z}^t$ is not feasible. For $\hat{z}^t \leqslant 0$ for all t is possible, so that $z^t \leqslant 0$ for all t, whence one easily verifies that $a \in \hat{P}$, $b(a) \in B$.

The possibility of inefficient equilibria can be confirmed by simple examples. Suppose that the market technology uses labour and nothing else in transforming any given quantity of named good into the same quantity of anonymous good of the same type. By (M.1(iv)), the labour used has the same date as the transaction. For the purpose of this example assume also that labour is both anonymous and named; that is, I treat labour as if it were money. I shall also take the market technologies to be linear and equilibrium profits as zero.

We consider the given equilibrium situation and examine the following re-allocation. Let household h be enabled to consume one more unit of leisure at t by reducing the forward transactions in good (k, t') at t, $t' > t$, appropriately. By my special assumptions, giving labour the subscript o, the reduction in forward transactions in this market is given by $p^t_{ot}/(p^t_{kt'} - q^t_{kt'})$. By this reduction, the stock of named good (k, t') at t' will be reduced for some households, and I suppose that they are compensated for this by an equivalent quantity of anonymous good of that type. (We may suppose that all these households were consuming all of their named good of type (k, t') at t' on their equilibrium plan.) Household h is now required to provide the labour at t' required to make these new transactions at t' possible. We calculate that it must provide $((p^{t'}_{kt'} - q^{t'}_{kt'})/p^{t'}_{ot'})(p^{t'}_{ot}/(p^t_{kt'} - q^t_{kt'}))$ more units of labour at t' than it did on its equilibrium plan. In our experiment therefore we have allocated more labour to h at t and less at t' while changing the allocation of named and anonymous good of type (k, t') at t' to other households in such a manner as to keep their utilities constant. (Recall that household utility depends only on the type of good.)

Now if the equilibrium prices have the Debreu property, the calculations we have just carried out would lead to a substitution rate of labour at t for labour at t' for household h equal to $\lambda(t, t')$. The experiment which we have imagined was not possible for the decentralised economy (since it involves a violation by h of its budget constraint for t and by other households of their budget constraints for t'), although plainly feasible in its resource use, but it could not improve on the equilibrium allocation. For in this case the transformation rate given by the experiment is the same as the one already ruling in the market. This only confirms what is clear from Theorem 1 (and equation (4)), which can easily be used in the traditional way to show that an allocation that is strictly Pareto superior to the equilibrium one is not feasible.

However, if the equilibrium prices do not have the Debreu property, then the substitution rate established by our experiment may differ from that facing household h when it is constrained by a sequence of budgets. The possibility of equilibrium therefore being inefficient is clear.

The example that I have chosen is only a special case of a large class. When the equilibrium prices do not have the Debreu property the intertemporal transformation rates that are feasible for any household for a good of given type, given the resources of the economy and the utilities of all other households, will in general not be those that face the household in a decentralised economy. In such an economy these transformation rates will in general differ between households. It is also important to remember that while a household may, for a given consumption plan, have to engage in forward transactions to meet its budget constraint, the economy is only constrained by the resource use of transactions.

THEOREM 6: *An equilibrium of the pure exchange economy may be inefficient.*

I did not expect this result when I started, but in retrospect it is not surprising once one has understood why in this economy households are in general constrained by a sequence of budgets. Considering that all expectational matters and all uncertainty have been neglected, this shows that the recognition of transactions as activities has non-negligible consequences as such.

Let me now briefly take up the postponed discussion of the set B.

LEMMA 6: *B is a convex set.*

PROOF: Let b and $b' \in B$ and a and a' in $A(\hat{c})$ be such that $b = b(a)$, $b' = b(a')$. Let $a(\alpha) = \alpha a + (1 - \alpha)a'$, $\alpha \in (0, 1)$, etc. For each h,

$$v^{h-}(a^h(\alpha)) \geqslant \alpha v^{h-}(a^h) + (1 - \alpha)v^{h-}(a^h).$$

So

$$v^-(a(\alpha)) \geqslant \alpha v^-(a) + (1 - \alpha)v^-(a').$$

Since $A(\hat{c})$ is convex $a(\alpha) \in A(\hat{c})$ and $b(a(\alpha)) \leqslant b(\alpha)$. But $b(\alpha) \leqslant \tilde{m}(\alpha)$ and $\tilde{m}(\alpha) \in M$ from which $b(a(\alpha)) \leqslant \tilde{m}(\alpha)$ and $b(a(\alpha)) \in B$.

One may now use traditional arguments to show that every efficient point of B has associated with it a separating hyperplane,

$$(\mu^*, \lambda^*)(b^* - \tilde{m}^*) = 0. \tag{9}$$

Interpreting the first rT components of μ^* as the difference between the spot prices of anonymous and named goods, the remaining components as all forward (buying) prices of anonymous goods, and $\lambda^* = q$, we could obtain (7) from (9) if $v^-(a) = w^-(a) = \sum w^{h-}(a^h)$. But we may always choose a^* such that this equality holds. For suppose a household is, on the efficient plan, consuming some anonymous good type (i, t) although $w_{it}^{h}(t) < 0$. Then it must buy that much more of the anonymous good of that type. If instead we make this household consume none of the named good of that type and make it consume more of the anonymous good, its utility would be the same and the transactions would be the same. Hence for every b in B there is an a such that $v^{-}(a) = w^{-}(a)$, $b = b(a)$. Hence we can indeed obtain (7) from (9).

But this does not mean that the economy can be decentralised at these prices. For we are not allowed to redistribute endowments. (If we were allowed to do so the only efficient point would be one of zero transactions.) Even if at these efficiency prices the endowment of every household were such that the sum of its budget constraints over t were satisfied at the given allocation, that would not be enough since this would be consistent with the violation of a budget constraint at some t.

I have not been able to show that for any arbitrary $(\hat{c})$ there must exist an efficient allocation such that at its shadow prices the allocation is an equilibrium one. I conjecture that indeed this cannot be done and so that in general every equilibrium of the economy is inefficient.

The exceptional cases must be those for which an equilibrium with the Debreu property is possible.

6. MONEY

In this section the place of money in the kind of model here considered is examined briefly and somewhat discursively. The brevity is only partly due to lack of time. I am not at all clear what an appropriate theory, fully articulated, should look like. I hope to return to it at a future occasion.

Money will be written as a good of type (n, t), $t = 1, \ldots, T$. I use the following definition.

DEFINITION (D.5): A good of type (n, t), $t = 1, \ldots, T$, is called *money* if it has the following properties.

(i): For transactions at t, the good of type (n, t) is both named and anonymous. That is, no market is required to transform (n, h, t) into (n, t).

(ii): A given quantity of the good (n, t) can be transformed into an equivalent quantity of the good (n, t'), $t' > t$, by storage without the use of any resources.

(iii): $c_{nt}^{h} \equiv 0$ for all t and h. The good does not enter the utility function.

Property (i) does *not* abolish the distinction between named and anonymous for transactions at date t of quantities of goods (n, t'), $t' > t$. That is, the distinction continues to apply to transactions in money dated later than the transaction date. Property (iii) is used because all the interesting questions arise when money is intrinsically worthless and because I cannot appeal to a "convenience" yield of money when the purpose of the exercise is to discover what this might be from a study of transactions.

One of the consequences of (D.5(i)) is that agents, at a positive exchange value of money, are always willing to accept money in exchange for goods. The set of market activities feasible under this regime will in general be larger than the set when there is no such good. That is, the set of marketing activities in a monetary regime will contain the set under barter but not vice versa. I do not think it necessary to discuss this observation. But it gives rise to a technical problem which I can state but not resolve. If one supposes that in the usual sense, the activities involving a monetary exchange dominate those that do not, then when one considers the transition from a monetary to a non-monetary regime such as would be involved by setting all the prices of money in unit of account equal to zero, the activity transition may not be smooth—that is, there may be a discontinuity. Academic though this problem is it causes difficulties in the attempt to establish the existence of monetary equilibria.

One can calculate the rate of return in unit of account of buying (n, t') at t as $(p^{t'}_{nt'} - p^{t}_{nt'})/p^{t}_{nt'}$. The rate of return for storing money, given (D.5(ii)), is $(p^{t'}_{nt'} - p^{t}_{nt})/p^{t}_{nt}$. If the former rate exceeds the latter, no one will store money. Since money is durable (it cannot be consumed), someone must however store it if money is to have a positive price. Therefore one must show that the equilibrium of the economy does not at any t make the lending rate greater than the implicit storage rate for all $t' > t$ and in particular for t' closest to t. Indeed in monetary equilibrium it must always be more profitable to some agent to store money between two adjacent intervals than it is to buy forward in any market.

The question is whether an equilibrium with these properties can be shown to be possible or whether this requires one to change (D.5(iii)) and allow the storage of money to yield direct or indirect psychic returns.

Let us first of all note that the more finely time is divided, the more goods and transaction dates there are. If we had allowed for set up costs (and increasing returns), we could argue that to have markets at every t for all goods dated $t' \geqslant t$ **must** always use more resources when time is more finely divided. In that case one may be able to show that in any equilibrium many markets will be inactive and in particular all those at any t for goods dated t' when t' is sufficiently close to t. Indeed the Tobin-Baumol analysis of the transactions demand for money does rest on the assumption that forward purchases of money for short enough periods are always unprofitable. If such transactions do take place the lending rate is negative.

It will of course also be a requirement that at any t there are agents wishing to transfer resources to t' nearest to t. In my construction this causes a difficulty at $t = T$. But the assumption that all households have the same horizon is inessential (although an economy with an infinite horizon does pose well known problems), and I do not consider this further. However, a much more interesting question is raised.

Let me say that the economy is *intertemporally connected* if there is no t at which there are no intertemporal transfers between t and t' closest to t, with $t' > t$. In the absence of production there may be difficulties in showing that in every equilibrium the economy is intertemporarily connected, in which case there will be obvious difficulties for monetary theory. For money cannot act as a medium of exchange if it does not also act as a store of value for some agent. To avoid these difficulties it seems to me once again that the model which I have discussed must be modified.

If I had allowed for M to be non-convex, I could, for instance, have argued that a contract at t to sell (i, t) and (i, t') uses a different amount of resources than do the sum of separate contracts to sell $((i, t), (it + 1), \ldots, (it'))$. For instance, it is easier in practice to sell labour by the week than by the day and it may be impossible to sell it by the minute. Of course, to integrate this idea into a proper theory I should also have to allow marketing firms to be concerned intertemporarily with the attendant difficulties which I have discussed and which I cannot solve. In any event the possibility that the resource cost of a composite contract may be smaller than the resource cost of the sum of the component contracts seems to me to be important for monetary theory. Once again let me appeal to Tobin-Baumol. They have assumed that the agent's receipts are at discrete time intervals while their purchases are not. A proper money theory must explain why composite contracts of the kind I have been discussing are indeed a feature of an equilibrium. For if they are, the economy will certainly be intertemporally connected. It should be noted that composite contracts introduce new prices and goods.

All these arguments suggest that my description of M must be modified before one can hope to derive a satisfactory monetary theory. For instance, it would have been congenial, one suspects, to many monetary theorists if I had made the number of households concerned in any activity $\tilde{m}^t$ a relevant technological variable. For in that case the number of transactions would have been technologically relevant. So far I have not been able to do this without great damage to the result required by a theorist concerned with general equilibrium. But it needs somehow to be done since most of monetary theory takes it for granted that an equilibrium is possible.

I myself believe that further research on these problems will lead to a rigorous foundation of monetary theory. The alternative, of course, is to allow the holding of money to yield utility. To do this at all sensibly, of course, involves the dependence of the utility function on market prices as well.

If I am correct in my view that to obtain a theory in which money is not part of a household's ordering one requires a marketing set which lacks convexity properties, then there are good traditional grounds for the view that an equilibrium, if it exists, may be inefficient. These grounds are, of course, not those of the last section. On the other hand in such an equilibrium the intertemporal return on holding money is for each household just equal to the opportunity cost and the Friedman-like inefficiency is absent. If contrarily we use the model of the previous section and allow the holding of money to yield utility, then Friedmanesque inefficiency can be present while inefficiency arguments connected with non-convexity disappear. However, inefficiencies of the kind discussed in the previous section also remain possible. It should also be noted that since the opportunity costs of holding money differ between households the cure of Friedman inefficiency may not be possible in any simple manner.

7. EXPECTATIONS

If different states of the economy are possible, we enlarge the space of goods by adding states to their specification. In general one would not expect all markets to be active at every t for the reasons already discussed earlier. But there are other reasons. Radner [**3**] has noted that certain contingent futures contracts may be impossible because the observation of states must be partly deduced from information provided by the action of other agents, and it may be impossible to provide the same information to both parties of a potential contract.

So far I have taken all prices as known to every agent. But of course it will only be the prices ruling in the present which will be known. At any date t the agent may have a hypothesis associating the prices which will rule at $t' > t$, given any state of the economy. He may be taken to have a probability distribution over possible states. Both the hypothesis and the probability distribution may differ between agents if not all possible markets are active at t. Suppose all agents at every t have the same hypothesis but possibly different probability distributions. The following question has recently been studied by Radner (in a model without transaction costs) [**4**]: Does there exist a set of hypotheses linking prices to states, a price in the current period, and a set of contingent plans by all agents optimal for them such that for every state the excess demands for that state at all dates are zero? It will be desirable to study the same question for an economy described in this paper. It will also be very difficult.

One may wish to start far less ambitiously, however, by examining the short period equilibrium of an economy, that is, the existence of prices at t which, given the agents' expectations, clear all markets at t for the optimal choices made at t. Arrow and I [**1**] have studied this problem in a rather simple model without transaction costs. I have only time to discuss one aspect of this work here.

Radner, in his study to which I have referred [**4**], requires that a trader does not plan to deliver at any date-event pair more than he could meet out of his resources or spot purchases without violation of his budget constraint. This assumption, which is quite analogous to my (C.3) for the certainty case, rules out the possibility of bankruptcy.

Consider the simplest modification of the model. We examine the economy at t. All prices subsequent to t are expected prices. Suppose $(p^{t'h}, q^{t'h})$ is the single valued expectation of h at t of prices at $t' > t$. Assume that these are continuous functions of the prices ruling at t, (p^t, q^t). One wants to show that an equilibrium for t exists at every t. Assumption (H.3) is now plainly inappropriate. Without a Radner-like postulate, bankruptcy for some h at some (p^t, q^t) cannot be ruled out. Note that by its definition bankruptcy depends on the expectations of h, since it can always borrow at $t < T$. The creditor households may have quite different expectations. Consider a creditor household k which, for the sake of argument, receives all of the endowment of h at (p^t, q^t) where h is bankrupt. Then it is easy to see that the set of feasible choices open to k may fail to be continuous at these prices. Moreover, if h only has to hand over those goods which have a positive price, then its set of feasible choices may also fail to be continuous at these prices. This causes difficulties for an existence proof. In the present context, particularly in the absence of production, this difficulty may be academic. I believe, however, that it is of considerable interest in more realistic constructions. In any event the possibility of bankruptcy is one of the main obstacles a short period equilibrium existence proof would encounter in the simple form in which it is here given. It should be noted that this point would be reinforced if we allowed trade in the shares of market firms and if we could also permit intertemporal choices for these firms.

Of course a demonstration, if it is possible, of the existence of equilibrium at every t is quite different from the demonstration of a Radner equilibrium of self-fulfilling expectations. There is no reason to suppose that the first kind of sequence of equilibria will be efficient. Indeed here is a much more important source of inefficiency than that discussed earlier, in part at least ascribable to transaction costs. In so far as these latter costs are responsible for the sequence of markets, they are also responsible for the inefficiencies which arise at least out of "Radner-equilibrium." I do not at present know whether the existence of the latter kind of equilibrium can be established for the economy with transaction costs. But even if it can, I should be rather surprised if such an equilibrium would be a description of an actual economy. Radner himself has drawn attention to the formidable computation requirements which are another species of transaction costs.

London School of Economics and Political Science

REFERENCES

[1] ARROW, K. J., and F. H. HAHN: *General Equilibrium Analysis*, forthcoming.
[2] DEBREU, G.: *Theory of Value*. New York, Wiley, 1959.
[3] RADNER, R.: "Competitive Equilibrium Under Uncertainty," *Econometrica*, 38, No. 1 (January, 1968, pp. 31–58.
[4] ———: "Existence of Equilibrium of Plans, Prices, and Price Expectations in a Sequence of Markets, I and II," two mimeographed papers, 1970.

17

INEFFICIENCY AND THE DEMAND FOR "MONEY" IN A SEQUENCE ECONOMY

by David A. Starrett

In this paper, Starrett presents a full clear statement of the allocative inefficiency in equilibrium discovered by Hahn (selection 16). Further, a theory of money as a store of value is presented as an innovation that allows overcoming the inefficiency in equilibrium. A conceptual point on the idea of transaction costs and inefficiency is worth mentioning here. Transaction costs represent the scarce resources used in transferring goods between agents. Even on spot markets, trade is a resource-using activity. Merely incurring such costs is no evidence of inefficiency. Efficiency will usually require reallocation; reallocation is resource-using. Inefficiency arises when such costs are incurred unnecessarily.

The unnecessary cost that plagues sequence economy models comes from the sequence of budget constraints—one for each period—facing agents as they trade. This contrasts with the single lifetime budget constraint of the Arrow-Debreu model. In order to pay for purchases, agents who wish to buy goods in one period must sell goods in the same period and *vice versa*. Use of futures rather than spot markets may be imposed to overcome differences in the timing of consumption and endowment. In the event that futures markets are more costly to use than spot, the excess transaction costs incurred represent an efficiency loss. They are a cost incurred simply to satisfy the institutional requirement of a sequential budget constraint rather than being technically necessary to effect the reallocation. The loss is not limited to excess costs actualy incurred. Pareto-improving reallocations are discouraged by the implied high unnecessary transaction costs. Efficiency losses include the misallocation from the reduction of these impeded transactions.

ISBN 0-12-663970-1

Hahn correctly identified the condition he called the "Debreu property" as a sufficient (but not necessary) condition for allocative efficiency in equilibrium. The condition is that price ratios should be independent of transaction date, that is, independent of whether the goods are transacted on spot or futures markets. In the situation posited—where spot and futures transaction costs differ—we would not generally regard it as likely or desirable for the Debreu property to be fulfilled. Differences in spot and futures market transaction costs should show up in the price (including transaction cost) of the goods. Hence the Debreu property represents an uninteresting special case in the present setting (which Hahn subsequently labelled "inessential").

The solution of the inefficiency is somehow to sever the temporal link between commodity buying and selling transactions while continuing to fulfill the sequential budget constraint. The introduction of "money" is designed to achieve this. Money is defined as a commodity of positive price and zero transaction cost that does not directly enter in production or consumption. Rather than engage in costly futures trades to achieve budget balance at each trading date, traders use trade in money to bridge the gap in timing between desired sales and purchases. The assumption of zero money transaction cost is of course extreme but it captures the essential point: a major cost reduction relative to commodity trade.

Starrett thus successfully resolves the inquiry introduced by Hahn. When an intertemporal economy includes a time sequence of budget constraints, then transaction costs imply the possibility of inefficiency in equilibrium. The inefficiency results from misallocation due to the costs and reallocations incurred in fulfilling the sequence of budget constraints. These costs may be avoided by the introduction of a transaction costless carrier of value which allows re-establishment of the Arrow-Debreu lifetime budget constraint (net of necessary transaction costs) as the effective constraint on household reallocation. Money as a store of value allows intertemporal reallocation without the distortion implied by sequential budget constraint.

Reprinted from THE REVIEW OF ECONOMIC STUDIES, Vol. XL (4), October, 1973, DAVID STARRETT, pp. 437-448.

Inefficiency and the Demand for "Money" in a Sequence Economy[1,2]

DAVID STARRETT
Harvard University

Several authors have recently attempted to incorporate transactions costs and/or incomplete information into models of general equilibrium (see, for example, Foley [3], Radner [7] and Starr [9]). Of particular interest to us here is the model of Professor Hahn [4]. His model has the following properties (among others).

1. Perfect certainty; in particular, prices on all markets (both spot and future) are known for sure by all agents at the outset.
2. Convexity in the transactions technology; in the presentation transaction operations essentially take the place of production operations as there is no independent production sector.

A model with these properties seems, at first glance, to be isomorphic to another in which " sold " goods and " bought " goods are different commodities, and there is a production technology for transforming the one into the other. In such a model we would surely expect that if efficiency is defined relative to the transactions technology, then a competitive equilibrium would be efficient (all the assumptions of the standard theory would seem to be satisfied).

However, Professor Hahn argued that competitive efficiency (in the sense defined above) was highly unlikely. The argument was persuasive, but not completely convincing, since no actual examples of inefficiency were given. In this paper we seek first to elucidate the inefficiency by example. Having done so, we discover that the inefficiency can provide a rational demand for a certain type of money. For ease of exposition, the analysis is carried out entirely by example in Part I. A general treatment is deferred until Part II.

I. INEFFICIENCY AND REMEDY—THE SPECIAL CASE

A. *Examples*

We present here an example which is simple and illustrates the inefficiency in a compelling way. Later we will argue that none of the special features in the example are actually necessary for inefficiency.

Our economic environment will consist of a one-commodity world and two individuals, each of whom lives two periods. Furthermore, each has a fixed-coefficients utility function $U = \min(c_1, c_2)$ on consumption in the two periods.

We begin with the following assumptions on the transactions technology.

1. There are no costs associated with spot transactions. Thus, if I want to deliver a unit of goods from one man to the other, it costs me nothing as long as the transaction is arranged in the period of delivery.

[1] *First version received August* 1972; *final version received March* 1973 (*Eds.*).

[2] Kurz [6] has independently developed a simplification of the Hahn model very similar to ours. He presents an example of inefficiency but does not explore the implications in any detail. Research supported in part by NSF Grant GS 33958. This is a revised version of HIER Discussion Paper #242, Harvard University (1972).

2. Transacting *forward* is costly. In particular, if I want to transact a unit of second-period goods in period one, then the operation requires a unit of the good in period one. (We assume that the transactions technology is constant returns to scale.)

With such a simple transactions technology we can easily determine the efficient allocations in the example. Suppose that one consumer starts out with the initial allocation $(A, 0)$ and the other with $(0, A)$ Then it is clear that society wants to avoid using forward markets, since by using spot markets alone it can obtain any desired reallocation costlessly. The " efficient " allocations are of the form (d, d), $(A-d, A-d)$, where d is the parameter of the Pareto frontier.

Let us now examine the alternatives available to our consumers in a competitive model. As Hahn pointed out, we can no longer assume ourselves to be in an Arrow-Debreu world in which all transactions take place simultaneously (indeed, in light of what was said about efficiency in the last paragraph, we clearly do not want such a restriction). Hence, consumers must decide when to make trades as well as what to trade.

Throughout the paper we will employ the following notation.[1]

y^i_{ja} purchases in period i of commodities for delivery in period j, by individual a.

q^i_j the price paid for such purchases.

x^i_{ja} sales in period i of commodities for delivery in period j by individual a.

p^i_j the price received for such sales.

Note that we assume that all agents face the same prices (though all agents naturally need not have the same options).

Returning to the example, our consumers must decide in the first period how much to buy and sell spot and also, how much to buy and sell forward (the household only engages in " transactions " in its role as a " firm "; we separate these roles here as elsewhere in economic theory). Since there are no paper assets in the model, the household must cover the value of all purchases by corresponding sales of some sort. This implies a first period budget constraint of the form

$$q^1_1y^1_1+q^1_2y^1_2 \leqq p^1_1x^1_1+p^1_2x^1_2. \qquad ...(1)$$

In the second period, the household has the chance to make some new transactions at the new prevailing prices. Since no one lives beyond two periods in the example, there is just a spot market in the second period. The budget constraint becomes

$$q^2_2y^2_2 \leqq p^2_2x^2_2. \qquad ...(2)$$

For the man with initial resources $(A, 0)$, consumption is given by

$$c_1 = A+y^1_1-x^1_1;\ c_2 = y^1_2-x^1_2+y^2_2-x^2_2. \qquad ...(3)$$

And given a set of prices, he will seek to maximize his welfare subject to the pair of budget constraints (1) and (2). The other consumer faces a similar problem from the opposite resource base.

The transaction-market brokers are assumed to maximize profits.[2] This places some restrictions on the prices which can prevail in equilibrium. The zero-profit condition on spot markets implies that

$$q^1_1 \leqq p^1_1;\ q^2_2 \leqq p^2_2 \text{ (and equality where there is spot trading),} \qquad ...(4)$$

while the corresponding condition for the forward market yields

$$q^1_2 \leqq p^1_2+p^1_1 \text{ (and equality if there is any forward trading).} \qquad ...(5)$$

1 Our notation differs somewhat from that of Hahn [4]. This is because we have restructured the model in such a way that the theorems of Part II are most easily stated and proved.

2 By assuming a constant returns transactions technology (which is slightly less general than that of Hahn), we avoid the problem of specifying the firm's optimality criteria.

Without actually computing the equilibrium, we can already argue that it must be inefficient. By examining (2), (3) and (4), we can see that no consumer can benefit from use of the second-period spot markets. From (4), if the market is used, then $q_2^2 = p_2^2$. But then, (2) implies that $y_2^2 \leqq x_2^2$, and since y and $-x$ are perfect substitutes in consumption, the consumer is always better off to consume $-x$ directly rather than trade it. It follows immediately that, if the initial situation is to be improved upon at all, the forward market must be used. But any use of the forward market is inefficient, so the competitive solution must be. The competitive mechanism just does not allow an efficient use of the transactions mechanism. Notice in particular this is a finite period market failure in contrast to the infinite period failure first studied by Samuelson [8] and summarized in Starrett [10].

It is a simple matter to actually compute the equilibrium in this example. We have one free normalization, so we may as well set $p_1^1 = 1$. Also, since we know that forward trading is going to take place, we can set $q_2^1 = 1+p_2^1 = 1+p$. We can save ourselves some effort by using common sense. The consumer with endowment in the first period will not buy anything in the first period or sell anything in the second (this could be proved, of course). And vice versa for the other consumer.

The first consumer's problem can then be stated as

$$\max y_2^1 \text{ such that } A-x_1^1 = y_2^1 \text{ and } (1+p)y_2^1 = x_1^1 \qquad \ldots(6)$$

(with appropriate non-negativity conditions). Demand functions derived from solving this problem are

$$y_2^1 = A/(2+p);\; x_1^1 = A(1+p)/(2+p). \qquad \ldots(7)$$

Solving the second consumer's problem similarly, we derive the demand functions (since from (7) we see that the first-period spot market is going to be used, we can set $q_1^1 = 1$):

$$y_1^1 = Ap/(1+p);\; x_2^1 = A/(1+p). \qquad \ldots(8)$$

Now, since no second-period goods are used for transactions purposes, one equilibrium condition would have it that $y_2^1 = x_2^1$. However, from (7) and (8), this cannot be satisfied for any positive p; no matter what p we choose, supply exceeds demand. Hence the equilibrium sellers price must be zero. This completes the determination of the equilibrium prices. From (7) and (8) we compute

$$y_2^1 = A/2;\; x_1^1 = A/2;\; y_1^1 = 0;\; x_2^1 = A/2. \qquad \ldots(9)$$

There is equilibrium on the first-period spot market, since the broker will require $A/2$ units in order to transact $A/2$ forward. Equilibrium consumptions are, for the first consumer, $(A/2, A/2)$; while for the second, $(0, A/2)$. The utility pair so attained is $(A/2, 0)$. Since the pair $(3A/4, A/4)$ was achievable, the competitive outcome can clearly be dominated.

Does the inefficiency depend on special features of our example? If we were to list the special features, we would surely want to include (i) no substitutability in consumption, (ii) zero incomes for some consumers in some periods and (iii) different transactions possibilities for spot versus forward trades. The last of these would seem to be particularly important since it was the inability to use a costless spot market which was blamed for inefficiency in the example. However, we can now argue that the inefficiency does not depend on such differences.

Let us modify the example by requiring that spot as well as forward trades require a unit of resources at the date of the transaction, for each unit traded. How does this affect the example? Clearly the profitability conditions (4) must be modified to read

$$q_1^1 \leqq 2p_1^1;\; q_2^2 \leqq 2p_2^2 \text{ (and equality where there is spot trading).} \qquad \ldots(10)$$

Again, there is no possible benefit to anyone from using the second-period spot market.

Now notice that the first consumer's problem is completely unchanged. He never considered the possibility of buying spot before, and certainly will not now. Therefore, his demand functions are as before. The second consumer's problem can now be stated as

$$\max y_1^1 \text{ such that } y_1^1 = A - x_2^1, \text{ and } 2y_1^1 = px_2^1 \qquad \text{...(11)}$$

(with appropriate non-negativity conditions). The demand functions derived from this problem are

$$y_1^1 = Ap/(2+p);\ x_2^1 = 2A/(2+p). \qquad \text{...(12)}$$

Supply still exceeds demand at every positive price on the forward market, so $p = 0$ is again the equilibrium forward sellers price. It follows that the equilibrium solution is exactly the same as before. But the efficient solutions are drastically reduced, so we must check whether the equilibrium solution can still be dominated. To demonstrate dominance, let us pick $A = 14$, implying an equilibrium allocation of (7, 7); (0, 7). Now consider the following series of transactions.

1. One unit is transacted spot from the first man to the second, in the first period; one unit of first-period resources is used up in the process.
2. Four units are transacted forward from the second man to the first; four first-period units are used up in the process.
3. Four units are transacted spot from the second man to the first, in the second period; four second-period units are used in the process.

The result is that five units of first-period goods are used up, one goes to the second man and the first man is left with eight. Four units of second-period goods are used up, eight go to the first man, and the second is left with two. The resulting consumption configuration: (8, 8); (1, 2) clearly dominates the equilibrium one.

Thus, it is not differences in the transactions technology which are necessarily responsible for inefficiency. More subtle matters of timing may be involved. Here, because of the shape of the utility functions, it is desirable to keep the amounts of resources available for distribution equal. However, as soon as the forward market must be used in lieu of the second-period spot market, it becomes impossible to maintain the correct balance (first-period goods become too scarce).

We can also argue that the first two special features mentioned above are not essential to inefficiency. This can be done by substituting Cobb-Douglas utility functions and giving the consumers positive but unequal endowments in the two periods. The analysis is somewhat tedious, but inefficiency can still be demonstrated. Indeed, it is difficult to construct any examples in which efficiency will hold.[1]

B. *Remedies*

Intuitively speaking, the inefficiency can be thought to generate a demand for some new type of asset. As it stands now, people are restricted to holding commodity assets (long purchases, etc.); these opportunities for borrowing and lending are not sufficient to allow consumers to time their transactions in a socially optimal way. The introduction of new assets creates new degrees of freedom and hence may be expected to improve efficiency.

Given the simplicity of our example, it is not too surprising to find that the addition of a single new asset will restore efficiency. However, we will show in Section II that this single new asset is in fact sufficient to restore efficiency to the general Hahn model. Before providing a general treatment, we explain the workings of the asset with reference to the example.

First, we must ask whether it is possible to introduce a new asset into the model without at the same time incurring " new " transactions costs. If not, then introduction

[1] Efficiency holds in the Foley [3] model of equilibrium with transactions costs only because recontracting on spot markets in the second period is not allowed.

of the asset can never be an efficient alternative since such introduction involves additional transactions costs which were avoidable in a first best world.

As it turns out, it is possible to introduce *one* asset into a Hahn-type model in such a way that it incurs no additional *transactions.* Intuitively, this asset has the properties of a " checking account balance " or a " credit card balance ". The usual story that is told about transactions in the Hahn model is as follows: when I sell something I get credits in unit of account at some clearing house and when I buy something, I get debits (and the seller gets credits). In the Hahn model with *no* paper assets, these must cancel at each trading date. Now, we can introduce a paper asset without incurring any additional transactions by simply allowing net credit positions at the clearing house. Interest rates on these paper assets will be determined by the condition that the supply and demand for credit be equal (the clearing house takes no position). And, of course, that all households end their lives with no net asset position.[1]

Let us see how this scheme works out in the example. We revert to the original case in which there are no spot transactions costs. a_a^1 will stand for the net credit position taken (in unit of account) by household a in period one. Since we are now in a two-period example, whatever position is taken in period one must be redeemed in period two. Let s stand for the redemption price. For convenience we let the asset be numeraire in current value pricing. The first consumer (who we will now refer to as consumer g) will now consider the following posibilities: he still will not buy anything for first-period delivery or sell anything for second-period delivery. However, after he sells spot in the first period he may either buy forward or borrow against account and buy spot in the second period. Thus, he faces the problem:

$$\max \min (A - x_{1g}^1, y_{2g}^1 + y_{2g}^2)$$

subject to

$$(1+p)y_{2g}^1 + a_g^1 = x_{1g}^1$$

$$y_{2g}^2 = sa_g^1$$

(and non-negativity conditions on all variables except a_g^1). After some substitution, this problem reduces to

$$\max \left\{ \frac{As}{s+1} + \left[1 - \frac{(2+p)s}{s+1} \right] y_{2g}^1 \right\}, \quad 0 \leqq y_{2g}^1 \leqq \frac{A}{2+p}.$$

Individual g buys forward or takes credits according to whether the coefficient of y_{2g}^1 is positive or negative. This leads to the two possible solutions summarized below.

1. $s < 1/(1+p)$; $a_g^1 = 0$, $y_{2g}^2 = 0$, $x_{1g}^1 = A(1+p)/(2+p)$, $y_{2g}^1 = A/(2+p)$
2. $s > 1/(1+p)$; $y_{2g}^1 = 0$, $a_g^1 = x_1^1 = A/(1+s)$, $y_{2g}^2 = As/(1+s)$.

The second consumer (whom we will call h) has a similar choice between selling short or taking a deficit on account and selling spot later. His problem can be stated as

$$\max \min (y_{1h}^1, A - x_{2h}^1 - x_{2h}^2)$$

subject to

$$y_{1h}^1 + a_h^1 = px_{2h}^1$$

$$0 = sa_h^1 + x_{2h}^2$$

(and non-negativity conditions on all but a_h^1).

After some substitution, this problem reduces to

$$\max \left\{ \frac{pA}{1+p} + \left[\frac{s+1}{s(1+p)} - 1 \right] x_{2h}^2 \right\}$$

$$0 \leqq x_{2h}^2 \leqq \frac{As}{1+s}.$$

[1] Running the new market may naturally be costly. We return to this difficulty later.

Again there are two possible solutions depending this time on the sign of the coefficient of x_{2h}^2.

1. $s<1/p$; $x_{2h}^1 = 0$, $a_h^1 = -A/(1+s)$, $y_{1h}^1 = A/(1+s)$, $x_{2h}^2 = As/(1+s)$

2. $s>1/p$; $x_{2h}^2 = a_h^1 = 0$, $y_{1h}^1 = Ap/(1+p)$, $x_{2h}^1 = A/(1+p)$.

Comparing the solutions for the two consumers, we see that three regimes are possible. In regime one, $s<1/(1+p)<1/p$. In this case, consumer h wishes to borrow on account, but g does not want to lend. Hence, s must rise and this regime cannot represent equilibrium. Similarly in the third regime (with $s>1/p>1/(1+p)$), g wishes to lend on account but h does not want to borrow, so s must fall. Equilibrium can only occur in the middle regime with $1/(1+p)<s<1/p$. And indeed, it occurs for any s in this region, since for any such s, supply and demand are equal on spot markets and on the asset market. The final solutions are

$$a_g^1 = A/(1+s) = -a_h^1;\ x_{1g}^1 = A/(1+s) = y_{1h}^1;\ x_{2h}^2 = As/(1+s) = y_{2g}^2.$$

The implied consumptions are for g: $(sA/(1+s), sA/(1+s))$ and for h, $(A/(1+s), A/(1+s))$ Obviously, any of these solutions is efficient and, indeed, by varying s (and p) we can trace out the entire Pareto frontier.

The indeterminacy of our solution is of course partly due to the special features of our example. But not entirely. We shall see later that even in the general case there is a region of indeterminacy in the asset equilibrium.

II. A GENERAL HAHN-TYPE MODEL

A. *Characterization of Efficiency*

We consider, now, an abstract model of exchange with transactions costs; the model presented is less general than that of Hahn, in that we do not allow storage. However, this ommission seems rather inconsequential as far as results are concerned. We introduce a commodity index into the notation of Section I. Thus y_{ivh}^w now stands for the purchases at date w of commodity i, deliverable in date v, by individual h; and similarly for the other variables. The indices i, v will be suppressed when we want to refer to the vector of purchases by h at w; and similarly for other variables.

We are now in the general framework of the Hahn commodity space. Goods are distinguished by (1) physical characteristics, (2) when they are traded and (3) when they are delivered.

Transactions possibilities are defined as follows: at each date, certain trading possibilities are open to society. Let T^w refer to the set of possible transactions at date w; that is (x^w, y^w) constitutes a feasible trading pair at date w if $(x^w, y^w) \in T^w$. Of course, T^w includes forward trades negotiated at w as well as spot trades. Let T be the direct sum of the T^w. We assume

P.1 T^w is a closed convex cone, for each w; T satisfies the condition: $(x, y) \in T$ and $x \leqq y$, implies $x = y = 0$. In addition $0 \in T^w$.

Some comment should be made about *P*.1. We agree with Hahn that convexity is totally unreasonable here, since most transactions costs are of the set-up kind. However, Hahn suggested that even with convexity, certain anomalies occur; it seems worth retaining the assumption of convexity in order to study these anomalies. Given that we must assume convexity, the further restriction to constant returns seems quite innocuous, since if large transactions are really more costly than small ones, the brokers would always make many small transactions and no large ones.

The second part of *P*.1 is a "no free lunch" stipulation. It says that you cannot get more out of an aggregate trade than you put into it. The condition also rules out the case of costless transactions, a case in which we have no interest here.

Nothing more need be said about the nature of the sets T^w. In particular, we do not need to specify (as Hahn did) at what dates transaction costs occur; they could occur at the date of the transaction, at the date of delivery, or both. Of course, for the sake of realism, we will want to specify that trades cannot be made after the date at which delivery is to occur ($y_{iv}^w = 0$, $v < w$; etc.). Furthermore, if the T^w are to be pure transactions sets, they must incorporate the condition that one cannot deliver more than one has. The sets T^w can obviously incorporate these conditions. Note that we have defined the sets T^w before knowing what institutions will be in existence. That is, costs of running institutions are not included. We will return to the implications of this specification in the last section.

Let z be a variable standing for household initial resources. Given a set of proposed trades, the consumption vector for household h is

$$c_h = z_h - \sum_w x_h^w + \sum_w y_h^w. \qquad \ldots(13)$$

It is assumed that the individual cares only about consumption and not at all about the transaction dates; that is, we postulate:

P.2 Household h has a preference ordering ($\underset{h}{\succsim}$) on c_h. This ordering is convex, continuous, monotone, and admits no point of satiation.

For our purposes, it is more convenient to think of the household ordering as being on the pair $(x_h, y_h) = (\sum_w x_h^w, \sum_w y_h^w)$. Clearly, this is possible, *given the resource endowments as fixed.*

We are now suitably prepared to define efficiency. As Hahn noted, efficiency can only be defined relative to a set of resource endowments. So the fact that these latter have been fixed is quite intentional. Since consumers do not have preferences on trading dates *per se* (but only on the net consumption vectors which result), efficiency must be defined in a reduced commodity space, the space in which we are blind to the date of transactions and sum all sales and purchases vectors over the w index. Intuitively, a trade is efficient if no alternative trade which is available in the trading technology is Pareto preferred. To be more precise, define the following (closed, convex) set.

$$D = \{x, y \mid \text{there exists } (x_h, y_h) \geqq 0 \text{ such that } x = \sum_h x_h,\ y = \sum_h y_h,\ c_h \geqq 0 \text{ and}$$
$$(x_h, y_h) \underset{h}{\succsim} (\bar{x}_h, \bar{y}_h), \text{ all } h\}.$$

The set D consists of those aggregate trades which can be distributed in a way which is Pareto preferred or indifferent to a reference programme $(\bar{x}_h, \bar{y}_h)$. $(\bar{x}_h, \bar{y}_h)$ is efficient when and only when $(\bar{x}, \bar{y}) \in T$ (the set of aggregate trades which can be achieved by an appropriate set of dated transactions) and D contains no interior points of T.

Some remarks should be made concerning the set of feasible trades allowed in the model. The assumption $c_h \geqq 0$ implies that

$$\sum_w x_h^w \leqq \sum_w y_h^w + z_h.$$

According to this constraint, there is nothing to prevent the consumer from selling goods which he has just bought (although he clearly cannot sell goods which he does not have). If transactions are costly, he presumably will not choose to do so at equilibrium, but we impose no such restrictions *a priori*. Further, it should be noted that our requirement $c_h \geqq 0$ is a special case of the more general requirement that c_h lie in some feasible "survival" set. Again, the simplification is for convenience only. Finally, notice that the consumer is restricted from "buying at the selling price" by the requirement that $x_h \geqq 0$.

Since we have assumed convexity, we can immediately obtain from the separation theorem a price theory characterization of efficient distributions.

Theorem 1. *If* $(\bar{x}_h, \bar{y}_h)$ *is an efficient distribution, then there exists* $p, q \neq 0$ *such that (we have made the obvious choice of signs so that* $p \geqq 0, q \geqq 0$*):*

$$qy^w - px^w \leqq q\bar{y}^w - p\bar{x}^w, \text{ all } (x^w, y^w) \in T^w, \text{ all } w \quad \ldots(14)$$

and

$$qy_h - px_h \geqq q\bar{y}_h - p\bar{x}_h, \text{ all } (x_h, y_h) \underset{h}{\succsim} (\bar{x}_h, \bar{y}_h), \text{ with } x_h, y_h, c_h \geqq 0, \text{ all } h. \quad \ldots(15)$$

Proof. After applying the separation theorem, we use the decentralized structure of sets T and D in the usual way.

Theorem 1 provides us with " Debreu type " prices. Indeed, (14) tells us that the $\{x^w, y^w\}$ are profit maximizing at prices which do not depend on the transaction date. In other words, the relative price at which two goods can be traded does not depend on which date is chosen for making the transaction. (Recall that in the Hahn [4] model, equilibrium prices generally do depend on w). Since independence is an important property of the Debreu equilibrium, we will refer to the " prices " having this property as Debreu prices.

Conditions (15) can be given a pseudo-competitive interpretation. Suppose that households face Debreu-type prices instead of a sequence of budget constraints (let us not worry for the moment about how such a scheme could be administered). Then if household h is provided a subsidy (or taxed) the amount $q\bar{y}_h - p\bar{x}_h$ in present value, conditions (15) would say that the distribution $(\bar{x}_h, \bar{y}_h)$ is cost minimizing for each h at the Arrow-Debreu prices (q, p). We should be careful not to say that this is equivalent to competitiveness after a redistribution of income, since the initial endowment must be taken as fixed.[1]

It is somewhat surprising to find that the Debreu property should be characteristic of efficiency, particularly since we have not assumed that the trading possibility sets are the same at each trading date. One might argue, for example, that apples could be more expensive than oranges if contracted in advance than if contracted spot because the forward transaction is more costly. However, the answer to this is that if forward transactions are really more costly, then society should not be using them. And it is precisely the fact that individuals may have to use them that makes the competitive sequence economy inefficient. Indeed, we can now say that whenever equilibrium in the sequence economy is inconsistent with the Debreu property, then that equilibrium is inefficient. Clearly, this was the case in our examples.

When we consider various " asset equilibria " in the next section, we will find that there is a one-to-one correspondence between asset equilibria and equilibria of the type described in Theorem 1, *with no taxes or subsidies*, that is, output-price configurations satisfying (14) and

$$qy_h - px_h \geqq 0, \text{ all } (x_h, y_h) \underset{h}{\succsim} (\bar{x}_h, \bar{y}_h), \text{ with } x_h, y_h, c_h \geqq 0, \text{ all } h. \quad \ldots(16)$$

Such an equilibrium can be interpreted as a standard Debreu equilibrium for a model in which households and traders face present-value prices (p, q). (This is a statement in pure mathematics; there may be no set of institutions which make present value pricing possible.) Our model with households and traders is isomorphic to Debreu's model [2] with households and producers (the functions of producers and traders are mathematically indistinguishable). Therefore, we can assert the existence and efficiency of equilibria

[1] In a subsequent paper, Hahn [5] shows that Theorem 1 can be extended to the statement that our sequence economy is equivalent to a " Debreu " economy if and only if sequence prices have the Debreu property.

satisfying (14) and (16) (we will refer to such equilibria in the sequel as Debreu equilibria) by quoting the appropriate theorems from Debreu [2].[1]

B. *Asset Amended Equilibria*

We now introduce the idea of an " evergreen cash reserve " into the accounting system. People may borrow (or lend) against account simply by incurring a deficit (surplus) on account. No repayment date is specified (i.e. no specific forward contract is made); but interest will be charged (paid) and agents are required to end their lives with no net asset position.

Let d_h^w stand for the deficit of h in period w. The increment in the deficit in period $w+1$ will include interest payments plus the deficit position in $w+1$. Letting S^w stand for the interest factor on account, we obtain the recursive relation:

$$d_h^{w+1} = d_h^w S^w + q^{w+1} y_h^{w+1} - p^{w+1} x_h^{w+1} \qquad \text{...(17)}$$

d_h^w is of course sign unrestricted since h could take either a positive or a negative position. One may ask why we have not imposed the obvious conditions

$$y_{ivh}^w = x_{ivh}^w = 0,\ w > v.$$

The answer is that it is irrelevant whether or not we write in these conditions since they will automatically be satisfied at any feasible equilibrium (given that the transaction technology incorporates those conditions); it is notationally simpler to ignore those constraints and set up fictitious prices on the associated markets. Of course, it is possible that allowing this additional (fictitious) degree of freedom would make it more difficult to prove the existence of an asset amended equilibrium. However, we shall see below that this is not the case.

Each household begins its life with no net position and must end it with no net debit. We write these additional restrictions as

$$d_h^{b(h)-1} = 0;\ d_h^{n(h)} \leqq 0, \qquad \text{...(18)}$$

where $b(h)$ and $n(h)$ are the first and last periods of h's life, respectively.

The array $(p^w, q^w, \bar{x}_h^w, \bar{y}_h^w, \bar{d}_h^w)$ will be called an Asset Amended equilibrium if $(\bar{x}_h^w, \bar{y}_h^w, \bar{d}_h^w)$ maximizes

$$U^h(\ldots, z_{ish} - \sum_{t<s} (x_{ish}^t - y_{ish}^t), \ldots) \qquad \text{...(19)}$$

subject to

constraints (17), (18),

non-negativity on c_h, x_{iv}^w and y_{iv}^w,

$$(\bar{x}^w, \bar{y}^w) = \left(\sum_h \bar{x}_h^w, \sum_h \bar{y}_h^w\right) \in T^w \text{ (each } w) \qquad \text{...(20)}$$

and

$$q^w y^w - p^w x^w \leqq q^w \bar{y}^w - p^w \bar{x}^w, \text{ all } (x^w, y^w) \in T^w, \text{ each } w.$$

The asset feasibility condition $\sum_h d_h^w = 0$ (each w) is satisfied. ...(21)

[1] As it stands, equilibria satisfying (14)-(16) are not necessarily efficient because of a problem known as the " Arrow Corner ". This problem has to do with the fact that minimizing the cost of achieving given utility is not the same (necessarily) as maximizing utility subject to the associated present value constraint. If Debreu equilibrium is defined to mean the latter (call this Debreu *full* equilibrium), then such equilibria must be efficient.

The standard method of eliminating the distinction between Arrow-Debreu equilibria and Arrow-Debreu full equilibria is to assume some connectedness in the economy. Distinctions arise only in cases where some individuals wind up with zero income; this outcome can be eliminated by assuming that each individual has in his initial endowment goods which are desirable either directly or indirectly by others. The same condition could be used here, but we must be careful. It is not enough that I have goods which you would like to have. It would also have to be true that there was some way these goods could be delivered to you. We will not pursue this matter further here. For a general discussion see Arrow-Hahn [1, ch. 5].

The remainder of this section is devoted to establishing a set of conditions under which every Debreu equilibrium can be generated as an Asset Amended equilibrium and vice versa. This equivalence is interesting in itself, but our main purpose in presenting it is to establish the existence and efficiency of Asset Amended equilibria.

We prove first two lemmas.

Lemma 1. *The problem* (19) *is equivalent to*

$$(x_h^w, y_h^w) \text{ maximizes } U^h \qquad \text{...(22)}$$

subject to

$$\sum_w [S_w^n q^w y_h^w - S_w^n p^w x_h^w] \geqq 0, \qquad \text{...(23)}$$

and non-negativity on c_h, x_h^w, *and* y_h^w, *where* $S_w^n = \prod_{t=n}^{w} s^t$ *(and n is an arbitrary base date).*[1]

Proof. (23) is obtained from (17), (18) by substituting recursively for the d_h^w in (17), using (18) and multiplying by a term: $\prod_{t=n}^{b(h)-1} s^t$. To obtain (17) and (18) from (23), start with $d_h^{b(h)-1} = 0$, and define the d_h^w's recursively according to (17) (any d's are possible since there are no non-negativity restrictions on the d's). (23) then implies $d_h^{n(h)} \leqq 0$, so (20) must be satisfied.

Lemma 1 tells us that the consumer problem essentially reduces to one with a single budget constraint. Intuitively, this happens because the asset allows one to trade between the budget constraints of the different transaction dates.

Lemma 2. *Condition* (21) *is redundant in the sense that* (19) *and* (20) *imply* (21).

Proof. If we sum up (17) over all households at the equilibrium values, and use the fact that there are constant returns to scale in the trading technology, we obtain the relationship:

$$\sum_h \bar{d}_h^w = s^{w-1}\left(\sum_h \bar{d}_h^{w-1}\right). \qquad \text{...(24)}$$

Now, if $t = 1$ is the " initial " date of the model, we can arbitrarily set $\bar{d}_h^0 = 0$, all h. Then, the recursive relationship (24) implies that (21) is satisfied.

Theorem 2. *Assuming P.1 and P.2, every Debreu full equilibrium can be generated as an Asset Amended equilibrium.*

Proof. Let p, q be the Debreu prices, and define p^w, q^w, s_w^n as

$$q^w = q/S_w^n; \; p^w = p/S_w^n.$$

Clearly, there is one degree of freedom for defining these prices at each date, corresponding to the arbitrariness of the current value numeraire at each date. With these definitions, the Debreu problem for consumer h is identical to (22). Furthermore, profit maximization at prices (p, q) clearly implies (20) since (p^w, q^w) is a constant multiple of (p, q). The Theorem now follows from Lemmas 1 and 2.

The converse of Theorem 2 is not true in general. Indeed, society could perhaps be made better off if some trades were made for people before they were born. The simplest example involves two individuals, one born in the first period and one in the second; their preferences are such that they want to make an exchange of commodities x and y for delivery in period two. Now, if a forward transaction in period one uses fewer resources than a spot transaction at period two, an efficient outcome cannot be reached unless the second individual is somehow represented in period one. Clearly, inclusion of our asset does not help. Furthermore, there is no way that the necessary information could be made available to society at the time that it is needed, so for a model of overlapping generations, our definition of efficiency is too stringent.

[1] S_w^n should be interpreted as the interest factor on an appropriate long-term asset.

Thus, we must restrict ourselves to models which are either short term, or in which preferences of future generations are correctly reflected in the asset choices of their ancestors; that is, we assume

P.3 all families live concurrent finite lifetimes.

Theorem 3. *Assuming P.1-P.3, every Asset Amended equilibrium can be generated as a Debreu full equilibrium.*

Proof. Given Asset Amended prices, p^w, q^w, S^n_w, define corresponding Debreu prices by the rules:

$$q_{iv} = \min_w S^n_w q^w_{iv} \qquad \text{(each } i\text{)} \qquad \ldots(25)$$

$$p_{jv} = \max_w S^n_w p^w_{jv} \qquad \text{(each } j\text{)}. \qquad \ldots(26)$$

We claim first that the new Debreu problem is equivalent to (22) for the consumer: since y^w_{hiv} and y^z_{hiv} are perfect substitutes for h, he will make all his purchases at that transaction date for which $S^n_w q^w_{iv}$ is minimized. (Of course, he must be alive at that date; hence the need for *P*.3.) Lowering the other "prices" to this minimum value cannot change his real purchasing possibilities. A similar statement holds for sales.

Now, it follows that the new Debreu problem for producers must be equivalent to (20) also, since the effect of (25) is to lower the price of some delivered goods which were not traded (and therefore could not have been profitable in the Asset Amended equilibrium); such a change clearly could not make profitable in the Debreu world something which was not already profitable in the Asset Amended world. A similar statement holds for (28) and the associated sales.

The theorem now follows from Lemmas 1 and 2.

CONCLUSIONS

The results of this paper can be summarized as follows. We began by giving some examples to illustrate the generality of inefficiency in a Hahn-type sequence economy. Then, we showed that we could introduce an asset into the model in such a way that equilibrium would exist and always be efficient. Any time the economy would have otherwise been inefficient, this new equilibrium must surely generate positive demands for these assets. Since the assets involved are essentially privately created interest-bearing money, we are provided with a rationale for the introduction of a certain kind of "paper money" into the "real" world.

A few remarks should be made concerning some special features of the analysis. We argued earlier that the asset could be introduced without anyone being involved in any extra *transactions*. However, this does not necessarily imply (as we assumed) that no new *transactions costs* will be incurred. Indeed, we can imagine that it will take more effort to keep track of interest payments and to quote interest rates, than to simply operate a clearing house. If this is so, we cannot argue for sure that the introduction of such an asset will be a good thing; whether or not it is will depend on whether or not the extra transactions costs incurred are more than offset by the efficiency savings (our theorem would be false as it stands, since such costs will drive a wedge between borrowing and lending interest rates).

Hahn [5] shows that our "account balance" money can be replaced by a more conventional story. In his version, people are given fiat money at the beginning of their lives and required to give it up at the end; in the meantime, they may draw down or build up their assets by making transactions on "costless" spot markets. While this version is more realistic, Hahn is no more immune than we are from the criticism that he is ignoring the costs of running institutions, since he must have new spot prices for money at each date (the relative spot prices at adjacent dates take the place of our interest rates).

The trouble is that we both took the position that the transactions technology (like a production technology) reflected costs of delivering goods quite apart from the costs of running the institutions needed to effect the delivery. With this definition, it should be clear that no solution can be efficient which requires the setting up of " costly " institutions. We can only argue for the introduction of a paper asset if the institutional costs of doing so are outweighed by the efficiency savings we have discussed above, and no better alternative is available. The more general problem of choosing an optimal set of institutions is beyond the scope of this paper.

The same remark applies to the introduction of other types of paper assets which may require extra transactions.

Finally, we would like to return and reconsider the characterization of efficiency. The characterization in terms of Arrow-Debreu prices seems to rest squarely on our assumption that the roles of consumers and commodity brokers can be separated; more specifically, it depends on the assumption that the feasibility of an aggregate trade pair does not depend on who is doing the trading. This seems to be the appropriate assumption in a world in which it is always possible to pay someone else to do your shopping for you. However, in situations where people have a positive desire to shop for themselves (as many of us do), it is inappropriate since, then, whether I can trade my wares for a television set will depend on (among other things) whether I have enough time to go shopping.

These remarks are particularly telling when we introduce set-up costs into the transactions technology (as we eventually must). Of course, one consequence would be that we lose the property of convexity. But more than that, the presence of set-up costs surely means that we cannot talk about an " aggregate trading set "; the amount of goods which can be transacted depends now on how many individual transactions are made. This observation suggests that dropping the Hahn assumptions of convexity may lead to models with radically different properties from the ones reported here. We hope to analyze such models in future research.

REFERENCES

[1] Arrow, K. J. and Hahn, F. H. *General Competitive Analysis* (Holden Day, 1971).

[2] Debreu, G. *Theory of Value* (Wiley, 1957).

[3] Foley, D. K. " Economic Equilibrium with Costly Marketing ", *Journal of Economic Theory* (1970).

[4] Hahn, F. H. " Equilibrium with Transactions Costs ", *Econometrica* (1970).

[5] Hahn, F. H. " On Transactions Costs, Inessential Sequence Economies and Money ", *Review of Economic Studies* (This issue).

[6] Kurz, M. " Equilibrium in a Finite Sequence of Markets with Transaction Costs ", Technical Report No. 52; IMSSS Stanford University (1972).

[7] Radner, R. " Existence of Equilibrium of Plans, Prices and Price Expectations in a Sequence of Markets " I and II; two mimeographed papers (1970).

[8] Samuelson, P. " An Exact Consumption Loans Model of Interest With or Without the Social Contrivance of Money ", *Journal of Political Economy* (1958).

[9] Starr, R. M. " The Price of Money in a Pure Exchange Monetary Economy with Taxation ", *Cowles Foundation Preliminary Paper* No. 310 (1971).

[10] Starrett, D. A. " On Golden Rules, the ' Biological Theory of Interest ' and Competitive Inefficiency ", *Journal of Political Economy* (1972)

Reprinted from THE REVIEW OF ECONOMIC STUDIES, Vol. XLV (2), June, 1978, ROSS M. STARR, p. 391.

Money in a Sequence Economy: A Correction

ROSS M. STARR
University of California, Davis

In Starrett's [1] elegant and important study, there is an oversight in the statement of Lemma 1 (p. 446). The sense of the inequality in equation (23) and the definition of the interest factor S_w^n are incorrect as printed. An alternative correct formulation of the Lemma is:

Lemma 1 (*corrected*). *The problem* (19) *is equivalent to*

$$(x_h^w, y_h^w) \text{ maximizes } U^h \qquad \ldots(22)$$

subject to non-negativity of c_h, x_h^w, y_h^w, *and subject to*

$$\sum_w S_w^n(q^w y_h^w - p^w x_h^w) \leqq 0, \qquad \ldots(23) \text{ (corrected)}$$

where

$$S_w^n \equiv \prod_{t=n}^{w-1} 1/S^t, \quad \text{for } n \text{ an arbitrary base date } (n \leqq b(h)-1).$$

The original statement in Starrett [1] differs in the sense of the inequality and by defining S_w^n as $\prod_{t=n}^{w} S^t$. The proof follows as outlined in Starrett [1] with a change in multiplicative constant: "(23) is obtained from (17), (18) by substituting recursively for the d_h^w in (17) using (18) and multiplying by a constant:" $\prod_{t=n}^{n(h)-1} 1/S^t$. The rest of the proof is identical.

The new definition of S_w^n is formally very similar to Starrett's and represents what the term was intended to convey. S_w^n (corrected) $= S^w/S_w^n$ (original). Theorems 2 and 3 follow as before.

First version received November 1976; *final version accepted June* 1977 (*Eds.*).

Notation and the numbering of equations are taken from Starrett [1]. I am indebted to Rhonda Price for assistance in research and to David Starrett for a helpful conversation. Errors are my responsibility.

REFERENCE

[1] Starrett, D, "Inefficiency and the Demand for 'Money' in a Sequence Economy", *Review of Economic Studies*, **40** (1973), 437-448.

SECTION 3

Intertemporal Market Equilibrium with Transaction Costs

18

EQUILIBRIUM IN A FINITE SEQUENCE OF MARKETS WITH TRANSACTION COST

by Mordecai Kurz

This paper introduces the concept of an individual transaction technology in a well organized model of a sequence economy. Each household is endowed with its own transaction technology specifying the resource requirements for purchase and sale transactions. A household's consumption then is endowment plus purchases less sales and transaction costs incurred. On the basis of prices, endowment, and transaction technology the household faces an implied consumption opportunity set, and makes an optimizing choice. This implies a choice both of transaction date and among transaction techniques. Hence activity of markets and transaction costs incurred are the endogenous result of optimizing decisions. The emphasis on optimization and transaction technology at the level of the individual transactor is a distinctive contribution of the article. This becomes particularly helpful for consideration of nonconvex transaction costs (Heller-Starr, selection 19).

Reflecting a still unfilled gap in the literature, there is no explicit account of brokers, wholesalers, and retailers—agents whose business it is to create a market. Rather, the market is taken as a datum. It may be costly to get to the market and trade on it, but the market itself is a costless constant requiring no resources and no decisions.

The familiar problem of the Arrow corner, positivity of income, takes a distinctive form here. In order to avoid discontinuity of opportunity sets, the usual positivity of income considerations are strengthened to overcome the

General Equilibrium
Models of
Monetary Economies

ISBN 0-12-663970-1

effects of transaction costs. For example, it is not immediate that a good desired by everyone will trade at a positive equilibrium price—it must be desired net of transaction cost. The article develops in detail a weak family of sufficient conditions.

ECONOMETRICA

VOLUME 42 January, 1974 NUMBER 1

EQUILIBRIUM IN A FINITE SEQUENCE OF MARKETS WITH TRANSACTION COST

BY MORDECAI KURZ[1]

The work extends the results of an earlier paper by Hahn; it presents a model of a barter economy with a sequence of markets in which each trader operates with his own transaction technology. An equilibrium is proved to exist and the efficiency of equilibrium is discussed.

1. INTRODUCTION

THE MOST INVESTIGATED approach to general equilibrium theory has developed along the lines of the Arrow-Debreu model where all present and future decisions are made in a single market in the present. This model has raised a significant number of issues, some of which have been discussed by Radner [**6**]. The idea of viewing the economy as a sequence of markets rather than an extensive single market was introduced in order to overcome some of the difficulties mentioned above. Radner [**7**] worked with a sequence of markets in the context of analysis of behavior under uncertainty. Hahn [**3**] proposed a similar model for any economy with transaction cost and no uncertainty. Thus with transaction cost present and without uncertainty, the theory attempts to explain the distribution of transactions over time and the economic rationalization for the existence or non-existence of markets.

The present paper proceeeds further into the analysis of equilibrium in a sequence of markets with transaction cost. The paper has two basic aims: (i) to provide an analysis of Hahn's theory with a great simplification of his model; and (ii) to push the theory much further by investigating the technology of transactions and the motivation for selection of optimal transaction activities. Hahn left question (ii) above in an unresolved state, although in our opinion the study of this question is the essential part of the analysis.

Before proceeding into our analysis let us note some important differences between the concepts used in the conventional theory of general equilibrium and the concepts used here for the analysis of equilibrium with transaction cost.

The primitive concepts in the conventional theory of exchange equilibrium are "bundles of goods" or "allocations." These are vectors of goods with which an individual either starts the process or ends it. When transaction cost and transaction

[1] This work was supported by the Ford Foundation Faculty (1971/72) and by National Science Foundation Grant GS-3269 at the Institute for Mathematical Studies in the Social Sciences, Stanford University. The author benefited greatly from extensive conversations with Professor Bezalel Peleg. The Seminar in Mathematical Economics at the Hebrew University led by Professor R. Aumann provided very valuable critical suggestions.

technology are introduced, the focus shifts to a different primitive concept, the "exchange vectors." In the conventional theory of exchange, one can always define the exchange to be the difference between the initial allocation and the final allocation. When transaction costs are present such simple transformations are not possible since the basic material identities do not hold, and the choice of transaction *activities* is an economic issue of its own. In Hahn's treatment [**3**] he arrives at those concepts by making a distinction between "named" and "anonymous" goods. Thus every good may have its owner's name on it or it may be "in the market" without a name. The act of transaction becomes, in fact, a change in category, and thus the structure of budget constraints revolves around those changes in the two categories. Although appealing, the Hahn structure ultimately becomes too complicated and thus fails to clarify the main issues.

It appears to us that the critical distinction is to be made between the stock of goods at hand and the flow of transactions. This distinction allows us to keep the dimensionality of the commodity space at its conventional level, yet it makes it possible to study in a rich fashion the structure of transactions over time and the budget constraints associated with transactions in each market.

2. DESCRIPTION AND NOTATION

We shall deal here with an exchange economy in which there are H households, each making decisions over T periods. Thus the index h runs from 1 to H and t runs from 1 to T. At each moment of time t there are potential spot markets for the N commodities and future markets for delivery of these N commodities in times $t + 1, t + 2, t + 3, \ldots, T$. The horizon being fixed leads to a rather peculiar situation where the number of potential futures markets is greatest at $t = 1$ and smallest (in fact, equal to zero) at $t = T$, at which time only spot markets can be held. Let us now introduce some notation:

$\omega^h(t)$ is the vector of endowment at t for household h.

$\omega^h = (\omega^h(1), \omega^h(2), \ldots, \omega^h(T))$.

$x_\tau^h(t)$ is the vector of purchases made at time t for delivery at time $\tau \geqslant t$. This is purchased in the τ futures market at t.

$x^{ht} = (x_t^h(t), x_{t+1}^h(t), x_{t+2}^h(t), \ldots, x_T^h(t))$.

$y_\tau^h(t)$ is the vector of sales at time t for delivery at time $\tau \geqslant t$.

$y^{ht} = (y_t^h(t), y_{t+1}^h(t), y_{t+2}^h(t), \ldots, y_T^h(t))$.

$g_\tau^h(t)$ is the vector of transaction cost registered at the transaction time t and will occur at time $\tau \geqslant t$.

$g^{ht} = (g_t^h(t), g_{t+1}^h(t), \ldots, g_T^h(t))$.

$\bar{x}_t^h = \Sigma_{\tau=1}^{t-1} x_t^h(\tau)$ is the vector of past accumulated futures purchases whose delivery date is t.

$\bar{y}_t^h = \Sigma_{\tau=1}^{t-1} y_t^h(\tau)$ is the vector of past accumulated futures sales whose delivery date is t.

$s^h(t)$ is the vector of commodities coming out of storage at t.

$s^{ht} = (s^h(t), 0, 0, \ldots, 0)$.

$s^h = (s^{h1}, s^{h2}, \ldots, s^{hT})$.

$z^h(t)$ is the vector of commodities placed into storage at t.
$z^{ht} = (z^h(t), 0, 0, \ldots, 0)$.
$z^h = (z^{h1}, z^{h2}, \ldots, z^{hT})$.
$c^h(t)$ is the vector of consumption at t.
$c^h = (c^h(1), c^h(2), \ldots, c^h(T))$.

Sometimes we shall find useful the distinction between spot and futures transactions; thus for y^{ht} or x^{ht} we shall write

$$y^{ht} \equiv (y_t^h(t), \bar{y}^{ht}), \qquad \bar{y}^{ht} \equiv (y_{t+1}^h(t), y_{t+2}^h(t), \ldots, y_T^h(t)),$$
$$x^{ht} \equiv (x_t^h(t), \bar{x}^{ht}), \qquad \bar{x}^{ht} \equiv (x_{t+1}^h(t), x_{t+2}^h(t), \ldots, x_T^h(t)).$$

$p_\tau(t)$ is the price vector (futures if $\tau > t$) of commodities traded at time t and delivered at time τ.
$p^t = (p_t(t), p_{t+1}(t), \ldots, p_T(t))$.

Finally we introduce the following global vectors:

$$x^h = (x^{h1}, x^{h2}, x^{h3}, \ldots, x^{hT}),$$
$$y^h = (y^{h1}, y^{h2}, y^{h3}, \ldots, y^{hT}),$$
$$g^h = (g^{h1}, g^{h2}, g^{h3}, \ldots, g^{hT}),$$

and

$$p = (p^1, p^2, p^3, \ldots, p^T).$$

Note that all the vectors $x_\tau^h(t)$, $y_\tau^h(t)$, $g_\tau^h(t)$, $\bar{x}_t^h$, $\bar{y}_t^h$, $s^h(t)$, $z^h(t)$, $c^h(t)$, and $\omega^h(t)$ are in E_+^N while ω^h, s^h, z^h, and c^h are in E_+^{NT}. The vectors x^{ht}, y^{ht}, g^{ht}, and p^t are of ranging dimensions $N(T - t + 1)$ and thus x^h, y^h, g^h, and p belong to $E^{NT(T+1)/2}$.

In this model we do not introduce any uncertainty; thus a household receives a sequence of spot endowments $\omega^h(t)$, it wishes to make a sequence of spot consumptions $c^h(t)$, and it is allowed at any market date to engage in any spot or future exchange that is available. We shall investigate the existence and characteristics of such a sequence of equilibria.

3. THE TRANSACTION TECHNOLOGY[2]

The transaction technology from which optimal transaction activities are selected is the main tool of this paper. The name "transaction technology" is perhaps misleading since it is only intended to specify the technological possibilities of transacting goods while incurring transaction cost. On a deeper level the "transaction technology" and the way it is used provide a complete characterization of the nature of exchange. Thus, an exchange economy and a monetary economy have different transaction technologies, and they are used differently. In separate papers (Kurz [**4** and **5**]), we discuss the issue of a monetary economy, but here we shall restrict our attention to a barter economy where money is not present, either as a medium of exchange or as a store of value.

[2] The concept of "transaction technology" was also employed in our papers [**4** and **5**].

In any economy with transaction cost, the transaction technology incorporates the social arrangements and conventions. It also reflects the legal system since it may specify the legal requirements concerning changes in titles to commodities. Thus different social arrangements result in different transaction technologies purely as a result of legal ways of protecting property rights. It is thus obvious that the transaction technology will reflect the level of commercial development and the degree of sophistication of the exchange process. For example, in a primitive society where bilateral exchanges are the only way to trade, the structure of the transaction technology will be different than in an exchange economy with a well organized market.

It is important to specify the degree of commercial development of the economy which we study in this paper since this is the basic justification for our assumptions regarding the transaction technology. We view the exchange process as taking place in a "market." The existence of such a "market" means two fundamental things. First, all conceivable multilateral exchanges are possible, and since all the commodities are "brought" to the market it really makes no difference if the exchange is made between one person and n others. Thus, the distribution of initial holdings does not influence the transaction technology itself. Second, the market itself provides the basic pool of resources from which services and commodities needed to carry out the transactions can be contracted. This interpretation of a "market" is critical, since without a market an individual may have a bundle of commodities to trade but may not have at his disposal those specific services and commodities needed (as real transaction cost) to carry out the exchange. Without a "market" an exchange cannot take place, while one of the fundamental functions of the market is to provide the possibilities of exchange.

The second interpretation above points out our conception of a market in a more developed commercial economy. In the next level of development the "market" provides money as a medium of exchange, and in a further level of development it will also provide money as a store of value.

In our economy each household is thus endowed at time t with a transaction technology T^{ht} which is the set of all triples (x^{ht}, y^{ht}, g^{ht}) which are technically possible: If the household buys x^{ht} and sells y^{ht}, then it must incur g^{ht} in transaction cost. Here all exchanges and cost are in terms of real (spot and futures) commodities. The set T^{ht} incorporates all the elements discussed earlier. Note, however, that T^{ht} also incorporates the customary way buyers and sellers divide the transaction cost, since g^{ht} is household h's share of the total transaction cost involved while the rest of these costs are being borne by other members in the market. We allow T^{ht} to be different for different households in order to take into account differences among individuals. The reader may wish to assume $T^{ht} \equiv T^{t}$ for all h. A more important fact, which we shall elaborate below, is that in this paper we do not assume that the "market" takes on the function of a trading agent. Thus each individual carries out his own transactions subject to his own transaction technology. We return to this point below.

As for dimensionality note that T^{ht} has a larger dimension than $T^{h(t+1)}$ because of the same reasons given above. In fact, we have that $T^{ht} \subset E_{+}^{3N(T+1-t)}$.

Finally, we have the storage activities. We wish to simplify this matter and thus assume the existence of a set $S \subset E^{2N}$ such that $(z(t), s(t+1))$ is a feasible storage pair if $(z(t), s(t + 1)) \in S$.

4. SOME ASSUMPTIONS

We shall distinguish between assumptions which we maintain throughout and those which we modify later. Some assumptions will be presented in the proper context below. The following assumptions *will be maintained throughout*.

ASSUMPTION T.1: *T^{ht} is a closed convex set.*

ASSUMPTION T.2: *If $(x^{ht}, y^{ht}, g^{ht}) \in T^{ht}$, then $x^{ht'} \leqslant x^{ht}$, $y^{ht'} \leqslant y^{ht}$, and $g^{ht'} \geqslant g^{ht}$ imply $(x^{ht'}, y^{ht'}, g^{ht'}) \in T^{ht}$.*

ASSUMPTION T.3: $(0, 0, 0) \in T^{ht}$.

ASSUMPTION T.4: *There exist $\hat{x}^{ht} \gg 0$, $\hat{y}^{ht}$, and $\hat{g}^{ht}$ such that $(\hat{x}^{ht}, \hat{y}^{ht}, \hat{g}^{ht}) \in T^{ht}$ and $\hat{y}^{ht} - \hat{g}^{ht} \gg 0$.*

ASSUMPTION D.1: *$\underset{h}{\lesssim}$ is a continuous preference ordering over E_{+}^{NT}.*

ASSUMPTION D.2: *$\underset{h}{\lesssim}$ is convex.*

ASSUMPTION E.1: *$\Sigma_{h=1}^{H} \omega^h(t) \gg 0$ for all t.*

ASSUMPTION S.1: *S is a closed convex set.*

ASSUMPTION I.1: *$x_\tau^h(t) = y_\tau^h(t) = 0$ for all $\tau \geqslant 1, t < 1$, all h.*

ASSUMPTION I.2: $s^h(1) = 0$, *all h.*

It is clear that T.1–T.4 are the special assumptions of this work. Assumption T.4 essentially says that some trade is possible where the net amount sold is less than the vector of transaction cost.

We shall see below that some additional assumptions may be needed to ensure the existence of equilibrium. For the purpose of designation only, let us now introduce some alternative assumptions that may be used below. Whenever they are used we shall explicitly state so.

ASSUMPTION D.3 (Desirability): *If $c^{h'} \gg c^h$, then $c^{h'} \underset{h}{\succ} c^h$.*

ASSUMPTION E.2: *$\omega^h(t) \gg 0$ for all t and all h.*

ASSUMPTION T.2: *If $z \gg 0$, then there exists $s \gg 0$ such that $(z, s) \in S$.*

5. BUDGET AND DEMAND CORRESPONDENCES

The individual consumer wishes to buy vectors x^{ht} and sell vectors y^{ht} while incurring g^{ht} as transaction cost. At any market date t he is faced with the following level of consumption:

$$c^h(t) = \tilde{\omega}^h(t) + x_t^h(t) - y_t^h(t) + s^h(t) - z^h(t) \qquad (t = 1, 2, \ldots, T), \tag{1}$$

where

$$\tilde{\omega}^h(t) = \omega^h(t) + \tilde{x}_t^h - \tilde{y}_t^h \qquad (t = 1, 2, \ldots, T),$$

and his budget constraint for exchange and storage is simply

$$p^t x^{ht} \leqslant p^t y^{ht} - p^t g^{ht} \qquad (t = 1, 2, \ldots, T), \tag{2}$$

$$(x^{ht}, y^{ht}, g^{ht}) \in T^{ht} \qquad (t = 1, 2, \ldots, T),$$

$$(z^h(t), s^h(t + 1)) \in S \qquad (t = 1, 2, \ldots, T).$$

It is important to note that it is the individual who regards the transaction technology T^{ht} to be his own. The level of development of the market under analysis calls for the individual to select his $(x^{ht}, y^{ht}, g^{ht}) \in T^{ht}$ but *without insisting that* $g_t^h(t) \leqslant \omega^h(t)$; this was the basic point we made earlier. One may consider a more developed market where a retailing activity is organized within the market. This producer has a technology T^t and all individual transactions must satisfy $(x^{ht}, y^{ht}, g^{ht}) \in T^t$. In this economy the retailer becomes a regular profit maximizing agent, and because of his transaction cost it becomes necessary to introduce a dual price system p^{bt} and p^{st}, where p^{bt} are buying prices and p^{st} are selling prices. In such an economy the retailer's profits are derived from the differences between p^{bt} and p^{st}, and in equilibrium these differences reflect transaction cost. From the viewpoint of the household the budget constraint becomes

$$p^{bt} x^{ht} \leqslant p^{st} y^{ht}, \tag{2'}$$

where the requirement $(x^{ht}, y^{ht}, g^{ht}) \in T^t$ is an equilibrium condition only.

The above economy is clearly an interesting one but we postpone its study to a separate paper. It is our belief that the introduction of a profit maximizing trader is intrinsically related to the separation of the act of buying from the act of selling and thus the introduction of money at least as a medium of exchange. This point and its implications are discussed by Kurz [**4**]. Here we want to confine ourself to a barter exchange economy.

Let us now introduce some additional notation:

$$px^h = (p^1 x^{h1}, p^2 x^{h2}, \ldots, p^T x^{hT}),^3$$

$$py^h = (p^1 y^{h1}, p^2 y^{h2}, \ldots, p^T y^{hT}),$$

and

$$pg^h = (p^1 g^{h1}, p^2 g^{h2}, \ldots, p^T g^{hT}).$$

[3] This is a very special kind of an "inner product" operation.

The "budget set correspondence" will be defined for the set of feasible actions (x, y, g) and (z, s). We thus define

$$(3) \qquad B^h(p) = \left\{ (x, y, g, z, s) \;\middle|\; \begin{array}{l} px \leqslant py - pg \text{ [4]} \\ (x^{ht}, y^{ht}, g^{ht}) \in T^{ht}, (z(t), s(t+1)) \in S \\ \hfill (t = 1, 2, \ldots, T) \\ 0 \leqslant \omega^h(t) + \tilde{x}_t + x_t(t) + s(t) - \tilde{y}_t - y_t(t) - z(t) \\ \hfill (t = 1, 2, \ldots, T) \end{array} \right\}.$$

Given a point $(x, y, g, z, s) \in B^h(p)$, we define

$$(4) \qquad c^h(x, y, g, z, s) = \omega^h(t) + x_t + \tilde{x}_t(t) + s(t) - \tilde{y}_t - y_t(t) - z(t) \qquad (t = 1, 2, \ldots, T);$$

then we define the demand correspondence

$$(5) \qquad \gamma^h(p) = \left\{ (x^h, y^h, g^h, z^h, s^h) \in B^h(p) \;\middle|\; \begin{array}{l} c^h(x^h, y^h, g^h, z^h, s^h) \underset{h}{\succsim} c^h(x, y, g, z, s) \\ \text{for all } (x, y, g, z, s) \in B^h(p) \end{array} \right\};$$

finally we introduce the following definition:

DEFINITION: A vector $\{p^*, (x^{*h}, y^{*h}, g^{*h}, z^{*h}, s^{*h}), h = 1, 2, \ldots, H\}$ is a *competitive equilibrium* if

(i) $\qquad (x^{*h}, y^{*h}, g^{*h}, z^{*h}, x^{*h}) \in \gamma^h(p^*)$,

(ii) $\qquad x^* \leqslant y^* - g^*$,

$$x^* = \sum_{h=1}^{H} x^{*h},$$

$$y^* = \sum_{h=}^{H} y^{*h},$$

$$g^* = \sum_{h=1}^{H} g^{*h}.$$

It is of critical importance to note that the budget set $B^h(p)$ is invariant under T positive constants which can multiply $p^t, t = 1, 2, \ldots, T$. This means that in each one of the T time periods only relative spot and futures prices matter. This may appear peculiar in view of the possibility of storage. It appears that, say, relative spot prices in two successive spot markets should be a determining factor in the profitability of storage. This is not the case since relative prices and the subjective exchange rates between consumption at t and $t + 1$ are sufficient to allow the consumer to make intertemporal allocations. In fact, this only brings out a fundamental principle for the theory of sequence of markets: Without money as a store of value only relative prices in each period matter. Thus *the demand correspondence*

[4] Note: $px \equiv (p^1x^1, p^2x^2, \ldots, p^Tx^T)$.

in our economy without money as a store of value is homogeneous of degree zero in T positive scalars that multiply the price vectors p^t.

This means that we can restrict our search for equilibrium to the set of simplexes P_t so that

$$P_t = \{p^t | p^t > 0, \|p^t\| = 1\} \qquad (t = 1, 2, \ldots, T), \tag{6}$$

and

$$p \in P_1 \times P_2 \times \ldots \times P_T \equiv P.$$

Before proceeding to prove the existence of equilibrium, it may be desirable to review the notion of equilibrium used in this work. Keeping in mind that at time τ only markets dated τ are actually open, the idea of clearing markets before they actually open means that the present theory deals with consistency of plans and expectations. Thus the notion of sequential equilibrium which is discussed here can be viewed as the precise concept of perfect and correct foresight.

6. EQUILIBRIUM WHEN $\omega^h(t) \gg 0$, ALL h AND ALL t

In spite of the fact that x^h, y^h, g^h, z^h, s^h, and p have special intertemporal structure, we have reduced the analysis of equilibrium to a point where conventional equilibrium techniques can be applied. Let us then consider the economy under assumption E.2 according to which $\omega^h(t) \gg 0$ for all h and t.

LEMMA 1: *The budget set correspondence $B^h(p)$ is a closed convex set for all $p \in P$; under Assumptions E.2 and T.4, $B^h(p)$ is also continuous at all $p \in P$.*

PROOF: Convexity and closedness is straightforward. Also upper semi-continuity follows from Assumptions T.1, D.1, and S.1. To prove lower semi-continuity, it is sufficient to prove that for any p, $B^h(p)$ contains a point which satisfies all the constraints with strict inequalities. Thus let $z = 0$ and $s = 0$.

First consider $t = 1$. By Assumption T.4 there exists $(\hat{x}^1, \hat{y}^1, \hat{g}^1) \in T^{h1}$ such that $\hat{x}^1 \gg 0$ and $\hat{y}^1 - \hat{g}^1 \gg 0$. By Assumptions T.2 and T.3 for any $0 < \varepsilon_1 < 1$ and $\delta_1 \leqslant \varepsilon_1$ we also have $(\delta_1 \hat{x}^1, \varepsilon_1 \hat{y}^1, \varepsilon_1 \hat{g}^1) \in T^{h1}$. Since $\omega^h(1) \gg 0$, then for a given p^1 there exists a small ε_1 and $\delta_1(p^1, \varepsilon_1) \lesseqgtr \varepsilon_1$ such that

$$\begin{aligned} &0 \ll \omega^h(1) + \delta_1 \hat{x}_1(1) - \varepsilon_1 \hat{y}_1(1), \\ &\delta_1 p^1 \hat{x}^1 < \varepsilon_1 p^1 \hat{y}^1 - \varepsilon_1 p^1 \hat{g}^1. \end{aligned} \tag{7}$$

The last inequality in (7) follows from the fact that $\|p^1\| = 1$ and $\hat{y}^1 - \hat{g}^1 \gg 0$.

The above argument was based on Assumptions T.2, T.3, T.4, and $\omega^h(1) \gg 0$; since the same conditions prevail for all t, it can be repeated for all t. Thus a sequence $\varepsilon_1, \varepsilon_2, \ldots, \varepsilon_T$ and $\delta_1, \delta_2, \ldots, \delta_T$ can be found such that

$$\delta_t p^t \hat{x}^t < \varepsilon_t p^t \hat{y}^t - \varepsilon_t p^t \hat{g}^t, \tag{8a}$$

when ε_t can be chosen to be as small as we please and $\delta_t \equiv \delta_t(p^t, \varepsilon_t)$ is chosen accordingly.

Now we have to scale ε_t down so that for each t

(8b) $$0 \ll \omega^h(t) + \delta_t \hat{x}_t(t) - \varepsilon_t \hat{y}_t(t) + \tilde{x}_t - \tilde{y}_t.$$

However, to do that note that

$$\varepsilon_t \hat{y}_t(t) + \tilde{y}_t = \sum_{\tau=1}^{t} \varepsilon_\tau \hat{y}_t(\tau),$$

and since $\hat{x}_t(\tau) \gg 0$, $\tau = 1, \ldots, t$, and $\omega^h(t) \gg 0$ by assumption, (8b) can be satisfied by simply choosing $(\varepsilon_1, \varepsilon_2, \ldots, \varepsilon_T)$ such that

$$\tfrac{1}{2}\omega^h(t) \gg \sum_{\tau=1}^{t} \varepsilon_\tau \hat{y}_t(\tau) \quad \text{for} \quad t = 1, 2, \ldots, T. \qquad Q.E.D.$$

COROLLARY: *If we replace Assumption E.2 by the assumption* $\omega^h(1) \gg 0$, *all* h, *and add Assumption S.2, the possibility of storing all commodities, then the conclusions of Lemma* 1 *are not changed.*

In order to proceed we have to follow the standard procedure of equilibrium theory and bound our economy. We let

$$\omega(t) = \sum_{h=1}^{H} \omega^h(t),$$

$$\omega^t = (\omega(t), \omega(t+1), \ldots, \omega(T)),$$

$$\omega = (\omega(1), \omega(2), \ldots, \omega(T)) \quad (\text{thus } \omega \equiv \omega^1),$$

and

$$W = (\omega^1, \omega^2, \omega^3, \ldots, \omega^T),$$

and define a large cube K_ρ which is defined by

$$K_\rho = \{(x, y, g, z, s) | x \leqq \rho W, y \leqq \rho W, g \leqq \rho W, z \leqq \rho W, s \leqq \rho W\}$$

with $\rho > 1$. Now we restrict the budget set to K_ρ so that

$$B_\rho^h(p) = B^h(p) \cap K_\rho.$$

Similarly we redefine the demand correspondence

$$\gamma_\rho^h(p) = \left\{ (x^h, y^h, g^h, z^h, s^h) \in B_\rho^h(p) \,\middle|\, \begin{array}{l} c^h(x^h, y^h, g^h, z^h, s^h) \underset{h}{\gtrsim} c^h(x, y, g, z, s) \\ \text{for all } (x, y, g, z, s) \in B_\rho^h(p) \end{array} \right\};$$

with this definition we have the following lemma:

LEMMA 2: *Under the conditions of Lemma* 1 *the demand correspondence* $\gamma_\rho^h(p)$ *is non-empty, compact, convex, and upper semi-continuous for all* $p \in P$.

With the two lemmas at hand we can now prove the following lemma:

LEMMA 3: *Under the conditions E.2 and T.4 the bounded exchange economy under consideration has a competitive equilibrium.*

PROOF: First we define

$$\gamma_\rho(p) = \sum_{h=1}^{H} \gamma_\rho(p). \tag{9}$$

For any vector $\{(x^h, y^h, g^h, z^h, s^h), h = 1, 2, \ldots, H\}$ define

$$\begin{aligned}\mu_t\{(x^h, y^h, g^h, z^h, s^h), h = 1, \ldots, H\} \\ = \left\{p^t \in P_t \,\middle|\, p^t \sum_{h=1}^{H} (x^{ht} - y^{ht} + g^{ht}) \text{ is maximum}\right\}.\end{aligned} \tag{10}$$

Let

$$\mu(x, y, g, z, s) = \mathop{\times}_{t=1}^{T} \mu_t(x, y, g, z, s). \tag{11}$$

Now consider the mapping

$$\Phi[(x, y, g, z, s), p] = \gamma_\rho(p) \times \mu[(x, y, g, z, s)]. \tag{12}$$

From (9), Lemma 2, and the definitions (10) and (11), it follows that Φ is a non-empty convex, compact, and upper semi-continuous correspondence. Under these conditions Φ satisfies all the conditions of the Kakutani fixed point theorem. Thus there exists $(x^*, y^*, g^*, z^*, s^*, p^*)$ such that

$$p^* \in \mu[(x^*, y^*, g^*, z^*, s^*)] \tag{13a}$$

and

$$(x^*, y^*, g^*, z^*, s^*) \in \gamma_\rho(p^*). \tag{13b}$$

But (13b) means that there exists

$$(x^{*h}, y^{*h}, g^{*h}, z^{*h}, s^{*h}) \in \gamma_\rho^h(p^*) \qquad (h = 1, 2, \ldots, H), \tag{14}$$

and thus

$$p^{*t} x^{*ht} \leqslant p^{*t} y^{*ht} - p^{*t} g^{*ht}. \tag{15}$$

Expression (13a) means that for all $p^t \in P_t$,

$$p^{*t} \sum_{h=1}^{H} (x^{*ht} - y^{*ht} + g^{*ht}) \geqslant p^t \sum_{h=1}^{H} (x^{*ht} - y^{*ht} + g^{*ht}). \tag{16}$$

Using the budget constraint (15) we have that

$$p^t \sum_{h=1}^{H} (x^{*ht} - y^{*ht} + g^{*ht}) \leqslant 0 \quad \text{for all } p^t \in P_t. \tag{17}$$

From (6) it follows that $p^t > 0$; thus (17) implies

$$\sum_{h=1}^{H} (x^{*ht} - y^{*ht} + g^{*ht}) \leqq 0, \tag{18}$$

or

$$x^{*t} - y^{*t} + g^{*t} \leqq 0 \qquad (t = 1, 2, \ldots, T).$$

Combining (14) and (18) we find that $\{p^*, (x^{*h}, y^{*h}, g^{*h}, z^{*h}, s^{*h}), h = 1, 2, \ldots, T\}$ satisfy (i) $(x^{*h}, y^{*h}, g^{*h}, z^{*h}, s^{*h}) \in \gamma_\rho^h(p^*)$, and (ii) $x^* \leqq y^* - g^*$. *Q.E.D.*

We note that if the weaker form of desirability D.3 is assumed, then $x^* \ll y^* - g^*$ is not possible, and then from the definition (10) of μ_t above it is clear that $p^{*t}(x^{*t} - y^{*t} + g^{*t}) = 0$, all t.

Now we need to prove that equilibrium in the bounded economy leads to an equilibrium in the unbounded economy. Thus we have the following theorem:

THEOREM 1: *Under the maintained assumptions and E.2, the exchange economy under consideration has a competitive equilibrium.*

PROOF: By Lemma 3 any K_ρ-bounded economy has a competitive equilibrium. Using the same procedure as in Kurz [**5**, Theorem 1], we show that the sequence of competitive equilibria are uniformly bounded and have a limit point which is a competitive equilibrium in the unbounded economy. *Q.E.D.*

7. EQUILIBRIUM II: $\omega^h(t) \gg 0$, ALL h and t, DOES NOT HOLD

In Section 6 we showed that, except for the maintained assumptions, equilibrium will exist in two cases: (i) if $\omega^h(t) \gg 0$, all h all t, and (ii) if $\omega^h(1) \gg 0$, all h, and positive storage is possible (Assumption S.2). It is interesting to discover that when we do not assume these two conditions, our equilibrium analysis changes significantly. It is here that the structure of the transaction technology becomes critical and the study of equilibrium requires a deep analysis of the transaction possibilities sets. In order to motivate our discussion below let us first review some examples of issues which cause difficulties. These are not to be viewed as problems which necessarily lead to non-existence of equilibrium, but rather as problems arising from the fact that the structure which we have introduced in this paper is sufficiently new that it needs further enrichment.

EXAMPLE 1: When $\omega^h(t) > 0$ but not $\omega^h(t) \gg 0$, it is possible that $p^t\omega^{ht} = 0$ (where $\omega^{ht} = (\omega^h(t), \omega^h(t+1), \ldots, \omega^h(T))$. However even if $p^t\omega^{ht} > 0$, it is not clear that anything of value can feasibly be purchased. Thus there may not exist $(x^t, y^t, g^t) \in T^{ht}$ such that $p^t x^t \leqq p^t y^t - p^t g^t$ and (ignoring storage), $\omega^h(t) + \tilde{x}_t(t) + x_t - y_t(t) - \tilde{y}_t \geqslant 0$. In fact, for $y^t \leqslant \omega^{ht}$ there may be no vector in T^{ht} such that $p^t y^t - p^t g^t > 0$. The economic meaning of the problem is very simple: The endowment may be such that, given the price system, *any* exchange plan will use up in transaction cost more than the value of the endowment.

EXAMPLE 2: At times the issue of exchanging present goods for future goods arises. Thus sometimes it is desired to sell a fraction of the endowment $\omega^h(t)$ and purchase a vector $x^t = (0, \bar{x}^t)$ where $\bar{x}^t \gg 0$, while incurring spot transaction cost $g^t = (g_t(t), 0)$. This means that we wish to sell a vector $y^t = (y_t(t), 0)$ with $p^t y^t > 0$ and buy a vector $x^t = (0, \bar{x}^t)$ such that $(x^t, y^t, g^t) \in T^{ht}$ with $g^t = (g_t(t), 0)$. The feasibility of such a transaction is not necessarily assumed.

EXAMPLE 3: If we even assume *strong* desirability it still does not follow that all prices are positive. If $p_{t_i}(t) = 0$, then we wish to increase the purchases of $x_{t_i}(t)$ and make it large. However, the purchase of large $x_{t_i}(t)$ involves a transaction cost which may not be free, and therefore such an increase in the spot commodity purchases at time t will violate the budget constraint even when the commodity has zero price. This last problem is really not surprising and to some extent is natural for a world with transaction cost.

Turning now to the analysis of equilibrium, let us first raise the natural question: Under what alternative conditions would the budget set correspondence be continuous?

ASSUMPTION T.5: *For every y^1 and for any p^1 with $p^1 y^1 > 0$ there exists $(x^1, y^1, g^1) \in T^{h1}$ such that $p^1 y^1 > p^1 g^1$ and $x^1 \gg 0$.*

Assumption T.5 covers all the cases of intertemporal exchanges. For example, consider $y^1 = (y_1(1), 0)$. Then T.5 says that there exists feasible $y^1 = (y_1(1), 0)$, $x^1 \gg 0$, and g^1 such that $p^1 y^1 > p^1 g^1$. However, T.5 requires the existence of x^1 and g^1 for any choice of p^1. Thus if $p^1 = (p_1(1), 0)$, then T.5 says that $p_1(1) y_1(1) > p_1(1) g_1(1)$ and $x \gg 0$.

From the argument above it follows that the following lemma is true:

LEMMA 4: *The following two conditions are equivalent:*

ASSUMPTION T.5: *For every y^1 and for any p^1 with $p^1 y^1 > 0$, there exist $(x^1, y^1, g^1) \in T^{h1}$ (x^1 and g^1 may depend upon p^1) such that $x^1 \gg 0$ and $p^1 y^1 > p^1 g^1$.*

ASSUMPTION T.5′: *For every y^1 there exist $(x^1, y^1, g^1) \in T^{h1}$ such that $x^1 \gg 0$, $y^1 > g^1$, and for any $y_{\tau_j}(1) > 0$ we have $y_{\tau_j}(1) > g_{\tau_j}(1)$.*

One more approach to this issue is to isolate a special commodity, say 1, and think of it as "leisure services" with which everybody is endowed; thus $\omega_1^h(t) > 0$ for all h and t. Now we can introduce an assumption based on this structure. To start with, consider any vector $y^1 = (y_1(1), y_2(1), y_3(1), \ldots, y_T(1))$ with $y_{\tau 1}(1) > 0$ for all $\tau = 1, 2, \ldots, T$. Define, for $0 < \lambda \leqslant 1$, $y_\lambda^1 \equiv (y_{\lambda 1}(1), y_{\lambda 2}(1), \ldots, y_{\lambda T}(1))$

where[5]

$$(19)\qquad y^1_{\lambda\tau j} = \begin{cases} y_{\tau 1}(1) & \text{for all } \tau = 1, 2, \ldots, T, \\ \lambda y_{\tau j}(1) & \text{for all } \tau = 1, 2, \ldots, T \text{ and all } j \neq 1. \end{cases}$$

Thus y^1_λ is a sales vector where the present and future leisure components are unchanged while all other components are reduced by a factor λ.

ASSUMPTION T.5″: *For any* y^1 *with* $y_{\tau 1}(1) > 0, \tau = 1, 2, \ldots, T$, *there exist* $0 < \lambda \leqslant 1, x^1$, *and* g^1 *such that*:
(*i*) $(x^1, y^1_\lambda, g^1) \in T^{h1}$,
(*ii*) $x^1 \gg 0$,
(*iii*) $g_{\tau 1}(1) > 0, g_{\tau j}(1) = 0, j \neq 1$, *all* τ, *and*
(*iv*) $y_{\tau 1}(1) > g_{\tau 1}(1)$, *all* τ.

The above assumption says that if we have a sales vector y^1 with positive components of all present and future commodity 1 then we can scale down all other components and find a purchase vector $x^1 \gg 0$, and carry out this exchange using *only* present and future "leisure" such that the total "leisure" used up in every market is less than the total "leisure" offered for sale.

Assumption T.5″ allows us to conclude that at least vectors y^1 with positive present and future components of commodity 1 can be feasibly exchanged for some positive quantities of all present and future commodities.

LEMMA 5: *Under any of the following three assumptions the budget set correspondence is continuous for all* p^1 *with* $p^1\omega^{h1} > 0$ (*i.e.*, $p^1\omega^{h1} = \Sigma^T_{t=1} p_t(1)\omega^h(t)$ *and* $\omega^{h1} = (\omega^h(1), \omega^h(2), \ldots, \omega^h(T))$): (*i*) (*T.5*); (*ii*) (*T.5′*); (*iii*) (*T.5″*) *and* $\omega^h_1(t) > 0$ *for all h and t.*

PROOF: Upper semi-continuity of $B^h(p)$ is immediate. To prove lower semi-continuity we show the existence of a vector in $B^h(p)$ which satisfies all the constraints with strict inequalities.

Parts (i), (ii): Since T.5 and T.5′ are equivalent, we prove the lemma under T.5′. Thus assume $p^1\omega^{h1} > 0$. Now let $y^1 = (1/2)\omega^{h1}$; since $p^1y^1 > 0$, it follows from T.5′ that there exist $(x^1, y^1, g^1) \in T^{h1}$ such that $p^1y^1 > p^1g^1$ and $x^1 \gg 0$. By T.2 for any $0 < \varepsilon \leqslant 1$, $(\varepsilon x^1, y^1, g^1) \in T^{h1}$; thus we can choose ε small enough so that $\varepsilon p^1x^1 < p^1y^1 - p^1g^1$. Now consider the vector $\bar{\omega}^{h1} = \omega^{h1} - y^1 + \varepsilon x^1$; since $y^1 = (1/2)\omega^{h1}$, it follows that

$$\bar{\omega}^{h1} = 1/2\omega^{h1} + \varepsilon x^1 \gg 0.$$

We have thus demonstrated that an initial trade is feasible such that at the end of it $\bar{\omega}^h(t) \gg 0$ for all h and all t. However, from the proof of Lemma 1 it then follows that $B^h(p)$ is continuous.

[5] We use the notation $y_{\tau j}(1)$ to mean the jth component of the vector $y_\tau(1)$. This is used instead of the more common notation $y_{\tau_j}(1)$.

Part (iii): Using T.5″ we choose again $y^1 = (1/2)\omega^{h1}$. Here again $p^1 y^1 > 0$ and for any $0 < \lambda \leqslant 1$, $p^1 y^1_\lambda > 0$ and $y_{\tau 1}(1) > 0$, all τ. By T.5″ there exist $(x^1, y^1_\lambda, g^1) \in T^{h1}$ such that $p^1 y^1_\lambda - p^1 g^1 > 0$ and $x^1 \gg 0$. Again for small enough $\varepsilon > 0$, $(\varepsilon x^1, y^1_\lambda, g_1) \in T^{h1}$ and $\varepsilon p^1 x^1 < p^1 y^1_\lambda - p^1 g^1$. Repeating the same calculation as in the first part of the proof we find that after one trade we can assure $\bar{\omega}^h(t) \gg 0$ for all h and t, and thus by Lemma 1 $B^h(p)$ is continuous *Q.E.D.*

Now we define

$$\gamma^h(p) = \left\{(x^h, y^h, g^h, z^h, s^h) \in B^h(p) \,\middle|\, \begin{array}{l} c^h(x^h, y^h, g^h, z^h, s^h) \underset{h}{\gtrsim} c^h(x, y, g, z, s) \\ \text{for all } (x, y, g, z, s) \in B^h(p) \end{array}\right\}.$$

In order to proceed to the analysis of equilibrium we have to bound our economy in a large enough rectangle K_ρ which now must be defined. Let

$$\omega(t) = \sum_{h=1}^{H} \omega^h(t),$$

$$\omega^t = (\omega(t), \omega(t+1), \omega(t+2), \ldots, \omega(T)),$$

$$W = (\omega^1, \omega^2, \omega^3, \ldots, \omega^T),$$

$$K_\rho = \{(x, y, g, z, s) | x \leqslant \rho W, y \leqslant (\rho - 2/H)W, \\ g \leqslant (\rho - 1)W, z \leqslant \rho W, s \leqslant \rho W\},$$

and select $\rho > H + 2$. Then let

$$B^h_\rho(p) = B^h(p) \cap K_\rho,$$

$$\gamma^h_\rho(p) = \left\{(x^h, y^h, g^h, z^h, s^h) \in B^h_\rho(p) \,\middle|\, \begin{array}{l} c^h(x^h, y^h, g^h, z^h, s^h) \underset{h}{\gtrsim} c^h(x, y, g, z, s) \\ \text{for all } (x, y, g, z, s) \in B^h_\rho(p) \end{array}\right\},$$

and define

$$\hat{\gamma}^h_\rho(p) = \begin{cases} \gamma^h_\rho(p) & \text{if } p^1\omega^{h1} > 0, \\ B^h_\rho(p) & \text{if } p^1\omega^{h1} = 0. \end{cases} \tag{20}$$

From Lemma 5 it follows that if any of the assumptions T.5, T.5′, or T.5″ is satisfied, $\hat{\gamma}^h_\rho(p)$ is a non-empty, compact, convex, and upper semi-continuous correspondence. Using the same procedure as in Lemma 3 we can prove the following lemma:

LEMMA 6: *If any of the assumptions of Lemma 5 are satisfied, then the K_ρ-bounded exchange economy under consideration has a quasi-equilibrium.*

In order to prove that the quasi-equilibrium is an equilibrium, we have to establish $p^1\omega^{h1} > 0$ for all h, and this in general is not true with the structure that we have assumed so far.

Now let $e_\lambda = (\lambda, 0, 0, \ldots, 0)$ so that for any vector v we write $v + e$ to mean v plus λ in the first coordinate. With this notation we introduce the following assumption.

ASSUMPTION T.6: *If $(x^1, y^1, g^1) \in T^{h1}$, then for any $\lambda > 0$ there is a $\mu > 0$ such that if $\tilde{\tilde{x}}^1 = x^1 + e_\lambda$ and $\tilde{\tilde{g}}^1 = g^1 + e_\mu$, then $(\tilde{\tilde{x}}^1, y^1, \tilde{\tilde{g}}^1) \in T^{h1}$.*

Assumption T.6 simply says that it is possible to buy spot labor services using spot labor as the only needed transaction cost.

We now introduce our final assumption. To do that denote

$$c^h(x^h, y^h, g^h, z^h, s^h) \equiv c^h$$

and

$$c^h(x', y', g', z', s') \equiv c^{h'}.$$

Then we can make the following assumption:

ASSUMPTION D.3′: *If $c^h \geqslant c^{h'}$ with $c_1^h(1) > c_1^{h'}(1)$, then $c^h \underset{h}{\succ} c^{h'}$.*

Assumption D.3′ says that commodity 1 is always desirable.

LEMMA 7: *The quasi-equilibrium is a competitive equilibrium in the K_ρ-bounded economy if any of the assumptions T.5, T.5′, or T.5″ are satisfied and in addition (i) T.6 is satisfied for all h, (ii) $\omega_1^h(1) > 0$, all h, and (iii) D.3′ is satisfied for all h.*

PROOF: We prove that $p_{11}(1) > 0$. Let $\{p, (x^h, y^h, g^h, z^h, s^h), h = 1, 2, \ldots, H\}$ be a given quasi-equilibrium. Since $\Sigma_{h=1}^H \omega^h(t) \gg 0$ for all t, it follows that $p^1\omega^{h1} > 0$ for some h and for this h, $(x^h, y^h, g^h, z^h, s^h) \in \gamma_\rho^h(p)$. If $p_{11}(1) = 0$, then consider the following exhange at time 1:

$$\tilde{\tilde{x}}^{h1} = x^{h1} + e_\lambda,$$

$$\tilde{\tilde{y}}^{h1} = y^{h1},$$

and

$$\tilde{\tilde{g}}^{h1} = g^{h1} + e_\mu.$$

By T.6 for any $\lambda > 0$ there exists $\mu > 0$ such that $(\tilde{\tilde{x}}^{h1}, \tilde{\tilde{y}}^{h1}, \tilde{\tilde{g}}^{h1}) \in T^{h1}$, and since $p_{11}(1) = 0$ it follows that

$$p^1\tilde{\tilde{x}}^{h1} \leqslant p^1\tilde{\tilde{y}}^{h1} - p^1\tilde{\tilde{g}}^{h1}.$$

By D.3′ $c^h(\tilde{\tilde{x}}^h, \tilde{\tilde{y}}^h, \tilde{\tilde{g}}^h, z^h, s^h) \underset{h}{\succ} c^h(x^h, y^h, g^h, z^h, s^h)$, and since $c^h(x^h, y^h, g^h, z^h, s^h) \in \gamma_\rho^h(p)$ it follows that $(\tilde{\tilde{x}}^h, \tilde{\tilde{y}}^h, \tilde{\tilde{g}}^h, z^h, s^h) \in B_\rho^h(p)$. Since $(\tilde{\tilde{x}}^h, \tilde{\tilde{y}}^h, \tilde{\tilde{g}}^h, z^h, s^h)$ is technologically feasible and satisfies the budget constraint, it must be true that either $x_{11}^h(1) = \rho\omega_1(1)$ or $g_{11}^h = (\rho - 1)\omega_1(1)$.

Case (i): $x^h_{11}(1) = \rho\omega_1(1)$. In this case we have

$$(21) \qquad x_{11}(1) \geqslant \rho\omega_1(1).$$

Since $y^h_1(1) \leqslant ((\rho - 2)/H)\omega(1)$ and $g^h_1(1) \leqslant (\rho - 1)\omega(1)$, we must have

$$(22) \qquad y_1(1) \leqslant (\rho - 2)\omega(1)$$

and

$$(23) \qquad g_1(1) \leqslant (\rho - 1)H\omega(1).$$

From the conditions of quasi-equilibrium we know that

$$(24) \qquad x_1(1) \leqslant y_1(1) - g_1(1).$$

Combining (22), (23), and (24), we obtain

$$x_1(1) \leqslant y_1(1) - g_1(1) \leqslant (\rho - 2)\omega(1),$$

and particularly

$$(25) \qquad x_{11}(1) \leqslant y_{11}(1) - g_{11}(1) \leqslant (\rho - 2)\omega_1(1).$$

But (21) and (25) together imply

$$\rho\omega_1(1) \leqslant x_{11}(1) \leqslant (\rho - 2)\omega_1(1),$$

which is a contradiction.

Case (ii): $g^h_{11}(1) = (\rho - 1)\omega_1(1)$. Here again we have

$$y_{11}(1) \leqslant (\rho - 2)\omega_1(1),$$

and since $g^h_{11}(1) = (\rho - 1)\omega_1(1)$, we also have

$$g_{11}(1) \geqq (\rho - 1)\omega_1(1),$$

and, therefore,

$$0 \leqslant x_{11}(1) \leqslant y_{11}(1) - g_{11}(1) \leqslant (\rho - 2)\omega_1(1) - (\rho - 1)\omega_1(1) = -\omega_1(1),$$

which is again a contradiction.

This proves that $p_{11}(1) > 0$. Since $\omega^h_1(1) > 0$, all h, it follows that $p^1\omega^{h1} > 0$, all h, and therefore the given quasi-equilibrium is in fact an equilibrium. *Q.E.D.*

THEOREM 2: *The exchange economy has a competitive equilibrium if the following assumptions hold*: (*i*) *T.5, T.5′, or T.5″*; (*ii*) *T.6*; (*iii*) $\omega^h_1(1) > 0$, *all h*; *and* (*iv*) *D.3′*.

PROOF: Since by Lemmas 6 and 7 there exists a competitive equilibrium for any K_ρ-bounded economy, then what is left to prove is that as we let $\rho \to +\infty$ we obtain a competitive equilibrium in the unbounded economy. To do that we employ exactly the same procedure as the one used in the proof of Theorem 1. *Q.E.D.*

8. ALLOCATION OVER TIME, EFFICIENCY, AND MONEY

In establishing the existence of an equilibrium we have revealed some structure of the sets T^{ht}. There are a few fundamental questions related to the efficiency of the equilibrium and the structure of allocation over time which cannot be answered without a further understanding of the structure of T^{ht}.

DEFINITION: The price system p is said to have the "traditional property" if there exist $\mu(t) > 0$ such that

$$p^{t+1} = \mu(t)\bar{p}^{t}.$$

Hahn [3] calls the above property "the Debreu property." The property essentially says that relative futures prices at time t are exactly the same as the actual spot and future prices at any $\tau > t$.

The "traditional property" is precisely the kind of property a competitive equilibrium will satisfy when transaction costs are absent. We shall see below that in a world with transaction cost, the price system may not have this property. This observation is due to Hahn. Hahn states a theorem according to which when $p^{t+1} = \mu(t)\bar{p}^{t}$, households are indifferent between making a sequence of transactions and a single set of transactions at $t = 1$. This theorem is *not* true without further structure for the sets T^{ht}.

ASSUMPTION T.7: *(i) T^{ht} are closed convex cones for all t, and (ii)* $T^{h(t+1)} = \{(x^{t+1}, y^{t+1}, g^{t+1}) | ((0, x^{t+1}), (0, y^{t+1}), (0, g^{t+1})) \in T^{ht}\}$.

Assumption T.7 (ii) says essentially that $T^{h(t+1)}$ is nothing but the projection of T^{ht} on the $t+1, t+2, \ldots, T$ coordinates when $x_t(t) = y_t(t) = g_t(t) = 0$.

THEOREM 3 (Hahn): *For technologies satisfying T.7, households are indifferent between making a sequence of transactions over time and a single set of transactions at $t = 1$ if and only if the price system p has the traditional property.*

PROOF: If $p^{t+1} = \mu(t)\bar{p}^{t}$, $\mu(t) > 0$, one can multiply the $t + 1$ budget constraint by $1/\mu(t)$ and then add the budget constraints into one single constraint at $t = 1$. The resulting set of transactions is feasible at $t = 1$ because of T.7. The converse is the same as Hahn [3].

THEOREM 4: *If $p^{t+1} = \mu(t)\bar{p}^{t}$ holds and T.7 is satisfied, then the competitive equilibrium in a sequence of markets is efficient.*

PROOF: Under the conditions $p^{t+1} = \mu(t)\bar{p}^{t}$ and T.7, the household budget constraint is simply reduced to

$$p^{1}x^{h1} \leqslant p^{1}y^{h1} - p^{1}g^{h1}, \qquad (x^{h1}, g^{h1}, g^{h1}) \in T^{h1}.$$

Let $\{p^1, (x^{h1}, y^{h1}, g^{h1}), h = 1, 2, \ldots, H\}$ be a competitive equilibrium with

$$c = \omega + x^1 - y^1, \qquad x^1 = \sum_{h=1}^{H} x^{h1}, \qquad y^1 = \sum_{h=1}^{H} y^{h1}.$$

Assume that $c = (c^1, c^2, \ldots, c^H)$ is not efficient. Then there exists a feasible $\bar{c} = (\bar{c}^1, \bar{c}^2, \ldots, \bar{c}^H)$ with $\bar{c}^h \succsim_h c^h$ and $\bar{c}^{h^0} \succ c^{h^0}$ for some h^0. Consider that h^0. Since $\bar{c}^{h^0} \notin \gamma^{h^0}(p^1)$, it follows that $p^1\bar{x}^{h^01} > p^1\bar{\bar{y}}^{h^01} - p^1\bar{g}^{h^01}$. Since $\bar{c}^h \succsim_h c^h$, all h, it follows $p^1\bar{x}^{h1} \geqslant p^1\bar{\bar{y}}^{h1} - p^1\bar{g}^{h1}$; thus

$$p^1(\bar{x}^1 - \bar{\bar{y}}^1 + \bar{g}^1) > 0.$$

However, since c is feasible it follows that $\bar{x}^1 - \bar{\bar{y}}^1 - \bar{g}^1 \leqslant 0$. Since $p^1 \geqslant 0$, we have

$$p^1(\bar{x}^1 - \bar{\bar{y}}^1 + \bar{g}^1) \leqslant 0.$$

This is a contradiction; thus c is efficient. *Q.E.D.*

We are thus left with the question of the efficiency of competitive equilibrium when the economy has a sequence of markets and transaction costs. The answer which was provided by Hahn is that in general such competitive equilibria are not efficient. The reason for this fact is simply because the sequence of budget constraints,

$$\begin{aligned} &p^1(x^{h1} - y^{h1} + g^{h1}) \lesseqgtr 0, \qquad (x^{h1}, y^{h1}, g^{h1}) \in T^{h1},\\ &p^2(x^{h2} - y^{h2} + g^{h2}) \lesseqgtr 0, \qquad (x^{h2}, y^{h2}, g^{h2}) \in T^{h2},\\ &\vdots \qquad\qquad\qquad\qquad\qquad\quad \vdots\\ &p^T(x^{hT} - y^{hT} + g^{hT}) \lesseqgtr 0, \qquad (x^{hT}, y^{hT}, g^{hT}) \in T^{ht}, \end{aligned} \tag{26}$$

leads to a smaller budget set than the single budget constraint,

$$\sum_{t=1}^{H} p^t(x^{ht} - y^{ht} + g^{ht}) \lesseqgtr 0, \qquad (x^{ht}, y^{ht}, g^{ht}) \in T^{ht}, \tag{27}$$

and thus a maximal element in the budget set generated by (26) may be an interior point in the budget set generated by (27). The point is that any *efficient* point need not satisfy the budget constraints (26) but need only satisfy the constraints $(x^{ht}, y^{ht}, g^{ht}) \in T^{ht}$ and $x - y + g \lesseqgtr 0$.

There are two points to note. First, if transaction cost were not present the equilibrium in a sequence of markets would have had the traditional property and thus would have been efficient. Second, the inefficiency with which we are faced is a result of the nature of the transaction technology itself.

To see the last point consider an economy where the set T^{ht} will be represented by a cost function

$$g_\tau(t) = \alpha[x_\tau(t) + y_\tau(t)] \quad \text{all } t \text{ and } \tau \geqslant t. \tag{28}$$

Assume also that $\succsim_h$ is represented by a differentiable utility function $U^h(c(1), c(2), \ldots, c(T))$. Then the equilibrium conditions of the consumer would have been described by the following system of equations. Let

$$U_t = \left(\frac{\partial U}{\partial c_1(t)}, \frac{\partial U}{\partial c_2(t)}, \ldots, \frac{\partial U}{\partial c_N(t)}\right).$$

The multiplier associated with the budget at t is λ_t^h. Then

$$U_t - (\lambda_1 + \alpha)p_t(1) = 0 \qquad (t = 1, 2, \ldots, T),$$

$$U_t - (\lambda_2 + \alpha)p_t(2) = 0 \qquad (t = 2, \ldots, T),$$

and

$$U_t - (\lambda_N + \alpha)p_t(T) = 0 \qquad (t = T).$$

It is then clear that $p^{t+1} = (\lambda_t + \alpha)/(\lambda_{t+1} + \alpha)\bar{p}^t$. Also T.7 is satisfied; thus no inefficiency arises in this case.

It is clear that the transaction technology is usually more intricate than (28), and therefore it is possible that the sequence of budgets associated with the sequence of markets will constitute a sufficiently stringent set of restriction that will lead to an inefficient equilibrium.

To provide an intuitive understanding of the dependence of the inefficiency involved in the transaction technology, consider a case in which you and I found ourselves in the following situation: My endowments today and tomorrow are

today: $(0, 0, \omega_3, \omega_4, \omega_5, \ldots, \omega_N)$,

tomorrow: $(\text{apples}, 0, \omega_3, \omega_4, \omega_5, \ldots, \omega_N)$,

and your endowments are

today: $(0, \text{bread}, \omega_3, \omega_4, \omega_5, \ldots, \omega_N)$,

tomorrow: $(0, 0, \omega_3, \omega_4, \omega_5, \ldots, \omega_N)$,

where $(\omega_3, \omega_4, \ldots, \omega_N)$ are common to both of us. Now I want part of your "today bread" and you want part of my "apples tomorrow." Such an exchange is possible except that it calls for a futures contract where I shall buy spot bread and sell future apples while you do the opposite. If the cost of carrying out a futures transaction is higher than the cost of a spot transaction, then the trade involving futures markets is inefficient: You can give me spot bread today and I shall give you spot apples tomorrow all without a futures contract, but rather using spot transactions only. This leaves me with a debt to you until tomorrow. Such an act of creating a debt today will violate our budget constraints and is not feasible in the barter economy above without the introduction of money as a store of value.

On the basis of all this, how should we regard this inefficiency? Note first that if we allow the appearance of a medium of exchange and the emergence of credit in our economy, then the intertemporal transfer of obligations will bring our individual back to a budget constraint like (27) rather than (26). This means that if a costless money, which can be used as a store of value, is introduced, then the intertemporal efficiency of allocation is restored. However, one cannot assume that "money" and all the financial institutions needed to manage a monetary economy are all costless. For this reason the notion of efficiency itself must be understood to be defined relative to a specific set of institutional arrangements. This is clearly not the place to open this broad subject; our comments here have been made in order to encourage caution in interpreting our discussion of efficiency in this paper.

Stanford University

Manuscript received March, 1972; revision received September, 1972.

REFERENCES

[1] Debreu, Gerard: *Theory of Value*. New York: John Wiley, 1959.
[2] Hahn, F. H.: "On Some Problems of Proving the Existence of an Equilibrium in a Monetary Economy," in *Conference on the Theory of Interest and Money*, F. P. R. Brechling, ed. Royamount, France, 1962.
[3] ———: "Equilibrium with Transaction Cost," *Econometrica*, 39 (1971), 417–439.
[4] Kurz, M.: "Equilibrium with Transaction Cost and Money in a Single Market Exchange Economy," *Journal of Economic Theory*, 6 (1974), forthcoming.
[5] ———: "Arrow-Debreu Equilibrium of an Exchange Economy with Transaction Cost," Working Paper No. 7, Institute for Mathematical Studies in the Social Sciences, Stanford University, Stanford, Calif., April, 1972.
[6] Radner, R.: "Problems in the Theory of Markets under Uncertainty," *American Economic Review*, 60 (1970), 454–460.
[7] ———: "Existence of Equilibrium of Plans, Prices and Price Expectations in a Sequence of Markets," *Econometrica*, 40 (1972), 289–304.

19

EQUILIBRIUM WITH NON-CONVEX TRANSACTIONS COSTS: MONETARY AND NON-MONETARY ECONOMIES

by Walter P. Heller and Ross M. Starr

The idea that transaction costs display a scale economy is commonplace. This cost structure enters essentially as an explanation of the demand for inventories of goods, and for idle balances of money (Tobin, 1956; Baumol, 1952). Hence, a theory of a monetary economy with non-convex transaction costs is a necessary generalization of the transaction cost theory so far developed. Bounded non-convexities generally imply discontinuity[2] in demand behavior that precludes the direct application of fixed-point theorems. The now standard technique in a discrete finite economy is to approximate the non-convex economy by a convex economy. Equilibrium is established for the (artificial) convex economy, and finally it is shown that a small reallocation from this point represents an approximate equilibrium for the non-convex economy. The extent of disequilibrium has an upper bound independent of the number of traders (depending primarily on the dimensionality of the commodity space). Hence, in a large economy, the disequilibrium per head—the average shortage of goods—is correspondingly small.

The equilibrium includes idle balances of money and inventories of goods. Both are held to economize on transaction costs. The model uses the individualized transactions technologies of Kurz (selection 18) to formalize the idea of a non-convexity facing individual agents. The transactions technologies of Foley (selection 15) and Hahn (selection 16) would not allow so direct a representation. Bonds (more precisely, discounted notes) are simply futures

[2] More precisely, the demand is upper-hemicontinuous but not convex valued.

General Equilibrium
Models of
Monetary Economies

ISBN 0-12-663970-1

contracts for money. The holding of idle balances in equilibrium means that some major elements of the conventional characterization of a monetary economy are portrayed here in a fashion not available in the other transaction cost models of this section. Money is held as a stock. Velocity of circulation is determined by individual optimizing decision-makers trading off timing of purchases of goods and of bonds.

Absent from the model however are other predictable effects of scale economies in transactions. There is no representation of firms specializing in transactions: retailers, wholesalers, brokers. Hence, the financial structure is still primitive, but financial asset stocks enter in an essential way.

Reprinted from THE REVIEW OF ECONOMIC STUDIES, Vol. XLIII (2), June, 1976, WALTER PERRIN HELLER and ROSS M. STARR, pp. 195-215.

Equilibrium with Non-convex Transactions Costs: Monetary and Non-monetary Economies

WALTER PERRIN HELLER
University of California, San Diego

and

ROSS M. STARR
University of California, Davis

1. TRANSACTIONS COSTS IN A MONETARY ECONOMY

Transactions costs often possess the set-up property or some other form of diminishing marginal cost (i.e. a nonconvexity). The labour, time and other resources required to carry out an exchange involving a bushel of apples for money are not significantly greater than the resources required for the exchange of a single apple for money. Similarly, the resources needed to write a check for \$1000 are considerably less than 1000 times those required for a \$1 cheque. Such scale economies in the execution of transactions provide one of the main motives for holding inventories by households and firms. In a sequence economy where money acts as a medium of exchange, non-convex transactions costs of individuals will provide motivation for holding idle balances of money, i.e. inventories of the medium of exchange [15].[1] The willingness to hold idle balances is essential to obtain an equilibrium in an economy with a non-zero money supply and hence such behaviour is a cornerstone of monetary theory.

This poses a substantial problem in writing a general equilibrium theory of a monetary economy. The non-convexities involved generally imply that demand functions or correspondences will not fulfil the continuity or convexity conditions required for the application of the fixed point theorems used to prove the existence of equilibrium. There does not in general exist an equilibrium in the usual sense. Nevertheless, techniques developed in other contexts for the treatment of nonconvexity [1], [7], [13] allow us to demonstrate the existence of an approximate equilibrium. In an economy large and homogeneous enough, the approximation will be close enough to make the approximate equilibrium virtually indistinguishable from a true equilibrium. This is the principal result below. Non-convexities in transactions costs do not preclude the achievement of an allocation that is nearly a competitive equilibrium. The approximation theorem is surprising, since we allow the possibility of set-up costs to each individual transaction. Letting the number of agents become large does not, on the face of it, reduce the average number of transactions per agent. Although existence of an approximate equilibrium is proved, the effects of non-convexities are substantial; with economies of scale in transactions the equilibrium allocation will be characterized by a bunching of transactions into a few markets, and a corresponding bulge in inventory holdings.

The use of non-convex transactions costs is singularly appropriate to the study of costly transactions in a monetary economy since pure set-up cost (i.e. positive fixed cost with zero variable cost) permits cash transactions to be costly in such a way that these costs are invariant under a change in units. A currency reform that multiplies all currency values by 10^{-2} is unlikely also to multiply transactions costs by 10^{-2}.

The principal mathematical tool for treating non-convexity in this context is the theorem of Shapley and Folkman, Theorem A below, which says that the size of the non-convexity in the sum of a family of non-convex sets is bounded above in a fashion independent of the number of sets summed. The standard technique for treating non-convexities then is to convexify the problem, achieve an equilibrium in the convexified economy, and use the Shapley-Folkman theorem to relate the allocation of the non-convex economy to the market clearing allocation of the convexified economy. The non-convex economy is not too far from market clearing, and indeed the disequilibrium becomes negligible as the economy becomes large.

In studying non-convex preferences, the convexification used was to take the convex hull of " preferred or indifferent " sets [13]. In treating increasing returns in production, convex hulls of technology sets are used [1]. These approaches turn out to be equivalent to taking the convex hull of the household's or firm's demand or supply correspondences, and this is the essential point. In the present model we might convexify the transactions technology, the household's budget set, or the household's demand correspondence. The third alternative is the only one that allows convex approximation of the behaviour of the non-convex economy.[2] However, the demand correspondences may not satisfy the necessary continuity properties. We shall give a sufficient condition for demand correspondences arising out of non-convex opportunity sets to have the required continuity properties.

In a monetary economy, the supply of real outside money may enter essentially in the determination of the equilibrium. If periods are short and a set-up cost of labour is required by the transactions technology, a household may find it difficult or impossible to perform both buying and selling transactions during the same period. Purchases will then have to be paid for in money carried forward from previous periods. The volume of transactions that can take place will depend then on the real outside money supply. An increase in this quantity *ceteris paribus* may make additional transactions possible.

Non-convexities in transactions cost may provide a strong motive for making transactions and payments in large discrete amounts rather than smaller or, indeed, continuous amounts. In actual economies, many contracts consist of an agreement to provide goods at a sequence of future dates in exchange for deliveries, usually less frequent, of money at future dates. Such an exchange of futures contracts for futures contracts, all transacted at a single market date is an effect of non-convexities in transactions cost. The model allows—indeed, encourages—transactions to be made in composites that have lower unit transactions costs than would their constituents transacted separately. Long-term employment or rental agreements as well as the purchase of a shopping basket of goods together rather than each item separately are examples of exploitation of scale economies in transactions.

In the present model, trade takes place between individuals and the market, rather than between pairs of agents. It is not possible, therefore, to study within the context of the model the use of shops, retailers and other intermediary agents. It is worth while to note, however, that in a bilateral trade model the function of intermediary agents can be explained in part by scale economies on the size of transaction experienced by individual households. For example, if there are ten sellers of ten distinct commodities and twenty buyers each requiring some of each of the ten commodities, in the absence of intermediation 200 separate relatively small transactions will ensue. If a single intermediary is used there will be only thirty large transactions. The gross volume of trade is doubled (since each commodity is now traded twice), but if scale economies on transactions costs are present, the savings associated with the reduction in the number of separate transactions may more than compensate.

In Section 2 the model of a sequence economy with non-convex transactions costs is introduced. Section 3 develops the concept of local interiority needed for continuity of demand.

Section 4 gives further structure and contains a theorem establishing the existence of an equilibrium for a convexified version of the economy. In Section 5 we introduce the additional structure needed for a monetary version of the model, in particular to ensure positivity of the price of money. An equilibrium existence theorem is established for a convexified version of the monetary model. Section 6 uses the convexified equilibria from Sections 4 and 5 to establish approximate equilibria for the original non-convex economy. Proofs are gathered in Section 7.

2. MODEL OF A NON-MONETARY ECONOMY WITH NON-CONVEX TRANSACTIONS COSTS

The point of departure is the sequence economy of Heller [8] which is based on Kurz [11] and Hahn [6]. Thus, we are dealing with an economy with a sequence of markets: commodity i for delivery at date τ may be bought at date τ or $\tau-1$ or $\tau-2$... or date $t<\tau$ where t is today's date. Moreover, the complete system of spot and futures markets is open at each date (although some markets may be inactive). We shall suppose that time ends at date T and that each of H households is alive at time 0 and cares nothing about consumption after T. There are n physical commodities. At each date and for each commodity, the household has available the current spot market, and futures markets for deliveries at all future dates. Spot and futures markets will also be available at dates in the future and prices on the markets taking place in the future are currently known. Thus in making his purchase and sale decisions, the household considers without price uncertainty whether to transact on current markets or to postpone transactions to markets available at future dates. There is a sequence of budget constraints, one for the market at each date. That is, for every date the household faces a budget constraint on the spot and futures transactions taking place at that date.

In addition to a budget constraint, the agent's actions are restricted by a transactions technology. This technology specifies for each complex of purchases and sales at date t what resources will be consumed by the process of transaction: labour time, paper and pens, gasoline, telephone services, and so forth. It is because transactions costs may differ between spot and futures markets for the same good that we consider the reopening of markets allowed by the sequence economy model.

Though we will take the individual's transactions technology as fixed for the purpose of this model, it should be recognized that unlike the production technology of the firm in standard competitive equilibrium models, an individual's transaction technology should be made to depend on the actions of others in the economy. Thus, the structure of the economy (including for example the legal system and contract enforcement) will affect an individual's transaction possibilities. A more general model would allow endogenous specification of the individual transaction technology.

We shall use the following notation. All of the vectors below are restricted to be non-negative.

$x^h_\tau(t)$ = vector of purchases for any purpose at date t by household h for delivery at date τ.

$y^h_\tau(t)$ = vector of sales analogously defined.

$z^h_\tau(t)$ = vector of inputs necessary to transactions undertaken at time t. The index τ again refers to date at which these inputs are actually delivered.

$\omega^h(t)$ = vector of endowments at t for household h.

$s^h(t)$ = vector of goods coming out of storage at date t.

$r^h(t)$ = vector of goods put into storage at date t.

$p_\tau(t)$ = price vector on market at date t for goods deliverable at date τ.

With this notation, $p_{it}(t)$ is the spot price of good i at date t, and $p_{i\tau}(t)$ for $\tau > t$ is the futures price (for delivery at τ) of good i at date t.

The (non-negative) consumption vector for household h is

$$c^h(t) = \omega^h(t) + \sum_{\tau=1}^{t} (x_t^h(\tau) - y_t^h(\tau) - z_t^h(\tau)) + s^h(t) - r^h(t) \geqq 0 \quad (t = 1, \ldots, T). \qquad \ldots(2.1)$$

That is, consumption at date t is the sum of endowments plus all purchases past and present with delivery date t minus all sales for delivery at t minus transactions inputs with date t (including those previously committed) plus what comes out of storage at t minus what goes into storage. We suppose that households care only about consumption (and not about which market consumption comes from) and that preferences are convex, continuous and monotone. Thus, households maximize $U^h(c^h)$, where c^h is a vector of the $c^h(t)$'s, subject to constraint.

As discussed above, the household is constrained by its transaction technology, T^h, which specifies, for example, how much leisure time and shoeleather must be used to carry out any transaction. Let $x^h(t)$ denote the vector of $x_\tau^h(t)$'s (and similarly for $y^h(t)$ and $z^h(t)$). We insist

$$(x^h(t), y^h(t), z^h(t)) \in T^h(t) \quad (t = 1, \ldots, T). \qquad \ldots(2.2)$$

Naturally, storage input and output vectors must be feasible, so

$$(r^h(t), s^h(t+1)) \in S^h(t) \quad (t = 1, \ldots, T). \qquad \ldots(2.3)$$

For convenience, suppose that $s^h(1) \equiv 0$. Both $S^h(t)$ and $T^h(t)$ are closed. They are not assumed to be convex. We postpone further discussion of the $T^h(t)$.

Households may transfer purchasing power forward in time by using futures markets and by storage of goods that will be valuable in the future. Purchasing power may be carried backward by using futures markets. But these may be very costly transactions if set-up costs are present. If outside money and bonds were present, then the household could either hold outside money as a store of wealth, or it could buy or sell bonds. We will postpone to Section 5 consideration of the monetary version of this model. The budget constraints for household h are then:

$$p(t)x^h(t) \leqq p(t)y^h(t) \quad (t = 1, \ldots, T). \qquad \ldots(2.4)$$

We need more notation at this point. Let $a^h(t) \equiv (x^h(t), y^h(t), z^h(t), r^h(t), s^h(t))$, and let a^h be a vector of the $a^h(t)$'s, and define x^h, y^h, z^h, r^h and s^h similarly. Define $B^h(p)$ as the set of a^h's which satisfy constraints (2.1)-(2.4), and let $B^{ht}(p)$ be the projection onto t of $B^h(p)$. Clearly the household maximizes $U^h(c^h)$ over $B^h(p)$. Denote the demand correspondence (i.e. the set of maximizing a^h's) by $\gamma^h(p)$.

3. LOCAL INTERIORITY[3]

In order to prove existence of equilibrium, we will need to show that demand correspondences are upper semi-continuous. To do this, we need the continuity of the budget correspondences $B^h(p)$. Discontinuities in the budget set may arise in the absence of convexity. For example, suppose there are free goods whose acquisition requires a set-up transactions cost. There may be a convergent sequence of price vectors such that a household cannot afford the set-up cost for any point in the sequence but that at the limit of the sequence it can precisely afford the set-up cost. The budget set then makes a discontinuous change at the limit. A sufficient condition to avoid this discontinuity is that the non-degenerate part of the budget set ($\hat{B}^h(p)$ below) be locally interior. Local interiority is defined below, and the continuity implication is proved in Section 7.

Let $\hat{B}^{ht}(p) = \{(x, y, z, r, s) \mid (x, y, z, r, s) \in B^{ht}(p) \text{ and } x - y - z \nless 0\}$, where $u \nless v$ means that if every component of u is less than or equal to v, then $u = v$. Thus, $\hat{B}^{ht}(p)$ consists of points of $B^{ht}(p)$ which are not dominated by the no trade point. Note that $0 \in \hat{B}^{ht}(p)$. Also, $\hat{B}^{ht}(p)$ is not closed and not connected for the set-up cost case. We define $\hat{B}^h(p)$ to be the cross product of the $\hat{B}^{ht}(p)$'s. We show in Section 4 that (with monotonicity of preferences) there is no loss in restricting choices to $\hat{B}^h(p)$.

We shall now replace convexity of the sets T^h by local interiority and obtain the needed continuity of the correspondence $B^h(p)$. Recall how the Debreu proof [5] of lower semi-continuity of the convex budget correspondence goes. Given that $B^h(p)$ is convex and has an interior point a^* at p^0, one considers for any $a^0 \in B^h(p^0)$, the line segment, L, joining a^* and a^0. Since $B^h(p^0)$ is convex, this line segment also lies in the interior of $B^h(p)$ with the possible exception of a^0. Hence, for any $a \in L$, $a \neq a^0$, we have $a \in B^h(p)$ for p in some neighbourhood of p^0 (since $p^0a>0$ implies $pa>0$, for all p near p^0). Therefore, for any sequence (p^k), $p^k \to p^0$, there exists $a^k \in L$ such that $a^k \in B^h(p^k)$, whenever k is sufficiently large. Moreover, a^k can be chosen to converge to a^0. For, if $a^0 \notin B^h(p^k)$ let $a^k \in L$ be on the boundary of $B^h(p^k)$, i.e. $p^k a^k = 0$. Then $p^0\bar{a} = 0$ where $a^k \to \bar{a}$. But $\bar{a} \in L$ implies $\bar{a} \in \text{int } B(p^0)$ or $\bar{a} = a^0$. But $p^0\bar{a} = 0$ means that $\bar{a} \notin \text{int } B^h(p^0)$. Hence $a^k \to a^0$, as was to be shown.

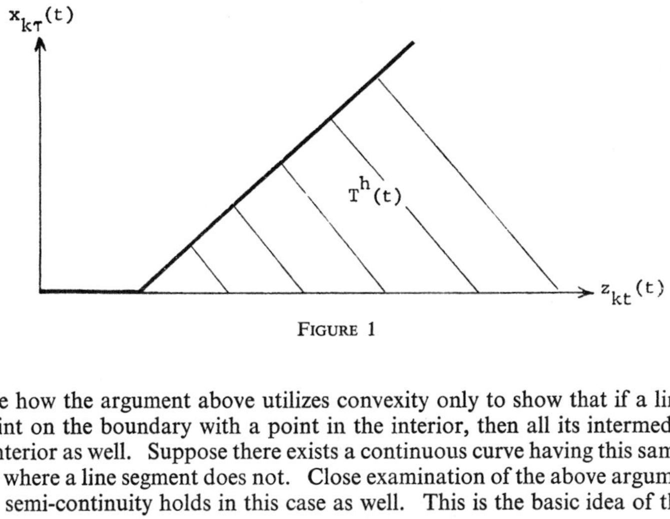

FIGURE 1

Notice how the argument above utilizes convexity only to show that if a line segment joins a point on the boundary with a point in the interior, then all its intermediate points lie in the interior as well. Suppose there exists a continuous curve having this same property in the case where a line segment does not. Close examination of the above argument reveals that lower semi-continuity holds in this case as well. This is the basic idea of this section.

Definition. $\hat{B}^h(p)$ is said to be *locally interior* if for each $a \neq 0$, $a \in \hat{B}^h(p)$ there is a^* so that

(i) $a^* \in \hat{B}^h(p)$.

(ii) a^* satisfies (2.4) with strict inequality, i.e. $p(t)(x^*(t) - y^*(t)) < 0$ for all t.

(iii) There is a continuous function $f:[0, 1] \to \hat{B}^h(p)$ so that $f(0) = a^*$, $f(1) = a$, and for all σ, $0 \leqq \sigma < 1$, $f(\sigma)$ satisfies (2.4) with strict inequality for all t.

The reason for restricting local interiority to $\hat{B}^h(p)$ is that we can include the case of set-up costs, since local interiority on $B^h(p)$ would rule out the technology depicted schematically in Figure 1. The horizontal portion of $T^h(t)$ is not included in $\hat{B}^{ht}(p)$.

Geometrically, local interiority of a set S means that any point (except 0) " faces " the interior of the set in the sense that any point is arc-connected to some point in the interior. Actually, our condition is a bit weaker than that since we only require that points be interior to the half-space (in lower dimension) defined by (2.4).

Naturally, the classical case of convexity of T^h and S^h plus

(E) $$\omega^h(t) \gg 0 \quad \text{for all } t \text{ and } h$$

implies local interiority. For then $a^* \in \text{int } \hat{B}^h(p)$ exists by (E) and $f(\sigma) = \sigma a^0 + (1-\sigma)a^*$ belongs to the interior of $\hat{B}^h(p)$ for $\sigma = 1$, by the usual arguments. Indeed, if T^h is strictly star-shaped with centre at $a^* = (\varepsilon, \varepsilon, \varepsilon, \ldots, \varepsilon)$ for some $\varepsilon > 0$, then $\hat{B}^h(p)$ is locally interior (cf. Arrow-Hahn for definition and discussion of strict star-shapedness). In this case, the function f is linear and a^* does not depend on a^0. Strictly star-shaped technologies may be of the U-shaped average cost curve type, although they cannot be of the set-up cost type.

What other economic conditions are sufficient for local interiority? If all transactions costs are purely set-up costs (i.e. no positive marginal transactions costs), if all transactions of the individual are strictly feasible using own resources, and storage technologies are convex, then local interiority also holds. For we then have that for all x, y there is a z such that $(x, y, z) \in T^h$ and $\sum_{\tau=1}^{t} z_t(\tau) \ll \omega^h(t)$. Hence, if a^1 and a^2 are both non-zero and both belong to $\hat{B}^h(p)$, for each σ there exists z such that $(\sigma x^1 + (1-\sigma)x^2, \sigma y^1 + (1-\sigma)y^2, z) \in T^h$ and $\sum_{\tau=1}^{t} z_t(\tau) \ll \omega^h(t)$. Thus, if $a(\sigma)$ is the convex combination of a^1 and a^2, $a(\sigma) \in \text{int } \hat{B}^h(p)$ whenever $a^1 \in \text{int } \hat{B}^h(p)$, since (2.1) and (2.4) are linear constraints. Hence, $\hat{B}^h(p)$ is locally interior (recall that although $0 \in \hat{B}^h(p)$, there is no requirement that 0 be connected to the interior of $\hat{B}^h(p)$ in the definition of local interiority).

Indeed, the argument used in the case of convexity can be used to show that $\hat{B}^h(p)$ is locally interior whenever T^h and S^h are locally convex and $\sum_{\tau=1}^{t} z_t(\tau) \ll \omega^h(t)$ for all $(x(t), y(t), z(t)) \in T^{ht}$. For in that case, there is easily seen to be a point interior to the constraint (2.4) and arbitrarily close to any $a \in \hat{B}^h(p)$. In fact, we can ask only that

$$\hat{T}^{ht} = \{(x(t), y(t), z(t)) \in T^{ht} \mid x(t) - y(t) - z(t) \lneq 0\} \quad (\text{note that } 0 \notin T^h)$$

be locally convex, thereby admitting set-up costs with positive marginal cost after the set-up. See Figure 1 above.

Proofs of all lemmas and theorems below are found in Section 7.

Lemma 3.1. *Let $\hat{B}^h(p^0)$ be locally interior. Then $\overline{\hat{B}^h(p^0)}$ (the bar denotes closure) is lower semi-continuous at p^0.*

Lemma 3.2. *$\overline{\hat{B}^h(p)}$ is upper semi-continuous for all $p \in P$.*

Lemma 3.3. *Let $\hat{B}^h(p^0)$ be locally interior for all p^0. Then $\gamma^h(p^0)$ is upper semi-continuous at p^0.*

4. EXISTENCE OF EQUILIBRIUM FOR THE CONVEXIFIED NON-MONETARY ECONOMY

Because of possible non-convexities in demand correspondences arising from the non-convex transactions technology, it will not in general be possible to prove the existence of an equilibrium. Rather, we will adopt a now familiar technique due to Starr [13] using mathematical tools developed by Shapley and Folkman (reported in [13]) and extended by Starr [13] and Heller [7]. An economy with convex behaviour (" convexified economy ") is described bearing a close relationship to the non-convex economy. Standard fixed-point techniques are used to discover an equilibrium for the convexified economy. Then it is shown that there is an allocation for the non-convex economy that approximates the behaviour of the convexified equilibrium. That is, there are allocations for the non-convex economy that are nearly equilibria.

The correspondences $\gamma_t^h(p)$ are always homogeneous of degree zero in $p(t)$, as is easily seen from the definition of $\hat{B}^h(p)$. We can therefore restrict the price space to the simplex. Let S^t denote the unit simplex of dimensionality, $n(T-t+1)$. Let $P = \displaystyle\mathop{\times}_{t=1}^{T} S^t$.

Lemma 4.1. *Let $a^h \in \gamma^h(p)$. Then $a^h \in \hat{B}^h(p)$.*

Proof. It is easy to show that if $a^h(t) \in B^{ht}(p)$, but $a^h(t) \notin \hat{B}^{ht}(p)$, then there exists $\hat{a}^h(t)$ such that $\hat{c}^h(t) > c^h(t)$. Hence, under monotonicity of preferences, a^h is dominated by $\hat{a}^h$.

QED

Therefore, we may restrict household decisions to $\hat{B}^h(p)$ without loss of generality. We now state formally the assumptions on the sets $T^h(t)$ and $S^h(t)$.

(A.1) $T^h(t)$ is a closed, but not necessarily convex set. The same holds for $S^h(t)$.

(A.2) (Free disposal.) If $(x^h(t), y^h(t), z^h(t)) \in T^h(t)$ then $x^{h'}(t) \leqq x^h(t)$, $y^{h'}(t) \leqq y^h(t)$ and $z^{h'}(t) \geqq z^h(t)$ imply $(x^{h'}(t), y^{h'}(t), z^{h'}(t)) \in T^h(t)$. Similarly, $S^h(t)$ exhibits free disposal.

(A.3) $0 \in T^h(t)$ and $0 \in S^h(t)$.

(A.4) (Local interiority.) For $p \in P$, $\hat{B}^h(p)$ is locally interior.

(A.5) (Boundedness.) $a^\nu \in T^h \times S^h$ and $\| a^\nu \| \to \infty$ implies $\| z^\nu \| \to \infty$.

Assumptions (A.1)-(A.3) are more or less self-explanatory and are not unreasonable. Assumption (A.5) is needed to make " wash sales " (the buying and selling of the same good at the same time) inefficient for the household. Positive marginal transactions cost for all commodities would certainly imply (A.5). An alternative to (A.5) would be to simply require that households not make wash sales. In that case, conventional arguments for pure exchange economies would guarantee the boundedness of consumption plans and (therefore) purchase and sale plans.

Define $B^h_\rho(p)$ to be the intersection of $B^h(p)$ with a cube of the same dimensionality as $B^h(p)$, where each side of the cube is of length ρ. Let $\gamma^h_\rho(p)$ be the set of utility-maximizing elements of $\overline{B^h_\rho(p)}$. Then $\gamma^h_\rho(p)$ is clearly compact-valued and upper semi-continuous.

Let $\hat{\gamma}^h_\rho(p) = \text{con}\, \gamma^h_\rho(p)$, where " con " indicates convex hull. Then $\hat{\gamma}^h_\rho(p)$ is a convex, compact set for all $p \in P$ (since $\gamma^h_\rho(p)$ is compact). Moreover, $\hat{\gamma}^h_\rho(p)$ is an upper semi-continuous correspondence since its values consist of convex combinations of points belonging to values of another correspondence possessing a compact graph. We are now in a position to apply the Kakutani fixed point theorem to show the existence of prices and an allocation that act as an equilibrium for the convexified economy. So far this is a technical convenience rather than an economically meaningful result since the actual economy is non-convex, but it will be shown in Section 6 that the non-convex economy with many agents approximates the behaviour of the convexified economy.

Theorem 4.1 (Existence of Equilibrium for the Closed Convexified Non-monetary Economy). *Under* (A.1)-(A.5), *there is a price vector $p^* \in P$ and an allocation $\langle a^{h*} \rangle_h$ such that*

$$a^{h*} \in \text{con}\, \gamma^h(p^*)$$

$$\sum_{h=1}^{H} x^{h*} \leqq \sum_{h=1}^{H} y^{h*}$$

with $p^*_{it}(\tau) = 0$ for i, t, τ such that the strict inequality holds.

5. A MONETARY ECONOMY[4]

The model may now be trivially modified to incorporate fiat money and bonds by introducing money as a 0th commodity for which the household has no direct utility (cf. Heller [8] for more discussion of the [convex] monetary model). The non-trivial modification is to ensure the existence of equilibrium with a *positive* price of money in each period. A futures contract for delivery of money is a bond. For convenience, let $x^h_{0t}(t)$ (the zero-th component of $x^h_t(t)$) denote the total amount of spot money acquired by household h in the market at date t. Similarly, let $y^h_{0t}(t)$ be the disbursement of spot money at t. Now if $\tau > t$, then $y^h_{0\tau}(t)$ is a commitment made at time t to deliver $y^h_{0\tau}(t)$ units of money at date τ. Suppose that by convention each bond promises one unit of money. Then $y_{0\tau}^h(t)$ is the number of bonds with maturity date τ sold by h. Similarly, $x^h_{0\tau}(t)$ is the number of bonds purchased by household h with maturity date τ.

One of the purposes of this section is to establish whether there are equilibria such that money can be exchanged for positive quantities of scarce goods. It would therefore be begging the question to make money the *numeraire*. Hence we say that spot money trades at a price of $p_{0t}(t)$ at date t (and $p_{0t}(t) = 0$ is thereby a possibility). The price of a bond maturing at τ is denoted $p_{0\tau}(t)$. With this convention we may write the budget constraints on the household as in (2.4), except that $p(t)$, $x(t)$, $y(t)$ all contain an added, zero-th component.[5]

The interpretation is that spot money on the market at t can be acquired by spot and futures sales of goods and bond sales. Similarly spot and future purchases of goods and bond purchases can be paid for in cash, goods, bonds or goods futures.[6]

What is to prevent a household from disbursing an unlimited amount of money $y^h_{0t}(t)$? The answer is to be found in constraint (2.1) for the zero-th component: " consumption " of money is a non-negative number. It is possible to disburse money for considerably more than one's current money holding without violating (2.1), but there must be corresponding receipts of money to balance out the discrepancy. This view of the budget constraint concentrates attention on the store of value rather than medium of exchange aspects of money.

Since we are dealing with fiat (rather than commodity) money, utility maximization will always imply zero consumption of money. We shall assume that there is a positive endowment of cash at least at the beginning and that at no time is there any input of cash being used up by the transaction process. Therefore, by (2.1),

$$r^h_0(t) - s^h_0(t) = \omega^h_0(t) + \sum_{\tau=1}^{t} [x^h_{0t}(\tau) - y^h_{0t}(\tau)].$$

Thus, net additions to storage of cash at t equals endowment plus total net acquisitions from the market place, where the total is taken over all previous transaction dates. Hence, a household needs to deliver cash only to the extent that his promises to others exceed the promises of others to him.

Transactions and storage technologies will also include money and bonds, since both of these are also costly to exchange. Some discussion of the interpretive difficulties of introducing money into the transaction technology is found in [8].

There is just one further constraint that the household must satisfy: the terminal condition that holdings of money at the end of time should be at least equal to the money endowment. Without this artificial requirement, no one would want to hold a positive money stock at the end. This would drive its terminal price to zero. But then no one would hold money at $T-1$, and so forth. The problem arises because of our initial artifice that $T < \infty$.

$$\sum_{\tau=1}^{T} [x^h_{0T}(\tau) - y^h_{0T}(\tau)] + s^h_0(T) \geqq \sum_{\tau=1}^{T} \omega^h_0(\tau) \equiv M^h. \qquad \text{...(5.1)}$$

Define $M = \Sigma_h M^h$.[7]

The constraint (5.1) says that the household is required to have at the economy's terminal date holdings of nominal money equal to its endowment thereof. One interpretation of this is that the government lends money at periods up to T and calls back its loan at the end of T. Because the model has a finite horizon, without this or a similar requirement the only equilibrium price of money would be zero [14], thereby demonetizing the economy. At any positive price there would be an excess supply of money in the final period leading to a fall in price in the last and all prior periods.[8] The artificial constraint against depletion of money balances arises because of the artificial specification of a finite horizon. The finite horizon is required to avoid well-known difficulties (inapplicability of fixed point theorems) associated with infinite horizon models. If the finite horizon were removed, then the economic reason for depletion of money balances and the resultant demonetization would disappear.

There is a variety of alternative more elaborate constructions that will achieve the same effect as (5.1) with no increase in analytic content, though some increase in plausibility. A bequest motive can generate sufficient terminal period demand for money to avoid demonetization. Agents alive at period T may have a derived utility from their stock of money at T reflecting their desire to make a bequest to their successors at $T+1$. Sufficiently exacting taxes payable in money can imply an arbitrary positive price of money [8], [12], [14]. If the present model were embedded in a temporary equilibrium treatment [1] with agents' preferences and expectations extending beyond the terminal date, this too would generate demand for terminal money balances if money were expected to be of positive value in succeeding periods.

The artificiality of these constructs means that we cannot conclude that money is useful simply because it has a positive equilibrium price.[9] Money will be useful only to the extent it enters into exchange. Money might not be traded in equilibrium, even when it has a positive price. This possibility seems unlikely if (1) money has lower transaction and storage costs than bonds, goods or futures and (2) households wish to make intertemporal transfers of purchasing power at equilibrium prices.

In the present model, as in all sequence economy models [6], [8], [11], the emphasis is on the role of money as a store of value, a means of transferring purchasing power forward and backward in time. Any durable good or futures contract can perform the function of shifting purchasing power forward or back, but transactions and storage costs associated with some commodities used for this purpose will be prohibitive. A distinguishing feature of money should be its low transactions and storage costs as compared to goods, bonds and futures contracts. Households may transfer purchasing power over time by accumulating and depleting their money balances and by the use of money futures contracts (loans). If the desired timing of purchase and sale transactions does not coincide, money acts as a carrier of purchasing power between the two transactions dates. If there are scale economies on the size of transactions (e.g. set-up transactions costs) the use of money will allow them to be exploited by concentrating in time transactions that might otherwise have to be more evenly spread. The smaller number of transactions should result in smaller total transactions cost. We now introduce assumptions on the monetary economy.

(M.1) (Durability of money.) For all t, τ, $z^h_{0\tau}(t) = 0$ is feasible for all vectors

$$(x^h(t), y^h(t), z^h(t)) \in T^h(t).$$

Storage of money is costless.

(M.2) (Transactions costs of sales.) For all $y(t)>0$, $(0, y(t), z(t)) \in T^h(t)$ implies $z_\tau(t) \neq 0$, for some $\tau \geqq t$.

(M.3) (Low transactions costs of money acquisitions.) For all t, there exists some h' and $(x^{h'}, y^{h'}, z^{h'})$ such that $(x^{h'}(t), y^{h'}(t), z^{h'}(t)) \in T^{h'}(t)$ with $x^{h'}_{0t}(t)$ as large as we please and $z^{h'}_\tau(t) \ll \omega^h(\tau)$.

(M.4) (Net productivity of terminal period monetary trade.) For all h there is

$$(x^h, y^h, z^h) \in T^h(T)$$

so that $y^h(T)$ is positive only in its 0th component and $x^h - y^h - z^h$ can assume any non-negative value.

Assumptions (M.1) and (M.2) are more or less self-explanatory and not unreasonable. (M.3) says that there is always at least one household with endowment great enough to cover the transactions costs of very large acquisitions of money. Clearly we could dispense with (M.3) (or rather, it would be trivially fulfilled) if money had zero transactions costs. (M.4) says that in the terminal period it is technologically possible for the household to make any arbitrary net purchase, with money the only means of payment. Together, (M.3) and (M.4) imply that if the price of money falls low enough in any preterminal period (the price in the terminal period being supposed positive) there is at least one household that can use this as an opportunity to acquire large stocks of money to be held until the terminal period when they can be converted to large net purchases of goods. If there is sufficient substitutability between preterminal and terminal period consumption (assumption (S) below), at least one household will exploit the opportunity. The result is to keep the equilibrium price of money positive in all periods.

(S) For some household h satisfying (M.3), any consumption vector c^h and for any date t, let $\bar{c}^h(t)$ be arbitrarily specified. Then there exists $\bar{c}^h(T)$ such that

$$U^h(c^h(1), \ldots, c^h(t-1), \bar{c}^h(t), c^h(t+1), \ldots, \bar{c}^h(T)) > U^h(c^h).$$

Property (S) is satisfied, for example, by any additive separable utility function which is unbounded above.

As before, $\gamma^h(p)$ is the demand correspondence of household h (but with the additional zero-th components corresponding to money and bonds). The correspondences $\gamma_t^h(p)$ are again homogeneous of degree zero in $p(t)$. Let S^t denote the unit simplex of dimensionality $(n+1)(T-t+1)$. Let S_α^T denote the unit simplex of dimensionality $n+1$ with the restriction that $p(T) \in S_\alpha^T$ implies $p_{0T}(T) = \alpha$, where $0<\alpha<1$. Define

$$P^\alpha = \{(p(1), p(2), \ldots, p(T)) \mid p(t) \in S^t, p(T) \in S_\alpha^T\}.$$

As in the previous section $\hat{\gamma}_\rho^h(p)$ is the convex hull of the demand correspondence of the economy bounded by ρ. By the same reasoning as in Sections 3 and 4, $\hat{\gamma}_\rho^h(p)$ is convex, compact and upper semi-continuous.

We can now establish the existence of an equilibrium with a positive price of money for the convexified monetary economy. As in the corresponding Theorem 4.1 for the non-monetary economy the result is in itself merely a convenience. However, it is the basis of establishing in Section 6 approximate equilibria for the nonconvex economy.

Theorem 5.1 (Existence of equilibrium for the convexified monetary economy). *Under* (A.1)-(A.5), (M.1)-(M.4) *and* (S), *for any* α, $0<\alpha<1$, *there is a price vector* $p^* \in P^\alpha$ *and an allocation* $\langle a^{h*}\rangle_h$ *such that*

$$a^{h*} \in \text{con}\, \gamma^h(p^*),$$

$$\sum_{h=1}^{H} x^{h*} \leqq \sum_{h=1}^{H} y^{h*}$$

with $p_{it}^*(\tau) = 0$ *for* i, t, τ *such that the strict inequality holds, and* $p_{0t}^*(t) \neq 0$ *for all* t.

The multiplicity of equilibria established by the theorem is really a case of the indeterminacy of the price of money. This occurs because of the absence of wealth effects (constraint (5.1)). For more discussion, see [8].

6. APPROXIMATE EQUILIBRIUM

An approximate equilibrium is generally defined as a price vector, p^*, and two allocations, w^* and $w^\dagger$. One, $w^\dagger$, is the allocation desired by households and firms at those prices, which may not clear the market. The other, w^*, is an allocation obeying a materials balance (market clearing) condition although it need not represent agents' optimizing behaviour. The equilibrium is approximate of modulus A if some suitably chosen norm of the difference between two allocations is no larger than A. The desired allocation represents an approximate equilibrium in the sense that the failure to clear the market at those prices is bounded by A. Conversely, should the economy be forced to the market clearing allocation the disparity between this allocation and a desired allocation is bounded by A. The outcome one has in mind in this formulation is that agents in the economy will seek *ex ante* the optimizing allocation. Since actual sales must equal actual purchases, *ex post*, the allocation must be market-clearing. It is of interest then that the discrepancy between intentions (*ex ante*) and realization (*ex post*) be small, so that incentive to change behaviour and hence upset the realized allocation be small.[10] In the results below, A is independent of the number of households in the economy. Thus, as the economy becomes large, disequilibrium becomes small relative to the size of the economy.

The only requirement of equilibrium in the usual sense that $w^{\dagger}$ fails to fulfil is the most essential, market clearing. In all other respects, particularly inclusion in the production and consumption possibility sets of firms and households respectively, $w^{\dagger}$ is well behaved. The same cannot generally be said of w^*, the market clearing allocation. w^* may require firms to produce technologically impossible input-output combinations or require households to have negative consumptions of some commodities. Restricting w^* to avoid these difficulties is possible under some assumptions. In an economy with non-convex preferences and production technologies and without transactions cost there exists an approximate equilibrium with a bound on the expression $|\Sigma w^{*i} - \Sigma w^{\dagger i}|$ where the index i runs over households and firms. At the allocation w^* firms are not restricted to remain in their technology sets. The bound is not on the amount by which individual agent actions in w^* depart from their desired actions $w^{\dagger}$ but rather on the disparity in aggregate behaviour between the two allocations. This bound is a measure of the extent to which markets fail to clear at $w^{\dagger}$, the desired allocation. Arrow and Hahn refer to such p^*, w^*, $w^{\dagger}$ as a social approximate equilibrium.

The social approximate equilibrium represents only part of the desired near equilibrium concept. The existence of such a price-allocation combination assures us that a norm of the aggregate excess demands is relatively small. By itself, this is only an interesting piece of arithmetic. What is actually required is a prescription of individual agents' behaviour that takes advantage of this smallness to achieve an allocation that is not only near by to agents' choices but also fulfils material balance and non-negativity constraints. If these constraints are not fulfilled then we are considering an allocation that cannot be a candidate for a worthwhile approximate equilibrium since it violates the most elementary conditions defining an achievable allocation.

Consider the case of the household depicted in Figure 2. The opportunity set determined by transactions technology and budget constraint is the kinked line. The household is indifferent between the two consumption choices $c^{\dagger}$ and ω (the endowment point), but neither of these is consistent with material balance of the market as a whole. Typically some convex combination of ω and $c^{\dagger}$ will fulfil material balance, c^{**} for example. But c^{**} is not in the household's opportunity set because c^{**} requires the household to transact outside the transactions technology. Is it possible to find an allocation near to the optimizing point fulfilling material balance and transactions technology requirements? In the case of the figure the answer is " yes "; $c^{\dagger\dagger}$ achieves these objectives by acceptance of a small reduction in consumption. Such a reduction is not always possible. If $c^{\dagger}$ were on the boundary of the quadrant, reduction of consumption of some commodities would require negative consumptions, another violation of constraint.

In a pure exchange economy with non-convex preferences and without transactions costs there is an approximate equilibrium with a bound on $(\Sigma|w^{*i} - w^{\dagger i}|^2)^{1/2}$. The sum over households of the squared disparities between the allocations is bounded. In large economies the two allocations for a typical individual will be nearly identical. Arrow and Hahn call such an allocation an individual approximate equilibrium. It is possible, in fact, to find w^{*h} non-negative, so that no household is required to consume a negative amount of any commodity.[11]

In the analysis below we distinguish between social approximate equilibrium, individual approximate equilibrium, attainable individual approximate equilibrium, and attainable

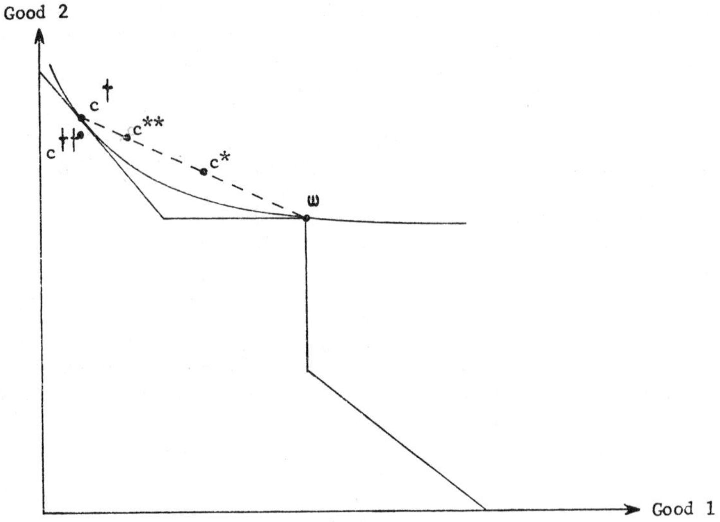

FIGURE 2

individual uniformly approximate equilibrium (the uniformity is on the Euclidean length of disappointment among households). The last two concepts are the more interesting since they describe achievable allocations. The first two are used mainly as technical aids to proving the existence of the latter.

The approximate equilibrium allocation $w^{\dagger}$ involves a choice of behaviour among households so that aggregate behaviour is approximately convex though individual behaviour is non-convex. The smoothing of aggregate behaviour comes from balancing one agent's behaviour off against another's. Thus identical households may have very different actions (though nearly equal utilities) specifically chosen so that the sum of their actions is well balanced. A household may be indifferent among making a given transaction on any of five days of the week but with set-up costs, making 20 per cent of the transaction on each day would be inferior because of the increased transactions costs incurred. To approximate convexified behaviour the allocation will prescribe that of five such households each make its transaction on a different day. Thus the approximate equilibrium implies a theory of the distribution of individual behaviour partially independent of the distribution of individual characteristics. It is often observed that only one of the many possible actions among which an agent is indifferent at given prices is consistent with equilibrium allocation. In the present model, the Shapley-Folkman theorem chooses one or several constellations of such indifferent points to limit the extent of disequilibrium.

Definition. The inner distance of a set S is defined as

$$\rho(S) = \sup_{x \in \text{con } S} \inf_{y \in S} |x - y|.$$

Theorem A (Shapley-Folkman). *Let* $S_1, \ldots, S_m$ *be compact sets in* E^n *and let* $x \in \text{con } S$. $S = \sum_{i=1}^{m} S_i$. *Then there are points* $b_i \in S_i$, $i = 1, \ldots, m$, *such that* $| x - \sum_{i=1}^{m} b_i | \leq R$. *Let* R *be the sum of the n largest* $\rho(S_i)$.

Proof. See [7].

The limits supplied by the Shapley-Folkman theorem depend on the dimensionality of the space. In the present models, for each commodity there are $[T(T-1)]/2$ spot and futures markets on which it may be traded. Further, each commodity and contract is subject to five separate decisions: buy, sell, incur a transactions cost, place in storage, remove from storage. There are n commodities and money. Thus the dimensionality of the spaces involved is

$$N = \begin{cases} \frac{5}{2}T(T-1)n & \text{for the non-monetary economy} \\ \frac{5}{2}T(T-1)(n+1) & \text{for the monetary economy.} \end{cases}$$

Analytically identical results are developed below for both monetary and non-monetary economies. To avoid repetition, N will be used to represent the dimensionality in both cases.

Definition. A social approximate equilibrium of modulus A is a price vector $p^* \in P$ (for the non-monetary economy) or $p^* \in P^\alpha$ (for the monetary economy) and two allocations a^{h*} and $a^{h\dagger}$ such that

(a) $\sum_h x^{h*} \leqq \sum_h y^{h*}$,

(b) $p^*_{it}(\tau) = 0$ if $\sum_h x^{h*}_{it}(\tau) < \sum_h y^{h*}_{it}(\tau)$,

(c) $a^{h\dagger} \in \gamma^h(p^*)$,

(d) a^{h*} satisfies (2.4) at p^* all t,

(e) $|\sum_h a^{h*} - \sum_h a^{h\dagger}| \leqq A$.

The usual technique for demonstrating the existence of an approximate equilibrium is to take convex hulls of the preference and technology sets, apply conventional techniques suitable for analysing the newly convex economy, and finally bound the disparity between the convexified economy and the non-convex economy by use of the Shapley-Folkman theorem. Following the approach successful in other contexts one would be led to convexify the household transactions technologies. The result, however, would be a serious oversight, since the household optimizing behaviour in an economy thus convexified is very different from behaviour in the actual economy. Households facing convexified transactions technologies will have no set-up cost induced behaviour such as bunching of purchases and sales with the resultant inventory holding. Convexification of the household demand correspondence is far more helpful, since it convexifies the behaviour, not the initial conditions, of the non-convex economy.

Let $R(p) = \sup_h \rho(\gamma_h(p))$. $R(p)$ is the maximum over all households at prices p of the inner distance of the household demand correspondence $\rho(\gamma^h(p))$. Recall that p^* is the convexified equilibrium price vector. Is it reasonable to suppose that $R(p^*)$ be finite? Since the number of households is finite, the only way this condition can fail to hold is if some household's demand correspondence at prices p^* includes points arbitrarily far from one another and excludes intermediate points. Such a condition could arise only if (i) there were unbounded scale economies in the transactions technology, and (ii) the household were indifferent among isolated bundles arbitrarily far apart all consistent with budget constraint (hence requiring free goods) and transactions technology. The possibility seems remote enough to exclude. We can then approximate points in the convex hull as the average of points in the original non-convex sets.

We may wish to consider the behaviour of the economy as the number of agents becomes large. How will $R(p^*)$ react? The addition of new endowments, tastes, and technologies may of course cause the convexified equilibrium price vector, p^*, to change. Even for p^* constant, new tastes and technologies may cause $R(p^*)$ to increase. To take the simplest case, if the economy grows by replication $R(p^*)$ will remain unchanged since tastes, technologies, and convexified equilibrium prices remain constant. Addition of other households depending on their endowments, tastes and technologies may make $R(p^*)$ increase or decline. To the extent that the growth is in households similar to those already in the economy, there is a presumption that $R(p^*)$ will remain relatively constant. For expository purposes below we will suppose that $R(p^*)$ is independent of the number of households in the economy.

Theorem 6.1. *Let p^* be an equilibrium price vector for the convexified economy. Let $R(p^*)$ exist, and be finite. Then at p^* there is a social approximate equilibrium of modulus $NR(p^*)$.*

Theorem 6.1 says that if $R(p^*)$ exists and is finite, for p^* the convexified equilibrium price vector, then there is a social approximate equilibrium at prices p^* of modulus $NR(p^*)$. Thus, there is a bound on the difference between aggregate demand and supply. Further, the bound is independent of the number of households in the economy so that in a large economy the disequilibrium is proportionately small. However, Theorem 6.1 provides no guarantee that the discrepancy between $a^{h\dagger}$ and a^{h*} be small for the households involved. The subsequent Theorem 6.2 uses the bound on aggregate disequilibrium established in Theorem 6.1 to show existence of the individual approximate equilibrium, an approximate equilibrium with a bound on the sum of the lengths of individual discrepancies. As the number of households increases the average discrepancy becomes correspondingly small.

Definition. An individual approximate equilibrium of modulus A is a price vector $p^* \in P$ (for the non-monetary economy) or $p^* \in P^\alpha$ (for the monetary economy) and two allocations a^{h**}, $a^{h\dagger}$ such that

(a) $\sum_h x^{h**} \leqq \sum_h y^{h**}$,

(b) $p^*_{it}(\tau) = 0$ if $\sum_h x^{h**}_{it}(\tau) < \sum_h y^{h**}_{it}(\tau)$,

(c) $a^{h\dagger} \in \gamma^h(p^*)$,

(d) a^{h**} fulfils (2.4) at p^*,

(e) $(\sum_h | a^{h**} - a^{h\dagger} |^2)^{1/2} \leqq A$.

Theorem 6.2. *Let p^* be an equilibrium price vector for the convexified economy. Let finite $R(p^*)$ exist. Then at p^* there is an individual approximate equilibrium of modulus $NR(p^*)$.*

The individual approximate equilibrium specifies for each agent an action a^{h**} that results in fulfilment of the material balance requirement and (on average across households) imposes a relatively small disparity between the agents' desired and market clearing actions. If the economy becomes large, the disparity for a typical household converges to zero. Because of non-convexity, a^{h**} may not be in the household's transactions technology, and as such does not represent an attainable allocation. Theorem 6.3 provides conditions under which it is possible to find individual approximate equilibria that are also elements of the household transactions technologies and provide for non-negative consumptions. Again, in a large economy, the difference between the two allocations for each household is correspondingly small.

Definition. An attainable individual approximate equilibrium of modulus A is a price vector $p^* \in P$ (for the non-monetary economy) or $p^* \in P^\alpha$ (for the monetary economy) and two allocations $a^\dagger$, $a^{\dagger\dagger}$, such that:

(a) $\sum_h x^{h\dagger\dagger} \leqq \sum_h y^{h\dagger\dagger}$,

(b) $c^{h\dagger\dagger} \geqq 0$,

(c) $a^{h\dagger} \in \gamma_h(p^*)$ all h,

(d) $a^{h\dagger\dagger}$ fulfils (2.4) at p^*,

(e) $a^{h\dagger\dagger} \in T^h \times S^h$,

(f) $(\sum_h | a^{h\dagger} - a^{h\dagger\dagger} |^2)^{1/2} \leqq A$.

Figure 2 shows typical consumption choices available to a household. ω is the endowment point, c^* is the consumption associated with a^*, c^{**} with a^{**}, $c^\dagger$ with $a^\dagger$, and $c^{\dagger\dagger}$ with $a^{\dagger\dagger}$. The dotted line represents the convex hull of the set of chosen consumptions. Households are indifferent between the two separated chosen points, ω, $c^\dagger$; no point between them is achievable and so cannot be chosen. A large number of such households distributed among the chosen points can approximate in their average behaviour any point in the convex hull of the chosen points.

In seeking an attainable individual approximate equilibrium we have to find an allocation near to $a^\dagger$ that is market clearing, leaves each household within its transactions technology, and assures it of non-negative consumption. The defect of $a^\dagger$ is that the allocation implies shortages; intended purchases of some commodities are greater than intended sales. The solution is then either to increase sales or reduce purchases. Increasing sales, even by a small amount, may cause a discrete increase in transactions cost, moving the allocation even farther from market clearing. A reduction in purchases will not increase transactions costs but if the purchases so reduced are of inputs to the transactions technology large changes in purchases and sales may be made necessary by small reductions in inputs to transactions. Again, this may result in a large move away from equilibrium. A reduction in purchases of goods going to consumption can have no such disruptive effect, but the reduction must not be so large as to cause households to have negative consumption. The conclusion is that if the goods in short supply at $a^\dagger$ are consumed at $a^\dagger$ from purchases (not from endowment) in amounts larger than the shortage, then there is an attainable individual approximate equilibrium.

This is the significance of the inequality in Theorem 6.3 below. $(x^{h\dagger} - y^{h\dagger} - z^{h\dagger})$ is the household's purchases net of sales and transactions costs. $(r^{h\dagger} - s^{h\dagger} - w^h)$ is the net input to storage not coming from endowment. The difference between the two is the portion of purchases going to consumption (rather than into storage or transactions costs). The inequality requires that the sum over households of purchases intended for consumption exceed the shortage of goods implied by the allocation $a^{h\dagger}$.

Theorem 6.3. *Let p^*, $a^{h\dagger}$, a^{h**} be an individual approximate equilibrium of modulus A and let $[\Sigma((x^{h\dagger} - y^{h\dagger} - z^{h\dagger})^+ - (r^{h\dagger} - s^{h\dagger} - \omega^h)^+)] \geqq \Sigma(x^{h\dagger} - y^{h\dagger})$. Then there is an attainable individual approximate equilibrium of modulus A.*

We may wish to consider attainable individual approximate equilibrium where the discrepancy between the attainable allocation and the desired allocation is spread evenly across households, so that no household bears a disproportionately large burden of the disequilibrium. An attainable approximate equilibrium with a uniform bound on Euclidean length of the disparity between the two allocations is defined below.

Definition. An attainable individual *uniformly* approximate equilibrium of modulus ε is a price vector $p^* \in P$ (for the non-monetary economy) or $p^* \in P^\alpha$ (for the monetary economy) and two allocations $a^\dagger$, $a^{\dagger\dagger\dagger}$ such that

(a) $\sum_h x^{h\dagger\dagger\dagger} \leqq \sum_h y^{h\dagger\dagger\dagger}$,

(b) $a^{h\dagger} \in \gamma_h(p^*)$ all h,

(c) $a^{h\dagger\dagger\dagger}$ fulfils (2.4) at p^*,

(d) $a^{h\dagger\dagger\dagger} \in T^h \times S^h$,

(e) $c^{h\dagger\dagger\dagger} \geqq 0$,

(f) $| a^{h\dagger} - a^{h\dagger\dagger\dagger} | \leqq \varepsilon$ for all h.

Theorem 6.4. *Let p^*, $a^\dagger$, $a^{\dagger\dagger}$ be an individual attainable approximate equilibrium of modulus A and suppose there is for each household h, $e^h \in R^N$, so that*

(i) $| e^h | \leqq \varepsilon$,

(ii) $\sum_h e^h = (\sum_h x^{h\dagger} - \sum_h y^{h\dagger})^+$

(iii) $(x^{h\dagger} - y^{h\dagger} - z^{h\dagger})^+ - (r^{h\dagger} - s^{h\dagger} - \omega^h)^+ \geqq e^h \geqq 0$.

Then there is $a^{\dagger\dagger\dagger}$ so that p^*, $a^\dagger$, $a^{\dagger\dagger\dagger}$ is an attainable individual uniformly approximate transactions equilibrium of modulus ε.

As in Theorem 6.3 above, the conditions of Theorem 6.4, particularly (ii) and (iii), ensure that the sum over households of purchases intended for consumption exceed shortages at allocation $a^{h\dagger}$. Condition (i) requires, further, that for each commodity in short supply there is a substantial number of households with purchases in excess of those required for storage or transactions costs. Thus the implied adjustment in consumption need not be large for any household. (i) may require that relatively large numbers of agents have positive levels of purchases on each market. Such a requirement is contrary to the tendency toward specialization in agents' actions that is implied by increasing returns in the transactions technology.

Under the assumptions of Sections 4 and 5, and if $R(p^*)$ is finite, we have:

(i) there exists at p^* a social approximate equilibrium of modulus $NR(p^*)$ and an individual approximate equilibrium of the same modulus;

(ii) if intended consumption out of purchases is large enough at p^* there exists an attainable individual approximate equilibrium of modulus $NR(p^*)$;

(iii) if all households have large enough intended consumption out of purchases at p^* there is an attainable individual uniformly approximate equilibrium of modulus ε where ε varies inversely with the number of households.

7. PROOFS

Lemma 3.1. *Let $\hat{B}^h(p^0)$ be locally interior. Then $\overline{\hat{B}^h(p^0)}$ is lower semi-continuous at p^0.*

Proof. Since $0 \in \hat{B}^h(p)$ for all p, we know that $\hat{B}^h(p^0)$ is lower semi-continuous at 0.

By local interiority, there is a continuous function f such that (for $\sigma < 1$) $f(\sigma)$ strictly satisfies the budget constraints (2.4) at p^0 and lies in $\hat{B}^h(p^0)$. It follows that for each $\sigma < 1$, $f(\sigma)$ also satisfies (2.4) with strict inequality for all p in some neighbourhood U_σ of p^0. Thus $f(\sigma) \in \hat{B}^h(p)$ for $p \in U_\sigma$.

For convenience, we make use of an alternative definition of l.s.c.: For all p^0 and open sets G such that $\hat{B}^h(p^0) \cap G \neq \varnothing$ there exists a neighbourhood $U(p^0)$ such that $p \in U(p^0)$ implies $\hat{B}^h(p) \cap G \neq \varnothing$.

Let $a^0 \in \hat{B}^h(p) \cap G$. Let f be a continuous function such that $f(1) = a^0$. Thus $f(\sigma) \in G$ for σ close to one, and $f(\sigma) \in \hat{B}^h(p)$ for $p \in U_\sigma$. Thus, for such σ and p, $f(\sigma) \in \hat{B}^h(p) \cap G$.

The l.s.c. of $\overline{\hat{B}^h(p)}$ follows immediately from that of $\hat{B}^h(p)$. QED

Lemma 3.2. *$\overline{\hat{B}^h(p)}$ is upper semi-continuous for all $p \in P$.*

Proof. Let $p^\nu \to p^0$. Let $a^\nu \in \hat{B}^h(p^\nu)$, $a^\nu \to a^0$. We seek to show that $a^0 \in \overline{\hat{B}^h(p^0)}$, that is, that a^0 fulfils (2.1)-(2.4) at p^0 and that $x^0 - y^0 - z^0$ is not less than zero in every component. This last follows from continuity of inequalities. (2.1) is fulfilled by the continuity of the addition operation. (2.2) and (2.3) follow from closedness of $S^h(t)$, $T^h(t)$. (2.4) follows from continuity of the dot product and addition. QED

Lemma 3.3. *Let $\hat{B}^h(p^0)$ be locally interior for all p^0. Then $\gamma^h(p^0)$ is upper semi-continuous at p^0.*

Proof. Obvious in view of the previous lemmas, the fact that utility functions are continuous, and the theorem ([3], p. 116) that sets of maximizing points of a continuous function constrained by a continuous correspondence are upper semi-continuous. QED

Theorem 4.1 (Existence of equilibrium for the convexified non-monetary economy). *Under* (A.1)-(A.5), *there is a price vector $p^* \in P$ and an allocation $\langle a^{h*}\rangle_h$ such that*

$$a^{h*} \in \operatorname{con} \gamma^h(p^*),$$

$$\sum_{h=1}^{H} x^{h*} \leqq \sum_{h=1}^{H} y^{h*}$$

with $p^*_{it}(\tau) = 0$ for i, t, τ such that the strict inequality holds

Proof. Define $a(t) = \langle a^h(t)\rangle_{h=1}^H$, $a = \langle a(t)\rangle_{t=1}^T$, and $\hat{\gamma}_\rho(p) = \sum_{h=1}^H \hat{\gamma}^h_\rho(p)$. Let

$$\mu_t(a(t)) = \{p(t) \in S^t \mid p(t)(x(t)-y(t)) \text{ is maximal in } S^t\}$$

and $\mu_T(a(T)) = \{p(T) \in S^T \mid p(T)(x(T)-y(T)) \text{ is maximal in } S^T\}$ and define

$$\mu(a) = \mathop{\times}_{t=1}^{T} \mu_t(a(t)).$$

Consider the transformation $\Phi(a, p) = \hat{\gamma}_\rho(p) \times \mu(a)$.

As we have seen, this transformation satisfies all the properties required to apply the Kakutani Theorem and so there is a fixed point

$$(a^*, p^*) \in \hat{\gamma}_\rho(p^*) \times \mu(a^*).$$

Thus, $a^* \in \hat{\gamma}_\rho(p^*)$ is such that $(a^* = (x^*, y^*, z^*, r^*, s^*))$

$$0 \geqq p^*(t)(x^*(t)-y^*(t)) \geqq p(t)(x^*(t)-y^*(t)), \text{ for all } p(t) \in S^t. \quad \ldots(7.1)$$

For $t \leqq T$, successively use the inequalities (7.1) for the vectors

$$p^i(t) = (0, \ldots, 0, 1, 0, \ldots, 0) \in S^t$$

where unity occurs in the ith component. Thus, $x^*(t) \leqq y^*(t)$ for $t \leqq T$.

All that remains to be shown is that an equilibrium in the ρ-economy is an equilibrium in the unbounded economy, for sufficiently large ρ. Let a^ρ denote an equilibrium in the economy with ρ as an upper bound. If $\| a^\rho \| \to \infty$ as $\rho \to \infty$, then $\| z^\rho \| \to \infty$, by our boundedness assumption (A.5). But, as is easy to verify, $c+z \leqq \omega$ in any equilibrium, a contradiction. Thus, the constraint that a^h lie in the cube defined by ρ is not binding for sufficiently large ρ. QED

Theorem 5.1 (Existence of equilibrium for the convexified monetary economy). *Under* (A.1)-(A.5), (M.1)-(M.4), *and* (S), *for any α, $0<\alpha<1$, there is a price vector $p^* \in P^\alpha$ and an allocation $\langle a^{h*}\rangle_h$ such that*

$$a^{h*} \in \operatorname{con} \gamma^h(p^*),$$

$$\sum_{h=1}^{H} x^{h*} \leqq \sum_{h=1}^{H} y^{h*}$$

with $p^*_{it}(\tau) = 0$ for i, t, τ such that the strict inequality holds, and

$$p^*_{0t}(t) \neq 0 \text{ for all } t.$$

Proof. As in the proof of Theorem 4.1, we obtain a fixed point $(a^*, p^*) \in \hat{\gamma}_\rho(p^*) \times \mu(a^*)$, where now $\mu_T(a(T)) = \{p(T) \in S^T_\alpha \mid p(T)(x(T)-y(T)) \text{ is maximal in } S^T_\alpha\}$. From this we again obtain the inequalities (7.1) except that $p^*(T)$ and $p(T)$ belong to S^T_α rather than S^T.

O—43/2

For $t<T$, successively use the inequalities (7.1) for the vectors

$$p^i(t) = (0, \ldots, 0, 1, 0, \ldots, 0) \in S^t$$

where unity occurs in the ith component. Thus, $x^*(t) \leqq y^*(t)$ for $t<T$. We cannot use this argument for $t = T$ because $p_{OT}(T) \geqq \alpha>0$, for $p(T) \in S_\alpha^T$.

Now, if $p_{kt}^*(v) = 0$, we claim that $y_{kt}^*(v) = 0$. For, we know that $y_{kt}^{h*}(v)$ is a convex combination of utility-maximizing vectors for each h. But any $y_{kt}^h(v)>0$ is transactions-costly, so that it is better that excess amounts of good (k, t) be freely disposed of (through the storage-technology) if its marginal utility is negative. Hence $y_{kt}^*(v) = 0$ because a convex combination of zeroes is still zero. It follows that $x_{kt}^*(v)<y_{kt}^*(v)$ is impossible, because then $p_{kt}^*(v) = 0$ (by the definition of $\mu_t(\cdot)$) and so $x_{kt}^*(v)<0$, a contradiction. In particular, we can now say that $x_{kT}^*(v) = y_{kT}^*(v)$, for $v<T$.

However, we can still show that $x_{0T}^*(T) = y_{0T}^*(T)$. Because of constraint (5.1), the fact that $c_0^*(T) = 0$, and $x_{0T}^*(v) = y_{0T}^*(v)$ (for $v<T$), we have $(M = \Sigma_h M^h)$

$$0 = c_0^*(T) = \omega_0(T)+s_0^*(T)+\sum_{v=1}^{T-1} [x_{0T}^*(v)-y_{0T}^*(v)]+x_{0T}^*(T)-y_{0T}^*(T)-M$$

$$= \omega_0(T)+s_0^*(T)-M+x_{0T}^*(T)-y_{0T}^*(T). \qquad \ldots(7.2)$$

But, $\omega_0(T)+s_0^*(T) = M$, because of (5.1), the durability of money (M.1) and because there is equilibrium in all periods prior to T. Thus, $x_{0T}^*(T) = y_{0T}^*(T)$.

This means that

$$0 \geqq p^*(T)(x^*(T)-y^*(T)) = \sum_{k=1}^{n} p_{kT}^*(T)(x_{kT}^*(T)-y_{kT}^*(T))$$

$$\geqq \sum_{k=1}^{n} p_{kT}(T)(x_{kT}^*(T)-y_{kT}^*(T))$$

for all $p(T) \in S_\alpha^T$. But $(\alpha, 0, \ldots, 0, 1-\alpha, 0, \ldots, 0) \in S_\alpha^T$ and so $x^*(T) \leqq y^*(T)$.

To show the positivity of the spot price of money, we argue the contrapositive. If $p_{0t}^*(t) = 0$, for some t, then we will argue that large positive values of $x_{0t}(t)$ are possible for some household. This is not trivial because there are transactions costs to positive $x_{0t}(t)$ and there may be only zero prices for goods the household owns. However, (M.3) guarantees that some household (h', let us say) can acquire arbitrarily large $x_{0t}(t)$ using his own resources. Hence, household h' may acquire arbitrarily large amounts of cash at t and store it until T whereupon, by assumption (M.4), he may trade it at price $p_{0T}^*(T) = \alpha>0$, thereby acquiring arbitrarily large amounts of goods at T. By assumption (S) (used repeatedly for t, $t+1$, ..., $T-1$, if necessary), this is always preferable to any consumption plan with $x_{0t}^h(t) = 0$. But $x_{0t}^*(t) = y_{0t}^*(t) = 0$, if $p_{0t}^*(t) = 0$, as was shown earlier. Yet, $x_{0t}^{*h'}$ is the convex combination of maximizing plans. But any maximizing plan must have positive $x_{0t}^{h'}(t)$ and so $x_{0t}^{*h'}(t)>0$, a contradiction.

All that remains to be shown is that an equilibrium in the ρ-economy is an equilibrium in the unbounded economy, for sufficiently large ρ.

Let a^ρ denote an equilibrium in the economy with ρ as an upper bound. If $\| a^\rho \| \to \infty$ as $\rho \to \infty$, then $\| z^\rho \| \to \infty$, by our boundedness assumption (A.5). But, as is easy to verify, $c+z \leqq \omega$ in any equilibrium, a contradiction. Thus, the constraint that a^h lie in the cube defined by ρ is not binding for sufficiently large ρ. QED

Theorem 6.1. *Let p^* be an equilibrium price vector for the convexified economy. Let $R(p^*)$ exist, and be finite. Then at p^* there is a social approximate equilibrium of modulus $NR(p^*)$.*

Proof. We have $a^{h*} \in \text{con } \gamma^h(p^*)$, $\Sigma x^{h*} < \Sigma y^{h*}$, $p^*_{it}(\tau) = 0$ if $\sum_h x^{h*}_{it}(\tau) < y^{h*}_{it}(\tau)$. This gives properties (a), (b), (d). Applying Theorem A gives the existence of $a^{h\dagger}$ satisfying (c) and (e). QED

Theorem 6.2. *Let p^* be an equilibrium price vector for the convexified economy. Let finite $R(p^*)$ exist. Then at p^* there is an individual approximate equilibrium of modulus $NR(p^*)$.*

Proof. Let a^{h*} be the equilibrium allocation for the convexified economy, and let $a^{h\dagger}$ be a social approximate equilibrium of modulus $NR(p^*)$. Choose $e^h \in R^N$ so that

(i) $\sum_h e^h = \sum_h a^{h*} - \sum_h a^{h\dagger}$

(ii) no coordinate of e^h is opposed in sign to the corresponding coordinate of

$$\sum_h a^{h*} - \sum_h a^{h\dagger};$$

(iii) e^h fulfils (2.4) at p^*.

These conditions are compatible since a^{h*}, $a^{h\dagger}$ fulfil (2.4).

Let $a^{h**} = a^{h\dagger} + e^h$.

$$\sum_h x^{h**} = \sum_h x^{h\dagger} + \sum_h (x^{h*} - x^{h\dagger}) = \sum_h x^{h*}.$$

$$\sum_h y^{h**} = \sum_h y^{h\dagger} + \sum_h (y^{h*} - y^{h\dagger}) = \sum_h y^{h*}:$$

Since p^*, a^{h*}, $a^{h\dagger}$ is a social approximate equilibrium, we have $\Sigma x^{h*} \leqq \Sigma y^{h*}$ and $p^*_{it}(\tau) = 0$ if $\Sigma_h x^{h*}_{it}(\tau) < \Sigma_h y^{h*}_{it}(\tau)$. But since $\Sigma x^{h**} = \Sigma x^{h*}$, $\Sigma y^{h**} = \Sigma y^{h*}$, we have

(a) $\sum_h x^{h**} \leqq \sum_h y^{h**}$, and

(b) $p^*_{it}(\tau) = 0$ if $\sum_h x^{h**}_{it}(\tau) < \sum_h y^{h**}_{it}(\tau)$.

Since p^*, a^*, $a^\dagger$ is a social approximate equilibrium

(c) $a^{h\dagger} \in \gamma^h(p^*)$.

This gives that $a^{h\dagger}$ fulfils (2.4) at p^*, as does e^h by (iii). Hence

(d) $a^{h**}(= a^{h\dagger} + e^h)$ fulfils (2.4) at p^*.

(i) and (ii) give $(\Sigma \mid e^h \mid^2)^{1/2} \leqq \mid \Sigma a^{h*} - \Sigma a^{h\dagger} \mid$.

But $\mid \Sigma a^{h*} - \Sigma a^{h\dagger} \mid \leqq NR(p^*)$ and $e^h = a^{h**} - a^h$, so

(e) $(\Sigma \mid a^{h**} - a^{h\dagger} \mid^2)^{1/2} \leqq NR(p^*)$. QED

Theorem 6.3. *Let p^*, $a^{h\dagger}$ a^{h**} be an individual approximate equilibrium of modulus A and let $[\Sigma((x^{h\dagger} - y^{h\dagger} - z^{h\dagger})^+ - (r^{h\dagger} - s^{h\dagger} - \omega^h)^+)] \geqq \Sigma(x^{h\dagger} - y^{h\dagger})$. Then there is an attainable individual approximate equilibrium of modulus A.*

Proof. Choose $\alpha^h \in R^N$ so that

(i) $\Sigma\alpha^h = (\Sigma(x^{h\dagger} - y^{h\dagger}))^+$,

(ii) $x^h \geqq \alpha^h \geqq 0$, all h, and

(iii) $(x^{h\dagger} - y^{h\dagger} - z^{h\dagger})^+ - (r^{h\dagger} - s^{h\dagger} - \omega^h)^+ \geqq \alpha^h$ all h.

The existence of such α^h is guaranteed by hypothesis. Let

$$a^{h\dagger\dagger} = (x^{h\dagger} - \alpha^h, y^{h\dagger}, z^{h\dagger}, r^{h\dagger}, s^{h\dagger}).$$

$a^{h\dagger} \in \gamma^h(p^*)$ implies $a^{h\dagger} \in T^h \times S^h$. Thus by free disposal $a^{h\dagger\dagger} \in T^h \times S^h$. $a^{h\dagger\dagger}$ satisfies (2.4) since $a^{h\dagger}$ fulfils (2.4) and $a^{h\dagger\dagger}$ merely reduces the smaller side of the inequality.

$$\sum_h x^{h\dagger\dagger} = \sum_h x^{h\dagger} - \sum_h \alpha^h = \sum_h x^{h\dagger} - (\sum_h (x^{h\dagger} - y^{h\dagger}))^+ \leqq \sum_h y^{h\dagger} = \sum_h y^{h\dagger\dagger}$$

so $a^{h\dagger}$ fulfils (a). $a^{h\dagger} \in \gamma^h(p^*)$ so $c^{h\dagger} \geqq 0$, but $c^{h\dagger} \geqq \alpha^h \geqq 0$ so $c^{h\dagger\dagger} = c^{h\dagger} - \alpha^h \geqq 0$. p^*, $a^{h\dagger}$, a^{h**} is an individual approximate equilibrium, so $a^{h\dagger} \in \gamma^h(p^*)$ and (c) and (d) are ful lled. To satisfy (f), note that p^*, $a^{h\dagger}$, a^{h**} is an individual approximate equilibrium of modulus A. But since

$$(\sum_h | a^{h\dagger} - a^{h**} |^2)^{1/2} \leqq A \quad \text{and} \quad \sum_h x^{h**} \leqq \sum_h y^{h**},$$

$$| \sum_h x^{h\dagger} - \sum_h y^{h\dagger} | \leqq A$$

so

$$(\sum_h | \alpha^h |^2)^{1/2} \leqq A.$$

But

$$a^{h\dagger\dagger} - a^{h\dagger} = (\alpha^h, 0, 0, 0, 0)$$

so

$$(\sum_h | a^{h\dagger\dagger} - a^{h\dagger} |^2)^{1/2} \leqq A,$$

fulfilling (f). QED

Theorem 6.4. *Let p^*, $a^\dagger$, $a^{\dagger\dagger}$ be an individual attainable approximate transactions equilibrium of modulus A and suppose there is for each household h, $e^h \in R^N$, so that*

(i) $| e^h | \leqq \varepsilon$,

(ii) $\Sigma e^h = (\Sigma x^{h\dagger} - \Sigma y^{h\dagger})^+$,

(iii) $(x^{h\dagger} - y^{h\dagger} - z^{h\dagger})^+ - (r^{h\dagger} - s^{h\dagger} - \omega^h)^+ \geqq e^h \geqq 0$.

Then there is $a^{\dagger\dagger\dagger}$ so that p^*, $a^\dagger$, $a^{\dagger\dagger\dagger}$ is an attainable individual uniformly approximate transactions equilibrium of modulus ε.

Proof. Let $a^{h\dagger\dagger\dagger} = a^{h\dagger} - (e^h, 0, 0, 0, 0)$. Since $a^{h\dagger} \in T^h \times S^h$, $a^{h\dagger\dagger\dagger} \in T^h \times S^h$ by free disposal. (ii) implies (a). Since $a^{h\dagger}$ fulfils (2.4), the reduced purchases of $a^{h\dagger\dagger\dagger}$ must also fulfil (2.4). (iii) ensures (e) and (f) follow from (i). QED

First version received September 1973; *final version accepted February* 1975 (*Eds.*).

Research support for W. P. Heller came from NSF Grant GS-2421.1. Support for R. Starr from the National Science Foundation and the Ford Foundation in grants to the Cowles Foundation for Research in Economics is gratefully acknowledged. This work was supported in part by National Science Foundation Grant GS-3269-A2 to the Institute for Mathematical Studies in the Social Sciences, Stanford University. The present essay is a revised version of [10].

NOTES

1. Non-convex transactions costs are not the only possible motivation for holding stocks of money. Because of transactions costs (convex or non-convex), holding stocks of money may be the least costly way of transferring purchasing power from one period to the next, or such stocks may be held for speculative gains due to expected decline in the price level.

2. In a continuum model the issue of individual convexification does not arise since convexification in aggregate is assured by the Lyapunov theorem [2].

3. Readers not interested in development of the mathematical structure may skip this section without loss of continuity; they should note only Lemma 3.3, that local interiority of the budget correspondence is a sufficient condition for upper semi-continuity of the demand correspondence. Extensions and further discussion of the ideas in this section are contained in [9].

4. Readers not interested in the introduction of money to this model may skip this section and proceed to Section 6 without loss of continuity.

5. Note that these constraints imply that forward contracts require payment today and delivery in the future, rather than an exchange of both money and goods in the future. Also, bonds here are not annuities, they are discounted notes.

6. For an analysis of a model similar to this one, but where (as emphasized in [4]) goods cannot buy goods, see [10].

7. Constraint (5.1) could be replaced by the requirement that $r_0^h(T) \geqq M^h$, where

$$\Sigma_h M^h = M = \Sigma_h \Sigma_t \omega_0^h(t).$$

8. The price need not fall strictly to 0 but merely to a positive value so low that no monetary trade takes place because gains from trade are swamped by transactions costs.

9. Though the converse does hold; if its price is zero, money is surely useless.

10. If we suppose that consumers, producers, and price formation are insensitive to disequilibria small as a proportion of total activity, then an approximate equilibrium of sufficiently small modulus (bound on the discrepancy between supply and demand) would be virtually indistinguishable from a true equilibrium. If, on the contrary, agents and markets are very sensitive to proportionally small discrepancies between supply and demand, then the distinction between a true equilibrium and an approximate equilibrium will be of major importance and the latter will be a very poor substitute for the former.

11. Arrow and Hahn spend several pages demonstrating this point without explicitly announcing it as a result.

REFERENCES

[1] Arrow, K. J. and Hahn, F. H. *General Competitive Analysis* (San Francisco: Holden-Day, 1972).

[2] Aumann, R. J. " Existence of Competitive Equilibrium in Markets with a Continuum of Traders ", *Econometrica*, **34**, No. 1 (January 1966), 1-17.

[3] Berge, C. *Topological Spaces* (New York: MacMillan Co., 1963).

[4] Clower, R. W. " A Reconsideration of the Microfoundations of Monetary Theory ", *Western Economic Journal*, **6** (1967), 1-9.

[5] Debreu, G. *Theory of value* (New York: Wiley, 1959).

[6] Hahn, F. H. " Equilibrium with Transactions Costs ", *Econometrica*, **39**, No. 3 (1971), 417-444.

[7] Heller, W. P. " Transactions with Set-up Cost ", *Journal of Economic Theory*, **4** (1972), 465-478.

[8] Heller, W. P. " The Holding of Money Balances in General Equilibrium ", *Journal of Economic Theory*, **7**, No. 1 (January 1974), 93-108.

[9] Heller, W. P. " Continuity in Nonconvex Economies ", *Vienna Conference on Equilibrium and Disequilibrium* (proceedings forthcoming).

[10] Heller, W. P. and Starr, R. M. " Equilibrium in a Monetary Economy with Non-Convex Transactions Costs ", Technical Report No. 110, IMSSS, Encina Hall, Stanford University (September 1973).

[11] Kurz, M. " Equilibrium in a Finite Sequence of Markets with Transaction Cost ", *Econometrica*, **42**, No. 1 (1974), 1-20.

[12] Lerner, A. P. " Money as a Creature of the State ", *American Economic Review*, **37**, No. 2 (May 1947), 312-317.

[13] Starr, R. M. " Quasi-Equilibria in Markets with Non-Convex Preferences ", *Econometrica*, **37**, No. 1 (1969), 25-38.

[14] Starr, R. M. " The Price of Money in a Pure Exchange Monetary Economy with Taxation ", *Econometrica*, **42**, No. 1 (1974), 45-54.

[15] Tobin, J. " The Interest Elasticity of the Transactions Demand for Cash ", *Review of Economics and Statistics* (1956).

Part IV

The Value of Money

20

DETERMINACY OF THE PRICE LEVEL, POSITIVITY OF THE PRICE OF MONEY

The studies presented in Parts II and III demonstrate a distinctive role for a medium of exchange and for a store of value. This does not explain the widespread use of non-interest-bearing unbacked government notes as money. The reason for using fiat money in an economy is not simply convention or low-cost government finance. There is a significant resource saving in the use of a fiduciary money rather than a commodity money. Since money is held as a stock, a commodity money requires that the economy hold a large fraction of capital whose sole function is to act as a financial instrument. Replacement of these real assets, e.g., gold, by a corresponding low-cost fiduciary asset, fiat money or private banknotes, implies that provision of a stock asset to facilitate reallocation between agents and over time can be achieved at a significantly lower real resource cost. As Adam Smith notes[3]

> When paper is substituted in the room of gold and silver money, the quantity of the materials, tools, and maintenance, which the whole circulating capital can supply, may be increased by the whole value of gold and silver which used to be employed in purchasing them. . . The operation, in some measure resembles that of the undertaker of some great work, who, in consequence of some improvement in mechanics, takes down his old machinery, and adds the difference between its price and that of the new to his circulating capital, to the fund from which he furnishes materials and wages to his workmen. . . The gold and silver money which circulates in any country, and by means

[3] I am indebted to Mark Thoma for bringing Smith's views on this point to my attention.

ISBN 0-12-663970-1

of which the produce of its land and labour is annually circulated and distributed to the proper consumers, is all dead stock. It is a very valuable part of the capital of the country, which produces nothing to the country. The judicious operations of banking, by substituting paper in the room of a great part of this gold and silver, enables the country to convert a great part of this dead stock into active and productive stock; into stock which produces something to the country. (*Wealth of Nations*, Bk II, chap. ii).

Supposing a fiduciary money to be desirable as a medium of exchange and store of value, what properties should it have, and is the central government an appropriate issuer? The classical characteristics are portability, cognizability, divisibility, and acceptability. In terms of the studies of Part III, the first three characteristics would be summarized simply as low transaction cost. As Prof. Tobin reminds us, acceptability is not so much a property of the asset as of the equilibrium; acceptability in exchange is self-justifying.[4] The studies of Part II, however, suggest additional properties that the monetary instrument should have. It should be unique, and it should be available in a quantity proportionate to the volume of trade to be sustained (Feldman, selection 8; Ostroy-Starr, selection 12; Starr, selection 13). Hence, the single issuer of the fiduciary asset should be capable of sustaining an issue proportionate to the volume of trade, a description fitting modern central government, among a small number of other large institutions. There is a final advantage of government issue in this regard: The taxing power of the state is capable of providing a form of backing to sustain the value of fiat money by guaranteeing that fiat money be acceptable for payment of taxes (Lerner, 1947).

An unbacked currency, a fiat money, is a particular problem in a model that includes endogenous price determination. There is always the possibility (in some models, the necessity) of the equilibrium price of fiat money to be nil (equivalently, for the price level expressed in terms of the fiat money to be arbitrarily high). A nil price of money effectively demonetizes the model. Thus, formal general equilibrium models of monetary economies using fiat money have to confront the question of how its price is determined and how in equilibrium the price can be positive (Hahn, selection 21). This problem is particularly troubling in a single period or finite-horizon model, where, because there is a terminal date on economic activity, the lack of backing to the currency will actually be experienced. In a finite-horizon model, unless there

[4] "The principal reason, then, that Treasury bills [for example] are not media of exchange is that they are not generally acceptable. This unsatisfactory circular conclusion underlines the essential point, that general acceptability in exchange is one of those phenomena—like language, rules of the road, fashion in dress—where the fact of social consensus is much more important and much more predictable than the content. Whether or not an asset is a generally acceptable means of payment will have to be taken as a datum determined by legal institutions and social conventions, rather than as something to be explained by economic theory." (James Tobin, *The Tobin Manuscript*, 1959)

is an additional element exogenously preventing the price of money from going to zero, zero may be the only equilibrium price of money.[5]

Quoting from Cass and Shell (1980):

> "It is obvious (and well-known) that money cannot have a positive price—that is, cannot be a store of value—in the conventional finite-horizon model in which the "end of the world" is known with certainty. The reason is simple. At the end of the last period, money is worthless. Therefore, in the next-to-last period, all individuals desire to dispose of money holdings in order to avoid capital losses. This drives the price of money to zero at the end of the next-to-last period. And so on. Individuals with foresight, not wanting to be stuck with the monetary "hot potato", thus drive the price of money to zero in each period. We know that money is not just another commodity. Tastes and endowments (including production possibilities) determine the relative price of apples in terms of oranges in the simple equilibrium model. But unlike ordinary Walrasian goods, the usefulness or "productivity" of money depends on its price. In particular, suppose that a barter equilibrium exists for a given market economy (with a given payments mechanism) without nominal money. Then it must be the case that, when such money is introduced into the economy, one of the new equilibria will be the old barter equilibrium with positive nominal money bearing a zero price. It could be that all households would be better off if the price of money were positive. But this does not imply that zero price is a disequilibrium price. Trust in fiat money is only a recent development, and even today such faith is hardly universal.

It is sometimes argued that fiat money, though not directly useful in itself, performs useful transaction services, and hence that usefulness creates the demand for money which sustains its equilibrium price. The argument is correct as long as the price of money is positive; the argument abruptly and completely breaks down when the value in exchange of the money commodity is zero. When money's price is zero, it can perform no transaction function. There is no financial demand for money when its price is zero, hence an equilibrium with a zero price can be sustained. The argument that money performs transaction functions is a correct explanation of the value of money in equilibrium at a positive price, but it does not explain the positivity of the price, merely its level assuming positivity. If money is what money does, then when money doesn't, it isn't. If money is acceptable because it is accepted, then when it's not accepted, it won't be acceptable.

A model of fiat money may be expected then to include an equilibrium where the price of money is nil. The question remaining is how to establish

[5]This is not a horror story of runaway inflation nor an unrealistic technicality. Rather it represents the technical requirements of our models which do in fact have practical counterparts. For example, in wartime in areas subject to military conquest, a former government's money may become valueless discontinuously and the money issued by a conquering power become valuable. Once the old government's currency loses its ability to pay taxes it loses the one form of backing it possessed, and its price becomes zero. The economy thus demonetized still has a strong need for a medium of exchange. A good that is necessarily incapable of fulfilling that need is one whose price is zero.

the existence of equilibrium in a fiat-money economy with a positive price of money (equivalently, with a bounded determinate price level). Three answers have been presented in the literature: infinite horizon, expectations of positive value, and taxes. In a finite-horizon, fiat-money economy the lack of backing for the unbacked currency will actually be experienced. This drives the price of fiat money to zero. One solution to this problem is to posit an infinite horizon, for example an overlapping generations model (Cass-Shell, 1980), where the lack of backing need never be experienced. Further it is useful in that model to have an intertemporal asset for the transfer of purchasing power from one period and generation to the next. Hence there is a class of equilibria where money trades at a positive price and serves an extremely useful function as a portfolio asset for interperiod and intergenerational transfer of purchasing power. Overlapping generation studies represent a rich and distinctive class of models, beyond the scope of this book.

A temporary equilibrium model, Grandmont (selection 22), looks at the behavior of the economy at a single date with limited foresight. One way to think of the temporary equilibrium model is as an extract of a single period from an overlapping generations model. Actions are taken in the current period with a view to optimization in the current and succeeding period. There is foresight for a finite horizon. If the price of money is expected to be positive in the succeeding period, that expectation provides sufficient backing to maintain positivity of the price in the current period. If the price of money ever approached zero in the current period, arbitrage between the two periods would ensure sufficient demand for money to drive the price back up. This requires, however, inelastic expectations of the future price of money as a function of the current price. For example, if the price of money had unitary elasticity, i.e., if the price were always expected to be in the succeeding period what it is in the present, then the arbitrage would not take place. The requirement rather is that future price expectations be sufficiently inelastic to ensure expected strict positivity of price in the succeeding period. This inelastic expectation then provides sufficient basis for sustaining positive price in the current period.

A finite-horizon fiat-money model typically requires in some form that the money be turned in at the end of the finite horizon. This ensures that the money won't be a drug on the market and drive its price to zero. This may be taken as an arbitrary technical constraint that chips be cashed in at the end of play, or a more explicitly economic interpretation may be given. The economic interpretation is that the same government that issues money also has the power to levy taxes (Starr, selection 23). Equilibrium requires that the taxes be paid and the state will accept tax payment in money. If the taxes were purely nominal, this would not quite be sufficient to guarantee the existence of a positive price equilibrium. After all, the taxes might require a smaller payment than the available money. But if the taxes are real, so that the nominal value of money required to pay them varies inversely with the price of money (directly with the price level), then the problem is solved. Equilibrium occurs with payment of real taxes at a price level so that the volume of available money is just sufficient to pay the volume of taxes.

The artificiality of these constructs implies an additional point. That money—when its price is positive—promotes allocative efficiency was established in the studies of Parts II and III. Nothing in the studies there ensured positivity of the price of fiat money based on more fundamental considerations than by assumption. Positivity is a necessary condition for usefulness. However, the property that money would be useful if its price were positive does nothing to ensure positivity. Conversely, in the models of taxation and temporary equilibrium a positive equilibrium price of money can be sustained with no necessary efficiency gain. Hence, we conclude that positivity of the price of money is a necessary but not a sufficient condition for money to promote allocative efficiency in a general equilibrium model; the conditions are not equivalent.

21

ON SOME PROBLEMS OF PROVING THE EXISTENCE OF AN EQUILIBRIUM IN A MONETARY ECONOMY

by F. H. Hahn

This is a pioneering essay. Prof. Hahn puts forth the suggestion (novel at the time) that monetary theory, and hence the theory of equilibrium of a monetary economy, should be subject to the same requirements of formal modelling as the non-monetary Arrow-Debreu style models. He then proposes a bewildering outcome of such a model: money may be worthless.

Money is characterized by the quality that it is desired for what it will buy. If, for some reason, it were worthless, it could not be valuable in this way. Hence there would be no excess demand for it. But this means that the nil value in exchange is an equilibrium "price" of money. There is an equilibrium where the economy is effectively demonetized; it no longer appears to be a monetary economy. There are (or may be) other equilibria where the price is positive.

Additional assumptions are then developed, sufficient to preclude this class of equilibria, but the essential points remain. Positivity of the value of money is to be a conclusion—not an assumption—of a well formulated general equilibrium model of a monetary economy. The presence of a demand or an excess demand for money at some positive price is not sufficient to imply positivity of the price of money. Positivity of the price is not equivalent to the desirability of having a monetary economy.

The following is reprinted with permission from *The Theory of Interest Rates*, F. Hahn and F. Brechling, eds. © 1966, Macmillan, London and Basingstoke.

ISBN 0-12-663970-1

ON SOME PROBLEMS OF PROVING THE EXISTENCE OF AN EQUILIBRIUM IN A MONETARY ECONOMY

BY

F. H. HAHN

Churchill College, Cambridge

I. THE PROBLEM

RECENT work on the existence of an equilibrium has been concerned with a world without money while all work in monetary theory has ignored the 'existence' question. In this paper I propose to investigate some of the problems of rectifying this omission. Before doing so let us ask ourselves whether the task is worth undertaking.

Most theories in economics involve the equilibrium solutions of certain models. These solutions are used as benchmarks, or as states to which an economic system is believed to tend or as means for making long-term predictions. Implicitly or explicitly most economists, whether 'practical' or 'airy fairy', use the notion of an equilibrium. It will also be agreed that very few of our models have as yet been exposed to exhaustive empirical tests. It therefore does not seem unreasonable or useless to expose them to some logical tests in the meantime.

Suppose we found that a given model has no equilibrium solution. This in itself need not mean that we should reject it, but it would surely mean that we should not continue to use it to describe equilibrium states. Take the well-known example of an economy with strongly increasing returns to scale. It is agreed that in this case the assumption that all units of decision take prices as given may mean that no equilibrium solution exists. This, it seems to me, is valuable information to have. It means that if we judge increasing returns to scale to be prevalent and if we also wish to discuss the working of the price mechanism by comparing equilibrium states, or given situations with equilibrium situations, that the perfect competition model will not be of much use. This is texbook stuff, but it is also the kind of question existence proofs are concerned with and which has been illuminated by them.

To take an example nearer home, consider Patinkin's model of general equilibrium. Suppose it were shown that it possessed no equilibrium solution. Can it be argued that Patinkin and economists in general could reasonably be indifferent to this result? What would become of the various exercises in Comparative Statics which are the flesh and bones of Patinkin's argument? As it turns out, the problem is particularly interesting in this case since we must show not only that a solution exists but also that it is one in which money has positive exchange value. It is no good saying, 'We know from everyday experience that we live in a world described by Patinkin's model'. Indeed that is precisely the point at issue. We wish to enquire whether the model satisfies the minimal requirements of everyday experience. If economists are willing to count equations they should also be willing to investigate the existence of a solution to their equations.

After these rather self-evident remarks, let us get down to work.

II. EQUILIBRIUM IN A MONETARY ECONOMY

(1) Let us first formulate the problem in the abstract. Let $P = \{P_0 \ldots P_n\}$, $X = \{X_o \ldots X_n\}$ be two vectors. Suppose that we have $X_i = X_i(P)$ $(i = 0 \ldots n)$ or more compactly $X = X(P)$. The following assumptions[1] are made (I give them their economic names):

A.1: Homogeneity (*H*): $X(P) = X(kP) \quad k > 0,\ P \geq 0$
Walras' Law (*W*): $P'X(P) = 0 \quad P \geq 0$
Continuity (*C*): $X(P)$ is continuous over $P \geq 0$
Boundedness (*B*): $X(P)$ is bounded from below
Scarcity (*S*): $X(0) > 0$

Given A.1 it can then be shown that there exists $P^* \geq 0$ such that $X(P^*) \leq 0$. The following obvious points should be noted:

(i) By (*W*) if $P_i^* > 0$, $X_i(P^*) = 0$ while only if $P_i^* = 0$ can we have $X_i(P^*) < 0$.
(ii) By (*H*) if P^* gives $X_i(P^*) \leq 0$ then so does kP^*, $k > 0$.

We refer to P^* as a solution of the system $X(P) \leq 0$.

(2) Suppose we wished to ensure that some particular component of any solution P^* is strictly positive. Let us write $P(i)$ as the vector P with its ith component identically equal to zero. If it were true that $X_i(P(i)) > 0$ all $P(i) \geq 0$ then evidently $P_i^* > 0$ and our task would have been accomplished.

[1] The notation '$\geq$' denotes a weak vector inequality. E.g. $X_i \geq 0$ means $X_i \geq 0$ all i, $X_i > 0$ some i.

But now let us suppose that the 0th component of X has the property

$$X_0(P(0)) \leqq 0 \text{ all } P(0) \geq 0 \qquad 2.1$$

then it can easily be shown that there exists some $P^*(0) \geq 0$ such that $X(P^*(0)) \leq 0$.

For let us set $P_0 \equiv 0$ and concentrate on the vector $P(0)$. By (H) we may confine ourselves to only those $P(0)$ contained within an n dimensional simplex. Also by (W), $\sum_{i \neq 0} P_i X_i = 0$ all $P(0) \geq 0$. Also if we write $\hat{P} = \{P_1 \ldots P_n\}$ we may substitute $X_i'(\hat{P})$ for $X_i(P(0))$ all i. A.1 will therefore hold for the problem $X' = \{X_1 \ldots X_n'\}$, $X'(\hat{P}) = X'$ and this has a solution $\hat{P}^* \geq 0$. But then evidently our original problem must have a solution $P^*(0)$ where this vector has the same components as $\hat{P}^*$ and an additional zero component.

(3) We may now consider an economic interpretation of the argument in (1) and (2). Let all economic agents have a two-period horizon and let the expected price of goods be always identically equal to their current price. Let there be no price uncertainty and let the initial endowments of all the agents be given. Let one of the goods have a futures market and interpret P_n as the present price for the future delivery of that good and P_{n-1} as its current price. Let all prices be expressed in fictional units of account. Assume that households maximize continuous quasi concave utility functions and that they are not satiated at any $P \geq 0$ and that they have positive initial endowments of every good. Suppose that the economy's production set is compact and that production without inputs is impossible. All profits are distributed to households and production agents maximize profits. They always have the choice of not producing at all and of costless disposal. We may then interpret P as a price vector and X as an excess demand vector for the current period and A.1 will hold. Note that the future market defines an interest rate $\frac{P_{n-1}}{P_n} - 1$. The solution P^* gives the equilibrium prices for the current period.

The model just given is in all respects similar to Patinkin's except that it as yet contains no money. Let us designate the good with the label '0' as fiat money. We are told that the demand for fiat money depends on its exchange value (absence of 'money illusion'). It follows that no money will be demanded if its exchange value is zero. But that means that X_0 has the property 2.1. We therefore reach the rather displeasing conclusion (based on the argument in (2)), that the Patinkin model always contains a 'non-monetary' solution. Moreover it is not at once clear how we could establish that it also contains a solution with $P_0^* > 0$. For evidently we cannot make use of the device discussed in (2) for ensuring this. Something has gone wrong.

(4) Now Patinkin—and others—assume that money always has positive exchange value and it can be argued that his model is not defined for the case

where it has not. For if there were no money we would have to specify more closely the activities connected with exchange. That is we are asked to replace A.1 by

A.1′: (H), (W), (C) and (B) hold for all $P \geq 0$, $P_0 > 0$.

The question is: can we prove that an equilibrium exists when A.1 is replaced by A.1′? Curiously enough Patinkin introduces two further assumptions which make the answer to this question affirmative. I say curiously enough, because at least one of these assumptions was introduced with a quite different end in view. Let us examine this in a little more detail.

(5) We write $\bar{x}_{0\alpha}$ as the initial endowment of cash of individual α and $X_{i\alpha}$ as this individual's excess demand for the ith good. Given the absence of 'money illusion' it is well known that we may write, using the notation introduced in (2),

$$X_{i\alpha} = X_{i\alpha}(\hat{P},\ P_{o}\bar{x}_{0\alpha}) \text{ all } i.$$

Moreover, $X_{i\alpha}$ possesses (H) in the given arguments. Write $\bar{x}_0 = \Sigma \bar{x}_{0\alpha}$. Patinkin's two further assumptions are:

A.2: We may write $X_i = \Sigma X_{i\alpha} = X_i(\hat{P},\ P_0\bar{x}_0)$ all i.

A.3: $X_0(\hat{P},\ P_0\bar{x}_0) >$ for all $P \geq 0$, $P_0 > 0$, $\bar{x}_0 = 0$.

A.2 states that all individuals are exactly alike so that the total excess demand for any good is independent of the distribution of initial cash balances between them. By 'exactly alike' we here mean that they all have parallel linear Engel curves going through the origin. A.3 states that the demand for money is always strictly positive for all prices admissible by A.1′.

Now using A.1′, A.2, and A.3 the existence of an equilibrium can be established. Here I shall only sketch a proof. Set $P_0 = 1$ and consider the simplex

$$S = \{P,\ \bar{x}_0 / P_i \geq 0, \text{ all } i, x_0 \geq 0, \Sigma P_i + \bar{x}_0 = 1\}.$$

A.1′ holds over S. We may now use a slightly modified mapping of S into itself first proposed by Uzawa

$$P_j = \frac{1}{k}\max\,[0, P_j + hX_j] \text{ all } j \neq 0$$

$$\bar{x}_0 = \frac{1}{k}\max\,[0, \bar{x}_0 + hX_0] \qquad 5.1$$

$$k = \sum_{j \neq 0} \max\,[0, P_j + hX_j] + \max\,[0, \bar{x}_0 + hX_0]$$

where h is taken sufficiently small to ensure $k > 0$. (Recall (B) of A.1′.) The mapping 5.1 can be shown to have at least one fixed point $\hat{P}^*, \bar{x}_0^*$. Using (W)

we easily find

$$(k-1)\left[\sum_{i\neq 0}(P_i^*)^2+\bar{x}_0^*\right]=h[\sum P_i^* \, X_i(P^*\bar{x}_0^*) + X_0(P^*\bar{x}_0^*)] = 0$$

so that at the fixed point $k=1$. It is now easy to see that, using A.3, $X_i(\hat{P}^*\bar{x}_0^*)\leq 0$ and $P_i^*X_i=0$ all $i\neq 0$ and $X_0\,(\hat{P}^*\bar{x}_0^*)=0$.

Since by A.3,, $\bar{x}_0^*>0$ and by A.2 its redistribution between individuals leaves all excess demand functions unaffected, we may redistribute it between individuals in the ratio of their actual initial endowments. A simple scale change (of $\hat{P}^*$ and $\bar{x}_0^*$) will then give us the money stocks for each individual which he started out with and the problem is solved.

It is evident that a proof of the existence of equilibrium which turns crucially on a supposition such as A.2 is hardly acceptable. Indeed the role of this assumption is simply to enable us to employ a technical trick to ensure that we can use a fixed point theorem and one cannot believe that it has any fundamental significance to the whole problem. The trick of course was to keep the exchange value of money strictly positive throughout so that money was always 'desirable' and to obtain the desired continuity be varying initial total stocks knowing that once an equilibrium was found the actual initial stock distribution could be restored without upsetting the equilibrium. But quite apart from A.2, A.3 too will repay further scrutiny.

(6) The supposition that the demand for money will always be positive when $P_0>0$ is justified by Patinkin by an appeal to the alleged uncertainty of the exact instant of sales and purchases within a given time period. We are also asked to imagine there to be a 'penalty' for being out of cash when a given purchase comes due. Tobin and Baumol justify the same assumption by the existence of transaction costs (brokerage fees). All assume that no transactions are possible without the intermediate use of money. It is, I think, evident that none of these rationalizations can be taken as an explanation of the positive exchange value of money since that is already assumed.

Now explanations which turn on 'brokerage' fees and the 'inconvenience' of indirect transactions are not easy to accommodate in a model such as Patinkin's. These are all 'imperfections' which find no place in the model. Indeed the notion of 'liquidity' would be hard to accommodate in Patinkin's world for that, as Marschak has pointed out, turns rather crucially on the imperfections of markets. But even Patinkin's own preferred acount is not easy to understand. We are told that there exist claims to debt. A unit of these is the promise to pay one unit of account in perpetuity. Let us suppose that they are (or have been) issued by the Government which otherwise plays no rôle in the economy other than financing its interest payments by lump sum taxes. There is no price uncertainty. Why should transactions not be carried out by means of these claims to debt? But even if that is not granted it is not clear why when I come to make a purchase, being out of cash, (having miscalculated the timing of my receipts), I could not offer to pay a little later (after I have cashed my claim), a litle more (offer interest). In Patinkin's world such an offer should always be acceptable, and if trade credits cause no social embarassment in the world we live in why should it in the abstract world of the textbook?

All this suggests that while Patinkin has rendered signal services he has failed to provide a model which can serve as an adequate foundation for a monetary theory. Such a model, it seems to me, must have two essential features beside price uncertainty. It must distinguish between abstract exchange opportunities at some notionally called prices and actual transaction opportunities. The latter requires a precise statement of the methods of transactions open to an individual with their attendant costs. Secondly it must specify rather precisely the conditions in which futures markets for various commodities would arise. For if there were future markets in all goods and services and no price uncertainty there would, as in Debreu's world, be only need for one single set of transactions over an individual's lifetime and there would be no problem of the non-coincidence of payments and receipts. This involves questions of costs of storage, etc. But it also involves questions of the 'standardization' of commodities. It forces one to recognize that there is no commodity called 'a second hand car' and makes the unsuitability of 'perfect competition models' to monetary theory rather obvious.

(7) The reason why I do not propose to attempt the construction of such a model here is as follows: In the usual existence problem the 'initial' position of the participants can be described independently of prices, i.e. in terms of the initial endowment of goods, technological knowledge etc. The interesting point of a monetary economy is that we cannot do so. For it is one of the features of such an economy that contracts, as Keynes noted, are made in terms of money. In particular, debt obligations are of this kind. By postulating the possibility of 'recontract' etc. this difficulty could be overcome—but it would then, it seems to me, turn out to be a somewhat arid exercise. In any case it is on this aspect of the problem that I wish to dwell in the remainder of this paper.

Before doing so, however, it might just be worth while to sketch a procedure which could be used to establish the existence of an equilibrium in Patinkin's world if his basic assumptions are granted, but A.2 is not used.

We imagine a world without money. Each individual attaches certain probabilities to being able to effect a given exchange at the exchange rates 'called'. However, he may, if he wishes, take out insurance. A unit of insurance is the guarantee of being able to carry out a transaction worth one unit of account at a given moment of time. One may suppose that as long as exchange is desired at all and as long as the price per unit of insurance is not equal to unity, some insurance is demanded. Insurance is supplied by some outside agency, say the government. The price charged per unit of insurance per unit time is $\left(\frac{P_{n-1}}{P_n} - 1\right)$, the rate of interest. At any price the amount of insurance supplied is just equal to what is demanded. The government redistributes the proceeds from its activity to households. It can then be shown with the aid of a number of purely technical assumptions that an equilibrium exists. It can then further be shown that corresponding to this fictional economy there would exist an actual one in which individuals 'bought' the same amount of insurance as in the fictional equilibrium by holding certain stocks of cash. Notice that this procedure begs the question: is the government service the only way by means of which economic agents could insure their transactions?

III. ARE THERE SOLUTIONS OF REALISTIC MONETARY MODELS?

(8) So far I have been concerned with the question of whether it is possible to construct an abstract model of economic exchange and activity in which money is used and whether the existence of an equilibrium can be proved for such a model. I hope to have shown that even for this task the difficulties are fairly formidable and that they have not yet been faced. I now wish to concern myself with the more interesting question of the existence of a solution to monetary models which are to be taken not as idealized but as in some sense as representing actual relationships. The most famous of these is of course the Keynesian short period flow equilibrium model.

It will be recalled that Keynes argued that if we set up a model which included the requirement that everyone willing to work at the going money wage should be able to do so, then whatever the money wage specified, no equilibrium solution may exist. Keynes further maintained that it was the existence of money in the economy, or more precisely the fact that wage bargains were made in terms of money and that money was always the preferred asset at a rate of interest 'low enough' which was responsible for that conclusion.

This has been widely rationalized in a way best given by a quotation taken from Modigliani. 'Since securities are inferior to money as a form of holding assets, there must be some positive level of the rate of interest (previously denoted by r) at which the demand for money becomes infinitely elastic or practically so. We have the Keynesian case when 'the full employment rate of interest is less than r''.... From the analytical point of view the situation is characterised by the fact that we must add to our system a new equation, namely $r = r''$. The system is therefore overdetermined . . . .'[1]

That this way of putting the case is wrong seems quite clear. The hypothesis that the equilibrium rate of interest cannot fall below a certain minimum is not an additional restriction on our system and provides no new independent relation between any of the unknowns. It is simply a hypothesis concerning the form of one or more of the excess demand functions of the system. Provided these satisfied A.1 and there were as many excess demand functions as unknowns the 'liquidity stop' would not prevent the existence of an equilibrium.

This has been recognized by a large number of writers although the objection is not usually put in this way. Instead it is argued that Keynes ignored the connection between real cash balances and consumption. It is now widely believed that there always exists a level of money wages low enough which will ensure the existence of a 'full employment' solution. The argument is as follows: we are concerned with the technical problem of the existence of a solution. Thus while the 'Pigou effect' may be small in practice, by making money prices and wages low enough we can always make the Pigou effect 'large enough'. Indeed since at zero money wages and prices there will always be excess demand (non-satiation and scarcity) for goods and labour, there will be some positive set of prices at which the excess demand for goods and labour is zero. I now wish to give reasons why this argument rests on some rather shaky foundations.

(9) One of the main problems faced in establishing the existence of an equilibrium is to find acceptable assumptions which will ensure that the excess demand functions are continuous over the relevant domain. Amongst these the one that has caused most difficulty is the necessity of ensuring that at all admissible prices every individual can, if he wishes, participate in some exchange. Consider an individual who owns positive stocks of one good only: say $\bar{x}_1$. Let there be only two goods. Suppose that as long as he is able, our individual always prefers to have whatever quantities of the second good he can get, to the good he has. Then for all $1 > P_1 > 0$, he will demand nothing of the first good ($P_1 + P_2 = 1$). But at $P_1 = 0$ he has no choice but to hold the good he has. There will be a discontinuity in his demand function. To exclude this possibility we can either postulate that he has strictly positive stocks of every good or that, loosely speaking, he is always capable of supplying a service which can be transformed into a good with positive price.

[1] F. Modigliani, 'Liquidity Preference and The Theory of Interest and Money', *Econometrica*, XII, 1944, pp. 45–88.

One might equally well suppose that there is some suitable social redistribution mechanism at work which allows every individual to participate in exchange.

But now let us suppose that our individual has initial endowments which include debt fixed in terms of money at a rate of interest also so fixed. Then as the price of goods in terms of money is made lower and lower (i.e. in our earlier notation as $P_0 \to 1$) our individual will be unable to meet his obligations: he will go bankrupt. Since at that stage the creditors—even if they get all the debtor's assets—and even if debtors and creditors are similiar as in A.2—the value of these assets may be less than the money value of the debt. For the debtor being capable of rendering services will go 'bankrupt' when he can no longer meet his interest payments. At that stage his assets may already be negative. The possibility of 'bankruptcy' is therefore also a possibility for the occurrence of some rather sharp discontinuities. In a society where contracts are made in terms of money and recontract is not possible an equilibrium solution may not exist. Of course in the 'long run' all contracts are escapable but that is another story.

(10) The point just made is perhaps of more than purely academic interest since it focuses attention on what is probably one of the most important features of a monetary economy: namely that contracts are made in terms of money. The fact that money is the actual numéraire is of some significance. If the route from unemployment to high levels of demand is strewn with bankruptcies then the smooth curves of the textbooks will be harder to justify. No doubt some sort of story could be invented to get over this difficulty, but it would be a curious one. Let me emphasize again that the difficulty cannot be overcome by supposing creditors and debtors to be exactly alike. For as long as any debtor is not bankrupt the real value of his debt to me increases with lower money prices. When he goes bankrupt and I take over his assets their money value will be less than the value of the debt and so there is a discontinuous change in the real value of money assets. I conclude from all this that the assertion that the 'Pigou effect' ensures the existence of an equilibrium is unproven.

22

ON THE SHORT-RUN EQUILIBRIUM IN A MONETARY ECONOMY

by Jean-Michel Grandmont

Grandmont formalizes the model of a *temporary equilibrium*. At each date there is a market in goods and in money. Each agent has a subjective probability distribution on prices in the succeeding period. This subjective probability depends, in part, on current prices. Demand for goods and money on the current market then depends on current prices and future expectations. An equilibrium occurs at current prices such that—taking account of the effect of current prices on future price expectations and of expectations on current demand—markets clear. Money is taken to be the only intertemporal asset. Sufficient conditions for existence of equilibrium are developed representing the rather complex generalization to this context of the usual continuity and compactness requirements.

Some restriction on subjective probability distributions of agents is required in order to establish the existence of equilibrium with a finite price level (positive price of money). The supports—independent of current prices—of the distributions must lie in a compact set. Nominal prices may become arbitrarily large, but expected prices are not allowed to do so. This restriction is quite strong. It precludes unitary elastic expectations (current price = expected price). The reason for the restriction is that in its absence, expectations of higher future prices may cause money holders to seek to reduce current money holdings. This would drive current prices higher, and the process would be repeated *ad infinitum*. There might be no finite price level in nominal terms consistent with equilibrium.

The economic significance of the restriction on price expectations is to place an upper bound on the expected future price level (equivalently, a

General Equilibrium
Models of
Monetary Economies

ISBN 0-12-663970-1

lower bound on the expected future purchasing power of money) independent of the current price level. In addition there is an assumed substitutability between present and future consumption. The result is that, should current prices become very high, hoarding of money will occur, which, through a budget constraint, implies a reduction in current demands sufficient to restrain further price level explosion. Expectations of future purchasing power are used as a form of backing to put a floor on the value of fiat money. No explanation is provided for where this expectation comes from. Nevertheless, the study makes the point that money, as an intertemporal asset, can derive its current value from the expectation of future value.

The following is reprinted with permission from *Allocation under Uncertainty: Equilibrium and Optionality*, J. Drèze, ed., New York: John Wiley and Sons, 1974.

On the Short-Run Equilibrium in a Monetary Economy

Jean-Michel Grandmont[I]

CEPREMAP, PARIS

A model of an exchange economy is presented where money is the only asset. It is shown that, under some assumptions, a short-run equilibrium exists if the traders' price expectations do not depend 'too much' on current prices.

I. INTRODUCTION

In order to take into account financial phenomena in a formal model of the economy, it seems worthwhile to consider an abstract world where several successive markets are held, to study the conditions which determine the equilibrium of each market and to find how these equilibria are linked together. This is a very old idea indeed, which underlies almost all economic thinking; it was in particular advanced by J. Hicks in his book *Value and Capital* under the name of 'temporary' equilibrium within a 'week' (see also J. Hicks [17], chapter 6). The same idea is present in the Keynesian theory and Don Patinkin [22] explicitly used this framework in his attempt to integrate money and credit in a general equilibrium theory. In a similar context, the recent work of E. Drandakis [8], R. Radner [23], [24] and B. P. Stigum [26] is in the same spirit.

However, the present state of economic theory in this area is not satisfactory, and there are still many difficulties to be solved before we have a consistent, formal theory of the temporary, or *short-run Walrasian equilibrium* (for a good survey of some of these difficulties, the reader may consult F. H. Hahn [14]). The research which is reported here was intended to make some progress in that direction. The simplified economy which is used to this

[I] I would like to express my deep gratitude to Gérard Debreu for his encouragement throughout this research. I also wish to thank Truman Bewley, Richard Cornwall, Emmanuel Drandakis, Werner Hildenbrand, Henry Lavaill, Thierry de Montbrial and Roy Radner for many helpful suggestions. I am also indebted to Jacques Drèze, Roger Guesnerie, Frank Hahn, Serge-Christophe Kolm and Yves Younes for their comments on an earlier draft. They of course bear no responsibility for any remaining error.

effect is very similar to the economy which is studied by Don Patinkin in ([22], chapters 2 and 3) or M. Friedman in ([10], chapter 1). As the formal treatment of the model is somewhat technical, it is perhaps useful to give here a brief account of the basic structure of the model and of the main results.

We consider an exchange economy where money is the only store of value. Time is divided into an infinite sequence of 'Hicksian' weeks; each week is indicated by an integer t. Markets are held on each 'Monday'; they are of the Walrasian type. All commodities which can be traded on any Monday are either consumption goods or (fiat) money. Consumption goods are perishable and cannot be stored from one week to the next; their number is N. Accordingly, a trader's consumption in the t-th week is noted by q_t, a point of R^N. Further, the consumption goods' *monetary* prices at time t are represented by a price system p_t; all prices considered in this study must be positive (formally, p_t must belong to $P_t = \{p \in R^N | p \gg 0\}$).[1] On the other hand, money has no 'direct' utility but is the only means to store wealth (at no cost) from one market to the next one. Finally, the total stock of money is invariant through time.

As in Patinkin's world, each trader receives on the t-th Monday a real income in kind, which is represented by a consumption bundle ω_t. His stock of money m_{t-1} was carried over from the previous week. The object of the t-th market is to allow for a reallocation of these endowments among traders. One of the objectives of our study is, precisely, to find sufficient conditions ensuring the existence of a short-run market equilibrium at time t.

A preliminary task is obviously to define the traders' behaviour on the t-th Monday. In order to do so, we consider a particular trader and assume that p_t is quoted on the floor of exchange. The consumer must choose his current consumption q_t and the money balances m_t he wishes to carry over until the next market. For the sake of simplicity, we assume that the trader makes plans only for the current week and for the next one. It follows that our trader must forecast next week's prices in order to make his choice. In this expository introduction, we shall take the trader's price expectations as certain (in the text, they will take the form of a probability distribution). They are based upon the consumer's information, which in our model consists only of past price systems and of p_t. Since past price systems are fixed, we shall not mention them and we shall note these price expectations $\psi(p_t)$, an element of P_{t+1}. Now let the consumer's intertemporal preferences at time t be represented by the 'direct' utility function $u(q_t, q_{t+1})$. If we assume that he knows with certainty next week's endowment ω_{t+1}, the trader's problem is to

[1] The following notation is used. If p, q belong to R^N, $p \geqq q$ means $p_n \geqq q_n$ for all n in N, $p > q$ means $p \geqq q$ and $p \neq q$, and $p \gg q$ means $p_n > q_n$ for all n.

maximise $u(q_t, q_{t+1})$ subject to[1] $p_t . q_t + m_t \; p_t . \omega_t + m_{t-1}$ and $\psi(p_t) . q_{t+1} \; \psi(p_t) . \omega_{t-1} + m_t$, where q_t, q_{t+1}, m_t are unknown. The optimal solution (s) gives us the trader's demand for consumption goods q_t, and money balances m_t, in response to p_t.

This demand can equivalently be obtained by a two-step procedure,[2] which allows us to introduce the concept of the 'indirect' or expected utility of money (a similar two-step procedure will actually be used in the text for the case of stochastic expectations). First, given p_t and for every $(\bar{q}_t, \bar{m}_t)$, choose $\bar{q}_{t+1}$ so as to maximise $u(\bar{q}_t, q_{t+1})$ subject to $\psi(p_t) . (q_{t+1} - \omega_{t+1}) \leqq \bar{m}_t$ with q_{t+1} as unknown. Then define $v(\bar{q}_t, \bar{m}_t, p_t) \equiv u(\bar{q}_t, \bar{q}_{t+1})$. This procedure gives us the expected utility v of the action $(\bar{q}_t, \bar{m}_t)$; this expected utility depends, through price expectations on current prices p_t (and implicitly on past prices). It is clear that the trader's demand in the t-th week is obtained by maximising $v(q_t, m_t, p_t)$ subject to $p_t . q_t + m_t \leqq p_t . \omega_t + m_{t+1}$ with q_t, m_t as unknowns.

This procedure 'introduces money in the utility function' as well as prices, and allows us to discuss an important question: is the expected utility v homogeneous of degree zero with respect to m_t and p_t? In general the answer is no; for instance price expectations may depend only on past prices and not at all on p_t, in which case v does not depend on p_t. On the other hand, this homogeneity property holds if the elasticity of price expectations with respect to current prices is unity, i.e. if $\psi(\lambda p_t) = \lambda \psi(p_t)$ for all positive λ (this condition is in particular satisfied by Patinkin's assumption of static expectations: $\psi(p_t) = p_t$ for all p_t). This is obvious if price expectations are certain; it will be shown in the text that the result is still valid when they are stochastic.

As was stated earlier, the main objective of the study is to find sufficient conditions which ensure the existence of a price system p_t^* which equilibrates demand and supply of all commodities (consumption goods and money) on the t-th Monday. We shall prove an existence theorem when, among other conditions, the traders' price expectations do not depend 'too much' on current prices. It must be noted that this condition is incompatible with the hypothesis of a unitary elasticity of price expectations which was discussed earlier. As a matter of fact, it is easy to construct counter-examples which show that an equilibrium may not exist when $\psi(\lambda p_t) = \lambda \psi(p_t)$ for all λ and p_t. Such a counter-example will be given in the text for the case of static expectations ($\psi(p_t) = p_t$ for all p_t). In that case if $\omega_t = \omega_{t+1}$ for all traders, and if the traders display a preference for present consumption, then the money market *cannot* be in equilibrium (if some other technical conditions are satisfied).

[1] For all p, q in R^N, $p.q$ denotes the inner product $\Sigma p_n q_n$.

[2] The reader will recognise a standard dynamic programming technique. It was used by B. P. Stigum in a similar context '[26].

The remainder of the study is devoted to a precise proof of these heuristic statements in the case of stochastic expectations. The paper is organised as follows. In section II we formally state the main definitions and assumptions. In section III we study the properties of an expected utility index. The traders' demand for consumption goods and money balances is analysed in section IV. The existence of a short-run market equilibrium is established in section V. Finally, conclusions are briefly given in section VI.

In what follows, it is taken for granted that the trader is well acquainted with the techniques which are used in G. Debreu's book *Theory of Value*. In addition, the reader should be familiar with the basic concepts of probability theory. References for additional material will be given in the text. Finally, a mathematical appendix gathers a few results for which no reference could be found.

II. DEFINITIONS AND ASSUMPTIONS

We fix t and focus the attention on the t-th week. There are by assumption K consumers (or traders) each of whom is indicated by an index k which varies from 1 to K. The symbol K will also denote the set $\{1, \dots K\}$.

The set of all consumption bundles available in the j-th week ($j = t,\ t+1$) which are admissible for the k-th consumer (his consumption set for the j-th week) is noted Q_{kj}. By assumption, Q_{kj} is equal to $R_+{}^N$, for all j (this assumption is inessential). The k-th trader's endowment of real goods at the beginning of the j-th week is noted ω_{kj}, a point of $R_+{}^N$. We shall always assume that ω_{kt} and $\omega_{k,t+1}$ are known with certainty by the k-th consumer on the t-th Monday. The k-th consumer's endowment of money at time t is $m_{k,t-1}$, a non-negative real number. The whole endowment is noted $e_{kt} = (\omega_{kt},\ m_{k,t-1})$, a point of $R_+{}^{N+1}$. We shall make the following assumption. For all k in K,

(a) $\omega_{kj} > 0, \qquad j = t,\ t+1.$

An *action* x_{kt} of the k-th trader on the t-th market is a complete description of his consumption q_{kt} (a point of Q_{kt}) in the t-th week and of the money balance m_{kt} (a non-negative real number) he wants to carry over from the current week to the next one. Formally, $x_{kt} = (q_{kt},\ m_{kt})$ is an element of the action space $X_{kt} = Q_{kt} \times R_+$. The purpose of this section is to decribe the k-th consumer's preferences among actions on the t-th Monday.

We assume for the simplicity of the exposition that the trader makes plans only for the t-th week and the next one. Then, the trader's *intertemporal preferences* at time t are defined on the space of consumption streams $Y_{kt} = Q_{kt} \times Q_{k,t+1}$. A generic element $y_{kt} = (q_{kt}, q_{k,t+1})$ of Y_{kt} describes the trader's consumption at time t and $t+1$. It will be assumed that the trader's intertemporal preferences can be represented by a complete preordering $\precsim_{kt}$

defined on Y_{kt}. Then $y \gtrsim_{kt} y'$ is to be read: y is preferred or indifferent to y'. Note that this preference relation can depend upon past consumption. We shall assume for all k:

(b.1) *For all* y_0 *in* Y_{kt}, the sets $\{y \in Y_{kt} | y \gtrsim_{kt} y_0\}$ *and* $\{y \in Y_{kt} | y_0 \gtrsim_{kt} y\}$ *are closed in* Y_{kt}.

(b.2) *For all* y, y' *in* Y_{kt} *such that* $y > y'$, *one has* $y >_{kt} y'$.

When making his choice on the t-th market, the trader must forecast what his consumption will be in the following week, according to the price system p_{t+1} which will prevail on the next Monday, if he now takes the action $\bar{x}_t = (\bar{q}_t, \bar{m}_t)$ in X_{kt}. Given any $\bar{x}_t$ in X_{kt} and any p_{t+1} in P_{t+1}, let the set of feasible consumption streams $y_{kt}(\bar{x}_t, p_{t+1})$ be defined as the set of elements $y_{kt} = (q_t, q_{t+1})$ of Y_{kt} such that $q_t = \bar{q}_t$ and $p_{t+1} \cdot (q_{t+1} - \omega_{k,t+1}) < \bar{m}_t$. Next week's consumption will then be determined by the maximisation of the consumer's preferences $\gtrsim_{kt}$ over $\gamma_{kt}(\bar{x}_t, p_{t+1})$. This procedure gives a set $\phi_{kt}(\bar{x}_t, p_{t+1})$, a subset of Y_{kt}, which is interpreted as the set of *conditional consumption programs* associated with the action $\bar{x}_t$ and the price system p_{t+1}. When $\bar{x}_t$ and p_{t+1} vary, this defines a correspondence ϕ_{kt} from $X_{kt} \times P_{t+1}$ into Y_{kt}. One shows by a standard argument:[1]

Proposition 2.1. The correspondence ϕ_{kt} *is nonempty-, compact-valued and u.h.c.*[2] *on* $X_{kt} \times P_{t+1}$.

In order to make a choice at time t, the trader must also forecast next week's equilibrium price system. This forecast will depend upon the consumer's information, which in our model consists only of the sequence of past equilibrium prices and of the price system p_t which is currently quoted. Past prices are fixed in our analysis: we shall omit them. For each p_t in P_t, the trader's forecast will take the form of a probability measure defined on P_{t+1}. Loosely speaking, a forecast is a random variable on R^N which assigns probability one to P_{t+1}. Formally, let $B(P_{t+1})$ be the Borel σ-algebra of P_{t+1}, i.e. the σ-algebra generated by its open subsets. Let $M(P_{t+1})$ be the set of probability measures defined on the measurable space $(P_{t+1}, B(P_{t+1}))$ (see K. R. Parthasarathy ([21], p. 1) for a definition). By assumption, the k-th trader's pattern of expectations at time t is given by a mapping ψ_{kt} which takes P_t into $M(P_{t+1})$. Then, for every E in $B(P_{t+1})$, $\psi_{kt}(p_t, E)$ is the probability assigned by the k-th consumer to the Borel set E if p_t is quoted on the t-th market.

[1] See G. Debreu ([6], chapter 4) which can be easily adapted.

[2] Let X (resp. Y) be a subspace of R^N (resp. R^M). A correspondence ϕ from X to Y is P-valued if $\phi(x)$ has the property P for all x in X. Further, ϕ is upper hemi-continuous (u.h.c.) on X if for all open sets G of Y, the set $\{x \varepsilon X | \phi(x) \subset G\}$ is open in X.

We shall use, later on, the 'continuity' of a consumer's expectations. We must therefore introduce a topology on the set $M(P_{t+1})$. We shall choose the usual topology of weak convergence of probability measures (K. R. Parthasarathy ([21], chapter 2, section 6) and make the following assumption. For all k:

(c.1) *The mapping* $\psi_{kt}: P_t \to M(P_{t+1})$ *is continuous.*

We are now able to describe the k-th consumer's *preferences among actions* on the t-th market. These preferences will reflect his tastes, his expectations and his attitude towards risk. Since the trader's expectations may vary according to the price system p_t, his preferences among actions may themselves depend upon it. They will be described by a *family of complete preorderings* $\{\pi_{kt}(p_t): p_t \in P_t\}$ defined on X_{kt}. Then $x[\pi_{kt}(p_t)]\, x'$ is to be read: 'the action x is preferred or indifferent to the action x' if p_t is quoted on the t-th market'.

The consumer's preferences will obey the so-called expected utility hypothesis,[1] which is now formally stated:

(d) *There exists a real-valued function* u_{kt} *defined on* Y_{kt} *such that*:
  (*i*) u_{kt} *is continuous, bounded, concave*[2] *and order preserving with respect to* $\succsim_{kt}$;
  (*ii*) *if for all* (x_t, p_{t+1}) *in* $X_{kt} \times P_{t+1}$, $u_{kt}(\phi_{kt}(x_t, p_{t+1}))$ *is defined as* $u_{kt}(y)$ *for some* y *in* $\phi_{kt}(x_t, p_{t+1})$, *the real-valued function* v_{kt} *defined on* $X_{kt} \times P_t$ *by* $v_{kt}(x_t, p_t) = \int_{P_{t+1}} u_{kt}(\phi_{kt}(x_t, .))\, d\psi_{kt}(p_t, .)$ *is for each* p_t *order preserving with respect to* $\pi_{kt}(p_t)$.

We remark that this assumption makes sense. First, $u_{kt}(\phi_{kt}(.\,,.))$ is a well-defined continuous function according to proposition 2.1. Since it is bounded, the function v_{kt} is well defined. The function u_{kt} is called a *von Neumann-Morgenstern utility* (for short, a von N.–M. utility) and $u_{kt}(y)$ is interpreted as the utility for the k-th consumer on the t-th week of the consumption stream y. Then $u_{kt}(\phi_{kt}(x_t, p_{t+1}))$ is the utility of the conditional consumption program associated with x_t and p_{t+1}, and $v_{kt}(x_t, p_t)$ is the expected utility of the action x_t if p_t is quoted on the t-th market. In what follows, such a function v_{kt} will be called an *expected utility index*. Although we wrote the expected utility index as a function of current prices alone, it must be emphasised that this index depends also on the past equilibrium price systems. Finally, the concavity of u_{kt} on Y_{kt} means that the trader is *risk-averse*.

[1] I greatly benefited from the work of J. Tobin [27] and K. J. Arrow [2].

[2] That is, for all λ in $[0, 1]$, and any y, y' in Y_{kt}, one has $u_{kt}(\lambda y + (1-\lambda)y') \geqq \lambda u_{kt}(y) + (1-\lambda)\, u_{kt}(y')$.

It must be noted that if we start from an *arbitrary* representation u of the preferences $\succsim_{kt}$ and we apply the formula given in (d), we shall not get, in general, a representation of the preordering $\pi_{kt}(p_t)$. What (d) says is that there exists *at least* one representation u of $\succsim_{kt}$ such that this is true (it can then be shown that the representations of $\succsim_{kt}$ which satisfy (d) are determined up to a linear transformation). In short,

Definition 2.2. A trader who satisfies (a), (b.1), (b.2), (c.1) *and* (d) *is called a regular trader.*

III. PROPERTIES OF AN EXPECTED UTILITY INDEX

We consider the k-th (regular) trader at time t. We choose a particular von N.–M. utility u_{kt} and focus the attention on the properties of the expected utility index v_{kt} which is derived from it as in (d). We shall drop the index k when no confusion is possible. We first establish a few technical properties of v_{kt}.

Proposition 3.1. Consider an expected utility index v_t.

(1) *v_t is continuous on $X_t \times P_t$;*
(2) *given p_t in P_t, the function $v_t(\,.\,,p_t)$ is concave on X_t;*
(3) *given p_t in P_t, for any x and x' such that $x > x'$ one has $v_t(x,p_t) > v_t(x',p_t)$.*

Proof. Assertions (2) and (3) are straightforward. We shall only prove (1). Fix (x^0,p^0) in $X_t \times P_t$ and consider a sequence (x^j,p^j) in $X_t \times P_t$ converging to (x^0,p^0). We wish $\lim v_t(x^j,p^j) = v_t(x^0,p^0)$. Now the sequence of functions $u_t(\phi_t(x^j,.))$ from P_{t+1} to R is uniformly bounded and converges continuously[1] to $u_t(\phi_t(x^0,.))$ on P_{t+1}. In addition, for each j, $u_t(\phi_t(x^j,.))$ is continuous on P_{t+1}. Finally, by (c.1), the sequence $\psi_t(p^j)$ converges weakly to $\psi_t(p^0)$. Therefore, according to [12, section 5, theorem A.3], $\lim v_t(x^j,p^j) = v_t(x^0,p^0)$. *Q.E.D.*

We now turn our attention to the *homogeneity properties* of v_{kt}. Monetary theorists often assume that only 'real' balances enter a typical trader's utility function (or in our terminology his expected utility index). In its most general form (see for instance P. A. Samuelson ([25], pp. 117–24)), this theory asserts that a trader's expected utility index must be homogeneous of degree zero in nominal money holdings and *current* prices. This property is often called 'absence of money illusion'. It should be clear that in our framework, a regular trader will not in general satisfy this requirement. In particular, if

[1] A sequence of functions f^j from a subspace Z or R^N to R converges continuously to f^0 on Z if for every z^0 in Z and all sequences z^j converging to z^0, one has $\lim f^j(z^j) = f^0(z^0)$.

there is a lag in the adjustment of a trader's expectations, these expectations—hence the expected utility index—will depend upon past equilibrium price systems, but not on the current one. In this case, the trader suffers from 'money illusion'. But one cannot say that he is inconsistent.

It is interesting to find a condition which implies the above homogeneity property of the expected utility index. We first give some definitions. Fix any positive real number λ. For any subset E of P_{t+1}, the meaning of λE is clear. For any element μ of $M(P_{t+1})$, define the probability measure $\lambda\mu$ of $M(P_{t+1})$ which assigns to any Borel set E of P_{t+1} the probability $\mu((1/\lambda)E)$. Finally for any x: (q, m) in X_t, define λ^*x as $(q, \lambda m)$. With these notations, the property we are looking for is $v_t(\lambda^*x, \lambda p) = v_t(x, p)$ for all positive real numbers λ, any action x in X_t and any price system p in P_t. It is intuitive that such a property will depend upon some kind of 'collinearity' between the trader's expectations and current prices. More precisely, let us consider:

(c.2) *For any* $\lambda > 0$ *and any* p_t *in* P_t, $\psi_{kt}(\lambda p_t) = \lambda\psi_{kt}(p_t)$.

This condition corresponds to the classical assumption of a 'unit elasticity of expectations with respect to current prices'; it is a very strong condition. We get as a particular case the assumption which is made by Don Patinkin in [22]: each trader is sure that p_{t+1} will be equal to p_t (from now on, this case will be called the case of *static expectations*).

Proposition 3.2. Under (c.2), *for any positive real number* λ, *any action* x *in* X_t, *and any* p_t *in* P_t, *one has* $v_t(\lambda^*x, \lambda p_t) = v_t(x, p_t)$ (*i.e. the expected utility index is homogeneous of degree zero with respect to nominal money holdings and current prices*).

Proof. Fix $\lambda > 0$, x in X_t and p in P_t. In order to simplify the notation, let $h(p_{t+1}) = u_t(\phi_t(x, p_{t+1}))$ and $\bar{h}(p_{t+1}) = u_t(\phi_t(\lambda^*x, p_{t+1}))$ for every p_{t+1} in P_{t+1}. It is easy to show that $\phi_t(x, p_{t+1}) = \phi_t(\lambda^*x, \lambda p_{t+1})$ in which case $h(p_{t+1}) = \bar{h}(\lambda p_{t+1})$. Then, the proposition follows immediately from proposition 1, section A.2 of the appendix. Q.E.D.

Is it true that the homogeneity of the expected utility index implies (c.2)? I have no definite answer to that question. If, however, we consider the case $N = 1$ and if the consumer's expectations are required to be certain (i.e. for each p_t in P_t, the probability measure $\psi_{kt}(p_t)$ is concentrated on a single element of P_{t+1}), it is easy to show that the homogeneity of v_{kt} implies (c.2).

The foregoing analysis suggests that the assumptions of 'static expectations' and of 'absence of money illusion' which Patinkin made in ([22], chapters 2 and 3) are consistent but too specific. On the other hand, our model, which allows for 'money illusion', seems to be in agreement with an idea which was put forward by, for instance, M. Allais [1], P. Cagan [4], or M. Friedman [9],

[10]. These authors assume that at any given point in time, the aggregate demand for real money balances depends, among other things, on the expected rate of inflation, which in turn is a function—a weighted average—of current and past actual rates. It is easy to see that such an assumption about the formation of expectations leads to 'money illusion' in the above sense.

Remarks. (1) The 'classical' homogeneity postulate can be interpreted as a proposition dealing with money balances and *expected* prices. One can show that this type of homogeneity holds in our model. We only sketch the argument. Consider a trader at time t and let $\psi \in M(P_{t+1})$ be any probability distribution defined on P_{t+1}. Choose a von N.—M. utility as in (d) and define

$$\bar{v}_t(x_t, \psi) = \int_{P_{+1}} u_t(\phi_t(x_t, .))d\psi.$$

Then $\bar{v}_t$ can be interpreted as representing the trader's preferences among actions when his price expectations are ψ. By the reasoning of proposition 3.2, one has $\bar{v}_t(x_t, \psi) = \bar{v}_t(\lambda^* x_t, \lambda\psi)$ for all λ.[1]

(2) Another interpretation is that the homogeneity postulate deals with stationary states. This type of homogeneity also holds in our model. We first recall that a trader's expected utility index depends, through his expectations, on past prices: it can be written $v_{kt}(x_t, p_t, p_{t-1}, \ldots)$. Now assume that past and current prices are stationary and equal to $p \gg 0$. Assume that the trader expects with certainty in that case p_{t+1} to be equal to p. Looking back at the formula giving v_{kt}, we find that $v_{kt}(x_t, p, p, \ldots) = u_{kt}(\phi_{kt}(x_t, p))$. Therefore, trivially, $v_{kt}(\lambda^* x_t, \lambda p, \lambda p, \ldots) = v_{kt}(x_t, p, p, \ldots)$ holds: v_{kt} is homogeneous of degree zero with respect to m_t and the *stationary sequence* of current and past price systems. Note that this result holds even if price expectations are independent of current prices (for instance if the trader expects with certainty p_{t+1} to be equal to p_{t-1}).

IV. DEMAND CORRESPONDENCES

Given p_t in P_t, the k-th (regular) trader must choose an action in his budget set $\beta_{kt}(p_t) = \{x \in X_{kt} | s_t . x \leqq s_t . e_{kt}\}$ (with $s_t = (p_t, 1)$). His gross demand is then as usual given by the satisfaction of the (conditional) preferences $\pi_{kt}(p_t)$ over $\beta_{kt}(p_t)$:

$$\xi_{kt}(p_t) = \{x^* \in \beta_{kt}(p_t) | x^*[\pi_{kt}(p_t)]x \text{ for all } x \text{ in } \beta_{kt}(p_t)\}.$$

Here again, it must be emphasised that the consumer's demand depends also on past equilibrium price systems. When p_t varies in P_t, this relation defines a

[1] This remark is due to F. Hahn.

correspondence ξ_{kt} from P_t into X_{kt}. One shows by a standard reasoning:

Proposition 4.1. For any regular trader, the correspondence ξ_{kt} is nonempty-, compact-, convex-valued and u.h.c. For all p_t in P_t and all x in ξ_{kt}, one has $s_t \,.\, (x - e_{kt}) = 0$.

We next study the behaviour of the correspondence ξ_{kt} when the price of the n-th good tends to zero, or when the price level tends to infinity on the t-th market. In the first case, in view of the monotonicity assumption (b.2), it would seem reasonable to expect that the consumer's demand for the n-th good increases indefinitely; in the second case, one would expect that the consumer's demand for money will tend to infinity. Unfortunately, it is easy to show that this may not be the case if no additional restriction is put on the agent's pattern of expectations (see below). In this case, an equilibrium on the t-th market may not exist. We need a new assumption.

(c.3) *The set* $\{\psi_{kt}(p_t) | p_t \in P_t\}$ *is relatively (weakly) compact.*

Formally, this means that the closure of the above set is a compact subset of $M(P_{t+1})$. This assumption is automatically fulfilled if the k-th trader's expectations are independent of p_t, or if there exists a compact C such that $\psi_{kt}(p_t, C) = 1$ for all p_t in P_t (K. R. Parthasarathy [21], chapter 2, theorem 6.4). These remarks show the economic meaning of the above assumption: although the trader's expectations can depend upon the price system which is currently quoted, the range of variation of these anticipations must not be 'too large' when p_t varies in P_t. Finally, it should be noted that the above condition and (c.2) are incompatible.

Proposition 4.2. Assume that the k-th (regular) trader satisfies (c.3) *and* $e_{kt} \gg 0$. *Consider any sequence p^j in P_t and any sequence $x^j \in \xi_{kt}(p^j)$. If p^j tends to $p^0 \in R_+{}^N \setminus P_t$, or if $\|p^j\|$ tends to $+\infty$, then $\|x^j\|$ tends to $+\infty$.*[1]

Proof. We omit the index k. Assume that the proposition is false. This means that there exists a subsequence (which can be taken to be equal to the original sequence) such that x^j converges to $x^0 = (q^0, m^0) \in X_t$. One can assume that there exists an element ψ^0 of $M(P_{t+1})$ such that $\psi_t(p^j)$ converges weakly to ψ^0. Choose a von N.—M. utility u_t and let v_t be the corresponding expected utility index. Define a function h on X_t by $h(x) = \int_{P_{t+1}} u_t(x,.))d\psi^0(.)$. As in proposition 3.1, one shows that for any x in X_t, one has $\lim v_t(x, p^j) = h(x)$ and $\lim v_t(x^j, p^j) = h(x^0)$. In addition, by the Dominated Convergence Theorem [3, A. 28 of the appendix], h is continuous. Finally, as in proposition 3.1, $h(x) > h(x')$ whenever $x > x'$. Let us distinguish the two cases.

$$\text{(i) } \lim p^j = p^0 \in R_+{}^N \quad P_t$$

[1] For any x in R^N, $\|x\|$ denotes the usual norm of x.

We have $p^0.q^0 + m^0 \geqq p^0.\omega_t + m_{t-1}$ and $p^0.\omega_t + m_{t-1} > 0$. It is not difficult to show, as in proposition 4.1, that $h(x^0) \geqq h(x)$ for all $x = (q, m)$ in X_t such that $p^0.q + m < p^0.\omega_t + m_{t-1}$. But this leads to a contradiction, since there exists an index n such that $p_n{}^0 = 0$.

$$\text{(ii)} \ \lim \|p^j\| = +\infty$$

We claim that $h(x^0) \geqq h(x)$ for all x in X_t such that $x = (q^0, m)$ where m is arbitrary. Fix such an x. Let for all j, $\mu^j = p^j/\|p^j\|$. Since $\|\mu^j\| = 1$, we can assume that μ^j converges to $\mu^0 > 0$. Clearly, $\mu^0.q^0 \geqq \mu^0.\omega_t$. Now $\mu^0.\omega_t > 0$ implies that there exists $\bar{q}$ in Q_t such that $\mu^0.\bar{q} < \mu^0\,\omega_t$. Choose λ in $[0, 1]$ and define $q^\lambda = \lambda\bar{q} + (1-\lambda)q^0$. Then $x^\lambda = (q^\lambda, m)$ belongs to X_t. We have $\mu^0.q^\lambda < \mu^0.\omega_t$, hence for j large enough, $p^j.q^\lambda + m < p^j.\omega_t + m_{t-1}$, which implies $v_t(x^j, p^j) \geqq v_t(x^\lambda, p^j)$. In the limit, $h(x^0) \geqq h(x^\lambda)$ and when λ tends to zero, $h(x^0) \geqq h(x)$. But this leads to a contradiction: if $x = (q^0, m)$ is such that $m > m^0$, then $h(x) > h(x^0)$. This proves the proposition. *Q.E.D.*

We now give an example which shows why an assumption such as (c.3) cannot be avoided. We shall assume, as Patinkin does in [22], that the consumer's expectations are static. In addition, we shall focus the attention on the case $\omega_{kt} = \omega_{k,t+1}$. Finally, we shall assume that the preferences $\succsim_{kt}$ are separable and that the preorderings induced on Q_{kt} and $Q_{k,t+1}$ are identical. Then, the following result says that if the consumer displays a preference for present consumption, he will not keep more than one-half of his stock of money $m_{k,t-1}$. If all traders are of this type, and if the total stock of money is positive, the money market cannot be in equilibrium.

Proposition 4.3. Consider the k-th (regular) trader and assume:

(1) $\psi_{kt}(p_t, \{p_t\}) = 1$ *for all* p_t *in* P_t;

(2) $\omega_{kt} = \omega_{k,t+1} = \omega_k$;

(3) *Given* q_{t+1} *(resp.* q_t*) in* $Q_{k,t+1}$ *(resp.* Q_{kt}*), the preordering* $\succsim_{kt}$ *induces a preordering on* Q_{kt} *(resp.* $Q_{k,t+1}$*) which is independent of* q_{t+1} *(resp.* q_t*). The two induced preorderings are identical and are noted* $\succsim_{kt}{}^*$;

(4) *for all* q_t *and* q_{t+1} *in* $R_+{}^N$ *with* $q_{t+1} \succ_{kt}{}^* q_t$, *one has* $(q_{t+1}, q_t) \succ_{kt} (q_t, q_{t+1})$;

Then, for every p_t *in* P_t *and every* $x_t = (q_t, m_t)$ *in* $\xi_{kt}(p_t)$, *one has* $m_t \leqq (\frac{1}{2})m_{k,t-1}$.

Proof. We drop the index k. Assume the contrary. Then, for some p_t in P_t, there is an $x_t = (q_t, m_t)$ in $\xi_t(p_t)$ with $m_t > (\frac{1}{2})m_{t-1}$. Let $y = (q_t, q_{t+1})$ in $\phi_t(x_t, p_t)$. Let u_t be a von N.–M. utility, and let $v_t(x, p_t) = u_t(\phi_t(x, p_t))$ for all x in X_t. Clearly, $v_t(x_t, p_t) = u_t(y)$. Since $p_t \cdot q_t = p_t \cdot \omega + m_{t-1} - m_t$ and $p_t \cdot q_{t+1} = p_t \cdot \omega + m_t$, one has $p_t \cdot q_t < p_t \cdot q_{t+1}$, hence $q_{t+1} \succ_t{}^* q_t$. Now, let

$\bar{q} = (\frac{1}{2})(q_t + q_{t+1})$, $\bar{y} = (\bar{q}, \bar{q})$ and $\bar{m} = (\frac{1}{2})m_{t-1}$. Consider $\bar{x} = (\bar{q}, \bar{m})$. From $p_t \cdot \bar{q} + \bar{m} = p_t \cdot \omega + m_{t-1}$, it follows that $\bar{x}$ belongs to $\beta_t(p_t)$, hence $v_t(x_t, p_t) \geqq v_t(\bar{x}, p_t)$. But $\bar{y}$ belongs to $\gamma_t(\bar{x}, p_t)$ which implies $v_t(\bar{x}, p_t) \geqq u_t(\bar{y})$. Now, by (4) and the concavity of u_t, $u_t(\bar{y}) > u_t(y)$. Therefore, $v_t(\bar{x}, p_t) > v_t(x_t, p_t)$. This contradiction completes the proof.

Q.E.D.

V. MARKET EQUILIBRIUM

We study the problem of the existence of an equilibrium on the t-th Monday. This study will allow us to test the logical consistency of the model which was presented in the preceding section. We first introduce some definitions.

A *regular economy* E_K is an economy composed of K regular traders. An *allocation* in the t-th week of the regular economy E_K is a K-tuple $x_t = (x_{1t}, \ldots, x_{Kt})$ where x_{kt} belongs to X_{kt} for all k, such that $\sum_k (x_{kt} - e_{kt}) = 0$.

An *equilibrium price system* of the t-th market is a price system p_t^* of P_t such that there exists an allocation $x_t^* = (x_{1t}^*, \ldots, x_{Kt}^*)$ with $x_{kt}^* \in \xi_{kt}(p_t^*)$ for all k.

Theorem 5.1. Consider a regular economy at the moment of the t-th market. Assume that for some trader k, (c.3) $e_{kt} \gg 0$ *both hold. Then, there exists an equilibrium price system* p_t^*.

Proof. Define $\bar{S} = \{s = (p, 1) \in R^{N+1} | p \in R_+^N\}$ and $S = \{s \in \bar{S} | s \gg 0\}$. For every $s = (p, 1)$ in S, define the aggregate excess demand correspondence ζ by $\zeta(s) = \sum_k \xi_{kt}(p) - \left\{\sum_k e_{kt}\right\}$.

It is easily seen that the correspondence ζ satisfies all the conditions of theorem 1 of section A.1 of the appendix. The result then follows by a standard argument. *Q.E.D.*

This result says that relative prices and the price level are *jointly* determined, provided the total stock of money is positive. Thus, we reach the same conclusion as Patinkin: the 'classical dichotomy' is invalid in the short run.

The foregoing existence theorem still holds for a regular economy when we assume $\sum_k e_{kt} \gg 0$ provided that *every* trader satisfies (c.3).

The details are left to the reader.[1]

[1] It should be noted that the assumption of strong monotonicity of preferences (b.2) is essential to our result. An example due to E. Drandakis shows that it might be difficult to weaken this assumption.

VI. CONCLUSIONS

We have presented a model of an exchange economy where money is the only store of value. We showed that a short-run market equilibrium exists if the traders' price expectations do not depend too much on current prices. This type of result and the methods we used to reach it should be useful for most sophisticated and more realistic models.

We assumed for the simplicity of the exposition that a trader made plans only for the current week and the next one. As a matter of fact it is not difficult to extend the analysis to the case of an arbitrary finite or infinite planning horizon when the traders' expectations are certain.[1] Our results are then still valid. The case of stochastic expectations is more complicated. Its study will probably require the use of stochastic dynamic programming techniques. However, it is likely that the main conclusions of this paper will continue to hold.

This research has been voluntarily restricted to a short-run analysis. The framework which was developed in this paper should, however, be useful for the study of the long-run properties of a monetary economy. The same type of approach should also be useful for the study of an economy with credit. It will then be possible to examine the effect of various monetary policies.

APPENDIX

Section A.1

The following theorem is an extension of a well-known result (see D. Gale [11], H. Nikaido [20], G. Debreu [5] or [6, (1) of 5.6]). A version of it is implicitly contained in L. McKenzie [19] (see also G. Debreu [7, Proposition]). The set $\{1, \ldots, N\}$ is noted N.

Theorem 1. Let I be a nonempty subset of N and define $\bar{S} = \{p \in R_+^N | \sum_{n \in I} p_n = 1\}$. Let S be any subset of S containing $S^0 = \{p \in \bar{S} | p \gg 0\}$. If $\xi: S \to R^N$ is a nonempty-valued correspondence whose graph is closed in $S \times R^N$ and which satisfies:

(a) *ξ is bounded below, i.e., there is an element b of R^N such that for each p in S and all x in $\xi(p)$, one has $x \geqq b$;*

(b) *for any p in S, $\xi(p)$ is convex and $p.x \leq 0$ for all x in $\xi(p)$;*

(c) *for any sequence $p^j \in S$ such that $\lim p^j = p^0 \in \bar{S} \backslash S$ or $\lim \|p^j\| = +\infty$ and for any sequence $x^j \in \xi(p^j)$, there is an index n in N such that $\lim x_n^j > 0$;*

then there exists p^* in S and x^* in $\xi(p^*)$ such that $x^* \leqq 0$.

[1] For the case of an infinite planning horizon, see [13].

Proof. Let S^j be a non-decreasing sequence of nonempty, compact, convex subsets of S^0 such that $S^0 \subset \bigcup_1^\infty S^j$. Then for each j, there is a compact X^j such that $\xi(p) \subset X^j$ for all p in S^j. One shows by a standard argument ([5], for instance) that there exists a p^j in S^j and an x^j in $\xi(p^j)$ such that $p \cdot x^j \leqq 0$ holds for all p in S^j.

The sequence x^j is bounded. Thus there is a subsequence (retain the same notation) such that $\lim x^j = x^* \in R^N$. For each p in $\bar{S}$, there is a sequence $\pi^j \in S^j$ such that $p = \lim \pi^j$. Since $\pi^j \cdot x^j \leqq 0$. This shows that the sequence p^j is bounded, for otherwise one could contradict (c). One can therefore assume that the sequence p^j converges to $p^* \in \bar{S}$. But $x^* \leqq 0$ and (c) together imply that p^* cannot belong to $\bar{S} \setminus S$. Therefore $p^* \in S$. Finally $x^* \in \xi(p^*)$ since ξ has a closed graph.

Q.E.D.

Section A.2

Let X be a subspace of R^N which is assumed to be a cone with vertex zero, i.e. if $x \in X$, then $\lambda x \in X$ for all positive real numbers λ. Let $B(X)$ be the Borel σ-algebra of X and $M(X)$ the set of all probability measures defined on the measurable space $(X, B(X))$. For any μ in $M(X)$ and any $\lambda > 0$, define the new element $\lambda\mu$ of $M(X)$ which assigns the probability $\mu((1/\lambda)E)$ to any Borel set E of $B(X)$.

Proposition 1. Let $\lambda > 0$ and consider two real-valued functions h and $\bar{h}$ defined on X such that $h(x) = \bar{h}(\lambda x)$ for all x in X. Choose μ in $M(X)$ and assume that h is μ-integrable. Then:

$$\int_X h\,d\mu = \int_X \bar{h}\,d(\lambda\mu)$$

Proof. We only sketch the proof which is elementary. First, it is clearly sufficient to consider only non-negative functions. Second, it is not difficult to show the proposition when h (hence $\bar{h}$) is a simple function. Finally, when h is arbitrary but non-negative, there exists a non-decreasing sequence of non-negative simple functions h^j which converges pointwise to h ([18, (C′) of 5.3)]. The sequence $\bar{h}^j$ of simple functions defined by $\bar{h}(x) = h^j((1/\lambda)x)$ is non-decreasing and converges pointwise to $\bar{h}^j$. The result then follows from the Monotone Convergence Theorem ([3], A.26 of the appendix).

Q.E.D.

REFERENCES

[1] M. Allais, 'A Restatement of the Quantity Theory of Money', *American Economic Review*, vol. LVI (1966), pp. 1123–57.
[2] K. J. Arrow, *Aspects of the Theory of Risk-Bearing* (Helsinki: Academic Bookstore, 1965).
[3] L. Breiman, *Probability* (Addison-Wesley: Reading (Mass.), 1968).
[4] P. D. Cagan, 'The Monetary Dynamics of Hyperinflation', pp. 25–117 in [9].

[5] G. Debreu, 'Market Equilibrium', *Proceedings of the National Academy of Sciences of the U.S.A.*, vol XLII (1956), pp. 876–8.
[6] G. Debreu, *Theory of Value* (New York: Wiley, 1959).
[7] G. Debreu, 'Economies with a Finite Set of Equilibria', *Econometrica*, vol. XXXVIII (1970), pp. 387–92; *ibid*, p. 790.
[8] E. M. Drandakis, 'On the Competitive Equilibrium in a Monetary Economy', *International Economic Review*, vol. VII (1966), pp. 304–28.
[9] M. Friedman (ed.), *Studies in the Quantity Theory of Money* (Chicago: University of Chicago Press, 1956).
[10] M. Friedman, *The Optimum Quantity of Money* (Chicago: Aldine, 1969).
[11] D. Gale, 'The Law of Supply and Demand', *Mathematica Scandinavica,* vol. III (1955), pp. 155–69.
[12] J.-M. Grandmont, 'Continuity Properties of a von Neumann-Morgenstern Utility', *Journal of Economic Theory*, vol. IV (1972), pp. 45–57.
[13] J-M. Grandmont and Y. Younès, 'On the Role of Money and the Existence of a Monetary Equilibrium', *Review of Economic Studies*, vol. XXXIX, (1972), pp. 799–803.
[14] F. H. Hahn, 'On Some Problems of Proving the Existence of an Equilibrium in a Monetary Economy', pp. 126–35 in [15].
[15] F. H. Hahn and F. P. R. Brechling (eds.), *The Theory of Interest Rates* (London: Macmillan, 1965).
[16] J. R. Hicks, *Value and Capital* (2nd edition) (Oxford: Clarendon Press, 1946).
[17] J. R. Hicks, *Capital and Growth* (New York: Oxford University Press, 1965).
[18] M. Loève, *Probability Theory* (3rd edition) (Princeton: van Nostrand, 1963).
[19] L. S. McKenzie, 'On Equilibrium in Graham's Model of World Trade and Other Competitive Systems', *Econometrica*, vol. XXII (1954), pp. 147–61.
[20] H. Nikaido, 'On the Classical Multilateral Exchange Problem', *Metroeconomica*, vol. VIII (1956), pp. 135–45.
[21] K. R. Parthasarathy, *Probability Measures on Metric Spaces* (New York: Academic Press, 1967).
[22] D.Patinkin, *Money, Interest and Prices* (2nd edition) (New York: Harper and Row, 1965).
[23] R. Radner, 'Equilibre des marchés à terme et au comptant en cas d'incertitude', *Cahiers du Séminaire d'Econométrie,* vol. IX (1966), pp. 35–52.
[24] R. Radner, 'Existence of Equilibrium of Plans, Prices and Price Expectations in a Sequence of Markets', *Econometrica*, vol. XL (1972), pp. 289–303.
[25] P. A. Samuelson, *Foundations of Economic Analysis* (Cambridge: Harvard University Press, 1966).
[26] B. P. Stigum, 'Competitive Equilibria under Uncertainty' *Quarterly Journal of Economics,* vol. LXXXIII (1969), pp. 533–61.
[27] J. Tobin, 'Liquidity Preference as Behaviour Towards Risk', *Review of Economic Studies*, vol. XXV (1958), pp. 65–86.

23

THE PRICE OF MONEY IN A PURE EXCHANGE MONETARY ECONOMY WITH TAXATION

by Ross M. Starr

The difficulty encountered in the studies by Hahn (selection 21) and Grandmont (selection 22) is that a fiat money is without external backing. Absent some additional structure, its equilibrium price may be nil (the price level may be arbitrarily high), effectively demonetizing the model. Hahn introduced explicit assumptions and Grandmont presented inelastic expectations as sufficient conditions to avoid the nil price.

The present essay uses a bit more institutional structure for the same purpose. A transactions demand for money is built into the model—but it is a flow demand, not a stock demand. Further, the demand becomes discontinuously inoperative when the nil price of money occurs, since nil-price money is useless in exchange. The discontinuity in demand behavior in this neighborhood is a technical problem. Fixed-point theorems may not be directly applicable over the unrestricted price space.

The transactions demand is not sufficient to ensure price positivity. But fiat money is issued by a government possessing taxing authority. Money can be used to pay taxes. Hence taxation—assuming households will wish to pay their taxes due—creates a demand for money independent of its functions as a medium of exchange or store of value; "the note debt of the state stands against a corresponding quantity of demands by the state which can be unconditionally satisfied by the notes" (Kaulla. 1920). The demand for fiat money to pay taxes—if tax levels are set sufficiently high—creates sufficient demand for fiat money so that there is a positive price equilibrium and the nil price is no longer an equilibrium.

The following is reprinted with permission from *Econometrica*, vol. 42, No. 1, 1974. © 1974, The Econometric Society.

ISBN 0-12-663970-1

Econometrica, Vol. 42, No. 1 (January, 1974)

THE PRICE OF MONEY IN A PURE EXCHANGE MONETARY ECONOMY WITH TAXATION

BY ROSS M. STARR[1]

Market determination of the value in exchange (price) of money is considered in a general equilibrium finite horizon model. The possibility of the price of money being zero in equilibrium and the role of taxes (payable in money) in preventing a zero price are considered.

1. THE ROLE OF MONEY AND ITS VALUE IN EXCHANGE

MONEY IS PECULIAR among commodities in that its usefulness depends on its price. It would not upset the theory of value if water or diamonds had a price of zero, but monetary theory depends on money having a positive value in exchange. The term "price of money" means here for money precisely what the "price" of any other commodity means for that commodity. Price is a real number which, taken in ratio with another such number, indicates a rate of exchange between two commodities. If $p^m > 0$ is the price of money and p^n is the price of good n, then p^n/p^m is the number of units of money which must be traded (spent) on the market in order to acquire (buy) one unit of good n. This usage is at variance with two standard practices: (i) taking money as numeraire, setting its "price" identically equal to unity, and (ii) referring to the interest rate as the "price of money." Neither of these two usages enters here. Unfortunately, it is far from clear that the equilibrium price will be positive [**3**, **7**, **9**, and **10**]. This follows, after all, since modern money (debt instruments rather than items decorative or useful in themselves) generally consists of useless pieces of paper or accounting units whose only use is to be exchanged eventually for some positive quantity of other goods. However, if the price of money were zero, then for even arbitrarily large amounts of money one could buy precisely nothing. If we say that money is accepted because it is accepted, then we must agree that if money were not accepted then it would not be accepted because it would not be accepted. When the price of money is zero there will be no unsatisfied demand for money; there is an equilibrium in which the price of money is zero.

It is distressingly easy to find economies in which zero is the only price of money consistent with equilibrium. Consider an economy over time with a finite horizon. Near the terminal period the economy will be imbued with a *Weltuntergangstimmung*. There is no point in having a positive money holding at the end of the last period; at any positive price of money, money holders will seek to trade money for goods to be consumed before the end of the world.

[1] It is a pleasure to acknowledge the advice and criticism of K. J. Arrow. He bears no responsibility for errors in this essay. The research described in this paper was carried out under grants from the National Science Foundation and the Ford Foundation.

However, no one with any sense will accept money during the last period in exchange for goods. You can't take it with you. Money in the last period is useless, so the price of money in the last period will be zero. But then in the next to last period traders should be wary of accepting money. Since the price of money is zero in the last period there is no point in getting stuck with any money at the end of the next to last period, so the price of money will be zero in the next to last period as well. This argument can regress indefinitely so that the price of money is zero in all periods. Thus, in a discrete time finite horizon model in equilibrium the price of money will be zero in all periods. This is the argument of [**9**].

Though finite horizons are convenient to work with, we do not really believe in the end of the world occurring at a definite future date. Thus it is not too unreasonable to impose terminal conditions on money holdings—vaguely analogous to terminal capital stock constraints in finite horizon growth models—to eliminate depletion of money balances in the terminal period. Unfortunately there still may be an equilibrium where the price of money is zero.

How can we eliminate the possibility of the price of money being zero in equilibrium? In order to do this we must arrange that there be a positive excess demand for money when the price of money is zero. One way to achieve this is to guarantee that money can always be used in payment of taxes; that is, "the note debt of the state stands against a corresponding quantity of demands by the state which can be unconditionally satisfied by the notes" [**5**].

> The modern state can make anything it chooses generally acceptable as money and thus establish its value quite apart from any connection, even of the most formal kind, with gold or with backing of any kind. It is true that a simple declaration that such and such is money will not do, even if backed by the most convincing constitutional evidence of the state's absolute sovereignty. But if the state is willing to accept the proposed money in payment of taxes and other obligations to itself the trick is done. Everyone who has obligations to the state will be willing to accept the pieces of paper with which he can settle the obligations, and all other people will be willing to accept these pieces of paper because they know that the taxpayers, etc., will be willing to accept them in turn [**6**].

Taxes can be used to create a demand for money independent of its usefulness as a medium of exchange, thereby ensuring that its price will not fall to zero.

2. TRADE IN A MONETARY ECONOMY

There are N real goods; money is the $N + 1$st good. The real goods will be denoted $n = 1, 2, \ldots, N$. The $N + 1$st good, money, is denoted m. Traders are elements of the set T. Each t in T has an endowment $\bar{x}^t \gg 0$, and a continuous utility function $u_t(x_t)$ on possible consumptions (elements of the nonnegative orthant of R^N).[2] We assume u_t is semi-strictly quasi-concave and fulfills strong monotonicity. That is, $x^1 > x^2$ implies $u_t(x^1) > u_t(x^2)$, and $\{y | u_t(y) \geqq u_t(x)\}$ is convex for all x. Further, one distinguishes between buying, β, and selling, α, transactions. An individual's trades are characterized by what goods he buys and what goods he sells. Trader t's trade will be represented by $y^t \in E^{2(N+1)+1}$; y^t has an entry $y^{t\delta n}$ for each of the

[2] Adopt the following convention on vector inequalities: $x \geqslant y$ means $x^i \geqslant y^i$ all i; $x > y$ means $x^i \geqslant y^i$ all i with $x^i > y^i$ some i; $x \gg y$ means $x^i > y^i$ all i.

$N + 1$ commodities n, and for each of the two possibilities, $\delta = \alpha, \beta$, selling or buying. The remaining co-ordinate of y^t represents the payment of taxes, $y^{t\tau}$. Trader t's selling transactions are represented by $y^{t\alpha}$, which is composed of flows of goods from t to the market, and flows of money from the market to t:

(1) $\quad y^{t\alpha n} \geqslant 0 \qquad (n = 1, \ldots, N),$

and

(1m) $\quad y^{t\alpha m} \leqslant 0.$

Trader t's buying transactions are represented by $y^{t\beta}$, which is composed of flows of goods from the market to t and flows of money from t to the market:

(2) $\quad y^{t\beta n} \geqslant 0, \quad \text{all} \quad n = 1, \ldots, N,$

and

(2m) $\quad y^{t\beta m} \leqslant 0.$

The vector of t's buying transactions, selling transactions, and tax payments is y^t:

$$y^t = (y^{t\alpha}, y^{t\beta}, y^{t\tau}).$$

At the end of trade, trader t's holdings will be subject to nonnegativity constraints. Trader t cannot sell what he did not have to start with and what he did not acquire in trade:

(3) $\quad \bar{x}^{tn} + y^{t\beta n} - y^{t\alpha n} \geqslant 0, \quad \text{for} \quad n = 1, \ldots, N.$

Price vectors will be elements of P, the unit simplex in E^{N+1}. Let $P = \{p | p \in E^{N+1}, p > 0, \Sigma_{n=1}^{N+1} p^n = 1\}$. Prices are the same for buying and selling. If one wished to extend the analysis to a model with transactions costs it should not be difficult to let buying and selling prices differ merely by doubling the dimensionality of the price space.

Taxes are paid in money and are distinct from other money expenditures only in that they do not buy anything for the trader. The nonnegativity constraint (3) should also be extended to money. Thus,

(4) $\quad \bar{x}^{tm} - y^{t\alpha m} + y^{t\beta m} - y^{t\tau} \geqslant 0.$

Further, introduce trader t's required tax payment function (which may vary with prices) $\theta_t(p)$; then another constraint on trade is that traders pay their taxes. That is,

(5) $\quad y^{t\tau} = \theta_t(p).$

Trader t's possible trades will be the set,

$$Y_t = \{y | y \in E^{2N+3}, y \text{ fulfills (1), (1m), (2), (2m), (3), (4), and (5)}\}.$$

Budget constraints apply separately to buying and selling transactions. In the standard general equilibrium model, of course, each trader faces only one budget constraint. The twofold budget constraint here reflects the two requirements that the trader must supply to the market commodities equal in value to his money receipts from the market at market prices, and that the trader must pay to the market money equal in value at market prices to the goods he receives from the market. The constraints then are

$$(6\alpha) \qquad p \cdot y^{t\alpha} = 0,$$

and

$$(6\beta) \qquad p \cdot y^{t\beta} = 0.$$

Given prices, we can now write t's trading opportunity set. This set consists of those trades consistent with payment of taxes, the budget constraints at prevailing prices, and the other requirements above ((1), (1m), (2), (2m), (3), and (4)). Thus, t's trading opportunity set is

$$\eta_t(p) = \{y | y \in Y_t,\ y \text{ fulfills } (6\alpha) \text{ and } (6\beta) \text{ at } p\}.$$

It is from $\eta_t(p)$ that trader t will choose what trade to make. If he chooses $y \in \eta_t(p)$, then his consumption bundle consists of his original endowment plus his net trade. Consumption is $w^t = \bar{x}^t - y^\alpha + y^\beta$. The trader gets no satisfaction from money; utility varies only with the first N elements of w^t. Then t's choice correspondence is $\gamma_t(p) = \{y | y \in \eta_t(p),\ w^t = \bar{x}^t - y^\alpha + y^\beta$ maximizes $u_t(w)$ subject to $y \in \eta_t(p)\}$.

It is fairly easy to see that the tax function, $\theta_t(p)$, if not suitably restricted, can make the analysis vacuous. For example, if $\theta_t(p)$ required trader t to make a large tax payment at unfavorable commodity prices—in particular if the value of the required tax payment were greater than the market value of the trader's endowment—then it might be impossible to satisfy simultaneously (1)–(6). In such a case $\eta_t(p)$ would be empty. To avoid this the following restriction is adopted:

RESTRICTION ON $\theta_t(p)$: *For all* $p \in P$,

$$p^m \theta_t(p) < p \cdot \bar{x}^t.$$

Also, to assure tractability assume strict positivity of endowment.

ASSUMPTION: $\bar{x}^t \gg 0$ *for all* $t \in T$.

The restriction says that no trader will be required to make a tax payment greater in value than his original endowment.

A recurrent problem in this family of models is that budget sets may fail to be continuous about $p^m = 0$. Consider $p^0 \in P$ with $p^{0m} = 0$, and for some commodities l, n, $p^{0n} > 0$, $p^{0l} = kp^{0n}$, $k > 0$. Then at prices p^0 a typical trader can buy none of good l. However, consider $p^\nu > p^0$ such that $p^{\nu m} > 0$ and $p^{\nu l} = kp^{\nu n}$. For any ν, if $\theta_t(p^\nu)$ is not too big, there is $y^\nu \in \eta_t(p^\nu)$ such that $y^{\nu\beta l} = (1/k)\bar{x}^{tn} > 0$. But $y^0 \in n_t(p^0)$ implies $y^{0\beta l} = 0$. Hence $\eta_t(p)$ is not upper semi-continuous about $p^m = 0$. If we artificially bound $\eta_t(p)$, upper semi-continuity may be restored but failures of lower semi-continuity arise. Hahn noted this problem in a slightly different context in [**3**]. It is also analogous to aspects of [**4**], where he found that budget sets may fail to be lower semi-continuous in some areas of the price space. The implication of this observation is that proofs of existence of equilibrium will not be able to rely on the continuity of demand functions, hence ruling out the direct application of fixed point theorems.

There is a formal identity between the model with taxation described above and a model lacking taxation but having some constraint on the depletion of the trader's money balance. Constraints (4) and (5) could be interpreted as a requirement that after completing trade the trader should have a money balance of at least $\theta_t(p)$. Special cases of this interpretation are $\theta_t(p) \equiv 0$ (nonnegativity of final balance) and $\theta_t(p) \equiv \bar{x}^{tm}$ (unchanged money holding). There are corresponding interpretations of the results below, relating the equilibrium price of money to the required final balance.

3. EQUILIBRIUM IN THE MONETARY ECONOMY

Let

$$\bar{\Omega} = X_{j \in T} Y_j.$$

On the basis of attempted trades we can compute excess demands. Let

$$\zeta(x) = \sum_{j \in T} x^{j\beta} - \sum_{j \in T} x^{j\alpha}, \quad \text{for } x \in \bar{\Omega}.$$

Thus for a proposed group of transactions $x^j, j \in T$, the excess demand $\zeta(x)$, is the amount sought for purchase, $\Sigma_{j \in T} x^{j\beta}$, less the amount traders seek to supply, $\Sigma_{j \in T} x^{j\alpha}$.

DEFINITION: Let $p^* \in P$, $y^* \in \bar{\Omega}$, $z^* \in R^N$. Then (p^*, y^*, z^*) is an equilibrium for the economy if for all $t \in T$ (i) $y^{*t} \in \eta_t(p^*)$, for all $t \in T$, (ii) $w^t = \bar{x}^t + y^{*t\beta} - y^{*t\alpha}$ maximizes $u_t(w)$ for all $y \in \eta_t(p)$, and (iii) $z^* = \zeta(y^*)$ and $z^* \leqslant 0$.

This is a traditional definition of equilibrium. One has an equilibrium when the results of individual maximizations subject to constraint imply non-positive excess demand. The novel elements are embodied in the constraints that transactions take place through money, (6.α) and (6.β), and that taxes be paid in full, in money, (4) and (5).

4. THE PRICE OF MONEY

We now note a curious property of the monetary economy. When the value in exchange of money is zero, no one can seek to trade. We have required that all trade take place using money as medium of exchange. If the price of money is zero, then money is literally worthless paper. What will one sell for worthless paper? Nothing. What can one buy with worthless paper? Nothing. Thus we have the following lemma.

LEMMA 1: *Let $p \in P$, $p^m = 0$. Then $y \in n_j(p)$ implies $p^n y^{\delta n} = 0$, $\delta = \alpha, \beta$ for all $j \in T$, $n = 1, \ldots, N$. The same holds for all $y \in \gamma_j(p)$.*

PROOF: $\gamma_j(p) \subset \eta_j(p)$. However, $y \in \eta_j(p)$ implies y fulfills (6.α) and (6.β) at p. Thus $p \cdot y^\alpha = 0$ and $p \cdot y^\beta = 0$. Let $y^{\delta c}$ denote the N-dimensional vector consisting of the first N components (the real goods elements) of y^δ, $\delta = \alpha, \beta$. Then

$$p \cdot y^\delta = 0, \qquad \delta = \alpha, \beta,$$

and

$$p \cdot y^\delta = p^c \cdot y^{\delta c} + p^m \cdot y^{\delta m}, \qquad p > 0.$$

By (1), (1m), (2), and (2m) we have $y^{\delta m} \lesseqgtr 0$, $y^{\delta c} \gtreqless 0$. However $p^m = 0$ implies $p^m \cdot y^{\delta m} = 0$,

$$0 = p \cdot y^\delta = p^c \cdot y^{\delta c} + p^m \cdot y^{\delta m} = p^c \cdot y^{\delta c}.$$

Thus $p^n \cdot y^{\delta n} = 0, n = 1, \ldots, N.$ *Q.E.D.*

Denote the first $2(N + 1)$ components of y, those dealing with market transactions, by y^π; the final component, that dealing with tax payments, is, of course, y^τ.

LEMMA 2: *Let $p \in P$; $p^m = 0$, $p^n > 0$, all $n = 1, \ldots, N$. Then for each $j \in T$, $y \in \eta_j(p)$ implies $y^c = 0$. If $\theta_j(p) \leqslant \bar{x}^{jm}$, then there is $y^0 \in \eta_j(p)$ and $\gamma_j(p)$ with $y^{0\pi} = 0$.*

PROOF: By Lemma 1 we have $y \in \eta_j(p)$ implies $p^n y^{\delta n} = 0$. However $p^n > 0$ for $n = 1, \ldots, N$, so $y^{\delta n} = 0$ for $n = 1, \ldots, N$. Thus $y^c = 0$ for $\theta_j(p) \lesseqgtr \bar{x}^{jm}$ implies we can satisfy (5) with $y^m = 0$; thus let $y^0 = (0, 0, \ldots, 0, \theta_j(p))$; $y^0 \in \eta_j(p)$. Further, since u_j does not vary with w^{jm}, j is indifferent among all elements of $\eta_j(p)$. Thus $y^0 \in \gamma_j(p)$. *Q.E.D.*

This leads us to the fundamental quandary of this study. Lemma 2 tells us that if we announce a price vector p for the market such that the price of money is zero, the price of goods is positive, and taxes are sufficiently small, then traders will demand and supply zero quantities of all goods. But if all individual demands and supplies are zero, then excess demands and supplies are zero in all markets. The markets are in equilibrium, and p is an equilibrium price vector. This is a very curious equilibrium, however, since it is an equilibrium with no trade. This is not to say that there are no mutually beneficial trades conceivable between traders. Rather, because it is required in the monetary economy that trade take place through money, there are no effective demands or supplies when the price of money is zero. I think there is a legitimate question as to the significance of the equilibrium with zero price of money. Within the bounds of the model the implication is explicit: no trade. An alternative interpretation, going outside the model, is that there is no monetary trade, but that there is probably recourse to barter (see [**10**]). The implication of the structure of our demand functions is the following theorem.

THEOREM 1: *Let* $p^0 \in P$, $p^{0m} = 0$, *and* $\theta_j(p^0) < \bar{x}^{jm}$, *all* $j \in T$. *Then there is an equilibrium* (p^0, y^0, z^0) *such that* $y^{0\pi} = 0$.

PROOF: Let $p^{0m} = 0$ and $p^{0n} > 0, n = 1, \ldots, N$. By Lemma 2, $y^{0j} \in \gamma_j(p^0)$ with $y^{0j\pi} = 0$. However $\zeta(0) = 0$, so $(p^0, y^0, 0)$ is an equilibrium. *Q.E.D.*

There is only one case in which the equilibrium $(p^0, y^0, 0)$ can be Pareto efficient. It will be Pareto efficient if and only if the original endowment of goods, $\bar{x}^j$, is a Pareto efficient allocation.

LEMMA 3: *Let* $p^m > 0$, $p^n > 0$ *for some* $n = 1, \ldots, N$. *Then let* $\gamma \in \gamma_j(p)$. *Then*

$$\bar{x}^{jm} - y^{\alpha m} + y^{\beta m} = \theta_j(p).$$

PROOF: Suppose (4) is overfulfilled by the amount a_j. Then there is $*y \in \eta_j(p)$ with $*y^{\alpha n} = y^{\alpha n}$, $*y^{\beta m} < y^{\beta m}$, and $*y^{\beta n} \geqslant y^{\beta n}$ with the strict inequality holding for some n. Further by strong monotonicity of u, $*y$ is preferred to y, so $y \notin \gamma_j(p)$ contrary to hypothesis. The contradiction proves the lemma. *Q.E.D.*

The gist of Lemma 3 is that when the price of money is positive the nonnegativity restriction (4) is binding. The mischief one gets into then when the tax functions θ_j are insufficiently exacting now arises. When the price of money is positive, traders will deplete their money holdings to the point where the nonnegativity constraint is binding. If the constraint is not restrictive enough, however, this will result in an excess supply of money on the market and an excess demand for goods, clearly a disequilibrium. If we do not make the tax functions more exacting, the sole alternative is to let the price of money become zero. This gives us an equilibrium of the sort described in Theorem 1.

THEOREM 2: Let $\Sigma_{j\in T}\, \theta_j(p) < \Sigma_{j \in T}\, \bar{x}^{jm}$ *for all* $p \in P$. *Let* (p, y, z) *be an equilibrium for the economy. Then* $p^m = 0$.

PROOF: By insatiability of u_j, $p^n > 0$, some n. Suppose the theorem is false; $p^m > 0$. Then by Lemma 3

$$\sum_{j \in T} (\bar{x}^{jm} - y^{j\alpha m} + y^{j\beta m}) < \sum_{j \in T} \bar{x}^{jm},$$

which implies $\Sigma_{j\in T}\, y^{j\alpha m} > \Sigma_{j\in T}\, y^{j\beta m}$. However, we have $0 = p \cdot y^{j\alpha} = p^0 \cdot y^{j\alpha c} + p^m \cdot y^{j\alpha m}$ and $0 = p \cdot y^{j\beta} = p^0 \cdot y^{j\beta c} + p^m \cdot y^{j\beta m}$. We have then

$$y^{j\beta m} = \frac{-p^c y^{j\beta c}}{p^m} \quad \text{and} \quad y^{j\alpha m} = \frac{-p^c y^{j\alpha c}}{p^m}.$$

By the inequality above, then,

$$\sum_{j \in T} \left(-\frac{p^c}{p^m}\right) \cdot y^{j\alpha c} > \sum_{j \in T} \left(-\frac{p^c}{p^m}\right) \cdot y^{j\beta c},$$

so for some $n = 1, \ldots, N$, $\Sigma_{j \in T} y^{j\alpha n} < \Sigma_{j \in T} y^{j\beta n}$. However, $z^n = \Sigma_{j \in T} y^{j\beta n} - \Sigma_{j \in T} y^{j\alpha n} > 0$, and therefore (p, y, z) is not an equilibrium. The contradiction shows that $p^m = 0$. *Q.E.D.*

Theorem 2 tells us that not only do we face the difficulty of Theorem 1 (that there exist equilibria with price of money equal to zero) but also that in a broad class of cases (those where the tax functions are not exacting enough) the *only* equilibria are those where the price of money is zero. Such a situation could make life in a monetary economy awkward indeed. In this model the final demand for money is based on taxes. As illustrated in Theorem 2, when that constraint does not require sufficiently large terminal money holdings, the demand for money is not sufficiently great to lift the equilibrium price above zero. It will appear below that the converse holds, at least partially; when taxes are sufficiently high, but not so great as to be impossible, the only equilibria will be those with a positive price of money. Thus, we can introduce the following theorem.

THEOREM 3: *Let $\theta_j(p)$ be $\theta_j(p^m)$, a function of p^m only. Let $\theta_j(p)$ be such that there is $0 \leqslant b < 1$ so that for all $p \in P$, $0 \leqslant p^m \leqslant b$ and $\Sigma_{j \in T} \theta_j(p) > \Sigma_{j \in T} \bar{x}^{jm}$. Then there is an equilibrium for the economy, and if (p^0, y^0, z^0) is such an equilibrium, then $p^{0m} > b$.*

PROOF: Note that the restriction on $\theta_j(p)$: (i) implies that if $p^m = 1$ and $p^c = 0$, then $\theta_j(p) < \bar{x}^{jm}$, and (ii) together with strict positivity of endowment implies that the requirement $\Sigma_{j \in T} \theta_j(p) > \Sigma_{j \in T} \bar{x}^{jm}$ and $p^m \theta_j(p) < p \cdot \bar{x}^j$, all $j \in T$ and all p so that $0 \leqslant p^m \leqslant b$, is not a contradiction. There exist such $\theta_j(p)$. Then by the intermediate value theorem there is p^{*m}, $b \leqslant p^{*m} < 1$, so that $\Sigma_{j \in T} \theta_j(p^{*m}) = \Sigma_{j \in T} \bar{x}^{jm}$. Consider the barter (Arrow-Debreu) economy with prices on the simplex,

$$S = \{p | p \in E^N, p \geqslant 0, \Sigma p^i = 1 - p^{*m}\}$$

where traders, $t \in T$, choose x^{tc} to maximize utility subject to the budget constraint

$$p \cdot x^{tc} \lesseqgtr p \cdot \bar{x}^{tc} - (p^{*m} \theta_t(p^{*m}) - p^{*m} \bar{x}^{tm}).$$

Then there is an equilibrium price vector $p^{*c} \in S$ in this economy [2]. Let

$$y^{t\alpha c} = (\bar{x}^{tc} - x^{tc})^+,$$

$$y^{t\alpha m} = \frac{-1}{p^{*m}} p^{*c} \cdot y^{y\alpha c},$$

$$y^{t\beta c} = (\bar{x}^{tc} - x^{tc})^-,$$

and

$$y^{t\beta m} = -\frac{1}{p^{*m}} p^* \cdot y^{t\beta c}.$$

Then $p^* = (p^{*c}, p^{*m})$ is an equilibrium price vector for the economy according to the definition given in Section 3. This gives existence.

Suppose, contrary to the theorem, $p^{0m} \leqslant b$. Then we have

$$\bar{x}^{0jm} - y^{0j\alpha m} + y^{0j\beta m} \geqq \theta_j(p),$$

$$\sum_{j\in T} \bar{x}^{0jm} - \sum_{j\in T} y^{0j\alpha m} + \sum_{j\in T} y^{0j\beta m} \geqq \sum_{j\in T} \theta_j(p) > \sum_{j\in T} \bar{x}^{jm},$$

and

$$\sum_{j\in T} y^{0j\beta m} - \sum_{j\in T} y^{0j\alpha m} > 0.$$

There is excess demand for m and hence (p^0, y^0, z^0) is not an equilibrium. The contradiction proves the theorem. *Q.E.D.*

Theorem 3 tells us that if we can get traders to fulfill the right sort of tax constraint, $\theta_j(p)$, the price of money will be positive.

In an equilibrium with a positive price of money, trade takes place unimpeded. Just as a competitive equilibrium is Pareto efficient in a barter economy [**1**], so a competitive equilibrium with a positive price of money is Pareto efficient.

THEOREM 4: *Let (p^0, y^0, z^0) be an equilibrium for the economy, and let $1 > p^{0m} > 0$. Then $w^{0t} = \bar{x}^t - y^{0t\alpha} + y^{0t\beta}$ is a Pareto efficient distribution of goods among $t \in T$.*

PROOF: By [**1**] it is sufficient to show that w^{0t} maximizes $u_t(x)$ subject to $p^{0c} \cdot w^{0tc} \geqslant p^{0c} \cdot x^c$. Suppose not; then there is $r \in T$, so that for some x^{rc}

$$p^{0c} \cdot x^{rc} \leqslant p^{0c} \cdot w^{0rc}, \qquad u_r(x^{rc}) > u_r(w^{0r}).$$

We will show that this implies that y^{0r} is not a maximizing choice in $\eta_r(p^0)$ and hence is a contradiction of the hypothesis. Without loss of generality take $p^{0c} \cdot x^{rc} = p^{0c} \cdot w^{0rc}$. Choose y^r so that

$$y^{r\alpha c} = (x^{rc} - \bar{x}^{rc})^-,$$

$$y^{r\alpha m} = -p^{0c} \cdot (x^{rc} - \bar{x}^{rc})^- \frac{1}{p^{0m}},$$

$$y^{r\beta c} = (x^{rc} - \bar{x}^{rc})^+,$$

and

$$y^{r\beta m} = -p^{0c} \cdot (x^{rc} - \bar{x}^{rc})^+ \frac{1}{p^{0m}}.$$

Since $p^{0c} \cdot (x^{rc} - \bar{x}^{rc}) = p^{0c} \cdot x^{rc} - p^{0c}\bar{x}^{rc} = p^{0c} \cdot w^{0rc} - p^{0c} \cdot \bar{x}^{rc} = 0$, $y^r \in \eta_t(p^0)$. Thus (p^0, y^0, z^0) cannot be an equilibrium. The contradiction proves the theorem. *Q.E.D.*

5. SUMMARY

In the pure exchange monetary ecnomy, we have the following statements:

(i) There exists an equilibrium (Theorems 1 and 3).

(ii) If taxation is insufficiently exacting, there is an equilibrium with the price of money equal to zero (Theorem 1); further, this may be the only price of money consistent with equilibrium (Theorem 2).

(iii) If taxes are sufficiently exacting, there are equilibria and they all have positive price of money (Theorem 3).

(iv) An equilibrium with positive price of money is Pareto efficient (Theorem 4).

Cowles Foundation, Yale University

Manuscript received October, 1971; revision received February, 1972.

REFERENCES

[1] ARROW, K. J.: "An Extension of the Basic Theorem of Classical Welfare Economics," in *Proceedings of the Second Berkeley Symposium on Mathematical Statistics and Probability*, ed. J. Neyman. Berkeley: University of California Press, 1951.

[2] DEBREU, GERARD: *Theory of Value*. New York: John Wiley, 1959.

[3] HAHN, FRANK H.: "On Some Problems of Proving the Existence of an Equilibrium in a Monetary Economy," in *Conference on the Theory of Interest and Money*, ed. F. P. R. Brechling. Royaumont, France, 1962.

[4] ———: "Equilibrium with Transactions Costs," *Econometrica*, 37 (1971), 417–439.

[5] KAULLA, RUDOLPH: *Grundlagen des Geldwerts*. Stuttgart, 1920. Passage translated in *German Monetary Theory: 1905–1933*, Howard S. Ellis. Cambridge, Mass.: Harvard University Press, 1934.

[6] LERNER, ABBA P.: "Money as a Creature of the State," *Proceedings of the American Economic Association*, 37 (1947), 312–317.

[7] MARSCHAK, JACOB: "Money and the Theory of Assets," *Econometrica*, 6 (1938), 311–325.

[8] ———: "The Rationale of the Demand for Money and of 'Money Illusion,'" *Metroeconomica*, (1950), 71–100.

[9] PATINKIN, DON: "The Indeterminacy of Absolute Prices in Classical Economic Theory," *Econometrica*, 17 (1949), 1–27.

[10] SONTHEIMER, KEVIN: "On the Determination of Money Prices," *Journal of Money Credit and Banking*, forthcoming.

Part V

Conclusion

24
OPEN QUESTIONS: A RESEARCH AGENDA

The viewpoint of the studies presented in this volume was foreseen by Hicks (selection 2). The strategy he prescribed was formally to model impediments to trade and to analyze money as a device for overcoming (or evading) them. The studies of Parts II and III suggest that the strategy has been successful in providing foundations for the traditional medium-of-exchange and store-of-value functions of money. Additional research foreseeable along this line can be described by the rule "find a transaction cost and avoid it." This suggests room for further research on the role of transaction costs in analysis of the following topics[6]:

(*i*) The demand for liquidity, with resultant implications for the equilibrium composition of the capital stock.
(*ii*) Banks and other financial intermediaries.
(*iii*) Scale economies and specialization in production in equilibrium.

In addition, the studies of the collection have left some unfinished business. Open questions on these topics include

(*iv*) Convergence of non-monetary multilateral trade and of monetary bilateral and multilateral trade.

(*i*) *The demand for liquidity*

The concept of liquidity is a staple of monetary analysis. Interest in the concept depends on uncertainty and transaction costs. Without uncertainty, there is no need for liquidity; without transaction costs, all goods are liquid.

[6] See also Hahn (1980)

ISBN 0-12-663970-1

Liquidity of an asset is its ready convertibility through sale without prior arrangement to a desired acquisition (or equivalently, in a monetary economy in equilibrium, to money)." Liquidity is a desirable property to wealth owners because they are uncertain of the timing of their acquisition requirements and (reflecting transaction costs and other market imperfections) cannot fully hedge the uncertainty. A distinct form of uncertainty entering the portfolio decision is price/yield uncertainty. There is unfortunately a great deal to be formalized here, including the foundations of the demand for liquidity and the resultant structure of asset demands. Recent contributions in this area, emphasizing the distinct importance of liquid assets in individual portfolios and market equilibrium, include Townsend (1980, 1982), Green (1987), Foley–Hellwig (1975), Kohn (1981, 1984), Lucas (1980), Scheinkman and Weiss (1986), Hahn (1988), and Ostroy and Starr (1988). A general equilibrium concern is the implications of the desire for liquidity on the composition of the capital stock. Nonnull covariation of demands for liquidation with asset market yields will result in the demand for liquidity skewing the equilibrium yield structure and the economy's equilibrium composition of capital. This suggests the elements of a family of questions. Additional issues to be formalized include a role for a law of large numbers, money, banks, financial intermediaries, and a central bank in satisfying the demand for liquidity with resultant implications for the equilibrium composition of the capital stock. These issues are by no means novel (Bewley, 1980; Goldman, 1978; Tobin, 1964, 1966). But they require formal general equilibrium modelling. The Arrow-Debreu model resolves all of the issues here through the use of contingent futures contracts, but recognition of information considerations (Radner, 1972) and transaction costs leads to the view that this solution is inappropriate, and there is ample room for additional formal investigation.

The class of results one would expect to develop here focuses on general equilibrium implications of demand for safe liquid assets, particularly money and financial institution liabilities, as buffer stocks in individual portfolios. By acting as insurance against individual risks that are not sources of aggregate uncertainty, money and financial intermediaries should allow the economy's capital structure to be composed in equilibrium in a pattern reflecting relevant aggregate uncertainty (monetization of capital) Tobin, 1964. Conversely, in the absence of a structure for providing individual assurance, we would expect individual risks to affect the composition of the economy's capital stock with attendant efficiency loss. For example, the individual demand for liquidity in a poorly intermediated economy could result in skewing the allocation of the economy's capital stock unnecessarily toward low-risk short-lived investments (Starr, 1987).

(ii) Banking and Financial Intermediaries

Conspicuous by their absence in the papers of this volume are banks and financial intermediaries. An appropriate structure of transaction costs on asset markets, including scale economies, should allow for their formal modelling. This can be combined with a distribution structure over time of liquidation/purchase requirements by the holders of the bank/intermediary's liabilities. It should be possible to develop sufficient conditions for the concentration of financial transactions in financial intermediaries. Banks and financial intermediaries purchase financial assets financed by the sale of their own liabilities to wealth holders. Absent transaction costs, equivalent transactions could be undertaken directly by wealth holders, eliminating the intermediary function. Superiority of the intermediaries over direct trade in financial assets arises from two sources. Evaluation of asset purchases is a fixed set-up cost at the time of acquisition. Savings are achieved then if a single buyer acquires the asset and holds it to maturity. These savings are more readily achieved by a relatively large agent whose transactions can be timed to avoid premature liquidation; hence the scale economy. If the intermediary's liabilities are acceptable as a medium of exchange, there is room for additional transaction cost savings. Trade of the intermediary liabilities between liability holders need not imply a change in the volume of outstanding intermediary liabilities. Hence the aggregate volume of intermediary liabilities may be subject to smaller variation than the proportionate variation of individual liability-holders' assets. This implies a correspondingly small required liquidation of intermediary assets to meet net liability liquidation. Hence a saving in transaction costs on the asset side is achieved through the reduction in the volume of asset liquidation implied.

These comments are by no means novel, but developing the formal treatment represents unfinished business that can be treated using the explicit emphasis on the structure of transaction costs and market equilibrium presented in this volume.

(iii) Scale Economies and the Medium of Exchange

Adam Smith (1775) argued that the use of money as a medium of exchange was essential to sustaining specialization in production activity (division of labor). Production may be specialized, but diverse consumption requirements of a specialized producer are provided through trade. In order to sustain specialization in equilibrium, it is essential that trade take place at relatively low transaction cost; high transaction costs may make autarchy preferable. To the extent that a common medium of exchange reduces transaction costs then Smith's argument should follow. Modelling advantageous division of labor requires some form of non-convexity in the use of labor by the firm: indivisibility of the work day, a set-up cost on moving between jobs, or a scale economy at the level of the individual worker in producing labor services for a specific firm (Edwards-Starr, 1987). The approaches to modelling firm and market behavior with scale economies and transactions costs developed in Arrow-Hahn (1971) using the Shapley-Folkman theorem should then allow demonstration of the presence of an approximate equilibrium.

The character of the equilibrium—in particular, how it varies with transaction cost—is the real focus of the inquiry. We would expect that if transaction costs are low, the equilibrium would involve a high degree of specialization and very active trade. When transaction costs are high, we would expect relatively little trade and correspondingly little specialization.

Formalizing this approach in general equilibrium would be a step toward confirming Smith's views on scale economies. We would expect to confirm two related statements on the role of exchange in facilitating specialization: the institution of money is useful to specialization because it facilitates exchange; division of labor is limited by the "extent of the market". Presumably the "extent of the market" varies inversely with transaction costs.

(*iv*) *Bilateral and Multilateral Trade Models*

In the trading models of Ostroy (selection 10), Starr (selection 11), and Ostroy-Starr (selection 12), the emphasis is on the coordination of the trading process after prices have been established. An obvious extension then is to incorporate a price determination mechanism to allow the models to be more fully self-contained. This would necessarily involve a *nontatonnement* adjustment process. The trading process out of equilibrium may be expected to maintain the asymmetric role of the medium of exchange. The remaining question though is whether this asymmetry is enhanced by the price adjustment process superimposed on the trading process.

Goldman-Starr (selection 9) weakens the Feldman (selection 8) conditions and applies them to an assumed outcome of a multilateral trading process. No such process is actually examined, however, and generalizing the Feldman convergence results to the multilateral case remains an open question. We would expect to find that under sufficient smoothness conditions the *t*-wise multilateral trading process will converge to a *t*-wise optimum. This would bring us to the starting point of the Goldman-Starr study.

A remaining question to be investigated is the role of money in the convergence of the trading process when we add to the structure of Feldman (selection 8) the assumption that at the start of trade there is a good that can be thought of as a medium of exchange. One simple way to do this would be to single out a particular universally valued commodity and to delete the nonnegativity requirement on holdings of that good. Denote the modified model "monetary." The hypothesis that a common medium of exchange facilitates the trading process would show up as the suggestion that the speed of convergence would be greater in the monetary model than in its nonmonetary counterpart.

This agenda is by no means exhaustive. The viewpoint consistently expressed here is to consider monetary and financial institutions and behavior that we observe in actual economies, and that could not survive in an Arrow-Debreu model. The first place to look for microeconomic foundations of those institutions is in suitably chosen market imperfections, particularly in transaction costs and the piecemeal enforcement of budget constraints. In itself, this approach provides no answers—it has already provided fertile questions.

25
CONCLUSION

Modern treatments of classic issues at the foundations of the theory of money are presented in the studies of this volume. The analytic framework of the Walrasian general equilibrium model proves to be a powerful effective framework for posing the relevant questions. A single essential modification of the Walrasian model is sufficient to provide the additional complexity of structure needed to provide a role for money in trade: the budget constraint applies separately at each date and to each transaction. The result is a powerful need for a token of value to carry between transactions. Further, the token should be unique and available in sufficient quantity to sustain trade. Clearly, if money didn't exist, we should have to invent it.

The formal studies presented treat three major topics: function of a medium of exchange; intertemporal trade and allocation with money as a store of value; sustaining the equilibrium value of money (price of money). Formalizing the model of bilateral exchange results in recognition of the complexity of the trading process. This makes precise the long-standing idea of the "difficulties of barter." The trading process is overdetermined by the multiple requirements of (*i*) trading in a particular direction or through a restricted class of processes to an equilibrium allocation, (*ii*) payment for value received (*quid pro quo*), and (*iii*) nonnegativity of holdings. The requirements cannot in general all be fulfilled. The use of a specific good to enter asymmetrically in the trading process—for which these restrictions do not represent a binding constraint—avoids the overdeterminacy and allows fulfillment of the multiple conditions.

Models of intertemporal trade with transaction cost make the timing of transactions a non-trivial economic decision in equilibrium. The within-period budget constraint implies that the timing of purchases must coincide

ISBN 0-12-663970-1

with that of sales. If we combine this restriction with a requirement that an efficient allocation be achieved, overdeterminacy once again results. Introduction of money here takes the form of abstract purchasing power of zero transaction cost. This relaxes the overdeterminacy by allowing separation of buying and selling decisions. Transactions can be timed to avoid waste of resources through excessive transaction cost or inappropriate intertemporal reallocation.

The remaining focus of the studies is the maintenance of a positive price of money (determinate price level) in equilibrium. In a fiat money economy this is a question that needs to be addressed. Inasmuch as the money is not desired in itself, there is always a possibility that its price will fall to zero, effectively demonetizing the model. Note that the usefulness of money and positivity of its price are not logically equivalent. When the price is zero it is surely useless because it has ceased to be money; when the price is positive, positivity is maintained not by its usefulness but rather by exogenous structures. Sufficient conditions for positivity are expectations of future positivity or the demand created by taxes payable in money.

The literature presented in this volume has succeeded in answering a family of questions basic to the theory of a monetary economy. A full analytic rationale is presented for the use of a medium of exchange, for the use of a store of value, and for the holding of idle balances in equilibrium. Open questions remain and are not limited to those suggested in selection 24. Nevertheless this body of literature has concluded a distinct achievement: by explicit modelling of the structure and difficulties of trade, a powerful class of models that had denied a role to money and finance has been shown to provide their foundation.

BIBLIOGRAPHY

ARROW, K. J. [1951]. "An Extension of the Basic Theorems of Classical Welfare Economics". In *Proceedings of the Second Berkeley Symposium on Mathematical Statistics and Probability,* ed. Jerzy Neyman. Berkeley: University of California Press.

ARROW, K. J. [1964]. "The Role of Securities in the Optimal Allocation of Risk-bearing". *Review of Economic Studies* **31**(April):91–96.

ARROW, K. J., and F. H. HAHN [1971]. *General Competitive Analysis.* San Francisco: Holden-Day.

BARRO, R. J., and S. FISCHER [1976]. "Recent Developments in Monetary Theory". *Journal of Monetary Economics* **2** (April):133–167.

BAUMOL, W. J. [1952]. "The Transactions Demand for Cash: An Inventory Theoretical Approach." *Quarterly Journal of Economics* **66**(November):545–556.

BEWELY, T. [1977]. "The Permanent Income Hypothesis: A Theoretical Formulation." *Journal of Economic Theory* **16**(December):252–292.

BEWLEY, T. [1980]. "The Optimum Quantity of Money," in Kareken and Wallace.

BEWLEY, T. [1983]. "A Difficulty with the Optimum Quantity of Money." *Econometrica* **51**(5):1485–1504.

BROCK, W. A. and J. A. SCHEINKMAN [1980]. "Some Remarks on Monetary Policy in an Overlapping Generations Model," in Kareken and Wallace.

BRUNNER, K. and A. H. MELTZER [1971]. "The Uses of Money: Money in the Theory of an Exchange Economy." *American Economic Review* **61**(December):784–805.

BRYANT, J. [1980]. "Transaction Demand for Money and Moral Hazard." in Kareken and Wallace.

CASS, D. [1980]. "Money in Consumption Loan Type Models: An Addendum," in Kareken and Wallace.

CASS, D., M. OKUNO and I. ZILCHA [1980]. "The Role of Money in Supporting the Pareto Optimality of Competitive Equilibrium in Consumption Loan Type Models," in Kareken and Wallace.

CASS, D. and K. SHELL [1980]. "In Defense of a Basic Approach," in Kareken and Wallace.

CASS, D. and M. YAARI [1966]. "A Re-Examination of the Pure Comsumption Loans Model." *Journal of Political Economy* **74**(August):353–367.

Chichilnisky, G. and P. J. Kalman [1978]. "Rothe Fixed-Point Theorem and Existence of Equilibria in Monetary Economies." *Journal of Mathematical Analysis and Applications* **65**(1):56–65.

Chick, V. [1978]. "Unresolved Questions in Monetary Theory-Critical Review." *Economist* **126**(1): 37–60.

Clower, R. W. [1965]. "The Keynesian Counterrevolution: A Theoretical Appraisal." In *The Theory of Interest Rates,* eds. F. H. Hahn and F. P. R. Brechling. London: Macmillan & Co.

Clower, R. W. [1967]. "A Reconsideration of the Microfoundations of Monetary Theory." *Western Economic Journal* **6**(December):1–8.

Clower, R.W. [1975]. "Reflections on Keynesian Perplex." *Zeitschrift für Nationalokonomie-Journal of Economics* **35**(1–2):1–24.

Clower, R. W. [1977]. "Anatomy of Monetary Theory." *American Economic Review* **67**(1):206–211.

Clower, R.W. and P. Howitt [1978]. "The Transactions Theory of the Demand for Money: A Reconsideration." *Journal of Political Economy* **86**(June):449–466.

Davidson, P. [1977]. "Money and General Equilibrium." *Economie Appliquée,* **30**(4):541–563.

Debreu, G. [1954]. "Valuation Equilibrium and Pareto Optimum." *Proceedings of the National Academy of Science* **40**:588–592.

Debreu, G. [1959]. *Theory of Value.* New York: Wiley.

Diamond, P. and J. Yellin [1985]. "The Distribution of Inventory Holdings in a Pure Exchange Barter Search Economy." *Econometrica* **53**(2):409–432.

Drandrakis, E. M. [1966]. "On the Competitive Equilibrium in a Monetary Economy." *International Economic Review,* **7**(September):304–328.

Dreze, J. H. ed., [1974]. *Allocation Under Uncertainty: Equilibrium and Optimality.* Edinburgh: Macmillan.

Eckalbar, J. C. [1984]. "Money, Barter, and Convergence to the Competitive Allocation: Menger's Problem." *Journal of Economic Theory* **32**(2):201–211.

Eckalbar, J. C. [1986]. "Bilateral Trade in a Monetized Pure Exchange Economy." *Economic Modelling,* **3**(2):135–139.

Eden, B. [1983]. "On the Unit of Account Function of Money–The Use of Local Currency When Less Inflationary Currencies Are Available." *Economic Inquiry* **21**(3):361–373.

Feldman, A. M. [1973]. "Bilateral Trading Processes, Pairwise Optimality and Pareto Optimality." *Review of Economic Studies* **XL**(4), No. 124, (October):463–474.

Fischer, S. [1975]. "Recent Developments in Monetary Theory." *American Economic Review,* **LXV**,2 157–166.

Foley, D. K. [1970]. "Equilibrium with Costly Marketing." *Journal of Economic Theory* **2**(September):276–291.

Foley, D. K. and M. Hellwig [1975]. "Asset Management with Trading Uncertainty." *Review of Economic Studies* **42**(July):327–346.

Friesen, P. H. [1979]. "Arrow-Debreu Model Extended to Financial Markets." *Econometrica* **47**(3):689–707.

Gale, D. [1978]. "The Core of a Monetary Economy without Trust." *Journal of Economic Theory* **18**(2): 456–491.

Gale, D. [1980]. "Money, Information and Equilibrium in Large Economies." *Journal of Economic Theory* **23**(1):28–65.

Gale, D. [1982]. *Money: In Equilibrium.* New York: Cambridge University Press.

Goldman, S. M. [1978]. "Portfolio Choice and Flexibility—Precautionary Motive." *Journal of Monetary Economics* **4**(2):263–279.

Goldman, S. M. and R. M. Starr [1982]. "Pairwise, t-wise, and Pareto Optimalities." *Econometrica* **50**(May):593–606.

Graham, D. A., L. P. Jennergen, D. W. Peterson and E. R. Weintraub [1976]. "Trade-Commodity Parity Theorems." *Journal of Economic Theory* **12**(3):443–454.

GRANDMONT, J. M. [1972]. "Role of Money and Existence of A Monetary Equilibrium." *Review of Economic Studies* **39**(119):355–372.

GRANDMONT, J. M. [1973]. "Efficiency of a Monetary Equilibrium." *Review of Economic Studies* **40**(2):149–165.

GRANDMONT, J. M. [1974]. "On the Short Run Equilibrium in a Monetary Economy." In *Allocation Under Certainty: Equilibrium and Optimality*. ed. Jacques H. Dreze. (Macmillan (UK), Halsted Press) New York: John Wiley & Sons.

GRANDMONT, J. M. [1983]. *Money and Value*. New York: Cambridge University Press.

GRANDMONT, J. M. [1977]. "Temporary General Equilibrium Theory." *Econometrica* **45**(April):535–572.

GRANDMONT, J. M. and G. LAROQUE [1975]. "On Money and Banking." *Review of Economic Studies* **42**:207–236.

GRANDMONT, J. M. and G. LAROQUE [1976]. "On the Liquidity Trap." *Econometrica* **44**:129–135.

GRANDMONT, J. M. and Y. YOUNES [1972]. "On the Role of the Money and the Existence of a Monetary Equilibrium." *Review of Economic Studies* **39**(July):355–372.

GRANDMONT, J. M. and Y. YOUNES [1973]. "On the Efficiency of a Monetary Equilibrium." *Review of Economic Studies* **40**(April):149–165.

GREEN, E. [1987]. "Lending and the Smoothing of Uninsurable Income." In *Contractural Arrangements for Intertemporal Trade* eds. Prescott and Wallace. Minneapolis: University of Minnesota Press.

GREEN, J. R. [1973]. "Temporary General Equilibrium in a Sequential Trading Model with Spot and Futures Transactions." *Econometrica* **41**(6):1103–1123.

GREEN, J. R. and H. POLEMARCHAKIS [1976]. "A Brief Note on the Efficiency of Equilibria with Costly Transactions." *Review of Economic Studies* **43**:537–542.

GREEN, J. R. and E. SHESHINSKI [1975]. "Competitive Inefficiencies in Presence of Constrained Transactions." *Journal of Economic Theory* **10**(3):343–357.

HAHN, F. H. [1965]. "On Some Problems of Proving the Existence of an Equilibrium in a Monetary Economy." In *The Theory of Interest Rates,* eds. F. H. Hahn and F. P. R. Brechling. London: Macmillan.

HAHN, F. H. [1971]. "Equilibrium with Transaction Costs." *Econometrica* **39**(3): 417–439.

HAHN, F. H. [1971a]. "Professor Friedman's Views on Money." *Economica* **38**(February): 61–80.

HAHN, F. H. [1973]. "On the Foundations of Monetary Theory." In *Essays in Modern Economics,* ed. Michael Parkin and A. R. Nobay. New York: Harper & Row.

HAHN, F. H. [1988]. "Liquidity," to appear in *Handbook of Monetary Economics*, eds. B. Friedman and F. Hahn. Amsterdam: North Holland, forthcoming.

HAHN, F. H., and F. P. R. BRECHLING, eds., [1965]. *The Theory of Interest Rates*. London: Macmillan.

HARRIS, M. [1979]. "Expectations and Money in a Dynamic Exchange Model." *Econometrica* **47**(6):1403–1419.

HASLINGER, F. [1979]. "Money and Barter in General Equilibrium—Review." *Zeitschrift für Nationalokomie–Journal of Economics* **39**(3–4):385–400.

HAYASHI, T. [1974]. "The Non-Pareto Efficiency of Initial Allocation of Commodities and Monetary Equilibrium: An Inside Money Economy." *Journal of Economic Theory* **7**:173–187.

HAYASHI, T. [1976]. "Monetary Equilibrium in 2 Classes of Stationary Economies." *Review of Economic Studies* **43**(2):269–284.

HAZOME, Y. [1976]. "Remark on Structure of Exchange in Barter and Monetary Economies." *Quaterly Journal of Economics* **90**(3):521.

HELLER, W. P. [1972]. "Transactions with Set-Up Costs." *Journal of Economic Theory* **4**(3):465–478.

Heller, W. P. [1974]. "The Holding of Money Balances in General Equilibrium." *Journal of Economic Theory* **7**(January):93–108.

Heller, W. P. and R. M. Starr [1976]. "Equilibrium with Non-Convex T ansactions Costs: Monetary and Non-Monetary Economies." *Review of Economic Studies* **XLII**(2):195–215.

Hirshleifer, J. [1973]. "Exchange Theory–Missing Chapter." *Western Economic Journal* **11**(2):129–146.

Hicks, J. R. [1935]. "A Suggestion for Simplifying the Theory of Money." *Economica* **II**(5) 1–19. Reprinted in 1967 in Hicks' *Critical Essays in Monetary Theory*. Oxford: Oxford University Press.

Honkapohja, S. [1977]. "Money and Core in a Sequence Economy with Transaction Costs." *European Economic Review* **10**(2):241–251.

Honkapohja, S. [1978]. "On the Efficiency of a Competitive Monetary Equilibrium with Transaction Costs." *Review of Economic Studies* **XLV**(3), No. 141, (October):405–416.

Honkapohja, S. [1978]. "A Re-Examination of the Store of Value in a Sequence Economy with Transaction Costs." *Journal of Economic Theory* **18**(2):278–293.

Hool, B. [1976]. "Money, Expectations and the Existence of a Temporary Equilibrium." *Review of Economic Studies* **43**(October):439–445.

Hool, B]1979]. "Liquidity, Speculation and the Demand for Money." *Journal of Economic Theory* **2**(1):73–87.

Howitt, P. W. [1973]. "Walras and Monetary Theory." *Western Economic Journal* **11**(4): 487–499.

Howitt, P. W. [1977]. "Intertemporal Utility Maximization and Timing of Transactions." *American Economic Review* **67**(2):156–165.

Howitt, P. W. [1985]. "Transaction Costs in the Theory of Unemployment." *American Economic Review* **75**(1):88–100.

Iwai, K. [1988]. "The Evolution of Money—A Search-Theoretic Foundation of Monetary Economics." CARESS Working Paper #88-03, University of Pennsylvania.

Jennergen, L. P. [1983]. "On the Role of a Money Commodity in a Trading Process." *Economics Letters* **11**(1–2):9–14.

Jevons, W. S. [1875]. *Money and the Mechanism of Exchange*. London: H. S. King.

Jones, R. A. [1976]. "The Origin and Development of Media of Exchange." *Journal of Political Economy* **84**(August):757–775.

Kareken, J. H. and N. Wallace, eds. [1980]. *Models of Monetary Economies*. Minneapolis: Federal Reserve Bank of Minneapolis.

Kareken, J. H. and N. Wallace [1980]. "Introduction," in Kareken and Wallace, above.

Karni, E. [1973]. "Transactions Costs and Demand for Media of Exchange." *Western Economic Journal* **11**(1):71–80.

Kaulla, R. [1920]. *Grundlagen des geldwerts. Stuttgart, Germany:* Deutsche Verlags-Anstalt.

Keynes, J. M. [1936]. *The General Theory of Employment, Interest, and Money*. New York: Harcourt, Brace.

King, R. G. [1983]. "On the Economics of Private Money." *Journal of Monetary Economics* **12**(1):127–158.

King, R. G. [1986]. "Money As the Mechanism of Exchange." *Journal of Monetary Economics* **17**(1):93–115.

Kiyotaki, N. and Randall Wright [1988]. "On Money as a Medium of Exchange." CARESS Working Paper #88-01, University of Pennsylvania.

Kohn, M. [1981]. "In Defense of the Finance Constraint." *Economic Inquiry* **19**(2):177–195.

Kohn, M. [1984]. "The Finance (Cash-in-Advance) Constraint Comes of Age: A Survey of Some Recent Developments in the Theory of Money." Working Paper Series, Dartmouth College.

Kurz, M. [1974]. "Equilibrium with Transaction Cost and Money in a Single Market Exchange Economy." *Journal of Economic Theory* **7**(April):418–452.

Kurz, M. [1974]. "Arrow-Debreu Equilibrium of an Exchange Economy with Transaction Cost." *International Economic Review* **15**:699–717.

KURZ. M. [1974]. "Structure of Trade." *Economic Inquiry* **12**(4):493–516.

KURZ, M. [1974]. "Equilibrium in a Finite Sequence of Markets with Transactions Cost." *Econometrica* **42**(1):1–20.

LEAPE, J. I. [1987]. "Taxes and Transaction Costs in Asset Market Equilibrium." *Journal of Public Economics* **33**(1):1–20.

LERNER, A. P. [1947]. "Money as a Creature of the State." *American Economic Review* **37**(May):312–317.

LUCAS, R. E., Jr. [1972]. "Expectations and the Neutrality of Money." *Journal of Economic Theory* **4**(April):103–124.

LUCAS, R. E., Jr. [1978]. "Asset Prices in an Exchange Economy." *Econometrica* **46**(November):1429–1446.

LUCAS, R. E., Jr. [1980]. "Equilibrium in a Pure Currency Economy," in Kareken and Wallace.

MADDEN, P. J. [1975]. Efficient Sequences of Non-Monetary Exchange." *Review of Economic Studies* **42**(October):581–596.

MADDEN, P. J. [1976]. "Theorem on Decentralized Exchange." *Econometrica* **44**(4): 787–791.

MENGER, K. [1892]. "On the Origin of Money." *Economic Journal* **2**:239–255.

MILNE, F. [1976]. "Default Risk in a General Equilibrium Asset Economy with Incomplete Markets." *International Economic Review* **17**(3):613–625.

MULLER, H. and U. SCHWEIZER [1978]. "Temporary Equilibrium in a Money Economy." *Journal of Economic Theory* **19**(December):267–286.

NIEHANS, J. [1969]. "Money in a Static Theory of Optimal Payment Arrangements." *Journal of Money, Credit and Banking* **1**(November):706–726.

NIEHANS, J. [1971]. "Money and Barter in General Equilibrium with Transactions Costs." *American Economic Review* **61**(December):773–783.

NIEHANS, J. [1975]. "Interest and Credit in General Equilibrium with Transactions." *American Economic Review* **65**(September):548–566.

NORMAN, A. L. [1987] "A Theory of Monetary Exchange." *Review of Economic Studies* **54**(3):499–517.

O'DRISCOLL, G. P. [1986]. "Money–Menger Evolutionary–Theory." *History of Political Economy* **18**(4):601–616.

OH, SEONGHWAN [1988]. "A Theory of a Generally Acceptable Medium of Exchange and Barter." *Journal of Monetary Economics,* forthcoming.

OKUNO, M. "General Equilibrium with Money: Indeterminacy of Private Level and Efficiency." *Economic Theory* **12**:402–415.

OSTROY, J. M. [1973]. "The Informational Efficiency of Monetary Exchange." *American Economic Review* **63**:597–610.

OSTROY, J. M. and R. M. STARR [1974]. "Money and the Decentralization of Exchange." *Econometrica* **42**(6): 1093–1113.

OSTROY, J. M. and R. M. STARR [1988]. "The Transaction Role of Money," to appear in *Handbook of Monetary Economics*, eds. B. Friedman and F. Hahn. Amsterdam: North Holland, forthcoming.

PERLMAN, M. [1971]. "The Roles of Money in an Economy and the Optimum Quantity of Money." *Economica* **38**(August):233–252.

PERLMAN, M. [1973]. "The Roles of Money in an Economy and the Optimum Quantity of Money: Reply." *Economica* **40**(November):432–441.

PETHIG, R. [1975]. "Microeconomic Analysis of Exchange Function of Money." *Zeitschrift für Wirtschafts-Und Sozialwissenchaften,* (4):305–325.

REPULLO, R. [1987]. "The Existence of Equilirbium without Free Disposal in Economies with Transaction Costs and Incomplete Markets." *International Economic Review* **28**(2):275–290.

ROGAWSKI, J. and M. SHUBIK [1986]. "A Strategic Market Game with Transactions Cost." *Mathematical Social Sciences* **11**(2):139–160.

SAMUELSON, P. A. [1958]. "An Exact Consumption-Loan Model of Interest with or without the Social Contrivance of Money." *Journal of Political Economy* **66**(December):467–482.

SAMUELSON, P. A. [1968]. "What Classical and Neoclassical Monetary Theory Really Was." *Canadian Journal of Economics* **1**(February): 1–15.

SCHEINKMAN, J. A. and L. WEISS [1986]. "Borrowing Constraints and Aggregate Economic Activity." *Econometrica* **54**, 23–45.

SHAPLEY, L. and M. SHUBIK [1977]. "Trade Using One Commodity as a Means of Payment." *Journal of Political Science* **85**(5):937–968.

SHEFRIN, H. M. [1979]. "Spot Trading. Efficiency, and Differential Information." *Journal of Economic Theory* **20**(3):281–299.

SHEFRIN, H. M. [1981]. "Transaction Costs, Uncertainty and Generally Inactive Future Markets." *Review of Economic Studies* **LXVIII**(1), No. 151, (January):131–138.

SHELL, K. [1971]. "Notes on the Economics of Infinity." *Journal of Political Economy* **79**(September-October):1002–1011.

SHUBIK, M. [1976]. "Theory of Money and Financial Institutions .27. Beyond General Equilibrium." *Economie Appliquée* **29**(2):319–337.

SHUBIK, M. and C. WILSON [1977]. "Optimal Bankruptcy Rule in a Trading Economy Using Fiat Money." *Zeitschrift für Nationalokonomie-Journal of Economics* **37**(3–4):337–354.

SHUBIK, M. [1980]. "The Capital Stock Modified Competitive Equilibrium," in Kareken and Wallace.

SHUBIK, M. [1980]. *Market Structure and Behavior.* Cambridge: Havard University Press.

SMITH, A. [1776]. *An Inquiry into the Nature and Causes of the Wealth of Nations.*

SMITH, B. D. [1984]. "Money, Nonconvex Preferences, and the Existence of Equilibrium: A Note." *Journal of Economic Theory* **32**(2):359–366.

SONTHEIMER, K. [1972]. "On the Determination of Money Prices." *Journal of Money, Credit and Banking* **4**(August):489–508.

SPIVAK, A. [1980]. "Efficient Allocations Under a General Transaction Technology." *Journal of Economic Theory* **22**(3):465–476.

STARR, R. M. [1972]. "The Structure of Exchange in Barter and Monetary Economies." *Quaterly Journal of Economics* **LXXXVI**(May):290–302.

STARR, R. M. [1974]. "The Price of Money in a Pure Exchange Monetary Economy with Taxation." *Econometrica* **42**(1):45–54.

STARR, R. M. [1976]. "Decentralized Non-Monetary Trade." *Econometrica* **44** (5): 1087–1089.

STARR, R. M. [1978]. "Money in a Sequence Economy: A Correction." *Review of Economic Studies*, **XLV** (June): 391.

STARR, R. M. [1980]. "General Equilibrium Approaches to the Study of Monetary Economies: Comments on Recent Developments," in Kareken and Wallace.

STARR, R. M. [1986]. "Decentralized Trade in a Credit Economy," in W. P. Heller, R. Starr and D. Starrett, eds., *Equilibrium Analysis: Essays in Honor of Kenneth J. Arrow II.* New York: Cambridge University Press.

STARRETT, D. [1973]. "Inefficiency and the Demand for 'Money' in a Sequence Economy." *Review of Economic Studies* **40**:437–448.

TIROLE, J. [1985]. "Asset Bubbles and Overlapping Generations." *Econometrica* **53**(6):1499–1528.

TOBIN, J. [1961]. "Money, Capital, and Other Stores of Value." *American Economic Review* **LI**(2):26–37. Reprinted with permission in 1971 in Tobin's Essays in Economics **1**. Amsterdam: North-Holland.

TOBIN, J. [1956]. "The Interest-Elasticity of Transactions Demand for Cash." *Review of Economics and Statistics* **38**(August):241–247.

TOBIN, J. [1964]. "The Tobin Manuscript," unpublished.

TOBIN, J. [1965]. "Money and Economic Growth." *Econometrica* **33**(October):671–684.

TOBIN, J. [1966]. "The Theory of Portfolio Selection," in *The Theory of Interest Rates*, eds. F. H. Hahn and F. P. R. Brechling. London: MacMillan.

TOBIN, J. [1982]. "Money and Finance in the Macroeconomic Process." *Journal of Money Credit and Banking* **14**(2):171–204.
TOWNSEND, R. M. [1978]. "Intermediation with Costly Bilateral Exchange." *Review of Economic Studies* **45**(October):417–425.
TOWNSEND, R. M. [1980]. "Models of Money with Spatially Separated Agents," in Kareken and Wallace.
TOWNSEND, R. M. [1982]. "Optimal Multiperiod Contracts and the Gain from Enduring Relationships Under Private Information." *Journal of Political Economy* **90**, 1166–1186.
TOWNSEND, R. M. [1987]. "Asset Return Anomalies in a Monetary Economy." *Journal of Economic Theory* **41**(2):219–247.
ULPH, A. M. and D. T. ULPH [1975]. "Transaction Costs in General Equilibrium Theory—A Survey." *Economica* **42**(November):355–372.
ULPH A. M. and D. T. ULPH [1975]. "Efficiency. Inessentiality and the Debreu Structure of Prices," in *Equilibrium and Disequilibrium in Economic Theory,* ed. G. Schwodiauer. Boston: D. Reidel.
VEENDORP, E. C. H. [1970]. "General Equilibrium Theory for a Barter Economy." *Western Economic Journal* **8**:1–23.
WALLACE, N. [1980]. "The Overlapping Generations Model of Fiat Money," in Kareken and Wallace.
WALLACE, N. [1981]. "A Hybrid Fiat-Commodity Monetary System." *Journal of Economic Theory* **25**(3):421–430.
WEDDEPOHL, C. [1983]. "Developments in the Theory of General Equilibrium." *Economist* **131**(3):373–399.
WEINTRAUB, E. R. [1977]. "Micro-Foundations of Macroeconomics—Critical Survey." *Journal of Economic Literature* **15**(1):1–23.
WELCH, R. L. [1980]. "Vertical and Horizontal Communication in Economic Processes." *Review of Economic Studies* **47**(4):733–746.

Economic Theory, Econometrics,
and Mathematical Economics

Edited by Karl Shell, *Cornell University*

Recent titles

Robert J. Barro, editor, *Money, Expectations, and Business Cycles: Essays in Macroeconomics*

Ryuzo Sato, *Theory of Technical Change and Economic Invariance: Application of Lie Groups*

Iosif A. Krass and Shawkat M. Hammoudeh, *The Theory of Positional Games: With Applications in Economics*

Giorgio Szego, editor, *New Quantitative Techniques for Economic Analysis*

John M. Letiche, editor, *International Economic Policies and Their Theoretical Foundation: A Source Book*

Murray C. Kemp, editor, *Production Sets*

Andreu Mas-Colell, editor, *Noncooperative Approaches to the Theory of Perfect Competition*

Jean-Pascal Benassy, *The Economics of Market Disequilibrium*

Tatsuro Ichiishi, *Game Theory for Economic Analysis*

David P. Baron, *The Export-Import Bank: An Economic Analysis*

Real P. Lavergne, *The Political Economy of U.S. Tariffs: An Empirical Analysis*

Halbert White, *Asymptotic Theory for Econometricians*

Thomas G. Cowing and Daniel L. McFadden, *Macroeconomic Modeling and Policy Analysis: Studies in Residential Energy Demand*

Svend Hylleberg, *Seasonality in Regression*

Jean-Pascal Benassy, *Macroeconomics: An Introduction to the Non-Walrasian Approach*

C.W.J. Granger and Paul Newbold, *Forecasting Economic Time Series, Second Edition*

Marc Nerlove, Assaf Razin, and Efraim Sadka, *Household and Economy: Welfare Economics and Endogenous Fertility*

Jean-Michel Grandmont, editor, *Nonlinear Economic Dynamics*

Thomas Sargent, *Macroeconomic Theory, Second Edition*

Yves Balasko, *Foundations of the Theory of General Equilibrium*

Jean-Michel Grandmont, editor, *Temporary Equilibrium: Selected Readings*

Darrell Duffie, *Security Markets, Stochastic Models*

Ross M. Starr, editor, *General Equilibrium Models of Monetary Economies*